# WHY SPENCER PERCEVAL HAD TO DIE

# WHY SPENCER PERCEVAL HAD TO DIE

The Assassination of a British Prime Minister

## Andro Linklater

WALKER & COMPANY

NEW YORK

Published by Walker Publishing Company, Inc., New York
A Division of Bloomsbury Publishing

All papers used by Walker & Company are natural, recyclable products made from
wood grown in well-managed forests. The manufacturing processes conform
to the environmental regulations of the country of origin.

LIBRARY OF CONGRESS CATALOGING-IN-PUBLICATION DATA HAS BEEN APPLIED FOR.

ISBN: 978-0-8027-7998-4

Visit Walker & Company's website at www.walkerbooks.com

First U.S. edition 2012

1 3 5 7 9 10 8 6 4 2

Typeset by Hewer Text UK Ltd, Edinburgh
Printed in the U.S.A. by Quad/Graphics, Fairfield, Pennsylvania

For Paul and Charlotte,
the great encouragers

*Amicus certus in re incerta cernitur*

# Contents

1  A Horrible Event  1

2  The Identity of an Unfortunate Man is Revealed  11

3  Riots Break Out amid Rumours of Revolution  21

4  A Free and Easy Conspiracy?  30

5  Examining the Enigma of the Assassin's Sanity  46

6  The Victim is Seen as a Fond Father and
 Attentive Husband  58

7  A Prime Minister Put There by Providence  72

8  The Pervasive Power of Little P  84

9  The Beauty of Double Bookkeeping  97

10  The Prosecution Presents its Case  115

11  Bellingham and the Absence of *malice prepense*  126

12  The Compelling Evidence of Miss Stevens  135

13  The Search for the Truth behind the Murder  148

14  Choking to Death the Illegal Slave Trade  163

15  How to Kill an Economy  181

16  The Russian Connection Returns  196

17  Where the Money Came From  208

18  An Execution Ends all Cares  224

19  Understanding Why it Happened  234

*Notes*  243

*Bibliography*  277

*Acknowledgements*  287

*Index*  289

# A Horrible Event

From our report of the Parliamentary proceedings of the two Houses will an indignant and sorrowful nation learn the occurrence of one of those horrible events with which the annals of Great Britain have not often been stained – the murder of Mr Perceval the Prime Minister of these realms; a man who, in his personal intercourse gave offence to none – in his private life was an example to all; and who, however firm and unbending in his principles, yet conducted political conflicts in a way that seemed to disarm them of their characteristic bitterness.

*The Times*, 12 May 1812

The assassin was late. That is the loose thread in the tapestry. Pull at it, and the neat little picture of the murder that everyone knows will unravel. Behind it stands the large, ugly truth of what happened on Monday, 11 May 1812.

At half past four in the afternoon, the Prime Minister was due to appear in the House of Commons. At that moment the man who meant to kill him was a mile away in Sidney's Alley on the north side of Leicester Square. The geography of London should have saved the Prime Minister's life. By the time his murderer reached the top of Whitehall, it was already a quarter to five. Still a ten-minute walk to the Houses of

Parliament. By then anxiety must have been his killer's dominant emotion.

Murder is not entered upon lightly. The assassin had prepared
himself with care for the great eventuality. His pistols had been
bought three weeks earlier so that he could practise shooting with
them. He had spent long evenings in the gallery of the House of
Commons. He had familiarised himself with the features of the
Prime Minister and checked his identity with knowledgeable journalists nearby. His chocolate-coloured coat had a secret pocket
specially designed to carry the murder weapon unobtrusively.
Another pistol nestled in his clay-coloured trousers. He had paced
out the journey to the House of Commons. He could estimate to the
minute how long it would take. But none of his rehearsals had taken
into account the unfortunate circumstance that he might be delayed.

His anxiety would have triggered self-pity. That was his usual
reaction to adversity. He was forty-one, and throughout his life bad
luck had dogged him. However much care he took, some unfore-
seen circumstance would occur at the critical moment wrecking
the whole enterprise. He might have grown rich in the service of
the East India Company but for a shipwreck. He could have made
money trading in Russian iron had it not been for the unexpected
jealousy of a Dutch rival. He would have won compensation for his
losses except that the British ambassador inexplicably refused to
help. And now this delay in his carefully laid plan.

He should have gone straight from St James's Square to Whitehall.
Instead, he had been forced to make a detour to Leicester Square,
almost in the opposite direction. There had been no choice. Debt
drove him there. For lack of money, he had had to walk two sides
of a triangle instead of one. 'It has always been my misfortune,' he
would confess to his wife Mary, 'to be thwarted, misrepresented
and ill-used in life.'

But he had never given up. Some termed it obstinacy, others

madness, but he had developed a talent for endurance, for putting his head down and ploughing on until he got what he wanted. However great the obstacles, he would perform what he had undertaken to do. When he came to explain his actions, no one could miss the sense of righteousness that pervaded his thoughts. He was proposing to administer justice not commit murder, and he was doing so less for himself than for Henry, his six-month-old son. 'What man,' he would shortly demand of a group of strangers, 'would not want to make provision for his family?'

He must have tried to quicken his pace against the unforgiving clock, but May was the beginning of the summer building season, and new government offices were being constructed around Henry VIII's old palace of Whitehall. The pavements were obstructed by scaffolding and builders' rubble. The stream of traffic that came across Westminster Bridge from south of the river prevented pedestrians from overflowing into the road. To keep the weighty pistol in its special pocket from swinging against the close-packed crowd, he must have clutched his brown coat closer to him, even as he pushed forward through the press of people.

At last he entered Parliament Square, crossed to Palace Yard, and ran up the steps of St Stephen's entrance to the House of Commons. The clock in the lobby showed the time to be five minutes before five o'clock. He was more than twenty minutes late. For the moment, his anxieties and thoughts were private and of no interest to the wider world.

Conflict is inseparable from politics. Interests have to be represented by those who sit on the green leather benches of the House of Commons. Naturally interests run into each other. Noise is inevitable. Voices are raised, and tempers rise with them. In the early summer of 1812, the arguments that erupted over the government's Orders in Council reached an unprecedented pitch of fury.

The ramifications were so complex that it was difficult even for parliamentarians to understand them fully. The original purpose of the Orders issued by the Privy Council in 1807, however, was simple – to impose a naval blockade on France and its ruler, the Corsican tyrant, Napoleon Bonaparte. To this end, the Royal Navy was authorised to remove goods intended for that country from any ship flying a neutral flag on the high seas that was not sailing to or from a British port. Across the Channel, Napoleon had retaliated with his own decrees against neutral ships intending to sail to British ports. And on the other side of the Atlantic the United States, whose shippers suffered most, proceeded to enact its own embargo on trade with belligerent powers.

The consequences were momentous and unexpected. Around the world, trade slowed to a trickle as ships were searched and their cargoes impounded. By 1811, an economic recession had descended on every country from the Baltic to the Mississippi, and the value of British exports and imports had dropped by more than three-quarters. Unemployment and social distress reached such a pitch that in 1812 the House of Commons was driven to conduct an investigation into the effects of the Orders in Council.

Hearings opened on 11 May, a Monday. The lobby of the Houses of Parliament seethed with Liverpool shippers, Manchester cotton spinners, East India merchants, Yorkshire woollen weavers, Staffordshire pottery makers, and Birmingham brassmakers. All had come to plead for the continuation or abolition of the Orders in Council. Only sixty Members of Parliament were present in the chamber, but the high-ceilinged lobby rang with voices of the public raised in genuine outrage.

The rawness of their feelings must have communicated itself to the chamber. Shortly before five o'clock, Henry Brougham, leading the attack on the Orders, suddenly demanded to know why the Prime Minister was not present to defend them. It was

Mr Perceval who had persuaded the Privy Council to impose the Orders, and his authority was needed to remove them. The House had recognised the gravity of the issue, by constituting itself a committee to hear the representations of those affected. The hearings had opened promptly at half past four as advertised. Brougham had already spent more than twenty minutes examining the first witness, Robert Hamilton, a potter from Staffordshire. Hamilton was now waiting to be cross-examined by James Stephen, famous for having masterminded the successful anti-slave trade campaign of 1807. But the man for whom the drama was staged had not yet appeared.

The anger in the chamber was enough to convince Thomas Babington, in the chair, that the honour of the House required Mr Perceval's immediate attendance. A low-voiced consultation with the Treasury clerk resulted in a messenger being despatched to 10 Downing Street with urgent instructions to hurry the Prime Minister on. Meanwhile, Mr Stephen was permitted to begin his cross-examination. The time was almost five o'clock.

From his place just inside the pair of folding doors that led into the lobby, the man in the chocolate-coloured coat would have seen the messenger push through the groups of delegates. The large expanse of the lobby acted as the meeting place and crossroads of Parliament. To the left lay the House of Commons, to the right the House of Lords. Anyone who came in from the street, whether to badger a Member of Parliament or to enter the chambers of the Commons or Lords, would have to pass through the doors into the lobby. Once the hearings had begun, the crowd started to drift towards the Commons and the public galleries, but around thirty or forty people remained in the lobby as the messenger came through.

The sharp sense of failure must have gripped the assassin right up to that moment. But then, from the scraps of talk that eddied in the messenger's wake, he would have learned that for once in his unfortunate life fate had been on his side: the Prime Minister had not yet arrived. He still sweated and breathed heavily from his hurried walk, but all had changed. His elaborate plan was back in place. Now it was necessary to nerve himself to the great event. A supreme effort was still demanded of him, but beyond it lay a future free of debt and worry.

He had studied Mr Perceval's features often enough from the Strangers' Gallery, peering down through opera glasses at the government benches below. For reassurance, he had repeatedly asked to have the Prime Minister and other members of the cabinet identified for him. No mistakes could be allowed. Again and again he had peered at the politician's oddly childish face until he was certain that he could recognise it.

At just after five o'clock, John Norris, an employee of the House of Commons, passed through the open door of the lobby to reach the stairs leading up to the Strangers' Gallery. He passed close to the tall man in the dark brown coat who stood by the closed part of the double doors. No more than an arm's length, Norris estimated. 'I thought he appeared to be anxiously watching,' he said later. 'And as my recollection serves me, his right hand was within the breast of his coat.'

Other people would also remember exactly where they were and what they were doing in those last few minutes of normality. Henry Burgess, a well-connected Mayfair solicitor with a brief to lobby against the Orders, recalled that he was waiting close to the doorway, a convenient place to buttonhole any late-arriving MP. William Smith, anti-slave trade MP for Norwich, would later describe how he paused in the exact centre of the lobby on his way to the Commons chamber to press the case for keeping the Orders, and was speaking to another anti-slavery activist, Francis Phillips. In a members' committee room high above the lobby, General

Isaac Gascoyne, the fanatically pro-slavery MP for Liverpool, was writing a letter to the Prime Minister about the economic misery in that city, and listening through an open window to the sounds of argument below.

The normality is important. When a national leader is assassinated, normality is always the second victim, but those final moments before it is obliterated contain a clue. Stare at them long enough and you may discern the purpose of the killing.

Julius Caesar walks confidently to attend a last meeting of the senate, knowing that he dominates Rome's constitutional elite, and that when he leaves the city on the morrow it will be to take command again of his all-conquering army. But to a republican, the ease of his gait reveals the imperial nature of Caesar's command over both civil and military power. Abraham Lincoln sits in Ford's theatre at the end of his first day of happiness following the surrender of the South: the play is trashy but to a Confederate the president's delight in its mindless entertainment rubs salt in the deep humiliation of defeat. The newsreel camera captures Archduke Franz Ferdinand as he is driven slowly and amicably through the narrow streets of Sarajevo in the newly annexed province of Bosnia: but to a Serbian patriot nothing could make more patronisingly obvious the reach of Austrian power than this parade in an open, vulnerable vehicle.

Observe what the victim does in his last moments. But note too the position of those who are most outraged by his actions.

No one had ever killed a British Prime Minister. The tall man in the chocolate-coloured coat knew what he was undertaking. It was Mr Perceval who determined that Lord Wellington should fight the French in Spain; Mr Perceval who insisted that taxes be raised to new, astonishing heights to finance his army; Mr Perceval who despatched a Royal Navy squadron to enforce the ban on trading in slaves; Mr Perceval who decided that extra troops should be sent to Ireland to compel the loyalty of dissident Roman Catholics; Mr Perceval who insisted that fresh, draconian laws be imposed to execute or imprison Luddites and rioters for breaking machinery; Mr Perceval who had single-handedly brought the economy to a standstill by his support for the Orders in Council. A notoriously dissolute Prince Regent occupied the monarch's role, but in effect Mr Perceval ruled the nation.

The enormity of the act must suddenly have struck the assassin. The sweat rolled off his forehead, his pounding heart caused him to pant, and the breath rasped through his mouth as though he were a runner struggling to reach the finishing line. Very soon all these physical reactions would become public knowledge.

The messenger encountered the Prime Minister as he strolled out into Downing Street. There was a brief exchange. It was noted that Mr Spencer Perceval hurried at first then, as though remembering the dignity of his office, relapsed into a swift walk. His clothes were plain, a blue coat, white waistcoat, charcoal breeches and a short-crowned hat, and his slight boyish figure, no more than five feet four inches tall, was unimpressive. Only those familiar with political figures would have recognised him as the most powerful politician in the land, the man who combined the post of Prime Minister, or more formally First Lord of the Treasury, with that of Chancellor of the Exchequer, who dominated the House of Commons, whose irresistible energy drove the civil service to execute the policies of the most conservative government since Parliament took power in the Glorious Revolution of 1688. He was a torment to the caricaturists who could find nothing to identify him except for his small size and wide, tilted eyes. He was as anonymous as any Prime Minister could be.

To William Wilberforce, gazing out of the window of Thomas Babington's house in Downing Street, Perceval was, however,

instantly recognisable. On many political issues, they were opponents, but not on the one that was most important to Wilberforce.
Where the slave trade was concerned, he and Perceval were united
in their determination to put an end to it, and Wilberforce, scourge
of the West India lobby that represented the interests of slave
owners, was happy to call the Prime Minister 'Friend'. With
genuine affection, he watched the diminutive figure hurry out of
Downing Street. 'A man of more real sweetness of temper,' he later
declared, 'a man more highly blest by nature, was never known or
one in whom goodness of disposition was more deeply rooted.'

Spencer Perceval started up the steps to the House of Commons
shortly after five o'clock, closely following the heavily built figure
of William Jerdan, a journalist who wrote for the *British Press*. As
they were about to pass through the folding doors into the lobby,
Jerdan noticed the Prime Minister behind him, and courteously
stepped aside to let him go first. Power usually attracts attention,
but Perceval's entrance was so unobtrusive that it was scarcely
noticed in the crowded lobby. Even Jerdan did not quite see what
happened next.

The tall man beside the door pulled his right hand from the
inside breast pocket of his brown coat. The short pistol was almost
lost in his large grasp. The weapon was inaccurate over more than
five yards, but he had no intention of putting anyone else in danger
by firing from that distance. The Prime Minister was hurrying past
him. The man crossed in front to stand in his path. Perceval
stopped, and looked up at him. He was so small that the assailant
towered over him.

The Prime Minister said something – perhaps asking him to move
aside, or more probably offering an apology for pushing past – but
the words were blotted out by the cataclysm of the next moment.
Wordlessly the man stretched out his arm, pushed the wide barrel of
the gun against Perceval's chest, and pressed the trigger.

There was a flash as the powder ignited, a muffled explosion, and the force of the bullet sent the victim stumbling across the lobby. 'Murder,' he exclaimed, 'oh, murder.' Where a knife point would pierce, and a small-calibre bullet penetrate, the projectile that killed Spencer Perceval was a ball of lead almost half an inch across that pulverised the ribs, breast and heart.

# The Identity of an Unfortunate Man is Revealed

John Bellingham, alias John Billingham, not having the fear of God before his Eyes but moved and seduced by the Instigation of the Devil . . . did make an Assault [with] a certain Pistol of the value of nine shillings, charged and loaded with Gunpowder and a Leaden Bullet, which he then and there had and held in his right hand to and against the Breast of him, the said Spencer Perceval and . . . then and there shot off and discharged out of the Pistol aforesaid by the force of the Gunpowder aforesaid in, upon and through the Breast of him, the said Spencer Perceval, one Mortal Wound . . .

Verdict of the Coroner's Jury – 12 May 1812

On no fewer than three occasions witnesses were called upon to describe what happened after the shot was fired. They told their first version in Parliament immediately following the murder. A day later the coroner held an inquest in a local pub and ordered three of them to tell their story again. Finally their testimony was heard for a third time in the Old Bailey when the murderer appeared in court. The sequence of events was always the same. But each time the killing was described from a new angle. Different people appeared in the foreground, while in the background there were half-obscured, tantalising hints of another, larger picture. Nothing was quite as it seemed. One witness was a government spy. Another palpably lied. They, like every other person present at the crime, had a political agenda. What follows is a composite of their testimonies, accurate as to what happened but hardly the full truth.

The most detailed testimony came from William Smith, Norwich's anti-slavery MP, given at the coroner's inquiry in the Rose & Crown tavern in Downing Street. In the moments after the shot was fired, events seemed to move with the close-up intensity of a dream. Smith said that when he heard the report of a pistol, he looked up from his conversation with Francis Phillips, and saw a crowd by the door:

> Almost at the same instant a person rushed hastily from among the crowd, and several voices cried out, 'Shut the door', and 'Let no one escape'. The person who came from among the crowd came towards me, looking first one way and then another, and, as I thought at the moment, rather like one seeking for shelter than as the person who had received the wound. But taking two or three steps towards me, as he approached he rather reeled by me, and almost instantly fell upon the floor, with his face downwards . . . When he first fell I thought he might be slightly wounded, and expected to see him make an effort to rise, but gazing at him a few moments, I observed that he did not stir at all; I therefore immediately stooped down to raise him from the ground, requesting the assistance of a gentleman who stood close by me for that purpose. As soon as we had turned his face towards us, and not till then, I perceived it was Mr. Perceval.

Phillips immediately knelt beside the fallen man and seeing the bullet hole, just above the heart and angled down, concluded that it must be fatal. There was no out-going wound. The bullet was still lodged deep in the victim's chest. Together Phillips and Smith pulled the little body upright, and each holding Perceval's arm over his shoulder carried him into the nearest room, an office used by the Speaker's clerk. In his own statement, Phillips confessed that before they could even lay Perceval down, he felt the body go limp in his arms.

With the help of some Commons officials, they gently lowered the Prime Minister onto a small table hurriedly swept clear of papers, so that he was seated upright, supported on either side with his legs resting on a chair. His face, Smith noted, 'was, by this time, perfectly pale, the blood issuing in small quantities from each corner of his mouth . . . His eyes were still open, but he did not appear to know me, nor to take any notice of any person about him, nor had he uttered the least articulate sound from the moment he fell. A few convulsive sobs which lasted, perhaps, three or four minutes, together with a scarcely perceptible pulse, were the only signs of life.'

Inside the office, the silence grew profound. Neither man dared speak aloud his thoughts. Then William Lynn, a surgeon who had been hastily summoned from his house in Great George Street, entered and having examined the body, delivered the verdict they had known but could not bring themselves to admit: 'He is dead.'

Outside in the lobby, the frozen moment of the murder had erupted into confusion. Every account refers to the shouts of 'Close the doors' to prevent the perpetrator escaping, but evidently they were not heeded. Some people ran in to investigate the shot, others raced away to inform peers and MPs of what they had seen, and soon they brought a torrent of anxious enquirers coming to check whether the Prime Minister still lived. It would have been easy, William Jerdan thought, for the assassin to get away unobserved. 'If he had risen in a minute or two afterwards,' he wrote in his autobiography, 'and walked quietly out into the street, he would have escaped, and the committer of the murder would never have been known unless he had chosen to divulge it.'

But Tom Eastaff, an official in the Vote Office, had risen from his place by the door. He had noticed the tall man approach Perceval and when voices began to call out 'Who did it?' Eastaff answered, 'That is the man,' and pointed to the figure in a deep brown coat slumped on a bench against the wall. Standing nearby, Jerdan followed the direction of Eastaff's hand and ran to catch hold of the murderer, seizing him by the collar. The man had a long face, dark hair, and when pulled to his feet appeared taller than those around him. But what Jerdan particularly noticed was the evidence of the man's distress. 'Large drops of agonizing sweat ran down his pallid face . . . [it] was of the cadaverous hue of the tomb; and from the bottom of his chest to his gorge, rose and fell a spasmodic action, as if a body as large as the hand were choking him with every breath. The miserable creature struck his chest repeatedly with his palm, as if to abate this sensation. Never on earth I believe was seen a more terrible example of over-wrought suffering.'

Henry Burgess was also nearby, and within seconds had joined Jerdan, snatching at the assassin's arms and tugging the warm pistol from his right hand. Then came a journalist, Vincent Dowling, who pulled open the chocolate-coloured coat and seized from it first a pair of opera glasses, then the second pistol out of its secret pocket. An angry scrum quickly pressed against the murderer, ripping his clothes apart. Suddenly those nearest were pushed aside as General Gascoyne drove forcefully into the crowd, and gripped the murderer's free hand so violently he cried out at the pain. In the other hand, the man held above his head a bundle of papers tied up in red tape. Gascoyne grabbed them, and tossed them over to another MP, Joseph Hume. While he was still pinioned, the man's pockets were emptied of their contents – a gold guinea, and a one-pound note, bank tokens for 8s 6d, a pocket-knife, a bunch of keys and a pencil. His captors were shouting incoherently at him when someone emerged from the Speaker's office and ran towards the murderer in a fury.

'Mr Perceval is dead,' he cried. 'Villain, how could you destroy so good a man?' The words produced a strange reaction.

'I am sorry for it,' the murderer said, and then he added something stranger still. 'I am the unfortunate man,' emphasising the word 'I'. 'I wish I were in Mr Perceval's place. My name is John Bellingham; it is a private injury – I know what I have done. It was a denial of justice.'

Although each witness remembered his words slightly differently, they all agreed on their import – the surprising claim to be a victim himself, and the implicit admission that he had killed in cold blood. What also struck them was his failure to offer any physical resistance to his arrest. 'A Mouse might have secured him with a bit of Thread,' observed Burgess.

With impressive rapidity, the forces of order started to reassert themselves. A death had been caused, and the perpetrator arrested, but to charge John Bellingham with murder, evidence that he was responsible had to be presented before magistrates.

There were enough lawyers present for this procedure to be quickly agreed and, since Parliament was technically a court of law, voices immediately called for Bellingham to be taken to the chamber of the House of Commons to be charged at the Bar of the House. He was hustled out of the crowded lobby and into the chamber. There, General Gascoyne approached the assassin again, and said with seeming surprise, 'I think I know the villain. Isn't your name Bellingham?'

Before this question could be followed up, other legal experts interrupted to point out that the proper procedure required the arrested man to be in custody before he could be charged. So, from the chamber he was hurried down long corridors and up narrow stairways into the prison-apartment of the serjeant-at-arms where he was formally arrested. Several MPs who were magistrates found seats, and in the hot, airless room the legal process began that should have revealed why John Bellingham had murdered the Right Honourable Spencer Perceval.

Among the crowd of MPs who jammed themselves into the confined space was William Jerdan of the *British Press*. He was there because no journalist would have missed the opportunity to hear the assassin explain his motives, and also because he recognised this was an historic drama. Jerdan was a failed poet, a would-be literary man. Despite his bulk, he felt himself to be an outsider perpetually under threat, 'a stricken deer' was the phrase he used to describe himself. In the committee room, he heard undercurrents that apparently escaped most others present.

The purpose of this first hearing was simply to establish that John Bellingham was indeed the man who had killed the Prime Minister. Accordingly two outside witnesses unconnected with Parliament, a journeyman printer from Lambeth and a clerk from Gower Street, were brought in to testify that they had been standing in the lobby. Each swore that he had seen the pistol fired by Bellingham at Perceval. Then Burgess and Gascoyne identified Bellingham as the man they had arrested. Another MP, Charles Burrell, produced the pistol that had fired the shot. Finally Phillips testified that Perceval had died in his arms. Having demonstrated the chain of evidence, the senior magistrate for the county of Middlesex, Harvey Combe MP, charged Bellingham with the murder.

The formalities of the law revealed less than the informalities. The most important information came from the forty-nine-year-old General Gascoyne MP, a ramrod-straight former officer in the Coldstream Guards. The general had inherited his Liverpool constituency from his elder brother, whose name, Bamber Gascoyne, represented the alliance of two of the city's leading slave-trading families. True to this double family tradition, Isaac Gascoyne made it his business to defend as forcefully as he could the trade on which Liverpool's wealth had been built. During the debates in 1807 to make it illegal to carry slaves on British ships, it was said of him that 'he considered the slave trade so great a blessing that if it were not in existence at present, he should propose to establish it'. For almost twenty years his forceful advocacy on this topic had earned him the loyalty of the city's voters, who repeatedly elected him to represent their interests in Parliament. Now, with military precision, he provided the first independent confirmation of the murderer's identity and background.

The arrested man, he informed the makeshift court, was a constituent of his from Liverpool, named John Bellingham. According to a newspaper report, the general testified that 'he had seen Bellingham often, and that he had received many petitions and memorials from him respecting some claims upon government which he ought to be allowed.' The latest interview with Bellingham had taken place barely three weeks earlier. Their discussions were always about these claims for compensation. '[They] originated in services alleged to be performed by the criminal in Russia for which he complains that he has obtained no remuneration.' The general also described how he had helped arrest Bellingham, gripping the hand that held the pistol so that he could not fire again. He gave his testimony crisply and clearly. His confidence managed to convey a sense that discipline was taking over from the chaos that had been let loose by the horrific crime.

Nevertheless, one person in the room had reservations. Although almost fainting in the airless room, William Jerdan found himself doubting the general's version of events in the lobby. Gascoyne had arrived more than a minute after the shot had been fired, after

Bellingham had been secured and after the pistol had been taken from the assassin's hand. It was possibly a mistake in the heat of the moment, Jerdan thought, and for the time being he kept his thoughts to himself.

When John Bellingham himself was questioned, he confirmed that he had indeed consulted the general on several occasions about his claim for compensation. Despite being warned to say nothing that might be incriminating at his trial, he then insisted on making known the motives for his crime: 'I have been denied the redress of my grievances by Government; I have been ill-treated . . . I was accused most wrongfully by a Governor-General in Russia in a letter from Archangel to Riga, and have sought redress in vain. I am a most unfortunate man, and feel here [putting his hand on his heart] sufficient justification for what I have done.'

Listening to what Bellingham had to say, the crowded audience in the tiny room must have felt they had missed the first half of the drama. So much appeared to have happened before the shooting, and the killer was apparently so well known to the authorities. His account suggested that he had badgered everyone possessing any influence, from the Prince Regent and the Privy Council to anonymous civil servants, with his grievances. 'They all know who I am and what I am,' he insisted. 'They knew of this fact six weeks ago through the magistrates of Bow Street.' Eventually tiring of his demands, one official had told him that nothing could be done for him, and that 'he might do his worst', but it would make no difference. 'I have obeyed them,' Bellingham concluded calmly. 'I have done my worst and I rejoice in the deed.' Incoherent though his argument was, he delivered it with a composure that shocked his audience, worse still he displayed 'not the slightest symptom of remorse'. The panting, sweating Bellingham had given way to a man at peace with his conscience.

Although fascinated by the man, and by his extraordinary

physical recovery from extreme stress, Jerdan quickly concluded that he must be mad. No sane man could be so calm after committing murder. Nevertheless, the journalist wondered whether there might be more to the tragedy than Bellingham's version of events. One piece of evidence, almost lost in the confusion of events, suggested a wider context.

Harvey Combe, in charge of the committal proceedings, was an experienced magistrate familiar with criminal investigations. He had at his disposal the services of two officers from the Bow Street magistrates' court, colloquially known as the Bow Street Runners. Their arrest records and the reports of those cases that came to the Old Bailey showed John Vickery and William Adkins to be outstandingly good detectives. Immediately before the hearing began, Combe had sent them to search Bellingham's lodgings at 9 New Millman Street. This turned out to be a quiet cul-de-sac in the almost-respectable area between Lincoln's Inn and Gray's Inn Road, where law clerks and other foot soldiers in the legal profession lived. Bellingham's room was on the first floor, and when searching it Vickery had found in the chest of drawers all the material needed by Bellingham for his crime – a powder horn, equipment for casting bullets, a pistol key for fitting an extension to the barrel, more ammunition, and a quantity of letters and papers relating to his grievances. All of these would subsequently become evidence at his trial, but only those present at the committal stage heard Vickery's account of his conversation with Bellingham's landlady, Mrs Rebecca Robarts.

When the Bow Street officer had completed his hurried search, he asked Mrs Robarts whether she could tell him anything more about her lodger. Her reply was not illuminating – simply that he was polite, regular in his habits and had been staying there for about four months – but in answer to Vickery's further enquiry, whether she had anything belonging to Bellingham in her possession, she answered that she did. As the officer related this part of the conversation, it was noted that the prisoner lost his self-possession and became visibly upset. Asked by Vickery what the object was, Mrs Robarts said it was a memorandum of twenty pounds due to Bellingham from a Mr Wilson.

Many pieces of evidence were introduced during this hurriedly cobbled-together committal hearing. Understandably it was difficult to tell which were important, and the significance of Vickery's conversation did not stand out.

Bellingham soon regained his calm, and in answer to Combe's question he confirmed that the money did belong to him, and that his landlady was holding it for him. Twenty pounds was not a small sum – in buying power today, roughly equivalent to about £8,000: Mrs Robarts' almost-respectable neighbours would have expected to work for about four months to earn £20. But at this stage the magistrate's task was simply to judge whether sufficient evidence had been presented to justify charging the prisoner. The money lay beyond Combe's immediate concerns. Nor was it relevant to question the assassin further, to ask how long he had been waiting in the lobby, what circumstances had led him there, or why he had been detained on his way to the Commons.

At approximately eight o'clock, having consulted other MPs with legal training, Combe decided they had heard enough. He formally charged John Bellingham with the murder of the Right Honourable Spencer Perceval, and informed him that he would be remanded in custody until his trial. Bellingham pulled together his dishevelled clothes and was handcuffed by Vickery and Adkins. With that, the committal proceedings and the first attempt to find out who was responsible for killing the Prime Minister ended.

# Riots Break Out amid Rumours of Revolution

Bellingham was a pleasant and inoffensive companion, but when
he had disputed accounts in business, which was often the case, he
then shewed his obstinate and unyielding disposition.

*Liverpool Mercury*, 29 May 1812

Not until the shooting of President John F. Kennedy on 22
November 1963 would a catastrophe of such significance occur
again – the assassination of the leader of the most powerful democracy in the world. In each event, two identical processes started
immediately, the criminal investigation required by murder and,
more vital for the structure of law and order, the restoration of
government's authority. Only for a brief period after the crime did
the discovery of guilt seem the more important. Very quickly, the
second priority came to swamp the first. With the murder of
Spencer Perceval, the need to restore authority became obvious
when a messenger was sent to find a hackney coach to take the
prisoner to Newgate prison.

About three hours had elapsed since Perceval's murder. Hidden
away in the bowels of the House of Commons, neither the magistrates nor Bellingham had any idea of the impact his pistol shot
had made upon the world outside. Only when the handcuffed prisoner and his escort emerged from the building into Lower Palace

Yard, between Westminster Hall and Westminster Bridge, did they realise that the murder of the Prime Minister was not just a crime.

To the crowds in Parliament Square, it was a source of jubilation. The mood spread as fast as the news. Eager to celebrate, people began to hurry north across the Thames and south from the honeycomb of slum dwellings between Soho and Drury Lane. Within an hour of the murder, they were streaming into Whitehall and packing into the streets and yards around Parliament itself. Inside the building, the law was beginning an orderly investigation into the killing. Outside a festival was taking place to mark the death of the Prime Minister.

There were loud cheers when the hackney coach that had been summoned pulled up outside the gate to Lower Palace Yard. Then, as Bellingham appeared, the mob surged forward. When he climbed into the coach, the nearest celebrators swarmed over the vehicle, and tried to get in at the other door. 'By main force only could they be prevented from mounting the coach-box, clinging to the wheels, and even entering the coach to shake hands with and congratulate the murderer on his deed,' reported one eyewitness, the diplomat Sir George Jackson. 'They were whipped off, beaten off – there was no other course left – amid the execrations of the mob on the police, and the vociferated applause and hurrahs for Bellingham.' In alarm, Vickery pulled his prisoner out of the coach, and hurried him back into the building.

There was no mistaking what London's mob felt about the assassination of Spencer Perceval. For them, it represented a liberation from tyranny, a cause for unrestrained rejoicing. Within two hours, flyers and news-sheets were being sold on the streets with news of the murder. Emerging from the Commons, Samuel Romilly, an MP and Perceval's political opponent, was alarmed to hear 'the most savage expressions of joy and exultation' in the streets around Parliament. And the extraordinary demonstration carried an even more sinister undertone.

What sent shivers of alarm through the nerves of those who exercised power in Westminster was the smell of revolution in the air. Bellingham had become the people's hero. 'Oh I will fire my gun tomorrow,' shouted one demonstrator enthusiastically. 'I did not think there was an Englishman left that had such a heart. He could not have shot a greater rascal!' A constable brought his outburst to a halt by arresting him, but most of the crowd shared the demonstrator's feelings. From the heaving bodies around Parliament emerged chants, 'Perceval is down, the Prince Regent must be down next.' Take out the Prime Minister, followed by the acting monarch, and what was left of government?

All across London, the forces of law and order were called out to contain the wild demonstrations erupting in the streets. On behalf of the Home Secretary, John Beckett, permanent under-secretary in the Home Office, authorised the regular troops responsible for the safety of the capital, the Foot Guards and Horse Guards, to be ordered from their barracks to preserve the peace. Members of Volunteer regiments reported to their quarters. In the City of London, the mayor called out the militia. Elsewhere, justices of the peace commanded the watch to be reinforced, and instructed parish beadles to enrol special constables, known as 'bludgeon men', to patrol with them.

By nightfall, repeated charges by the Horse Guards had at last cleared the crowds from around Parliament, and the frenzy began to die down. At about midnight, the streets were quiet enough for the magistrates in the Commons to make a second attempt to send Bellingham to prison in Newgate. Instead of a hired coach, Lord Clive, the well-heeled, twenty-seven-year-old grandson of the nabob, Robert Clive of India, offered them the use of his six-seater chariot in which he had raced across London to give assistance. With an escort of Life Guards clattering on either side, a pair of policemen acting as coachmen, and a party that included a magistrate, the two Bow Street officers and Lord Clive inside, the Prime Minister's murderer was taken up Whitehall and along the Strand. Despite the late hour, a crowd was waiting to cheer Bellingham's arrival at Newgate prison on the edge of Smithfield meat market, although the horsemen kept them at a distance as he was hurried into the great stone fortress.

Once the door of Newgate thudded shut, responsibility for Bellingham's security rested with John Newman, the chief keeper. The City of London's sheriffs ordered him to take every precaution to prevent the prisoner committing suicide or being poisoned. The legal machinery had reached the discovery stage. So Bellingham had to be kept alive until the law could find out why he had killed Perceval, and who else was involved.

The keeper loaded the prisoner's arms and legs with a double set of irons, and posted two keepers in his cell to watch him through the night so that he could not harm himself. But the precautions were unnecessary. Bellingham showed no signs of anguish or of wanting to escape. Even weighed down by two sets of manacles around his wrists, and two around his ankles, he eagerly consumed a light meal. Then, as though exhausted by the great challenge he had overcome, he fell into a deep, untroubled sleep.

By contrast, the members of Perceval's decapitated cabinet sat up late into the night. Eleven ministers were present, including the most senior, the Lord Chancellor, Lord Eldon, normally forthright in defence of conservative values, and Richard Ryder, the Home Secretary and Perceval's closest friend. But Eldon seemed momentarily too shocked to give a lead, while Ryder, responsible for internal security, was prostrated by grief and barely able to speak. Lord Castlereagh, the secretive Ulsterman newly appointed as Foreign Secretary, would soon emerge as a political force, but he was still feeling his way. In these first hours on their own, the ministers still seemed stunned by what had happened. A single bullet had deprived them of four officers in one person: Prime Minister, Chancellor of the Exchequer, leader of the House of Commons, and Chancellor of the Duchy of Lancaster. Such was Perceval's dominance, a colleague had termed him 'the Supreme Commander'.

Yet every minister was acutely aware that, even before the murder, rioting and violence were widespread in the Midlands and north of England. Weapons had been stolen, buildings torched and factory owners murdered. To many it seemed the country was lurching towards revolution. Luddites opposed to industrial modernisation provided the armed edge, but in the cities the chief threat came from the mischief stirred up in the teeming slums by democratic firebrands still inspired by the ideals of the French Revolution. Already stringent precautions had been taken to monitor these dangers.

Barely two months earlier, the House of Commons had voted to re-establish a Committee of Secrecy to coordinate information-gathering on political radicals. The Aliens Office was mandated to collate rumours of insurrection issuing from Ireland. The private office of the Post Office was authorised to open the letters of suspected troublemakers. The centre of intelligence relating to security, however, was the Home Office. A stream of reports arrived there from paid spies as well as unpaid sources such as magistrates, justices of the peace, and clergymen, supplemented by intelligence from the self-appointed Association for the Preservation of Liberty and Property against Republicans and Levellers.

Next to grief, the strongest emotion driving the cabinet was fear – that John Bellingham might be part of some wider circle, that the murder might be a signal, the opening shot in a plot to create a nationwide rebellion, that the riot in Parliament Square was a rehearsal for the violence that would engulf them all. Ministers who were peers had just come from the House of Lords where they had voted to send a message to the Prince Regent expressing their horror at the crime, and their hope that the prince would take 'the speediest and most effectual measures for bringing the *perpetrators* of the crime to justice'. The plural revealed what they, and everyone who heard the news of Spencer Perceval's murder, feared most – a conspiracy.

The first decision of the cabinet was to order the guards to be doubled at the Tower of London and the Bank of England. Then messengers were sent to warn the lord lieutenant of each county of what had happened. Most of these were peers, already assembled in the House of Lords, and they soon left the capital in a string of private carriages carrying them out into the dark countryside. Back at home, they would instruct the justices of the peace to arrest radicals, troublemakers and insurrectionists, and to have the yeomanry and volunteers ready for action against the mob. At about eight o'clock, another edict was issued forbidding mail coaches to leave London in order to delay news of the assassination getting out.

After that the ministers stalled. There was discussion about imposing martial law, and sending the Prince Regent away from London. But no decision was taken. The gap left by Spencer Perceval was too big to be filled. A messenger was sent to Viscount Sidmouth, a former Prime Minister, to help them in their deliberations. Eventually the cabinet turned to the easier questions of funeral arrangements and the provision of financial support for the Prime Minister's family.

Shortly after midnight, the ministers ended their meeting in order to join the Speaker, Charles Abbott, as he accompanied the body of Spencer Perceval back to Downing Street. Even at that hour, onlookers still clustered in Whitehall. They jeered derisively when the coffin and the procession of political leaders went by. Soldiers on the street prevented any more active demonstration, but the hatred felt for Perceval's ministry could not be doubted.

The body in its open coffin was placed in the drawing room of

10 Downing Street surrounded by tall candles. The Prime Minister's brother, Lord Arden, sat next to it crying without restraint, but his widow, Jane Perceval, could not bring herself to look at the body. At six o'clock that evening, she had been visiting her closest friend, Frederica Ryder, wife of the Home Secretary, when the news was brought to her that her husband had been shot. Neither then, nor in the hours since, had she wept. Now she lay on her bed upstairs, dry-eyed, too shocked to move.

While 10 Downing Street remained frozen in grief, the printing-rooms of London's daily newspapers were a frenzy of noise and activity. To the rapidly developing trade of journalism, the murder presented a challenge. In twenty years, the number of papers and magazines had doubled to more than 240 in Britain, with fifty-two in London alone, about a dozen of them dailies. But all were still hand-printed on iron-framed presses – the steam-driven, rotary presses that *The Times* was planning to install were still two years away. Given the need to compose lines of new type by hand, to ink the frame that held the lead letters, and to pull each four-page sheet individually from the press, workers were restricted to printing about 250 impressions an hour from each press. Such an important, late-breaking story strained the primitive technology to its limits.

By six o'clock, when news of the murder became public, the country editions had already been printed and bundled for the mail coach. The London editions were set up, even at *The Times* which boasted that the last edition did not go to the printing-bed before five minutes past six. But on that evening all the London dailies held the presses.

The majority took time only to insert a few paragraphs into the already closely packed columns of print. With a print run lasting most of the night, any longer delay threatened to deprive readers of their morning paper. *The Globe* managed to get an extra edition away on the last mail coach before the ban was announced with three stark lines of print, 'Mr Perceval was SHOT DEAD this evening in the House of Commons. It is said that the Assassin was a Liverpool Merchant. His name was John James Bellingham.' But at *The Times*, the editor John Stoddard pulled out three columns of type to make way for a detailed report that began with an emotional tribute to the victim, 'a man whose personal qualities gave offence to no one – whose private life was an example to all – and who, however firm and unbending in his principles, yet conducted political conflicts in a way that robbed them of their characteristic bitterness'.

Then Stoddard voiced the only question that needed to be answered, 'What could have excited the wretched assassin to the commission of so diabolical an act?' He did not speculate further about Bellingham's motives, but even in this warmly felt tribute, Stoddard felt bound to refer to the widespread conviction that Perceval's 'firm and unbending' principles were 'narrow and bigotted [*sic*]', and liable to be replaced by 'a more enlightened policy or more beneficial maxims'. Like the cabinet, *The Times* implicitly assumed that Perceval's murder must be connected to the policies his ministry had followed.

Stoddard's editorial was pushed in among reports of the war in Spain against the occupying French forces, and a worrying account of violent disturbances in the north of England. Two nights earlier, several gangs of Luddites, twenty or thirty strong, had raided scores of private houses around Huddersfield and demanded that the owners hand over any weapons they had. 'By this means they have obtained possession of upwards of 100 stand of arms, and not one night has passed without some arms having been so taken.'

It was not difficult to see a connection between the assassination of the Prime Minister in the House of Commons and the organisation of these sinister events. Across London, the talk at fashionable parties was of impending revolution. The Prince Regent was rumoured to have fled to the safety of Brighton. 'Nobody knows at present whether it was the sole act of this man, or whether it is a plot,' the Irish society hostess, the Honourable Frances Calvert, wrote nervously in her journal. 'At all events, independent of the horrible thing it is, it is very alarming, the guards were all out for fear of any tumult.'

Until the cabinet could reassemble its collective will, the immediate priority for everyone with influence, politician, journalist and metropolitan hostess, was the discovery of Bellingham's motives. Everything hinged on his sanity. *The Times* editorial referred to the widespread rumours that his behaviour showed 'proofs of temporary derangement'. That was the good outcome. A mad gunman could have acted alone. But if John Bellingham proved to be sane, then it seemed likely that he was part of a wider conspiracy among Spencer Perceval's many enemies to overthrow the government.

Long before the assassin woke from his tranquil sleep the following day, journalists had begun to congregate round the door to the evil-smelling fortress of Newgate prison.

4

# A Free and Easy Conspiracy?

Welcome Ned Ludd, your case is good,
Make Perceval your aim;
For by this Bill, 'tis understood
It's death to break a Frame.

Luddite poem pinned up in Nottingham, February 1812

The assassin awoke on Tuesday morning, 12 May, with an over-whelming sense of relief. He had been daunted by the difficulty of killing the Prime Minister. The prospect of it had oppressed him for weeks, and he had repeatedly put it off, been 'dilatory' as he himself put it. But Spencer Perceval had had to be killed. It was not something that could be avoided. Now he had done the deed a great weight of anxiety had slipped from his shoulders. News of the assassin's satisfied state of mind was passed on to waiting reporters by John Newman, the chief keeper at Newgate prison, and a constant source of information about John Bellingham's behaviour while in custody. Having slept soundly, Bellingham had risen on the morning following the murder, Newman revealed, and breakfasted with a good appetite off buttered rolls and a large basin of sweetened tea prepared by the keeper himself. The image the keeper conveyed to reporters was of someone sane and at ease with the world.

Nothing in his appearance suggested that he was mad. John Bellingham stood about five feet ten inches tall, with dark, curly hair, and deep blue eyes. He had a long, saturnine face which bore a surprising resemblance, as everyone who saw him remarked, to that of the aristocratic, aquiline-nosed, radical MP, Sir Francis Burdett. His clothes were good but not foppish – a dark brown coat, now torn by rough handling, a striped toilinet waistcoat, dusty yellow nankeen trousers, and Hessian boots. These, as it happened, were almost exactly what the fashion magazine, *Le Beau Monde*, advised for a gentleman's morning wear. The brown coat, calf-length Hessian boots and waistcoat made of toilinet, a woven mixture of silk, cotton and wool, were particularly specified by the *Monde*, although it permitted bottle-green as an alternative for the coat. Kerseymere, or twilled cotton, was what the magazine recommended for trousers, but nankeen, a hard-wearing cotton akin to denim, though a little coarser, did not destroy the overall effect.

The impression of respectability was underlined by the apparently reasonable letter that Bellingham wrote to his landlady, Rebecca Robarts, later that morning after breakfast:

Dear Madam, Yesterday midnight I was escorted to this neighbourhood by a noble troop of light horse, and delivered into the care of Mr Newman as a State Prisoner of the first class. For eight years I have never found my mind so tranquil as since this melancholy but necessary catastrophe. As the merits or demerits of my peculiar case must be regularly unfolded in a Criminal Court of Justice to ascertain the guilty party, by a jury of my countrymen, I have to request the favour of you to send me three or four shirts, some cravats, handkerchiefs, night-caps, stockings &c out of my drawers, together with comb, soap, toothbrush, with any other trifle that presents itself which you think I may have occasion for, and inclose them in my leather trunk. And the key please to send

sealed, per bearer; also my great coat, flannel gown, and black
waistcoat, which will much oblige, Dear Madam, your very
obedient servant,

John Bellingham

To the above, please to add the prayer book.

His handwriting was as neat and composed as the tone of the letter.
The meaning was lucid, and the phrasing regular. And the desire to
appear smart in court was understandable. Only the context made
the message bizarre. The 'neighbourhood' was Newgate prison
where he was confined, the 'noble troop' of cavalry had been guards
posted to prevent his escape, Newman was his jailer, the 'melancholy but necessary catastrophe' was murder, and the country was
in uproar. To be tranquil in such circumstances suggested that
either he suffered from an impaired sense of reality or he was a
genuinely wicked character. As Tuesday wore on the newspapers
grew more inclined to believe the latter.

The reporter on the Whig paper, the *Morning Chronicle*, clearly
had a source among the MPs who were present when John
Bellingham was charged. As a result, the paper was able to add
some detail to the prisoner's motives for killing the Prime Minister.
They concerned 'a dispute which he had with the Consul in
Archangel by which he incurred a loss of seven or £8,000, but in
which the British Government had nothing to do'. Bellingham, a
Liverpool merchant, had been imprisoned in Russia following the
dispute, the newspaper explained, and since his arrival back in
Britain had sought compensation from 'the public offices', but had
been told the government could not interfere in 'private affairs'.
'He says that he was driven to despair; that three weeks ago he
bought the pistols for the horrid deed, which he has at last
perpetrated.'

Throughout Tuesday, reporters questioned their political and social contacts, and especially keeper Newman, for any additional information they could offer about the murderer. All those who had encountered Bellingham in the hours since he pulled the trigger remarked upon his peace of mind, and most newspapers followed the keeper's line about his mental state.

'At first it was impossible to believe that such an act could be committed by any but an insane man,' *The Courier* declared, 'but it would be difficult to come to this conclusion from the manner and demeanour of the prisoner . . . nothing appeared in his conduct to induce a suspicion of his labouring under insanity. He has since been very much employed in writing, and there is nothing of that hurry in his action, or want of method in his style, to induce us to believe that he does now or has ever laboured under mental derangement.'

This was the crux of the problem facing the legal investigation. Was Bellingham sane, and if so was his crime committed with the help of others? These were the questions that the two Middlesex magistrates, Harvey Combe and Michael Angelo Taylor, posed when they arrived to question him at about nine o'clock that morning.

They too noted that Bellingham appeared calm, self-possessed and respectful. He was no longer burdened by chains. His room next to the chapel, reserved for distinguished prisoners awaiting trial, was large and well-lit. It overlooked the chapel yard, and was almost free from the rank odour of sewage and despair that visitors associated with Newgate. In answer to their questions, Bellingham firmly assured the magistrates that he had acted alone, without any accomplices. Furthermore, he had intended to kill no one but the Prime Minister. Other members of the cabinet, he made clear, were not his targets. Probing his behaviour, the magistrates suggested, because of the sharp downward trajectory of the bullet, that he

might have leaned over someone else to shoot. Bellingham indignantly rejected the suggestion, and for the only time in the interview
showed signs of being upset. He would never have dreamed of
putting anyone at risk except for the Prime Minister. It was a matter
of justice, he insisted, brought about by the business in Russia.

Unlike Newman, who thought there was nothing wrong in
Bellingham's mind, the magistrates went away uncertain about his
sanity. That doubt overshadowed everything they had learned from
him. However reasonable his manner, his motive for murder made
no sense. Until they could be sure about his state of mind, the
magistrates could not decide how much weight to attach to his
declaration of having acted alone. It became supremely important
to find out the murderer's background, and what he had been
doing in the days before he killed Spencer Perceval.

This was the focus of the investigation directed by Harvey
Combe, a former lord mayor of London notable for his staunchly
Whig politics. So long as the legal process continued to dominate,
the inquiry into Bellingham's character and contacts would remain
the top priority. The groundwork was handled by the Bow Street
Runners, William Adkins and his brother Richard, led by the
talented John Vickery. The wealth of information they discovered
about the killer in a very short time testified to their energy and
detective skills. But Combe had two other sources of information:
the surprising number of people who actually knew Bellingham
and the indefatigable journalists on the London papers.

The first information came from a visitor to Newgate prison known
only as Hokkirk, who claimed to be a friend of the Bellingham
family. Although forbidden to see the prisoner, he and Newman
obviously talked because reporters soon learned that when
Bellingham was a child, his father, a painter, had gone mad and
been confined in St Luke's mental asylum in London. The place of

confinement was significant. Unlike the better-known and older asylum of Bethlem, or Bedlam, St Luke's did not allow visitors to come round and gawp at its inmates, and for a good reason. It gave priority to violent lunatics who were, under the definition of the 1744 Vagrancy Act, 'furiously mad, or so far disordered in their Senses that [it] may be dangerous [for them] to be permitted to go Abroad'. Most of its 260 patients had to be physically restrained in some way.

The news gave ammunition to those, like Jerdan, who were convinced of the murderer's insanity. Madness obviously ran in the family. Bellingham's studiously calm behaviour now took on a different complexion. It could have been a mask to conceal the mental chaos within. The father's descent into furious madness had been more clear-cut, but at least he had not killed anyone. The son's derangement was undoubtedly more severe.

Then two other items of information emerged that appeared to tip the balance the other way. The first came from Bellingham himself. He revealed that he had been brought up in St Neots, a small market town in Huntingdonshire about sixty miles north of London where the surroundings could not have been more secure. As was soon confirmed, his mother came from a long-established, prosperous family in the area, and after his father's death he had grown up surrounded by loving and supportive relatives. A second pointer towards his stability was the discovery that he was married and the father of three children, all living in Liverpool.

The most revealing clue found on Tuesday, however, was more ambiguous. This was the discovery of a pamphlet that Bellingham had written in March, eight weeks earlier. It described his experiences in Russia from 1804 to 1809, and he had had it printed at a cost of £9 15s 0d shillings for distribution to every Member of Parliament. The pamphlet had made no impact at the time, but by Tuesday afternoon typesetters on every London daily were setting chunks of its text on their formes. The writing was clear, but it did not explain why misfortunes that took place in Russia in 1805 should have led to murder seven years later.

What the pamphlet did make obvious was how well known Bellingham was to the authorities. It revealed that he had taken his complaints to senior civil servants, like John Beckett, under-secretary at the Home Office, and Michael Herries, permanent secretary at the Treasury, and that while he was in Russia he had even tried to claim asylum in the home of Lord Granville Leveson-Gower, the wonderfully handsome, impossibly vain, former ambassador to Russia. To the well-connected Combe, it would have been obvious that one or more of these encounters might have offered some warning of Bellingham's intentions. In the structure of law enforcement, magistrates responsible for policing London occupied a pivotal position. Like all magistrates, they took charge of both the investigation of crime and the maintenance of order within their county. But the law officers of the capital carried an extra burden: to prevent any kind of subversive activity that might endanger the government of the land. This added responsibility brought them into frequent contact with the Home Office and its unrivalled resources for gathering intelligence. When Combe met Beckett, he must have expected the under-secretary to be able to supply him with background reports on the assassin.

The industrious, efficient Beckett had access to information from across Britain and Ireland. In those turbulent days, so much flowed in that it was impossible for him to see it all. Reports of arson and rioting came from the textile counties of Lancashire and Yorkshire as well as from the manufacturing hotbed of the Midlands. There were waves of rick-burning in the south, and industrial sabotage in Wales. The Napoleonic Wars had introduced large numbers of men to weapons and disciplined organisation, and what especially frightened local informants was the potential alliance between military experience and social insurrection. The most urgent reports always concerned the groups of men who arrived at night to smash up stocking-machines or mechanical threshers, declaring themselves to be under the command of 'Captain Ludd' or 'Captain Edward Ludd'.

One note recently forwarded to Beckett had linked threats of destruction to a wider plan to overthrow the government and 'that damned set of Rogues, Perceval & Co to whom we attribute all the miseries of our country . . . we hope for assistance from the French Emperor in shaking off the Yoke of the Rottenest, wickedest and most Tyrannical Government that ever existed'. It was signed 'General of the Army of Redeemers Ned Ludd'. In Yorkshire alone, if one frightened informant were to be believed, eight thousand men were already under arms, including many militia soldiers, whose plan for 'bringing about a revolution, would be to send parties to the different houses of the members of both Houses of Parliament, and destroy them'. Nor did it escape the attention of magistrates that such reports very often mentioned the muskets and pistols carried by the mob. 'What the danger of assassination is,' Earl Fitzwilliam, lord lieutenant of Yorkshire's West Riding, reported to a fellow peer, 'your Lordship will readily collect from the readiness with which this abominable *banditti* fires on every occasion.'

Guns had never been so plentifully available to anyone intent on resisting authority. During two decades of war with France, the army had trained thousands of men to use muskets and supplied them by the ton to both regular soldiers and the part-time militia. Most householders owned at least a blunderbuss, to protect their property, and a variety of more portable, sophisticated weapons were available to those who needed them. The popularity of duelling, hunting and travelling – especially on roads frequented by highwaymen and *banditti* – had created a demand for small arms that made their manufacture a thriving industry. For the magistrates, their production simply increased the danger in a time of turmoil, but for later generations this was the classic era made famous by firearms artists such as Durs Egg and Joseph Manton who produced beautiful, lethal flintlock pistols for duelling; by James Purdey who manufactured sporting shotguns for wildfowlers; and by William Beckwith of Snow Hill in London who, as the Bow Street Runner John Vickery would shortly discover, made squat, half-inch calibre, steel pistols for sale at the price of four guineas a pair.

Yet where revolution was concerned, it was urban rather than rural violence that caused the government the greatest anxiety. Every large town was growing fast as manufacturing and commercial work lured people from the country. The population of Glasgow had tripled since 1750 to 100,000 people, the thriving port of Liverpool had quadrupled to almost 80,000 inhabitants in barely forty years, Manchester and Birmingham were only a little smaller at 70,000. None, however, came close in size to London where the population had exploded to almost one million, forcing thousands of families to live crammed into 'rookeries', made up of hovels piled one on another, where a dozen or more people might share a single squalid room. Such conditions incubated sickness, drunkenness, crime and, the Home Office's many spies reported, insurrection.

When the poet Samuel Taylor Coleridge visited a London pub on the morning after Perceval's murder to investigate public reaction, he was horrified by the sheer bitterness expressed by ordinary people. No regret for Spencer Perceval's death. No anger at the murderer. Just a savage pleasure in what had been done. 'These were the very words,' Coleridge reported for the *Morning Post*. ' "This is but the beginning" – "More of these damned Scoundrels must go the same way & then poor people may live." '

Influenced by the French Revolution and the writings of Tom

Paine, the poor saw a direct connection between their misery and political corruption. 'Every man might maintain his family decent & comfortable,' one person asserted in Coleridge's hearing, 'if the money were not picked out of our pockets by them damned Placemen.'

Those were the sentiments of the Corresponding Societies, set up in 1789 to share the ideas of the French Revolution, but supposedly suppressed in the 1790s by laws against political dissent and unauthorised meetings. As a Whig, and a declared supporter of Charles James Fox's liberal policies, Harvey Combe had opposed this draconian legislation, but he knew that the societies' former members had found ways of getting round the bans. They now assembled informally in pubs, ostensibly for 'free and easy evenings' of singing and drinking, but in reality to keep alive dreams of replacing a corrupt society by one based on liberty and equality. 'Yes we must lay on a general plan of Insurrection,' one of these radicals declared, according to a government spy, 'which must be agreed to be acted upon, and not debated afterwards.' Fear of what might happen when guns and urban revolutionaries came together led the Home Office and London magistrates to flood the revolutionary underworld with paid informers. Their reports were filled with wild talk and plans to storm Parliament and kill all the cabinet, or to take over the Bank of England, or to invade Carlton House where the Prince Regent lived, hang him and set up a republican government that would serve the people. Anger at a government that oppressed the poor and rewarded its friends with pensions and well-paid jobs appeared in the extravagant toasts the radicals offered as they downed their porter and ale: 'May the guillotine be as common as a pawnbroker's shop and every tyrant's head a pledge', 'Let the barren land of our country be manured with the blood of our Tyranny', and, most popular of all, 'To the last king, strangled by the guts of the last priest'. It was apparent too in their songs, one of the most popular being sung to the tune of 'Sweet Lass on Richmond Hill':

Tis in Pall Mall there lives a Pig [the Prince Regent]
That doth this Mall adorn.
So fat, so plump, so monstrous Big,
A finer ne'er was born.
This Pig so sweet, so full of Meat,
He's one I wish to kill.
I'll fowls resign on thee to dine,
Sweet Pig of fine Pall Mall.

Among the violent graffiti scrawled on the walls along Whitehall was one at least that came from the free and easy clubs, 'Perceval's ribs are only fit to broil the Prince Regent's heart on'. Revolutionary words might quickly lead to revolution itself. A London magistrate had to know whether Bellingham's bullet could be the signal the revolutionaries were waiting for. In his meetings with Beckett, Combe would therefore have asked whether the assassin's name had been mentioned by any of the under-secretary's spies in the underworld. Almost inevitably, given their number, one of the government's spies had met the murderer in the weeks before the killing.

Sitting up in the narrow press gallery that overlooked the chamber of the House of Commons, Vincent Dowling, parliamentary reporter for *The Day*, had been joined by Bellingham who carried with him the same opera glasses that were seized from him in the lobby. At the committal hearing in the Commons, the reporter testified that the stranger had come there more than once, and had asked him to identify the different members of the cabinet sitting on the government benches below. Dowling particularly remembered pointing out Richard Ryder, the Home Secretary. As a reporter, he declared that he only appreciated the significance of these encounters in retrospect.

Dowling, however, had a secret that never emerged in his testimony. He was also paid by the Home Office to infiltrate the groups of political extremists who met in drinking clubs to talk and sing and plot ways of creating a new, radical society. He was sufficiently conscientious to pass on several long accounts of treasonable meetings to the Home Office. A stranger with an interest as persistent as Bellingham's in identifying senior ministers, including the spy's employer, should have aroused his suspicions, and Dowling admitted that on the second or third meeting he had had a long conversation with Bellingham. He must have asked the stranger his name and business. It is possible that Dowling filed no report of his encounter, certainly none exists today. But the presumption must be that he did provide some note of the meeting, because the Home Office continued to pay him for information after Perceval's murder, indicating that no blame had been attached to his conduct regarding the murderer. Perhaps Beckett missed the significance of the warning, but it is equally probable that he had passed the information on to the Home Secretary, and in that case Combe would have understood immediately why no further action had been taken. The inadequacies of the Home Secretary and the paperwork that accumulated on his desk were notorious in government circles.

Richard Ryder had been Perceval's friend since their days at university. He had been appointed Home Secretary because the Prime Minister wanted the post to be held by someone whose loyalty was beyond question. But, physically delicate and crippled by lack of confidence, Ryder was ill-suited to the demands of a brutal portfolio that placed him in charge of the internal security of the kingdom. The Home Secretary was widely rumoured to retire to bed with a headache rather than take a difficult decision to deploy troops on the streets or to order the round-up of suspected troublemakers. To keep the department functioning, much of the minister's work had in practice been shouldered by the Prime Minister. Amidst Spencer Perceval's many other duties, sifting significant information from the dross did not rank high. The possibility existed, nevertheless, that Perceval himself might have been ultimately responsible for failing to prevent his own murder.

Whatever the failures of the Home Office, Combe would have learned much about the case from his meetings with Beckett. The murder did not come out of the blue: Bellingham had approached many people and his demands were well-known to every area of government. His crime was not spontaneous, and his preparations had none of the disorder that would indicate madness. And all of his actions indicated that he had acted alone.

On the afternoon of Tuesday, 12 May, less than twenty-four hours after the murder, members of the House of Commons met to pay tribute to their murdered colleague. The most eloquent expression of their feelings came not in words but in uncontrollable weeping. It was an emotional society, the last before the responsibility of running an empire made it desirable for men to stiffen the upper lip and keep their feelings under control in public. But even so their demonstration of grief was remarkable. The Speaker, Charles Abbott, noted that Richard Ryder could not even speak for crying, and that 'in most faces there was an agony of tears; and neither Lord Castlereagh [Foreign Secretary], Ponsonby [leader of the Whig opposition], Whitbread [a radical Whig], nor Canning [Perceval's Tory rival] could give a dry utterance to their sentiments.'

Shock at the violence of the Prime Minister's death, and that it should have taken place within the palace of Westminster, contributed to the depth of emotion, but their tears sprang also from genuine affection. The Whig leader, George Ponsonby, declared in a choking voice that while he had opposed Perceval bitterly on political matters, there was no one 'of whose sense of honour he had a higher opinion, or for whom he had a greater personal affection', at which point according to the *Parliamentary Register*, 'the emotions of the right honourable gentleman were such as for a few moments to deprive him of the power of utterance'.

In the House of Lords, the Lord Chancellor, Lord Eldon, was so convulsed by tears that he had to let Lord Ellenborough, the Lord Chief Justice, take his place on the woolsack as Speaker. Even after his return, Eldon was, in the words of the *Register*, 'so overpowered by his feelings that he could not read the message [of condolence from the Prince Regent] audibly and it was with great difficulty his lordship got through it'.

Their anguish provided a sharp contrast to the scenes of riotous celebration that were already rippling outwards from London. From towns in Hertfordshire and Essex, reports came in of the joy and often of the wild gunfire that broke out as people learned of Spencer Perceval's death. In the days to come the Midlands, Yorkshire, Lancashire and the Lowlands of Scotland would be convulsed by a wave of outrageous delight at the Prime Minister's murder. The forces of law and order in the country seemed as powerless to contain it as those in London.

On Tuesday evening, according to the *Nottingham Journal*, a mob 'proceeded with a band of music all through the principal streets. They were soon joined by a numerous rabble who, in the most indecent and reprehensible manner, testified their joy at the horrid catastrophe by repeated shouts, the firing of guns and every species of exultation.' Similar demonstrations were reported in Birmingham as people heard what Bellingham had done, and crowds 'stood huzzaing and expressing their savage joy'. Bellingham's health was drunk in Glasgow, Liverpool and Manchester. In the Lake District, a shocked

William Wordsworth warned his sister, Dorothy, 'The country is no doubt in a most alarming situation; and if much firmness be not displayed by the Government, confusion & havoc & murder will break out and spread terribly.' From Cambridge, another poet, the Irishman Tom Moore, reported apprehensively that 'all the common people's heads are full of revolution'.

It was still possible that Perceval's murder might have been designed to detonate the bomb of revolution, but in London the first fears were receding. Combe's initial conclusion that Bellingham was a lone eccentric would have been reported to Beckett and others responsible for law and order. And the political forces in Westminster were already beginning to regroup. With each new report of riot and disorder, ministers like Castlereagh, Eldon and Ellenborough grew increasingly determined to demonstrate the might of government forcefully and without delay.

When the cabinet assembled late on Tuesday night, their uncontrollable grief gave way to anger, and a savage desire to wipe out the affront done both to Parliament and to them personally. Bellingham had to be executed as quickly as possible. In the Commons, Castlereagh, who had taken over leadership from the paralysed Ryder, made it plain that in his opinion the murder 'was confined to the individual who had perpetrated the act'. Time spent searching for accomplices would be wasted.

Eldon went further. In the Lords, he had been braced by a conversation with Ellenborough, a legal neanderthal notorious for being the last judge to sentence a man to be hanged, drawn and quartered. The Lord Chief Justice was convinced that Bellingham should not only be executed without delay, but that in order to demonstrate the power of government as dramatically as possible to the rioters who had dared celebrate his atrocious crime, he should be hanged publicly in Palace Yard before the House of Commons.

Not every minister sympathised with this suggestion, but there was no dispute within the cabinet that public policy and personal feeling demanded the death of the murderer. The case would be handled by the Attorney General, Sir Vicary Gibbs. The Lord Chief Justice would be told to set the earliest possible date for the trial. The political machine was about to swamp the criminal investigation.

# Examining the Enigma of the Assassin's Sanity

I must begin to explain the origin of this unhappy affair, which took place in 1804. I was a merchant at Liverpool, in that year I went to Russia on some mercantile business of importance to myself, and having finished that business I was about to take my departure from Archangel for England.

John Bellingham, 15 May 1812

Once it was decided to bring John Bellingham to trial, a solicitor had to be appointed to act for his defence. The choice was easily made. Most defence solicitors had a reputation for being as ignorant and disreputable as their criminal clients. But in London, there was one notable exception.

When James Harmer, the son of a Spitalfields weaver, apprenticed himself to a firm of lawyers in the early 1790s, he discovered that the defence of clients usually depended on invented alibis or suborned witnesses. From the moment he set up on his own, however, he built a reputation for knowing the law, and for the care he took in briefing barristers. By the early 1800s, his offices in Hatton Garden, within shouting distance of the law courts, had become the first place to go for anyone, as a contemporary put it, 'whose natural destination was the Old Bailey'. Portly and successful, Harmer was destined to become a pillar of the legal profession, and an alderman of the City of London, yet he never lost an edgy loyalty to the underdog. By the time he retired, his commitment to the overhaul of his seedy end of the law had transformed court-room practice in criminal trials. In the judgement of Charles Phillips, the outstanding attorney of the early Victorian law courts, Bellingham's solicitor was both 'a worthy and a clever man'.

With characteristic energy, Harmer read all the material avail-able about his client, and late on Wednesday morning interviewed him at length. He found the prisoner in triumphant mood. That morning the newspapers had printed large portions of Bellingham's pamphlet containing the petition that he had sent out to MPs in March. 'The people will now be able to judge my case,' he declared, 'and do me the justice to say, I have only done my duty.' This remained Bellingham's unshakable conviction, that once it was known how unjustly he had been treated, everyone would under-stand why he had been forced to kill the Prime Minister. When that was understood, no jury could possibly convict him of murder. With difficulty Harmer persuaded him that he still needed to mount a defence in court. Eventually, he got from Bellingham the names of several people who knew him and might be able to give evidence on his behalf.

Having promised to read the pamphlet himself, Harmer returned to his office, then sent a series of urgent messages by the evening mail coaches to Liverpool and Southampton. The former were directed to John Bourne, mayor of Liverpool, and to Bellingham's business partner in the city, John Parton; the latter was addressed to Bellingham's cousin, Mrs Ann Billett. All of them asked for evidence of John Bellingham's insanity.

Harmer had reasonable grounds for believing that his client could be defended on the grounds of insanity. That Bellingham was obsessive could hardly be doubted. A strong case could be made that he was also delusional. And with the right witnesses, it might be convincingly argued that he was indeed mad, at least so far as the law understood the word.

Until 1800, the definition had been unambiguous. At the trial of Lord Ferrers in 1760, it was held that his lordship, having killed an employee while in a state of paranoia, must be found guilty because only a 'total, permanent or temporary want of reason would acquit a prisoner'. To be judged insane, the criminal's mental state had to be akin to that of 'a wild beast', unable to distinguish between good and evil. But in 1800, James Hadfield, a veteran severely wounded in battle by sabre cuts to his head, stood up in a theatre and fired a pistol at King George III in the belief that his death would bring about the new millennium. In court, his lawyer, the brilliant Thomas Erskine, successfully pleaded that Hadfield was suffering from so profound a delusion that he was incapable of telling right from wrong simply at the moment of firing.

The Hadfield judgment was suspect, partly because of the sympathy aroused by his terrible wounds, and partly because the judge had stopped the trial rather than letting the jury decide. Nevertheless, it was enough to give a solicitor hope that Bellingham could mount a successful defence on the same grounds. Harmer next wrote to two of London's most eminent experts on mental health, Dr Thomas Munro, who had given testimony on behalf of Hadfield, and Dr Samuel Simmons, who had attended George III during the king's madness, asking them both to testify to his client's insanity. He then instructed the flamboyant Irish attorney, Peter Alley, to defend John Bellingham on the grounds that at the time of the murder he was out of his mind.

On the very day that Harmer's letters went out, however, two witnesses tracked down by the Bow Street Runners, John Vickery and the Adkins brothers, cast severe doubts on the line of defence he proposed to adopt. The first was the gun-maker, William Beckwith, who testified that he had sold the murder weapon to Bellingham on about 20 April, three weeks before it was used.

The type of pistol showed that it had been chosen specifically to be concealed. It was equipped with a detachable barrel so that if necessary the firing mechanism could be carried unobtrusively in one pocket and the barrel in another. Beckwith had advised his customer to get accustomed to how the weapon behaved when fired, and he also informed the officers that Bellingham had then gone to a park to practise shooting with the pistol.

The second witness found by Vickery and his colleagues added to the impression that the crime had been carefully premeditated. Evidently Bellingham had tried screwing the barrel into place – a special key was provided for the purpose – and found the process too complicated. William Taylor, suitably enough a tailor by trade, told the Runners that he had been asked by Bellingham on about 23 April to alter his brown coat so that he could carry a concealed weapon that was exactly the size of Beckwith's pistol with the barrel already attached.

The testimony of these two witnesses not only illustrated the murderer's unmistakably rational state of mind but the carefully thought-out steps he had taken in preparation for his deed. It confirmed the impression given by Rebecca Robarts, his landlady. Vickery, who had briefly questioned her, went back to New Millman Street for a more extensive interview. Her evidence showed that Bellingham had stayed in her lodging-house from the beginning of January 1812, and that throughout that time he had behaved quite normally, indeed had been a model tenant.

Potentially, Rebecca Robarts was the most damaging witness of them all. For more than four months, she had seen John Bellingham almost every day. On Sundays, she and her son would go with him to the fashionable church in the Foundlings' Hospital in Guilford Street. Often she and Bellingham would also visit exhibitions and museums together. They went out so frequently that Vickery must have guessed that the young widow had developed a certain tenderness for her tall, well-dressed lodger. On one occasion, she recalled, her son had gone missing. She had immediately run to Bellingham for help, and he had searched through the streets until he found the boy and brought him back to his mother. No jury who heard Mrs Robarts's testimony was likely to suppose that Bellingham was mad.

Yet Harmer's reading of the pamphlet revealed a man acting so obsessively in one particular circumstance that it did create a clear impression of madness. Where righting a personal wrong was concerned, Bellingham did not behave rationally. In pursuit of justice for himself, he knew no limits.

Bellingham's troubles had begun in the summer of 1804 when he chartered a ship to sail from Hull to Archangel in northern Russia. From there he intended to bring back a cargo of timber and iron but, in the words of his pamphlet, 'was illegally prevented from returning to England by the said ship, as was my intention, and also was so much injured as to be deprived of the opportunity of loading my own goods on board of her'. As a result he had 'suffered very serious losses'. What he sought was compensation from the government because the British ambassador to St Petersburg had failed to support his efforts to obtain justice in Russia.

In the context of conducting trade during a time of war, the detail of his business dealings contained a powerful logic. Bellingham was obeying the same rationale of taking risks to make a profit that had also created the gigantic edifice of Britain's world-encircling trade. From the top of Ludgate Hill, a short walk from Hatton Garden, Harmer could see a forest of masts and spars rising above the Pool of London where vessels waited to load cargoes for Russia, India, the United States and the West Indies. What drove their owners had also driven Bellingham. And like them he had expected the laws of international trade to protect him from wrongdoing.

Trade with Russia always carried risk, but it promised huge profits, because the country's main exports – timber, iron, hemp and tallow – were strategic materials needed for shipbuilding and lighting, and demand for them was always strong. The usual route in peacetime was through the narrow Skagerrak strait between Denmark and Sweden, and across the Baltic Sea to St Petersburg. But in wartime, French and Dutch privateers – privately owned ships authorised by their governments to attack enemy shipping for their own profit – preyed upon British-flagged vessels near the coasts of Europe, and once Denmark fell within Napoleon's empire in 1800, the Skagerrak route became exceptionally hazardous. Consequently, many 'charter-parties', the contracts made between cargo-owners and shipowners, specified that the vessels were to sail around the northernmost point of Scandinavia to the port of Archangel in northern Russia, far away from the dangers of privateers and Danish guns.

Despite these dangers, the Baltic trade as it was known had become the fastest-growing financial sector in the City of London. A new dock dedicated to Russia's four main exports had just been opened on the south bank of the Thames, and the dealers, brokers and shippers in the Royal Exchange who specialised in these commodities had set up an unofficial exchange in the Baltic Coffee House. But every profitable deal came with stories of St Petersburg's intolerable weather, its stultifying bureaucracy and its backward conditions. And the memoirs of diplomats posted to Russia suggested that everything was even worse in Archangel. Surrounded by dark forest and impenetrable swampland, its winter temperatures dropped far below freezing, and the brief summer boiled with black swarms of mosquitoes from the stagnant pools that bordered the slowly oozing River Dvina. To administer this remote corner of the empire, the tsars appointed not one but two governors, one civil the other military, each equipped with a retinue of officials to enforce a different set of regulations.

Nevertheless Archangel had been a considerable trading centre for more than two centuries, and Bellingham's pamphlet pointed to the reason why. The port gave access to a region with seemingly inexhaustible reserves of timber and iron ore, and its trade, though dominated by a few, long-established Dutch companies, was well-regulated. Several British companies kept permanent agents there.

Bellingham had sailed for Archangel in June 1804, taking with him his young wife Mary, and their six-month-old son, James. Open water at the port was guaranteed for only five months during the year. Since the Russian port was less than twenty days' sailing from Hull, Bellingham should easily have been able to return with his cargo before the autumn. But, as the pamphlet suggested, something went wrong in the negotiations, and he was prevented from loading his cargo of timber and iron. He was still there in November long after ice had closed the port. That month he decided to leave Archangel and travel to the Russian capital of St Petersburg. For this he needed a *petrovnik*, or pass, but as he prepared for his departure, 'the said *petrovnik* was forcibly taken from me by the police Master without any cause whatever, and soldiers and police officers were placed on [my] person day and night to prevent [my] quitting the place'.

For Harmer, trawling the pages for evidence of his client's mental unsoundness, there were two unmistakable conclusions to be drawn from Bellingham's story: the first was the author's conviction that he had been the victim of commercial blackmail, and the second was that the author possessed an almost infantile refusal to accept the reality of events outside his control.

Bellingham's arrest was brought about by an influential Dutch merchant, Solomon van Brienen, who was a friend of the mayor of Archangel, Vasiliy Popov. The ostensible cause was to recover a debt of 4,890 roubles, approximately £500. Another Dutch merchant, Conrad Dorbecker, had bought a consignment of iron on behalf of

Bellingham from van Brienen, but had gone bankrupt before paying for the goods. Because Dorbecker and Bellingham were business partners, the Englishman was deemed to have become liable for the debt.

The pamphlet made it plain, however, that van Brienen's real purpose was revenge. He and Popov had been partners in the *Soyuz*, a vessel insured with Lloyd's of London for £3,800. When it sank in 1804 their insurance claim was refused by Lloyd's, on grounds of fraud. According to information passed secretly to the insurers, the ship was still afloat under another name. Unfortunately for Bellingham, the ship's owners decided that he must have been the Lloyd's informant. And so for good measure, van Brienen and Popov also brought a second, criminal suit against the Englishman for illegally depriving them of the money for the *Soyuz*.

According to Bellingham, no documentary evidence was ever produced to show that he had ordered the iron. If the supposed contract was concocted, and Dorbecker had indeed acted in collusion with his fellow Dutchman, Bellingham's anger was understandable, but the injury so overwhelmed him that he could see nothing else. Throughout his time in Archangel, Bellingham never looked for any settlement, or compromise. He simply demanded justice.

At first his persistence was rewarded. In response to his barrage of complaints, officials agreed that Popov and van Brienen 'had all along acted beyond the Law' as the pamphlet put it; in March 1805, he was released and actually on the road for St Petersburg before being stopped and brought back after the influential Popov persuaded the military governor, General Furster, to issue new orders for his arrest. On that occasion, Bellingham lost his self-control, creating a scene that the governor called 'highly indecorous'. The victim himself only admitted to having been 'a little vociferous'. Nevertheless, his case was then submitted to a court of commercial arbitration made up of two British merchants and two

Russians. As a compromise – and it signified the weakness of van Brienen's suit – they decided that Bellingham should pay just 2,000 roubles, approximately £200, to van Brienen for the non-existent iron purchase. This proposal was indignantly spurned.

Until then, his quarrel was confined to Russia, but in his fury Bellingham next appealed for help to the British ambassador in St Petersburg, Lord Granville Leveson-Gower. Unfortunately for Bellingham, the ambassador was about to take an eighteen-month holiday, and his appeal was passed on to the consul, Stephen Shairpe. A long-time resident of St Petersburg, and leader of the British expatriate community there, Shairpe quickly established that the dispute concerned a civil debt, and concluded that neither he nor the ambassador could intervene. With that refusal to help, Shairpe had apparently set in motion the convoluted sequence of steps that led Bellingham to the lobby of the House of Commons seven years later. To Bellingham, the logic was compelling – he had been denied help by the British government in his hour of need, and was thus entitled to seek redress later – but to Harmer, scouring the pamphlet for symptoms of lunacy, it must have offered the first faint hopes of showing that his client was indeed deranged.

In October 1805 a new civil governor arrived in Archangel, to be greeted by a letter from Bellingham not only demanding his release from confinement but also payment of compensation for unlawful imprisonment. Surprisingly, the governor promised to take another look at his case. A fresh hearing in court was ordered where, as Bellingham reported triumphantly, 'I obtained judgment against the whole party, including the Military Governor who had injured me.' However, as Harmer could easily discover, this was not the entire truth. The criminal suit was thrown out, but the judgment for debt still stood. Nevertheless, Bellingham's *petrovnik* allowing him to leave Archangel was at last restored. It was too late in the season to sail back to Britain, so in November 1805, eighteen disastrous months after he had arrived, Bellingham departed for St Petersburg.

Waiting for him in the capital were his twenty-three-year-old wife Mary and his son James. They had been with him when he was stopped on the road to St Petersburg earlier in the year, but unlike him they had been allowed to travel on to their destination. During the summer, Mary might have returned to Britain, but she had refused to leave without her husband. As she later explained, she supported herself and James by making hats and dresses for the families of the Factory, the powerful, well-entrenched association of British merchants in St Petersburg.

To Harmer, it was obvious that the reunited family could then have obtained permission to leave for home. The Factory carried influence with the Russian government, and both British and Russians were only too anxious to be rid of an embarrassment to the trading community. Had he followed this rational course, Bellingham would have shown himself to be sane. Instead he took the mad option of issuing a *ukase*, or writ, in St Petersburg demanding compensation from the tsar and the impeachment of General Furster, the military governor of Archangel, for his illegal detention. It was such an extraordinary demand that he could not get his writ printed until he had indemnified the printer against the risk of being sent to Siberia. Outraged that a foreigner should impugn the integrity of the tsar's government, the *duma*, or Parliament, in St Petersburg ordered him back to jail.

By now Leveson-Gower had returned from his extended holiday. Occasionally, as Bellingham was moved from one prison to another, he passed along a route in front of the residence of the ambassador 'who might view from his window this degrading severity towards a British subject'. Increasingly embittered, Bellingham began to blame Leveson-Gower for all his woes. Finally he made a desperate attempt to escape his guards and ran to claim asylum in the ambassador's house. To Bellingham's utter despair, Leveson-Gower refused to allow him to stay. 'I must therefore request you to give yourself up again into custody,' he wrote to the fugitive, 'but shall think it my Duty to make representations to the Government upon your affair, & shall be happy to use any means in my Power towards forwarding an arrangement of the Business in which you are involved.'

But no arrangement was possible. In July 1807 Bellingham's case had become ensnared in international politics, when Tsar Alexander I signed the Treaty of Tilsit with Napoleon, thereby altering the balance of power in Europe. From being a neutral country, Russia was transformed into an ally of France and an enemy of Britain. Caught in these great events, Bellingham's appeals for justice became still more hopeless. He endured another year of confinement in the city prison before being released in October 1808. Even then he remained under house arrest. In December he desperately appealed to the tsar for permission to leave – and, characteristically, to be paid compensation – but another eleven months passed before the necessary permit was issued. Early in December 1809 John Bellingham finally returned to London, financially ruined.

For a lawyer searching for signs of insanity, the pamphlet demonstrated an unmistakable loss of any sense of proportion, and arguably a breakdown of reason in the face of intolerable misfortune. Bellingham's conclusion that he deserved compensation because the ambassador was responsible for his ill-treatment was utterly illogical, and his recourse to the same argument more than two years later showed that he was still in the grip of the same obsession. As a defence, it only offered a slim chance of success. Backed by affidavits from those who knew him personally and professionally, however, and buttressed by Alley's combative advocacy, Harmer could only be sure that the strongest possible case would be presented that his client was unable to tell right from wrong. Why so much time should have elapsed before Bellingham determined to exact retribution, and why his target should have been Spencer Perceval rather than Granville Leveson-Gower, was not the concern of a defence solicitor.

By Wednesday evening the Attorney General, Sir Vicary Gibbs, had heard enough from Combe and the Bow Street officers to become as convinced of Bellingham's sanity as Harmer was of his madness. Where the two sides did agree, however, was in the belief that he had acted alone. From the prosecution's point of view, the criminal investigation had done its work. The political priority was now to have Bellingham hanged as an example to others, and any consideration of an accomplice could only delay proceedings. Harmer was equally averse to the idea of a conspiracy. To convince a court that a solitary murderer was mad would be hard enough. It would become impossible if Bellingham had been acting in concert with others.

Neither side had any interest in extending the scope of their inquiries. There was no need to discover why Bellingham had suddenly decided to kill Spencer Perceval, no need to enquire how he had maintained himself while in London, and above all no need to learn whether anyone else had been involved in the murder.

# The Victim is Seen as a Fond Father
# and Attentive Husband

I was born of Parents, powerful, honourable and happy till a cruel
blow deprived my mother of a husband, and her family of a father.
John Perceval, *Narrative of the Treatment experienced by a*
*Gentleman, during a state of mental derangement,* 1838

On the same Wednesday afternoon that James Harmer set in
motion his plan to save the murderer's life, the House of Commons
took steps to look after the victim's family. Spencer Perceval had left
a widow and no fewer than eleven children, most of whom had still
to be educated. In an age when politicians were expected to make
money from their time in office, the Prime Minister was virtually
unique, as more than one speaker pointed out, in leaving his family
poorer at his death than when he first entered the cabinet. It was
fitting therefore, Lord Castlereagh told the Commons, that some
financial compensation should be offered for the terrible tragedy
they had suffered. He suggested a grant of £50,000 for the upkeep
of the late Prime Minister's family, together with an annuity of
£2,000 for his widow, Jane.

It was a phenomenal sum, the price of six warships, and yet to
many MPs it was not enough. There were calls to allocate £60,000,
even £100,000 for the benefit of the Percevals. Compared to the

undiluted hatred that was the Prime Minister's legacy in the street, the affection he aroused among his colleagues was truly astonishing. So far as Spencer Perceval as a private individual was concerned, all who knew him agreed on his virtues, from the admiring George III who labelled him 'the most straightforward man I have ever known', to the opposition MP, Samuel Romilly, who wrote, 'No man could be more generous, more kind or more friendly than he was. No man ever in private life had a nicer sense of honour. Never was there, I believe, a more affectionate husband or a more tender parent.' The Percevals were indeed the antithesis of Regency London, where young bucks gambled away their inheritance at Crockfords and Whites, and fashionable ladies spent fortunes in order to secure an invitation from the social arbiters who controlled entry to the dances held at Almack's Assembly Rooms.

As though the Victorian age had arrived a generation early, Spencer and Jane were earnest, ambitious and devoted to family values. They adored gardening, bought toys for the children, played practical jokes on one another, went to church, and put money aside for a rainy day. Defending the pleasure he took in his family, Perceval told a friend, 'I assure you that it is as great as anything in this world can produce.' Exasperated by his attachment to domestic life, the Princess of Wales once loftily declared that 'Perceval is entirely governed by that silly woman, his wife.' The truth, however, was that his priorities grew out of the kind of enduring love that always escaped the unfortunate princess.

Perceval's domestic happiness was famous, and to his admirers, such as the earnest essayist and politician, Robert Plumer Ward, it made him exceptional. He was, wrote Ward, 'so perfect in private life that to name him seemed to be to name virtue'. The sheer romance of how his happiness began ensured that the story was widely known.

In 1786, at the age of twenty-four, he and his elder brother Charles, Lord Arden, were invited to stay at Charlton House, on the south bank of the Thames. As boys, they had grown up in the house, a magnificent Jacobean mansion and the grandest building in the neighbourhood. Since then it had been sold, and now belonged to Sir Thomas Wilson, an old soldier who had been lucky enough to marry an exceptionally wealthy heiress. The Perceval brothers were attracted back to their former home, not simply by nostalgia but by the presence of the Wilsons' two high-spirited daughters, Margaretta and Jane. In due course, the two brothers fell in love with the two sisters but, as readers of Jane Austen's novels were constantly reminded, romance was inseparable from finance. As the younger son of an earl, Spencer Perceval had the right connections but, alas, the wrong income.

Older readers who preferred the previous fashion for the Gothic novel, with its hauntings and echoes of a mildewed past, were better able to understand Perceval's background. He had been born in 1762 the second son of the second marriage of the second Earl of Egmont, a peer whose outlook was so rooted in the past as to be generally termed medieval. The Percevals had originally been impoverished Irish landowners, but political connections gained the first earl his title, and inspired him to compile an imaginative genealogy showing the family to be descended from Norman aristocrats. This spurious background helped the second Lord Egmont to marry two wealthy wives in succession, and acquire an English title together with a valuable government sinecure, registrar of the high court of the admiralty, worth £12,000 a year. But his money and the sinecure had all gone to the eldest son of his second marriage, Lord Arden.

Consequently, Sir Thomas Wilson had no qualms about giving his elder daughter, Margaretta, immediate permission to marry her wealthy and titled suitor. In 1787 she became Lady Arden and scandalised her antediluvian in-laws by espousing the radical politics of William Cobbett. But Jane, then only eighteen, was forbidden to see the impoverished Spencer who was struggling to earn a living as a barrister. A miniature of her at that age reveals a proper Jane Austen heroine – all curls and muslin, wilful expression, large dark eyes and amused mouth – and on her twenty-first birthday she eloped through a drawing-room window dressed in riding clothes, and hurried with Spencer to East Grinstead where they were married.

That was the story they both delighted in telling. Nor was Spencer Perceval shy about confessing that their first home was in rented lodgings above a carpet shop in London's Bedford Row. According to his own account, after a wedding celebration at which £21-worth of port and sherry was consumed, they could afford to drink nothing more expensive than beer. Fortunately, Jane's father soon forgave his errant daughter and, as Perceval joyfully informed his friend Dudley Ryder, elder brother of Richard, 'He has also told me that he will make up her fortune to just what it would have been had she married with his consent. In short, everything that I could have wished and much more than I could have expected has concurred to make the step I have just taken the happiest and most prosperous event of my life.' But wine did not return to their table for several years.

In his early days as a lawyer, Samuel Romilly met Perceval frequently as they both ground out cases on the Midlands circuit between Nottingham and Birmingham. Charm and obstinacy were the qualities he remembered best. Perceval, he said, had been a high-spirited, half-educated young man 'with very little reading, of a conversation barren of instruction [and] with strong and invincible prejudices on many subjects . . . [Yet] by his excellent temper, his engaging manners, and his sprightly conversation, he was the delight of all that knew him.'

That blinkered vision of the world was derived from his father. The second Lord Egmont held strong views that ran clean contrary to the prevailing appetite for rationalism and enlightenment. What he wanted was the restoration of the absolute authority of monarch and Church together with the return of feudal society. It was said that when he built himself a mansion in the country, he designed it so that it could be defended by bow and arrow 'against the time in which the manufacture and use of gunpowder shall be forgotten'. Egmont died when his fifth child was only eight years old, an age when a boy is ready to take his father's beliefs as the bedrock of reality.

In the Whiggish opinion of Henry Brougham, Perceval's politics never really developed beyond that stage. His education at Harrow school left him with 'no information beyond what a classical education gives the common run of English youths'. His intellectual background was not materially altered by two years at Trinity College, Cambridge. And since the legal system was a conservative bastion, he found no reason to expand his views after he became a barrister. Any change from the status quo was, in his opinion, always for the worst.

'I am sorry to say,' Perceval declared to a lawyers' debating club in 1783, 'that we live at a time . . . when men adopt opinions as they choose their dresses, according to the mode of the hour, when nothing is followed but what is fashionable, and nothing esteemed fashionable but what is new'. Anyone who felt that it was 'desirable to preserve anything of our ancient and venerable establishments', he argued, had no choice but to resist 'every fresh attempt at innovation'. He was not expressing a mere point of view that might eventually be modified. It was a conviction that guided his life. To modify the social order was to tamper with God's estate.

Still in his twenties, he established his anti-liberal credentials beyond doubt by writing a pamphlet calling on magistrates to crack down on 'violations of the public peace', and by his own successful prosecution of the publisher of Tom Paine's *Rights of Man*, in the course of which he damned its democratic author as 'wicked, malicious, and ill-disposed'.

His income rapidly increased, partly from the law, partly from the interest on Jane's dowry, and partly from government sinecures that came his way such as the post of Clerk of the Irons and Surveyor of the Meltings in the Mint, which brought in £100 a year. Each time he returned home, however, Jane's passion and his excitement had their inevitable consequence. In the first fourteen years of their marriage, she gave birth to twelve children, eleven of whom survived, and the money went out almost as fast as it came in.

They had to rely on help from Perceval's brother to buy their next home, a semi-detached house in desirable Lincoln's Inn Fields, acquired in 1792. Eight years later, Perceval was wealthy enough to purchase the other half of it for his enormous family. In 1802, at the age of forty, he transferred from the criminal law to the more lucrative area of chancery law, dealing with property and commerce, and soon earned up to £10,000 a year. It allowed him to employ a coachman and liverymen clad in 'scarlet plush breeches'. He bought toys for the children, including a doll 'to dress and undress complete', from George Grosvenor's fashionable cosmetics and fashion shop in Chancery Lane. In search of fresh air for them, he and Jane first rented Belsize House and its park on the edge of Hampstead, at the time virtually in open country, then in 1807 bought a substantial manor in thirty-six acres of fields and parkland, Elm Grove in Ealing. By that date, he had become Chancellor of the Exchequer, and their town address was 10 Downing Street.

That Spencer Perceval would follow a political career was almost inevitable. Powerful families, like the Percevals, liked to have one of their kind in government to protect their interests, and from university onwards Perceval had gravitated naturally towards friends and colleagues, such as the Ryders, Charles Abbott and Samuel Romilly, who were parliamentarians in the making. And as would quickly become apparent, a rare combination of political and spiritual conviction gave him an almost limitless desire for power.

In 1796 his cousin, the earl of Northampton, found him a constituency in Northampton, conveniently within the Midlands law circuit. Although he had to fight an election, the earl's influence made victory certain. In the House of Commons, Perceval identified himself with the party of the Prime Minister, William Pitt the younger, out of which the modern Tory party was to grow.

From the moment he took his seat in the Commons among the followers of William Pitt, it is clear that Spencer Perceval fused the moral certainties of his faith with the expediencies of conservative politics as seamlessly as the Moral Majority in the United States wove its fundamentalism into the Republican programme almost two centuries later. But he did so at the very moment when steam was transforming Britain from an eighteenth-century rural society into a nineteenth-century industrial power.

Compared to the energy of wind or water, the power of the new machines was astonishing. Even a hostile observer like the American republican Thomas Jefferson, who visited Britain in 1784, was impressed. 'The most striking thing I saw there, new, was the application of the principle of the steam-engine to grist mills', he wrote in his journal. 'I saw 8 pair of [grinding-]stones which are worked by steam, and they are to set up 30 pair in the same house.'

What Jefferson did not mention was that each set of steam-driven grinding-stones put a traditional miller out of work. When the power of steam was applied to spinning, weaving and knitting, with enormous mechanical jennies, looms and stocking frames replacing hand-worked models, great numbers of skilled spinners, weavers and knitters found themselves deprived of a livelihood. Many left the countryside to find employment in the towns, others enlisted in the battalions of Captain Ned Ludd, but most went to work for a new, increasingly wealthy class, known generically as 'the manufacturers', who built and bought the great machines.

To be opposed to social change in such turbulent times was not a rare ambition. William Pitt himself had abandoned most of the liberal agenda of political reform and religious toleration he espoused in his early years. Alarmed by the democratic ideology spawned by the French Revolution in 1789, conservatives became convinced that any reform would constitute the first step on a road to mob rule. When war was declared against France in 1793, French ideas were seen to pose a greater, more insidious threat than French attack. To contain them, Pitt's government undertook a punitive programme curtailing civil liberties, including the suspension of habeas corpus, the censorship of printed material, and the severe restriction of public meetings.

Perceval committed himself to these measures with a passion that was evident in his first speech in the House of Commons. The country needed to be saved, he insisted, 'from the delusions of popular opinion, from the plausible fallacies of democratic theories . . . [and] from the spirit of democracy'. In 1798 he made a withering attack on the most effective of Pitt's opponents, the liberal Charles James Fox, who had called for 'a total and radical and fundamental reform of our late system'. Either Fox meant what he said, Perceval asserted, in which case he was encouraging 'revolutionary violence', or he meant tinkering with 'some parts of the system', thus showing himself to be a rhetorical windbag.

His attack was aimed at the man as much as the matter under discussion – a quality that became the hallmark of a Perceval speech – and its effectiveness marked him out. From the House of Lords,

Leveson-Gower deemed it 'incomparable', while William Pitt, a consummate debater himself, termed his speech 'in all respects one of the best I ever heard', and soon afterwards paid him an even greater tribute. Challenged to a duel in May that year by the Whig MP, George Tierney, for having accused him of 'a desire to obstruct the defence of this country', Pitt was asked who he felt should succeed him if he failed to survive Tierney's shot. 'He thought,' his second recorded solemnly, 'Mr Perceval was the most competent, and that he appeared the most equal to Mr. Fox.' Since both duellists missed their targets – Pitt intentionally firing his second shot in the air – the recommendation remained theoretical, but Perceval was on his way.

In public life, Perceval's adamant hostility to progress involved him in repeated confrontations. Within the walls of his house, on the other hand, his refusal to change anything and his unalloyed affection for his family promoted both harmony and happiness. His fourth son, John, carried into old age joyful memories of an untroubled childhood in Hampstead when he would dance with his mother and sisters in the dusty roadway to the tune of a barrel organ. As the childen grew older and more numerous they behaved increasingly like a tribe whose behaviour was ruled by unchanging rituals and precedents. Thus the entire family was united in the desire to keep everything the same.

The three eldest children were daughters, Jane, Frances (known as Fanny) and Maria, who operated as a trio, whether swooning over the same handsome man or skewering their father's political opponents with barbs of fizzing outrage. In 1809, at the height of a political scandal orchestrated by Gwillym Wardle, MP, over the sale of army commissions by the duke of York's mistress, Mrs Mary Clarke, eighteen-year-old Maria wrote to her brother, Spencer Perceval junior, then aged fifteen: 'Do not think by my silence on the subject that I am an unconcerned spectator of what is passing in the House of Commons. I assure you I am not but I have no remarks on it at present except that it is evidently false, that I hate and detest Mrs Clarke, a noisy toad, and that I am not over-partial to the Hon. Gentleman, Mr Wardle.' Her sisters were in total agreement. 'I think it was as clear as possible from the beginning that the Duke knew nothing about it,' Fanny, aged seventeen, told her brother, 'and that it was all an invention of that nasty wretch Clarke to get some money. Don't you hate her?'

They were in unison too about men. 'Fanny and I have found a most excellent, ridiculous and striking likeness,' Maria wrote excitedly after one of their father's uglier supporters had come to dinner with them in Downing Street, 'Mr Oldham in side-face to a fish. Any fish will do, but a cod particularly. He dined here the other day, and it was then we saw it. He opens and shuts his mouth just as fish do when they breathe.' And over an anonymous Greek god of a man known only as 'Him', all three were in a state of weak-kneed unanimity. At dances and visits to the ballet and theatre, they scanned the crowds for a glimpse of Him, and the then fifteen-year-old Maria was mortified when her two elder sisters met Him at a ball to which she had not been invited. Trying to divert her daughters from their endless discussion of His good looks, their mother invited an alternative attraction to dinner, the famously handsome Lord Granville Leveson-Gower, when he came back to London in 1805 from his duties as ambassador in St Petersburg.

'I never was so much disappointed except with Sir Arthur Wellesley,' Maria wrote scornfully. 'He is a tolerably good height, but he slouches horribly, and can that be compared to Him! His face is handsome enough, but his features are too pretty for a man and he is rather silly looking – and how can that possibly be compared to Him! Instead of His beautiful, exactly wellproportioned figure, he is too slim, and instead of

His lovely, divine, sensible, expressive face, he has a rather silly look.' In the face of her daughters' withering disdain, Jane threw in the towel, admitting that 'she never really thought him hand-somer than Him'.

By comparison, the boys were duller and lazier, but on them too, Perceval lavished a warmth quite unlike the stereotypes of the remote Georgian father or the stern Victorian paterfamilias. Not even his incorrigibly idle, and unappreciative, eldest son, Spencer junior, could make him irritable. When George Butler, Harrow's new, reforming headmaster, complained that he could not get the boy out of bed in time for his classes, Perceval wrote back good-humouredly, 'Do not let that make you uneasy, for I can promise you that he is far more advanced than I was at his age.' He paid the boy's debts without quibble, and could hardly have chosen a more delicate way of reminding him to acknowledge the gift. 'Papa desired me to tell you,' Maria wrote in 1811 to her brother, then approaching his last year at Harrow, 'that, without goading your tender conscience too much, he thinks he might expect when he sends you money to pay your debts, and only desires you to send him a receipt, that you should do so. So pray send it.'

Even when he had become both Prime Minister and Chancellor of the Exchequer, and shouldered the burden of running a wartime government with a wafer-thin, occasionally non-existent majority, Perceval still found time in 1811 to buy his son an anthology of poetry and send it with a letter giving him the gentlest of nudges about the need to work harder: 'Remember this is the last year of your schooling, and I have always told you more may be done in the last year than in any of the five years which have preceded it.' It was written more in hope than in confidence. 'From your mother's account of the heat in which she has twice found you,' he ended sadly, 'I fear that football is upon the whole a more favourite pursuit with you than your books.'

The private side of his life proved impossible to separate from the political. Physically, there were Perceval children scattered through almost every room in the sprawling, knocked-together double house that existed behind the door of 10 Downing Street. Apart from the housemaids, kitchenmaids and footmen who lived under the rafters, the family occupied not only all of the modern top-floor flat but today's staterooms on the first floor as well. Spencer Perceval worked on the ground floor, but when Spencer junior at last came home with some worthwhile school exercises, his gratified father was promptly summoned upstairs and 'seemed very much pleased at seeing so many, and said they were worth coming up for'.

At home Jane and Spencer said prayers every day, and lived simply. In an era when fashionable society left London to take the waters expensively at Bath and other spas, and the Prince Regent's friends journeyed from the opulence of Carlton House to the gilded dome of the Royal Pavilion in Brighton, the Percevals preferred to spend their free time together, either in Downing Street or at weekends in Elm Grove in Ealing. He gave generously and privately to charity, supporting the poor through donations to individuals and to organisations like the Shoreditch Refuge for the Destitute. When his friend, Dudley Ryder, later Lord Harrowby, lost £800 gambling at faro, Perceval wrote reprovingly to him, 'Only suppose that instead of having flung these £800 into the sink of a Pharaoh-bank, you had distributed them in equal shares to 80 poor housekeepers . . . How many units go to make that sum, 80 families with suppose only 4 to a family – 320 fellow creatures – think of it a little in its detail, of widows, orphans etc. raised from a pinching state of penury to a comfortable existence.'

His personal behaviour was all the more admirable when contrasted with that of other politicians. The haughty Marquess of Wellesley, for example, was so notorious for neglecting his business as foreign secretary in favour of his mistresses that even Wellington, his own brother, exclaimed, 'I wish that Wellesley was castrated or that he would, like other people, attend to his business and perform too.' For Perceval, the idea of 'performing' outside the marriage bed would have been unthinkable. 'Tricking in love and tricking the public are both unquestionably immoral,' he told the opposition MP, George Tierney, making a connection between private and public integrity that few in his time took seriously.

Yet, even at that period, the Prime Minister's obviously happy family produced an undeniable political advantage. Everyone recognised that he was, in the words of *The Courier*, 'at once an attentive husband, a fond and instructive father, an affectionate friend and an active servant of the public'. And Perceval had no compunction about using his private image to sway public opinion in favour of his policies. It was a tactic that infuriated his political opponents.

'You spend a great deal of ink about the character of the present Prime Minister,' the progressive-minded clergyman, Sydney Smith, wrote in his satire, *Peter Plymley's Letters*, addressed supposedly to a Perceval supporter. 'Grant you all that you write – I say, I fear he will pursue a line of policy destructive to the true interest of his country: and then you tell me, he is faithful to Mrs. Perceval, and kind to the Master Percevals! These are, undoubtedly, the first qualifications to be looked to in a time of the most serious public danger; but somehow or another (if public and private virtues must always be incompatible), I should prefer that he . . . whipped his boys, and saved his country.'

Sydney Smith's Whig readers laughed, and quoted his clever phrase as a criticism. They failed to appreciate the political calculation in Perceval's widely publicised domesticity. More astutely William Cobbett commented on the Prime Minister's shrewdness in building a reputation on 'the fact that he was wont to go to church, every Sunday, with a large quarto gilt prayer-book under one arm, his wife hanging on the other, and followed by a long brood of children'. However much he disliked innovation, Perceval became the first British politician to demonstrate how to exploit a happy family in the race for political power. To that extent, the principles that guided his private life are inseparable from his assassination.

# A Prime Minister Put There by Providence

Most people believe that the danger to the constitution of this
country arises from the spirit of democracy.
Spencer Perceval to the Benchers of Lincoln's Inn, 1802

At 7 a.m. on Thursday, 14 May, John Bellingham awoke 'obviously
refreshed and,' according to Newman's report, 'apparently unaffected
by the unfortunate circumstances of his situation'. He washed,
shaved, and had his usual breakfast of sweet tea and bread. Later in
the day, he would lunch heartily on minced veal, boiled potatoes and
a pint of porter. Soon afterwards he was visited by Charles Litchfield,
the Treasury solicitor, who informed him that he would be tried for
the murder of Spencer Perceval the following day.

This extraordinary rush to judgement, allowing the lapse of just
three days from the charge of murder, and less than forty-eight hours
from the appointment of a lawyer to represent him, represented the
triumph of the political agenda over the criminal investigation. It
also made a travesty of the trial. Since Bellingham's solicitor needed
to summon witnesses from Liverpool, and to call on expert testimony on the matter of insanity, the government's timetable prevented
the preparation of any adequate defence. Harmer's legal colleagues
reminded him sympathetically that had his client been charged with
treason, the law would have required a minimum of fifteen days

between the charge and the trial in order to give both prosecution and defence time to assemble their evidence.

The legal profession was not alone in being outraged. Those most frustrated by the government's indecent haste to kill the murderer were the late Prime Minister's closest companions. They more than anyone else needed to understand why Spencer Perceval had been murdered. To Robert Plumer Ward, it was a catastrophe beyond reason, so profound that it challenged the very idea of a benign God. In his novel, *Tremaine*, he put his doubts into the mouth of the main protagonist: 'that such a man, the delight of his friends, the adoration of his family, the admiration of his opponents; that one so mild, yet so brave; so single-hearted, yet so keen, should be cut off by murder . . . that such a thing should be, leads for ever to despair of that protection from Heaven, which . . . is afforded to mankind'. The Prime Minister's assassination had to have a meaning or serve a purpose, otherwise everything became meaningless and purposeless.

What gave Spencer Perceval's killing this resonance was his faith. Writing to George Butler, the headmaster of Harrow, the Prime Minister once said that his ambition for his eldest son was that he should be 'a champion of true religion in a careless world'. By this, he meant something quite specific. The true religion was that of the Evangelical Anglicans who in the 1780s had begun to shake an almost moribund Church of England into new life. Although divided in their methods – the brothers John and Charles Wesley preached to thousands in the open air, whereas the father and son pairing of Henry and John Venn restricted their message to middle-class church congregations – the founding Evangelicals were united in holding that true belief came from an immediate, personal experience of God, to be found in the Bible and expressed through action. It was a physical rather than an intellectual faith

– 'Experience,' declared Henry Venn, 'is a living proof, stronger than a thousand arguments' – and, unlike the careless world that agreed with Lord Melbourne's clever dictum that 'Things are coming to a pretty pass when religion is allowed to invade private life', Evangelicals believed that the whole point of religion was to transform both private and public life.

The word they used to describe God working in the world was 'Providence', and any action that made the world a better place was therefore termed providential. The spread of civilisation itself and the general improvement of mankind through laws and moral education could therefore be taken as evidence of a divinely ordered creation. 'God has so assigned to things their general tendencies,' declared William Wilberforce, a standard-bearer for the faith, 'and established such an order of causes and effects, as . . . loudly proclaim the principles of his moral government, and strongly suggest that vice and imprudence will finally terminate in misery'.

Thus to be good was not enough. In order to help the work of Providence, it was necessary to do good. 'Action is the life of virtue,' wrote Hannah More, the Evangelical poet and friend of Wilberforce, 'and the world is the theatre of action.' It was not just the Church of England that needed to be actively reformed, but society itself had to be cleaned up. Consequently, some Evangelicals, and especially the followers of the Wesleys who broke with the Church of England to form the Methodist Union, became radicals devoting their lives to the poorest in society.

At first glance, Perceval seemed an unlikely adherent to such a faith. Like so many other guiding principles in his life, however, his Evangelical beliefs originated with his father's example. The second Lord Egmont favoured the spread of Bible-based religion, not least because it would counter any desire among the lower classes for material progress. Other Evangelicals, including Wilberforce, took a similarly conservative view. Although they attacked slavery, few criticised the horrific conditions of factory-workers or the squalid housing of the poor. Political radicals jibed, not altogether fairly, that Evangelicals preferred 'to look abroad for examples of cruelty and oppression' in order to avoid tackling social injustice at home.

The faith that he had inherited moved to the centre of Perceval's life in 1796 soon after the birth of his eldest son, Spencer junior. The baby fell seriously ill, and seemed likely to die until, in despair, both Spencer and Jane knelt to pray for his recovery. Almost at once the child started to improve and, as Perceval reported to Dudley Ryder, 'by the blessing of God our boy was restored to us'. After that he never doubted. When he entered Parliament later that year in the September election, he did so in the assurance that he was to be an agent of Providence.

Perceval's political ascent was rapid, and he owed it not just to his speeches against change but to an unremitting hostility to Catholics, another symptom of his Evangelical beliefs. It led directly to his first promotion to be Solicitor General in 1801. Pitt had brought Ireland into the United Kingdom in order to prevent it becoming the backdoor for a French invasion. But when he attempted to repeal the anti-Catholic legislation that banned 80 per cent of Ireland's population from holding office as magistrates, army officers and MPs, Pitt ran into George III's adamant opposition. Forced to resign, Pitt handed over to his picked successor, the anti-Catholic, Henry Addington, who did not hesitate to appoint Perceval to the second most important law office in the cabinet.

As a minister Perceval won the approval of both Addington and the king. In 1802 he successfully prosecuted the Irish-born Colonel Edward Despard for treason, despite clear evidence that the colonel had been entrapped by government informers. Ignoring the jury's strong recommendation for mercy, the judge, Lord Ellenborough, then sentenced Despard and a confederate 'to be hanged by the neck, but not until you are dead; for while you are still living your bodies are to be taken down, your bowels torn out and burned before your faces, your heads then cut off, and your bodies divided each into four quarters, and your heads and quarters to be then at the King's disposal; and may the Almighty God have mercy on your souls!' The hangman proved more merciful, and allowed Despard to swing for twelve and a half minutes, long enough to ensure he was utterly dead, before cutting him down and chopping off his head. The disembowelling was dispensed with.

Having demonstrated his anti-Irish credentials, Perceval reinforced his anti-liberal reputation by prosecuting William Cobbett for an article he published in the *Political Register* criticising the government's Irish policy. As was his habit, Perceval attacked the person rather than the principle. 'Gentlemen,' he demanded of the jury with an arrogance that only a peer's son would attempt, 'who is Mr. Cobbett? Is he a man writing purely from motives of patriotism? *Quis homo hic est? Quo patre natus?* [Who is this man? Who's his father?].' Before being found guilty by a sycophantic jury, Cobbett had enough time to study his prosecutor, and retorted with a disparaging comment of his own, describing Perceval as 'a sort of understrapper to the Attorney-General . . . a short, spare, pale-faced, hard, keen, sour-looking man with a voice well-suited to the rest'.

When William Pitt returned to office in May 1804 after the collapse of Addington's administration, Perceval had his reward, promotion from understrapper to Attorney General. He was now back in the cabinet, but with too little influence to be more than a small fish in the parliamentary pond. Yet when his Evangelical friends looked at his career, this was the point where they recognised it to be unmistakably providential, a 'blessing' as Wilberforce put it, in the sense of being divinely shaped to achieve good.

Regardless of their class or politics, Evangelicals were united in their desire to achieve one good in particular. Their commitment to it was both humanitarian and the inevitable outgrowth of their belief that to find God was, in Charles Wesley's phrase, to be 'a slave redeemed from death and hell'. As a group they were unique in mainstream Christianity in finding slavery so morally abhorrent that destruction of the trade in humans had come to be of paramount importance.

The greatest demand for captured Africans came from plantations in the Americas and the Caribbean: in the southern states of the United States, the crop was cotton, and the work planting and picking, but elsewhere, in Brazil, Cuba and Europe's colonies in the West Indies, it was the near-factory requirements of sugar growing, cutting and refining that created the need for slave labour. In 1790 a total of almost 1.5 million slaves were held west of the Atlantic, but to meet the growing demand for the raw products of the plantations, and to make good the deaths that resulted from the cruelties practised especially by sugar growers, about 70,000 more were shipped across the ocean every year.

Slavery had existed since the earliest records were made, and however deplorable it was as a practice, to condemn it appeared to fly in the face of history. Tactically, therefore, its opponents sidestepped the institution and focused on the transport as the most vulnerable link in the system. The shipping was supplied by some six hundred vessels, especially adapted to carry cargoes of around 250 slaves lying prone and chained side by side. Their hulls were designed for maximum speed to reduce the extravagant death toll from disease and despair. Almost half of these specialised ships were registered in Britain, and about two hundred sailed out of Liverpool.

The Evangelicals' attack on the trade was carried out on many levels, through leaflets, public meetings, sugar boycotts and preaching, but its cutting edge was the political campaign. Its roots were in Clapham, where Henry and John Venn preached, and where many of the politicians most fervently committed to the cause lived. With unwavering persistence William Wilberforce, as leader of the Clapham Sect, or the Saints, had introduced a bill in Parliament almost every year from 1790 to abolish the trade, and on every occasion it failed. The fault lay not just with the lack of support in the Commons, but with the reluctance of the Prime Minister to give it his backing.

William Pitt had repeatedly expressed his sympathy for Wilberforce's attempts to ban the slave trade, but in practice would never confront the West India lobby, the powerful group representing the shippers who carried slaves from Africa, and the sugar planters in the Caribbean who bought them. Nor was anyone in cabinet sufficiently committed to the cause to push it forward. A note that Wilberforce made in his diary in 1805 was therefore of considerable significance: 'I have hopes Perceval will still prove a blessing in a high station.'

Perceval's hostility to slavery and its trade was of no conceivable interest to the millions who hated him and rejoiced at his murder. Nevertheless it was as integral to his beliefs as his die-hard opposition to change. From his first involvement as Attorney General he brought to it the same combination of moral passion and political cunning that infuriated Catholics and reformers, and by the time of his murder his efforts had saved as many as forty thousand Africans from shipment across the ocean into slavery. There was sound reason for Evangelicals to feel that his career must be providential, and for the question that occurred so urgently to them – How could Providence allow such a force for good to be eliminated?

In the summer of 1805 the Attorney General justified Wilberforce's optimism by finding a typically roundabout means of achieving a good end. As the government's law officer, Perceval pointed out that it would be possible to restrict the trade without recourse to new legislation. Instead of aiming at a complete ban on the trade, as Wilberforce had done in thirteen earlier bills, Perceval concentrated only on the new colony of Guiana, modern-day Guyana, recently captured in the course of the war. After a policy meeting with supporters in June 1805, Wilberforce made another note in his diary: 'Guiana slave-trade, Attorney-General Perceval honest, warm, steady and intelligent on the subject.'

Formerly a Dutch possession, Guiana had been taken because the Netherlands were allied to France. It was chosen as a target because up to fifteen thousand slaves were expected to be brought in to work the virgin, sugar-bearing soil. Pitt was too sick and physically worn out to conduct a bruising battle in Parliament, but Wilberforce's next diary entry indicated the tactic Perceval intended to employ: 'Busy with [James] Stephen and Attorney-General on Order in Council.'

An Order in the Privy Council allowed the government to adjust existing policy without the need for parliamentary approval. Unlike an Act, it was open to legal challenge and in the long term usually had to be backed by legislation, but as a temporary measure it took immediate effect. Perceval convinced the Prime Minister that such an Order could be used to ban the trade to Guiana on the grounds that it merely modified the regulations for the island's government. In August 1805, relieved of the need to introduce new legislation, Pitt finally committed his government to the abolitionist cause by issuing an Order in Council banning the import of slaves to Guiana. At a stroke, a trade that had already carried six thousand slaves in its first year was made illegal. But six months later William Pitt died and his Tory government collapsed.

The election that followed in 1806 was dominated by the single issue of the slave trade. It returned a majority of Members of Parliament committed to its abolition, and the one notable achievement of the Whig ministry formed under Lord Grenville was to pass the legislation in 1807 that finally banned British involvement in the slave trade. On the opposition benches, Perceval showed that he could still be a blessing to the cause. With the Grenville ministry on the verge of collapse, and the bill not yet passed by the House of Lords, Perceval intervened with the Tory peers and persuaded them individually not to block the legislation.

By then, it was clear how formidable Perceval had become as a politician. What made him uniquely effective, in a way that Wilberforce could never be, was his ruthlessness. To achieve ends he decided were right, he would adopt whatever means were at hand, regardless of the consequences. That there really were no limits he had demonstrated in his defence of the Princess of Wales, Caroline of Brunswick.

In 1806 the princess, who had separated from her husband, the future George IV, was alleged by close friends to have given birth to a son by an unknown lover. The allegations would have been explosive enough in her role as wife to the future king, but the unpopularity of the Prince of Wales and her own good looks, especially her 'quick, glancing, penetrating eyes . . . and a remarkably delicately formed mouth', gave Caroline a popular celebrity that made her the people's princess. The alleged affair not only became the subject of intense political argument but inflamed the public's contempt for the Prince of Wales. In an attempt to limit the damage, the new Prime Minister, Lord Grenville, who also happened to be a friend of the prince, immediately launched a high-powered investigation into the alleged affair.

The findings of the inquiry were politically convenient for Grenville and the Whigs. It decided that the princess was guilty of unbecoming conduct, especially in her flirtatious behaviour with unmarried men, but cleared her of bearing a child. Perceval, however, decided that the libertine prince was really to blame for having sent her away from court. In a moral crusade that had the added political convenience of embarrassing the government, he took up Caroline's cause.

First he compiled a minority report that exonerated the princess, and implicitly blamed the prince, then he had five thousand copies printed as pamphlets and held ready for distribution. At that point, Perceval let it be known that he intended to put them on sale unless the princess was publicly received back in court as an innocent woman. The Prince of Wales was said to have responded by swearing 'with most offensive personal abuse, and an oath which cannot be recited, that he felt he could jump on [Perceval], and stamp out his life with his feet'. Nevertheless, the blackmail was effective. Early in 1807 the princess was allowed back in court, and Perceval set a match to a bonfire of his pamphlets in Lincoln's Inn Fields.

In March Grenville's brief government collapsed, and in recognition of the influence he now commanded Perceval was appointed Chancellor of the Exchequer in the new Tory administration under the duke of Portland, and its leader in the House of Commons. In this position, Perceval suddenly became of supreme importance to the abolition campaign.

Even Wilberforce understood that making the slave trade illegal was only the first step. Unless the traders were physically stopped from reaching the coast of Africa, they would continue to buy humans as commodities. To enforce the law, a police force was needed on the high seas, incentives had to be offered for the arrest of law-breakers, a court was required in west Africa to try those charged with breaking the law, and an identification system for existing slaves had to be set up to prevent new ones being smuggled in. Each of these measures was expensive, none was popular, and so all required political clout to push them through. Whatever his gratitude to Grenville's ministry for passing the Abolition Act,

Wilberforce had no hesitation in pledging his loyalty to the new government. 'My principles would govern my vote,' he confessed to his diary, 'even if I did not think so favourably of . . . Perceval as I do.'

His good opinion was justified. Within the cabinet, the Chancellor of the Exchequer would become the scourge of the flourishing though now illegal slave trade. Indeed for the next five years, until the day he was shot, no one did more to give teeth to the Abolition Act than Spencer Perceval.

To the Evangelical mind, Perceval's final promotion to Prime Minister raised the extraordinary possibility that Providence intended to use him to end not just the trade but slavery itself. At least three of his colleagues in Portland's cabinet were not only younger, but more talented and experienced: Viscount Castlereagh, Lord Hawkesbury, shortly to become the second earl of Liverpool, and George Canning. The last two were both to become Prime Minister, but Perceval reached the top of the greasy pole ahead of them. Although not obvious, his personal abilities were effective. The ruthlessness that he demonstrated in defence of the princess was well disguised by his personal charm. He had neither intelligence nor depth, but his absence of doubt won him political battles that a cleverer man might have lost. And, as Charles Arbuthnot, the veteran Treasury secretary, remarked when Perceval finally manoeuvred his way into the premiership, 'He has the best regulated ambition I ever witnessed.'

He possessed, however, another, greater advantage. During the confusing cavalcade that saw five different administrations hold office in the seven years after 1801, the king became increasingly aware of Perceval's entrenched attitudes and happy domestic life. They reflected almost exactly the priorities that George III looked for in a minister and a man. When Castlereagh and Canning took themselves out of the running for the leadership by fighting a duel in the summer of 1809, the king no longer hesitated.

In October 1809, with Portland only three weeks from death, George III wrote to the one politician who shared all his views about the various dangers presented by Napoleon, Catholics and reform: 'Mr Perceval's conduct has so fully confirmed the impression which the King had early received of his zeal and abilitities, of the honourable principles by which he is invariably activated, that His Majesty cannot pause in the choice of the person he should intrust a situation at all times most important, but particularly so under the present arduous circumstances.'

That Providence should have promoted Spencer Perceval to become Prime Minister at the age of forty-seven only to allow him to be shot less than three years later challenged the deepest beliefs of the Saints. 'Of all the cases in which man seems to have been abandoned by Heaven, and which leave the upholder of Providence without hope,' Ward wrote in *Tremaine*, 'I have always thought this the clearest.' His bewilderment is forgivable. Unless John Bellingham was so mad as to make his actions entirely unpredictable, there had to be an explanation. One answer lay in the very ascendancy that appeared so providential to the Evangelicals.

# 8

## The Pervasive Power of Little P

If, therefore, we can accomplish our purposes, it will come to this, that either those countries will have no trade, or they must be content to accept it through us.

Spencer Perceval explaining the goal
of the Orders in Council, 1807

The choice of Spencer Perceval in 1809 as Prime Minister, so obvious to George III, came as a surprise to almost everyone else. The radical MP, Henry Hunt, only slightly exaggerated when he recorded in his memoirs, 'Mr. Perceval, an insignificant lawyer, now suddenly became First Lord of the Treasury, and Chancellor of the Exchequer, to the astonishment of the whole nation.' Tory peers, familiar with the difficulties faced by the duke of Portland, had advised the king to select the new Prime Minister from the Commons, and the clear favourite was the clever, ambitious George Canning, who had a personal following of about twenty MPs. By the most generous count, Perceval appeared able to rely on just five votes.

Behind his back, cabinet colleagues referred to him as 'little Perceval', while the Lord Chancellor, Lord Eldon, diminished him further by calling him 'little P'. His lack of influence was reflected in the reluctance of former ministers to serve in his cabinet. Not only did Canning prefer to sit on the backbenches, he was followed there by William Huskisson, the financial genius who had guided Perceval's policy as Chancellor of the Exchequer under the duke of Portland. Acknowledging the significance of losing him, Perceval exclaimed, 'This is the worst and most unexpected stroke of all.'

The absence of any other candidate willing to take on the job left Perceval with no option but to double up the chancellor's portfolio with the Prime Minister's. Four times in the first months after taking office, his makeshift government was defeated in the House of Commons, and there was a general expectation that one of his rivals, Canning or Liverpool, or even his predecessor Lord Grenville, must shortly take over.

The king refused to have second thoughts, however, telling Perceval that he had 'drawn his line, and no prospect of harrassment or opposition shall induce him to stray from it'. This was, as Perceval remarked, 'very fine, firm and noble – but not very helpful'. Yet, as awareness of the King's unwavering commitment to his new Prime Minister filtered through Parliament, it produced an effect that virtually made up for Perceval's own lack of a personal following.

Royal approval was the invisible glue that held a parliamentary majority together. Its adhesive effect was felt most strongly by the heart of the Commons, the roughly one hundred and twenty 'country gentlemen' with independent incomes who spent most of the year on their estates. When they came to Westminster, it was to represent the patriotic instincts of their patrons and fellow property-owners where important legislation was concerned. With the additional support of about eighty government office-holders, and a shifting number of MPs anxious to secure a government job for themselves or their family, Perceval could eventually count on a majority for the most crucial measures. But for day-to-day votes, it was his personal reputation that came to weigh most heavily.

Parliament usually only sat from January to June or July. Even in session, its business began in late afternoon when the working day was almost over, and continued if necessary into the early morning. Most of its deliberations took place in a building lit by huge banks of candles, hanging in candelabra from the dark, vaulted ceilings, or standing in tall sticks above the green benches of the chamber, or arranged in sconces along its shadowy corridors. The windows often had to be kept shut, for, with the regularity of the rising and falling tide, the Thames carried the sewage of almost one million Londoners up and down outside its walls. Trapped in the fetid, oxygen-starved atmosphere of the chamber, MPs listened to the rhetoric of the front benches emerging from circles of golden candlelight amid the gloom. In such surroundings, finely honed arguments rarely carried as much weight as the character of the speaker and the interests he represented.

Thus Perceval's irreproachable personal behaviour, well publicised by his friends, was crucial to his success. In 1810 the independent newspaper, *The Day*, decided that 'in these times of imputed corruption when everything is supposed to be vendible' they would rate leading politicians on a trustworthiness table measuring them against the value of a pound. Canning was judged to be 'worth a song', Castlereagh 'a bad shilling', and Tierney's price was 'known only to his political friends', but Perceval was valued at 25s, a premium of 20 per cent above par, making him the most trustworthy commoner in Parliament.

In the jaundiced view of Henry Hunt, the moral ascendancy that Spencer Perceval came to exercise over the country gentlemen and the government's placemen led directly to his assassination. 'It was the protection that he was sure of receiving, from a corrupt majority of a corrupt and packed House of Commons,' Hunt declared, 'that induced him to persevere in denying justice to Mr. Bellingham; and if ever a man received the reward of his own injustice, it was Mr. Perceval.' Hunt was a far from disinterested spectator, but his suggestion that outright control of the Commons corrupted Perceval's judgement is worth picking out. Writing to Wellington in Spain in the summer of 1811, Lord Liverpool declared the Prime Minister's command to be 'completely established in the House of Commons; he has acquired an authority there beyond any minister in my recollection, except Mr Pitt.' Not by chance was Wellington the person told, because one vital element that underpinned Perceval's authority was his unquestionable effectiveness as a war leader.

Viewed down the long avenue of two centuries of history, the significance of his premiership has diminished to near-invisibility. But in the judgement of the *Dictionary of National Biography*, by the day of his death Perceval had 'carried on the government single-handed, prosecuted the war, defeated his opponents and disarmed his critics'. That is a notable record, achieved during the most dangerous days of the Napoleonic war. Not until the summer of 1940, when Winston Churchill's government confronted a Nazi government in full control of Western Europe, would a British Prime Minister have to deal with a power comparable to that facing Spencer Perceval in 1809. Having defeated the Prussians at Jena in 1806, the Austrians at Wagram three years later, and then occupied Vienna, Napoleon's armies bestrode the continent from Spain to the borders of the Russian empire, and from Sicily to Sweden. And just as Britain's capitulation seemed the most probable outcome in 1940 following the failure of the campaign in Norway, so did the expulsion of British forces from Corunna and their defeat in the Walcheren expedition in 1809 appear to extinguish its last military opposition to Napoleon.

Unfortunately for his reputation in history, Perceval's leadership lacked both Churchill's flair and his rhetoric. But to his parliamentary colleagues, his command seemed peerless.

Efficiency was what Perceval prized. In 1809 he had no hesitation in sacking Lord Chatham, the ineffective general of the forty thousand troops despatched to Walcheren island in the Netherlands, who had achieved nothing but the loss of half his force to malaria. The Prime Minister battled equally hard in 1810 to keep in office the duke of York, the army's commander-in-chief and its most energetic and effective organiser, after he was found to have sold military commissions through his mistress, the 'noisy toad', Mary Ann Clarke. Despite the scandal, and his own disapproval of 'tricking in marriage', Perceval restored the duke as soon as possible, an event triumphantly announced in 1811 by Fanny Perceval – 'the dear duke of York has at last had justice done to him and he is what (in my opinion) he ought always to have been, Commander-in-Chief'.

His greatest achievement, and one that ultimately proved decisive in swinging the military balance against Napoleon, was to keep Sir Arthur Wellesley and a British army in the Iberian Peninsula when every financial and military expert pressed for their recall. That Perceval never received credit for this success was because it grew out of a cheese-paring approach to the dreary business of public finance. Neither a reformer nor an innovator, he was dogged, industrious, and above all committed to making the existing system work. Indeed nothing demonstrated better the single-minded, blinkered drive that encouraged people to contemplate murdering him than his success as Chancellor of the Exchequer.

The nature of the challenge he faced was obvious to both supporters and opponents. From 1807 to 1812 Perceval had to find enough money to cover the costs of the Royal Navy at £19 million a year and the army at £17 million, as well as paying annual subsidies averaging £3 million to keep Portugal, Prussia, Saxony and Austria in the war against France. Since this wartime annual expenditure of almost £40 million represented about three-quarters of the total national budget, it strained the financial resources of the country to breaking point.

Even under William Pitt, the great financial reformer, who

introduced income tax and levies on items like houses, windows and hats, it had not been possible to squeeze much more than £23 million from personal taxation. Another £24 million came from permanent taxes such as customs and excise duties. But the 1806 budget, the first after Pitt's death, projected an estimated expenditure of £68 million, leaving an enormous gap of £20 million that had to be filled by borrowing.

Where Perceval excelled was in squeezing. As Chancellor of the Exchequer in Portland's ministry, he pressed the Bank of England and City financiers to reduce their gouging fees for handling government finance, and forced the Bank to make an interest-free loan of £3 million repayable only after peace was restored as compensation for past profiteering. With the help of William Huskisson, the financial wizard who as Treasury secretary was responsible for war finance, Perceval tightened the Treasury's auditing system, clearing up a backlog of accounts reaching back to 1776; slashed wastage from the notoriously inefficient military bureaucracy, including an inflated barracks building programme; appointed his own private secretary, Michael Herries, to cut through the mass of corruption that bloated the army's commissariat; and sent teams of auditors to flush out unpaid arrears of revenue from the ports, bringing in £100,000 from Ipswich alone and another £30,000 from Bristol.

Under his relentless prodding, Treasury auditors generated a torrent of reports written in a clerkly sloping hand, most of which Perceval insisted on checking himself. He presided over twice-weekly Board of Treasury conferences, as well as daily cabinet meetings, and constantly urged his colleagues to behave less extravagantly. The nagging insistence on efficiency had its effect. Expenditure came down to nearly £54 million a year in 1807, and remained near that level throughout his lifetime, and annual borrowing was reduced to around £11 million.

The military importance of Perceval's parsimonious accountancy while Chancellor of the Exchequer was revealed in 1809 when he became Prime Minister, and virtually every economic expert warned him that the country could no longer afford to fund Sir Arthur Wellesley's small army in Portugal, the sole remaining British force on the continent. It cost £2.5 million a year to finance his operations, and the absence of banking facilities in Portugal meant that most of it had to be paid in silver dollars which could only be bought in sufficient numbers in South America and China. Not only did the added cost and complexity threaten to break Britain's tightly stretched economy, critics pointed out that despite the expense Wellesley remained pinned in a remote southwest corner of the Iberian peninsula.

'To carry on the war on the present scale of expense with the ordinary means of the country, or anything approaching to it,' the knowledgeable George Rose wrote with italicised urgency in November 1809 'is *utterly impossible*'. Military expenditure had to be cut by one-third, he warned, or the whole economy would begin to collapse. In effect, the Peninsula campaign must be ended. Rose's call was supported by the entire Whig opposition, as well as many Tory supporters on the backbenches. Even Richard Wellesley, Arthur's elder brother and Perceval's Foreign Secretary, privately condemned 'the impolicy of sending a regular English army to act permanently in Spain'.

Impervious to this mounting barrage of criticism, both military and financial, Perceval insisted that the Peninsula force remain in the field, whatever the cost, and he signalled his approval by persuading the king to make Sir Arthur Wellesley a viscount, taking the name of Wellington. But by the spring of 1810, Rose's dire forecast seemed to be justified. The exchange rate plummeted, the price of gold rose, and the value of a pound note fell – the classic signs of inflation running out of control.

A parliamentary inquiry, the Bullion committee, blamed the Bank of England for printing too many notes in order to cover the excess in government expenditure. The cure that it recommended was convertibility, keeping the value of a pound note equal to the value of a gold sovereign so that paper could always be converted to metal. Crudely speaking, this would require the government to reduce the number of notes sharply and to cut its own spending drastically. It was a recommendation supported by, among others, David Ricardo, the outstanding economist of the day, the doyen of City banking, Sir Francis Baring, and the fiscal wizard, William Huskisson, Perceval's former colleague.

Although admitting 'he was aware that he was not as well informed on the question as he hoped yet to be', Perceval was quite clear about the implication of the Bullion committee's proposed remedy: not only did it mean the end of Wellington's expensive campaign, but an acceptance that the country could not afford to wage war in Europe. It was, he said, 'tantamount to a Parliamentary declaration that we must submit to any terms of peace rather than continue the war'. Grimly declaring that 'I retain all the ignorance and [remain] under all the prejudice which influenced me', he flatly rejected its recommendation. Wellington's men would stay in the field. Yet no sooner had Perceval stated his position than the stakes were raised higher still.

In the summer of 1810, Wellington abruptly announced that the cost of the Peninsular army had doubled to £5 million. Even he, normally unconcerned about the storm of criticism at home, felt compelled to promise his supportive Prime Minister that he was doing his best not to overspend. Unperturbed, Perceval replied that he was sure Wellington must already have made all possible economies, knowing 'that the failure of our pecuniary means is one of the most probable causes of our being compelled to discontinue our assistance to the Peninsula'. Consequently, he could assure Wellington of his 'perfect and unaffected reliance upon you'.

That September, however, the Bullion committee published its report, and the stark warning of economic collapse produced a panic in the City. The value of a basket of blue-chip stocks dropped 10 per cent in two days. Abraham Goldsmid, the government's senior broker, who was holding £2 million worth of stocks, found himself facing bankruptcy. On 28 September he committed suicide by cutting his throat. The next day the stock exchange was in melt-down. 'We think this,' *The Day* reported with some restraint, 'one of the most trying circumstances in which the Government of this country was ever placed.'

At that point a more rational Prime Minister might have thrown in the towel. On the continent, Napoleon had destroyed Britain's coalition with Austria, so expensively put together the year before. Two of its former members, Sweden and Russia, had actually declared war on Britain, and Austria's place in the French camp was confirmed by Napoleon's marriage to the Archduchess Marie-Louise. Worst of all, Wellington's latest attempt to break out from his corner in Portugal had failed.

In the autumn of 1810, he again retreated with his ruinously expensive army behind the Torres Vedras, the line of fortifications he had built along a range of hills outside Lisbon. Territorially, he had gained nothing. London gossip was dominated by the defeatist opinions of 'croakers' – serving officers who had returned from the Peninsula convinced that Wellington could achieve nothing. And the markets had lost all confidence in a government committed to keeping such an ineffective force in the field at the expense of the nation's economy. Commonsense dictated that the Prime Minister should restore confidence at a stroke by announcing his intention to bring Wellington home.

Among the threads leading to the Prime Minister's murder, one

of the most notable was the motive that made Perceval so determined to defy the best financial advice and every logical argument,
and insist on keeping an army in Portugal.

The absence of reason from the Prime Minister's calculations has
encouraged historians to write his contribution out of the narrative
of Wellington's military triumph. But without Perceval's irrational
conviction that he was right, Wellington's victorious Peninsula
campaign would not have happened.

The whole of Spencer Perceval's political life was spent in the
shadow of the French Revolution, and he responded to it in a quite
specific way. The conventional Tory response was expressed by
Edmund Burke who condemned the revolution for attempting to
replace a flawed system with an experiment in democracy, which
was bound to lead to mob tyranny. 'Of this I am certain,' Burke
asserted, 'in a democracy the majority of the citizens is capable of
exercising the most cruel oppressions upon the minority . . . and
that oppression of the minority will extend to far greater numbers
and will be carried on with much greater fury than can almost ever
be apprehended from the dominion of a single scepter'. For him as
for most Tories, the French Revolution was a political failure. For
Perceval it was quite simply a manifestation of evil.

Since even evil was part of God's plan, the temporary success of
French armies against the Catholic powers of Spain, Austria and
Italy must serve a divine purpose – 'they [the French] have been
raised up by Providence for the overthrow of popish superstitions,'
the Prime Minister confided to a friend, 'for, with some few excep-
tions which may have been permitted to prevent this object of
God's Providence from being too strikingly apparent, you will find
their progress most destructive where the popish superstitions most
prevailed'. In the long run, however, Providence always worked to
improve the world, and so the French in turn would inevitably be

defeated. Perceval's confidence in this outcome sprang from an unexpected source. It was prophesied in the Book of Daniel, as he explained in a pamphlet published in 1800, *Observations intended to put the Application of a Prophecy in the eleventh Chapter of the Book of Daniel to the French Power.*

The particular part of chapter eleven that interested him was Daniel's vision of an epic war between 'the king of the north', easily identified with Britain, and 'the king of the south', clearly meaning France. What made it especially attractive was that it predicted victory for the king of the north. His trust in Daniel's prophecies was shared with his brother-in-law, Thomas Walpole, and together they regularly consulted the Bible for prophecies that would throw light on difficult policy decisions. He and Walpole were in complete agreement, for example, that the passage in the Book of Revelation about 'the woman who rides upon the beast, who is drunk with the blood of the saints, the mother of harlots', could only refer to their enemies on the other side of the Channel. The major difference between them was that Perceval felt sure she was Napoleon, whereas Walpole, who must have been something of a literalist, argued that being female she was probably France. On a lesser point, Walpole was convinced that the Pope was the entire beast with all its seven heads, whereas Perceval thought it obvious he could only be one of the heads. Neither doubted, however, that the Book of Revelation provided a reliable pointer to the overall shape of international politics.

'I have been so forcibly impressed with the advantages to be derived to the world from making that study a more general pursuit,' Perceval told the *Orthodox Churchman's Magazine* in a letter praising the values of Bible prophecy, 'that, if any observations of mine can have that effect, I am persuaded I cannot perform a more useful work for mankind.'

The sensible Victorians always deplored this habit of divination, exercised while Perceval occupied the supreme elected office. Most later commentators have followed their lead, adding it to the list of disreputable traits that have condemned him to historical oblivion. But the charge misses the point. Certainty is vital to leadership, and few politicians achieve power without learning to follow their convictions, however illogical. Biblical prophecy merely added to Perceval's unwavering purpose at a moment of crisis. What was reprehensible was that he never followed anything but his convictions. Yet that very fault paved the way for Wellington's glittering victories. In Perceval's favourite eleventh chapter in the Book of Daniel, the critical moment in the war between the king of the north and the king of the south was described in verse fifteen: 'So the king of the north shall come, and cast up a mount, and take the most fenced cities: and the arms of the south shall not withstand, neither his chosen people, neither shall there be any strength to withstand.'

It needed no great insight to see that the decision to cast up a mount could only refer to the fortifications that Wellington had cast up along the hills of the Torres Vedras line. Nor could Perceval doubt Daniel's revelation that it would prove to be the decisive move in winning the war. Thus, however powerful the logical arguments against the deployment of Wellington's Peninsular army, nothing could persuade the prime minister to summon the commander back home.

His solution to the 1810 financial crisis triggered by Abraham Goldsmid's suicide was less esoteric but equally effective. He persuaded the City's leading financiers to take over Goldsmid's affairs, and in return promised that the government would not sue his estate for the money that he owed the exchequer. In the short term, City confidence was swiftly restored by the knowledge that its own bankers were in charge. But in the longer term, it became clear that Perceval's lean budgeting was holding down government expenditure. There was inflation, but it was not uncontrolled. This meant that Wellington's costly force could continue to be financed.

When Perceval returned to borrow more money for his 1811 budget, the City demonstrated its trust in his economic management by lending him a larger sum than the year before, slightly more than £11 million, but at a lower rate of interest.

In January 1812, the Peninsular army finally left for good the mount it had cast up, and advanced into French-held territory. As one enemy fortress after another fell before it, praise replaced the criticism. The confidence of the country gentlemen in their Prime Minister became set in stone. The cabinet publicly declared they would resign en masse if he stepped down. 'People,' Wellington announced with satisfaction that summer 'are in great good humour with the affairs in Portugal.'

But by then Spencer Perceval had been killed.

# The Beauty of Double Bookkeeping

Do you suppose me the man to go with a deliberate design without cause or provocation with a pistol to put an end to the life of Mr Perceval? No, gentlemen! Far otherwise. I have strong reasons for my conduct, however extraordinary, reasons which when I have concluded, you will acknowledge to have fully justified me in this fatal act.

John Bellingham addressing the jury, 15 May 1812

On Thursday, 14 May, James Harmer had a break in his search for a defence for his client. Into his Hatton Garden office stepped a well-dressed, briskly competent lady in her mid-forties. Her name was Mrs Ann Billett. She was a property-owner in Southampton and, that rarity in the early 1800s, a woman accustomed to running her own affairs. More importantly from Harmer's point of view, she had been born Ann Scarbrow, first cousin to John Bellingham, and had grown up with him in St Neots, Huntingdonshire. Most importantly of all, Mrs Billett was adamant that her cousin was mad. The specific word she used was 'deranged'.

Of the women who found themselves alternately loving Bellingham and being driven to distraction by him, Ann Billett had the widest and longest experience of his different states of mind. She had known his family and played with him as a child, and remembered him with affection. She had seen him as a young man at the beginning of his career. And he had stayed with her immediately after his return from Russia. From her account of John Bellingham's emotional life, a pattern emerged of repeated, dizzying swings from security to anxiety. Time after time, he appeared to have reached a place of comfort only to slip back into penury and distress. From cousin Ann's point of view, Bellingham's grasp of reality was shot through with a sense of fragility.

Comfort came first from his mother, Elizabeth Scarbrow, who belonged to a solid, well-to-do family in St Neots. In the church records her father was described as a 'gentleman', and her elder brother was so notable a benefactor that on his death he was buried within the church itself. Elizabeth must have had an adventurous streak because in 1767 she escaped the provincial limitations of St Neots, and went to live amid the clamorous excitement of London's Fleet Street. There she married an artist, John Bellingham senior, who was then at the height of his small success as a painter of miniature portraits. His work was on show at the annual exhibition of the Society of Artists of Great Britain, and his patrons included Caleb Whitefoord, a friend of Benjamin Franklin and Samuel Johnson. Their son, John, was born, according to the Evangelical bishop, Daniel Wilson, 'in London about 1771'.

Bellingham's anxieties began simply as a consequence of his father's uncertain profession. To be an artist of any kind at that time was to be involved in the great battle of the day between defenders of the beautiful and advocates of the sublime. It was a conflict that convulsed music and literature as well as painting. Neutrality was impossible. On the one side was beauty, well-proportioned, pleasing and regular; on the other, the sublime – romantic, turbulent and awe-inspiring.

In his *Philosophical Enquiry into the Origin of Our Ideas of the Sublime and the Beautiful*, Edmund Burke offered an almost Freudian explanation of the battle. Our love of beauty has 'its origin in gratifications and pleasures,' he argued, specifically in sexual desire or 'the purposes of propagation', so that when we see people or places that we desire, they 'give us a sense of joy and pleasure in beholding them'. The sense of the sublime, by contrast, is grounded in the instinct for self-preservation. 'The passions belonging to the preservation of the individual turn wholly on pain and danger,' he insisted. Thus whatever tends 'to excite the ideas of pain and danger, that is to say, whatever is in any sort terrible, or is conversant about terrible objects, or operates in a manner analogous to terror, is a source of the sublime'. Such terror, created by threats of violence and death, was 'the strongest emotion which the mind is capable of feeling'.

In a strikingly modern way, which anticipated both Freud's theory about the conflict between the desires of sex and death, and the rival attractions of romantic and horror films, Burke compared the contrary appeals of beauty and the sublime. The latter, he concluded, created a sense of danger that gave rise to a pleasure more wild and powerful than that of beauty.

This struggle between the classical sense of beauty and the romantic sense of the sublime was fundamental to late eighteenth-century thought. And it offers a key to understanding the swings of John Bellingham's mental state. However much his fragile mind strove for the comfort of order and beauty, it would always be tempted by the all-consuming savagery of chaos.

As a miniaturist, Bellingham senior was enlisted on the side of beauty – small art was automatically debarred from being terrifying – but during the early 1770s he gradually slipped from the intensely controlled concentration that miniature painting required into the chaos of mental illness. The Bellinghams moved back to St Neots, presumably to receive support from Elizabeth's family, and there the anxious little boy became friends with his elder cousin, Ann Scarbrow, who all her life would maintain a protective affection for

him. As the painter's behaviour grew wilder, he must have required
some care or restraint, but no parish wanted the expense of main-
taining a madman from outside its boundaries. In 1780 Bellingham
senior was shuttled back to London to be confined as a pauper
lunatic in St Luke's charitable asylum for the violently insane.

The effect on the young John Bellingham of his father's lunacy
and increasingly violent behaviour can only be guessed, though his
self-contained manners and his neat, abnormally regular handwriting offer an indication of the rigid control he felt necessary to
impose upon himself. Even Daniel Wilson, who saw Bellingham as
an unregenerate sinner, felt bound to admit that despite everything, 'his manner was mild, not at all resembling the coarseness of
the ruffian'. He was not clever but, to judge by his literate, highly
formalised letters, he must have been a diligent schoolboy.
Eventually John Bellingham's father was discharged as incurable,
and died in lodgings in Titchfield Street, behind the thoroughfare
of Oxford Street, in 1781.

Security returned in the person of William Daw, who had
married Elizabeth's sister, and was not only a barrister but held a
handsome sinecure as Clerk of the King's Silver. Elderly, childless
and wealthy, he found the fifteen-year-old Bellingham an opening
as an apprentice goldsmith, a trade that conventionally led on to a
financial career. Daw had to lay out a large sum of money to secure
such a promising place, but it went for nothing because the boy ran
away within a few weeks. When the sententious Wilson came to
write up an account of his interview with Bellingham, he ascribed
this rebellion to the murderer's 'very perverse and troublesome'
character, and to 'that dreadful obstinacy which hurried him on at
last to the foulest of all crimes'.

More charitably it might also be called the behaviour of a trou-
bled teenager, and uncle William evidently sympathised, because
less than a year later he bought the boy a cadetship in the East India

Company. But this still more promising route to riches was cut off when the ship carrying him out to India, the 900-ton *Hartwell*, was wrecked on rocks in the Azores. Despite the cost, wealthy William Daw apparently stepped in a third time by helping him set up in Oxford Street as 'a tin-plate worker', that is, supplying the thin, glossy metal that artists, jewellers and others used for etching, ornaments and decorations.

Its outcome too followed a familiar pattern. In 1794 the tin-plate retail business failed when the premises burned down in a fire, and the twenty-three-year-old Bellingham went bankrupt. Records suggest that he or his uncle soon paid off his debts, but this latest disaster marked a turning point. Evidently deciding that he had no future in art or retailing, and with no further backing from his uncle, Bellingham chose the safest profession open to an impoverished young man, and became an accountant.

The evidence of his neat handwriting and the meticulous itemisation of his sufferings suggest that Bellingham was well-suited to the profession. But his absolute insistence on justice, his determination to be compensated for his wrongful arrest, indicates that the match went deeper. A loss had to be balanced out by a gain. Accounts needed to be evened. It was the opposite of his father's chaos. And his career proved that he did indeed make an excellent accountant.

Having apprenticed himself long enough to learn the skill of double-entry bookkeeping, he found work in the counting-room – the accounts department – of a commercial firm trading with Russia. It promised lifelong security. A growing army of dealers, brokers, insurers and shippers were engaged in the business of importing Baltic iron, hemp and tallow, and exporting textiles, pottery, glass and metal. But Russian merchants required credit to be extended up to twelve months, payment to be made with bills of exchange that might fluctuate by as much as 20 per cent, and cargoes of cloth to be bartered in one year for the delivery of timber in the next. To keep the records of these complex financial transactions, the rapidly developing Baltic trade desperately needed reliable counting clerks.

In terms of order, regularity and smallness, the business of the countinghouse was beautiful. That was precisely what Goethe meant in *Wilhem Meister*, when he put into the mouth of Werner, his prototypical businessman, the assertion that 'Double-entry bookkeeping is one of the most beautiful discoveries of the human spirit'. It was beautiful because it introduced order and regularity to the chaotic forces of fear and greed. 'What a thing it is to see the order which prevails throughout [the merchant's] business,' Werner asserted. 'What advantages does he derive from the system of book-keeping by double-entry!' Not only could he see the column of his assets balanced against those of his debits, Werner insisted, 'it organises perceptions into a system'.

The Russian business was particularly suited to Bellingham's orderly temperament because it dealt with items in constant demand. Timber, iron and hemp were essential to the fleets of great commercial enterpises like the East India Company and to those engaged in the West India sugar and slaving trades, and they were absolutely vital to the Royal Navy with its incessant hunger for ships and cannon and rigging. Tallow was even more valuable because everyone was in need of candles and artificial light. Wholesalers came to meet the brokers in London who had suppliers in St Petersburg and Archangel. Once the deal was made, a shipbroker would produce a vessel, an insurer would cover the risk of loss, and a financier would advance credit. In normal times, the deals were standard, and competition kept prices reasonable. It was only in war when the rapacity of privateers increased and the deals grew riskier, and prices soared, that a beautiful business became sublime.

As early as 1796, the French port of St Malo alone sent out twenty-nine privateers that captured thirty-eight British cargo ships. Once Napoleon's power spread across the continent, they were joined by Dutch and Danish raiders. The value of the losses could be measured in the insurance rates at Lloyd's of London, which doubled in ten years. In 1800 the trade faced a still greater threat when the Russian tsar, Paul I, created a league of armed neutrality that included Denmark, aimed at giving peaceful aid to France.

To safeguard their interests, several Baltic firms sent out representatives to St Petersburg and Archangel. Such was Bellingham's reputation for reliability, his London employers selected him to represent them in Archangel during this anxious period. Given the possibility that trade with Britain might be stopped altogether, he would not have been expected to do more than supervise the execution of existing contracts. When the armed neutrality league ended in 1801 with the tsar's assassination, and the destruction of the Danish fleet by Admiral Horatio Nelson, Bellingham was summoned back to London. He had been in Archangel less than a year, but the experience had given him a first taste of how business operated in the port.

For some reason, perhaps because his old job had become less attractive after working on his own in Archangel, he left London. With fateful consequences, he chose to move to Liverpool, a city that, in the boast of one of its two Members of Parliament, General Banastre Tarleton, had risen 'to become the second place in wealth and population in the British Empire'.

In his meticulously detailed petitions, John Bellingham always described himself as a 'Merchant of Liverpool'. Neither term was entirely accurate. When he first set foot there in 1801, he was still an accountant, and he lived in the city for less than five years. Yet from the moment he arrived, it was certainly his ambition to become a Liverpool merchant.

Within the memory of many people still living then, Liverpool had possessed only a single small dock on the River Mersey, and the streets were still 'tortuous and narrow, with pavements in the middle, skirted by mud or dirt as the season happened. The sidewalks [were] rough with sharp-pointed stones that made it misery to walk upon them.' By 1800 the port had expanded to include five docks capable of handling 20,000 tons of shipping at once. The port's tough, marine character still remained, especially down by the river, where taverns, brothels, pawnbrokers, and low-beamed, small-windowed houses were jammed into narrow lanes and round the dank backyards that hid behind chandlers' stores and tall warehouses. 'Scarcely a town by the margin of the ocean could be more salt in its people than the men of Liverpool of the last century;' wrote a nineteenth-century Liverpudlian, 'so barbarous were they in their amusements, bull-baitings and cock and dog-fightings, and pugilistic encounters.'

Yet already the city's phenomenal growth had tilted the balance decisively towards commercial grandeur. Away from the docks, magnificent public buildings had been constructed, such as the Exchange where commodity traders, brokers and their agents met, the Athenaeum with its superb library where financiers congregated, and the Lyceum for important shippers and merchants, their interests catered for by a weather-vane let through the ceiling that told them when the wind was set fair to take their vessels down the Mersey. Substantial houses with tall windows were being built at the top end of Hanover Strret, the wide, paved thoroughfare that climbed up the slope from the docks towards Mount Pleasant overlooking the Mersey. The population was less than a tenth of London's, but growing fast at 77,000, and per head the town's inhabitants were more prosperous by far than Londoners. Almost all of them depended for their earnings on the port – skippers, tide-waiters, customs officers and harbour masters; shipowners, bankers, insurers and brokers; riggers, carpenters, porters and dockers, even house-builders, shopkeepers and brickmakers.

Bellingham put his accounting skills to work for a company that specialised in trade with Ireland, importing linen, bacon and cattle, and exporting Lancashire cloth, Birmingham brass and Staffordshire pottery. The Irish trade had been a small, reliable, coastal business, until in 1801 Ireland was incorporated within the United Kingdom. Once customs duties were abolished, imports of wheat, linen and cattle jumped by 25 per cent. However, it never generated the sort of profits that came from the blue-water trade that made Liverpool merchants wealthy – raw sugar from the West Indies; Cheshire salt to Newfoundland; tobacco, cotton and wheat from the United States in exchange for machinery, glass, china and textiles; beads, iron and bolts of vividly dyed cotton for Africa to be traded for ivory, wax, spices and, the most profitable commodity of all, humans.

In the slave trade, Liverpool had long swamped rivals like London and Bristol. It sent out more than 120 slave ships a year from the Mersey, accounting for two-thirds of Britain's traffic in people, and nearly half of Europe's, and the city's dominance was becoming more marked. Not only had the number of ships increased by a fifth since the 1780s, their average size had grown from around 280 tons to close to 350 tons, each one representing an investment of up to £8,500. Strong demand from new markets such as Brazil and Cuba as well as from established buyers in the West Indies and the United States was driving up the sale price of each slave from around £40 in the early 1790s to £60 in the new century. It was the jewel in Liverpool's trading crown.

The town owed its success in the trade partly to its infrastructure. As its leading merchants explained in a 1788 petition to Parliament, they had invested heavily in 'the constructing of proper and convenient wet docks for shipping . . . [and] the numerous canals and other communications from the interior parts of this kingdom'. But the critical ingredient was Liverpool's unique network of shippers, bankers and insurers, who spread the risks of each twelve-month voyage so that none was wiped out by disaster, and all profited from success.

John Norris, a successful trader himself, estimated that altogether the town invested about £1 million annually in the slave trade. On average, investors could expect a healthy if not spectacular 10 per cent return, but with insurers taking another 6 per cent, and suppliers between 5 and 7 per cent, the overall return to Liverpool from the trade was around £220,000 a year. For someone like Thomas Leyland, one of Liverpool's richest men, worth almost £740,000 at his death, the rewards were so great that he gradually moved from being a shipper, personally responsible for transporting nearly 3,500 Africans across the Atlantic in twenty-five years, to advancing credit to other slavers, and eventually ended as the founder of one of Liverpool's largest banks.

Without capital or credit, it was impossible for Bellingham to earn money on so large a scale. No more than a week was required for a voyage to and from Dublin or Belfast, so any profits were made quickly and with little risk, but intense competition kept margins thin. The high returns from slaving reflected the dangers and length of time between investment and pay-off. Even in the United States trade, the fastest growing business sector in Liverpool, a round trip across the Atlantic taking four to six months meant a long delay before any return was seen.

Bellingham soon moved from the counting-room to become a trader on his own account, making a slim though predictable, and therefore beautiful, profit from dealing in livestock and cloth in one direction, and metal and pottery in the other. But it took money to make real money.

His reward came in a different fashion. One of his Irish business associates was an unsuccessful but histrionic shipbroker in Newry named John Nevill, who had been bankrupted once and was on the verge of going under a second time. He could hardly have made a congenial companion to the fastidious Bellingham, but he had a nineteen-year-old daughter, Mary, 'a very pleasant, affable woman' according to a later description, 'genteel in her manners: rather short, and inclined to be lusty [plump]'. Bellingham was almost fifteen years older, and five or six inches taller. He may have thought her youth and size would make her biddable, or he may simply have fallen in love. Her motives may have concerned nothing more than escape from Newry and a hopeless father, but her personality suggests a stronger drive. Mary Nevill would surely have responded to the attractions of John Bellingham's dark face, precise mind and elegant taste in clothes. She may even have fallen in love with him. Whatever the impulse, in 1803 they were married, and set up house together in Liverpool.

All of the few facts known about Mary, and each of her surviving letters, show her to have been feisty, jealous, energetic and enterprising. However disturbing her character may have been to her highly controlled husband, he obviously found her physically exciting and within months of the wedding Mary was pregnant. But in that summer of 1803, at the age of thirty-two, he took what turned out to be a life-changing choice in his career. He gave up the Irish business, and returned to Archangel, acting for a group of Liverpool traders. His presence there was proof of the flexibility and enterprise of Liverpool's trading culture.

In 1802 the Peace of Amiens had brought a brief halt to the war with France. Yet even in a year of peace when commodity prices and shipping rates had slumped, the value of timber, tallow, and iron that passed through Archangel reached five million roubles,

approximately £500,000. More than three-quarters of this trade
was destined for Britain, where its value would be doubled. In 1803
war with France broke out again, offering irresistible prospects for
business. The price of Russian timber, cut by serf labour from virgin
forests owned by the tsar or his nobles, could not have been cheaper,
and the demand could not have been more urgent. It was too good
an opportunity to leave to London traders. As they were accustomed to do in the slave trade, the group of Liverpool investors and
bankers for whom Bellingham acted as agent would have put up
the money to charter a ship, approximately £4,000. Although
based on the wrong side of England, they intended to ship the
timber to Hull on the east coast, the nearest convenient port to
Archangel, involving a round trip of no more than forty days. Since
Bellingham's experience of conditions in Archangel and his
accountant's knowledge of the Russian trade were essential – indeed
he may have suggested the enterprise – he would have been offered
a share in the profits.

Despite his experience, everything in Bellingham was psychologically attuned to the order and neatness of the counting clerk
rather than to the chaotic switches of fortune that a born trader
could exploit to make money. What he possessed was dogged determination and an attention to detail. He could read accounts, find
a broker to charter the cargo vessel, and arrange the insurance with
Lloyd's of London, but to negotiate the purchase of timber, assess
its quality, make a deal, and arrange delivery and finance required
other skills. Anyone trading in Archangel needed local contacts,
but Bellingham needed them more than most. From his earlier visit
there, he would have known most of the Dutch traders. The contact
he chose turned out to be the man who would become his nemesis,
Conrad Dorbecker.

Not only was Dorbecker highly experienced in the intricacies
of Russian business, as a Dutchman he was deeply integrated into

the expatriate community of Archangel with its unrivalled access to information and resources. It appears that his initial partnership in 1803 with Bellingham and the Liverpool backers was successful. The timber, bought in Archangel, was landed in Hull and sold at a profit.

Had Bellingham taken his earnings and returned home to Liverpool, the tranquillity of mind that he so valued might have remained intact. But that was not how a Liverpool merchant behaved. Risk, enterprise and the chance to become a second Thomas Leyland drove Liverpool traders on. And so, fatally misjudging his own capacities, Bellingham decided to undertake a second expedition, again in partnership with Dorbecker, but this time he himself would be in charge of the English side, organising the investment and trading on his own account.

While he had been in Archangel, his aunt, the widow of his wealthy uncle, William Daw, had died leaving £400 to Bellingham's mother. Since Elizabeth Bellingham was already dead, the money had come to him. He invested the inheritance and his earnings from the earlier voyage in chartering a vessel and, since it was a matter with which he was familiar, he presumably took personal charge of arranging insurance with Lloyd's of London. If he did alert the insurers to the *Soyuz* scam, as his Archangel enemies alleged, he certainly had the opportunity, and the information would have earned him a reward. But thousands more were needed to finance the purchase of iron and timber. Following the Liverpool model, he evidently raised the money by persuading a group of Hull merchants to invest in his project. Then, as befitted a potentially wealthy merchant, just before embarking, he made a generous contribution to charity. 'The debtors of Hull gaol,' the *Hull Advertiser* announced in May 1804, 'return thanks to Mr Billingham [*sic*] of Archangel for his kind donation of one guinea.'

When he set sail for Russia on this occasion, his young wife Mary accompanied him together with their new-born son, James. Her presence was living proof of her support and encouragement of his ambition to make his forturne.

Bellingham himself had no doubt about the profitable outcome of this venture. According to a confused account cobbled together by a pamphlet-writer in a hurry, he had in fact 'entered into engagements with the merchants of Hull for the delivery of deals to the amount of £12,000', implying that he intended to organise not one but several voyages. Thinking big was the mark of a Liverpool merchant.

The story that Ann Billett told James Harmer on the day before the trial mostly concerned Bellingham's behaviour after he was finally released from his St Petersburg prison in December 1809. On the day before Christmas, when he had at last set foot in London again, he appeared on her doorstep at 104 Sloane Street in a state of such anxiety that, despite the impropriety of a married man living under the same roof as an unmarried woman, she immediately took him in and insisted he spend Christmas with her.

While her cousin was lurching between triumph and disaster, Ann Scarbrow's life had followed a more conventional and less fraught pattern. After their childhood together, she had gone to live in London where she met and married Edward Billett, a property-owner originally from Hampshire. Although she had been widowed and left to bring up two young daughters alone, she possessed enough energy and intelligence to take over her late husband's large property near Southampton as well as the house in the newly fashionable west end of London, and run his estate herself. Her evidence was the more convincing because she was so obviously someone accustomed to taking charge of her life.

While Bellingham was still in Sloane Street, Ann insisted that he write home to his wife, now back in Liverpool, to tell her of his release. Then after Christmas she moved him into lodgings nearby in order to preserve the proprieties. Nevertheless, she continued to see him frequently for the next four months. The Bellingham she described was in an almost manic state. He blamed all his troubles and financial losses on the failure of the British ambassador, Lord Leveson-Gower, to intervene on his behalf. During the first months of 1810, he hurled himself into a furious round of petitions and visits to government offices in an attempt to gain compensation for his losses in Russia. Ann Billett remembered especially his wild talk of the great schemes he would undertake when the money was paid.

'He said he had realized more than an hundred thousand pounds with which he intended to buy an estate in the west of England, and to take a house in London,' she told Harmer. 'I asked him where the money was. He said he had not got the money, but it was the same as if he had, for that he had gained his cause in Russia [referring to the trial in Archangel that led to the return of his passport], and our government must make it good to him.' Ann Billett summoned her friend Mary Clarke to help reason with him. Both women came to the blunt conclusion that he was, as they later put it, 'in a state of perfect derangement'.

In February 1810 Mary Bellingham came down to London from Liverpool in response to her husband's letter. It was two years since she had last seen him in detention in St Petersburg. Heavily pregnant with their second child, she had been allowed to leave Russia with the young James, her voyage home being paid for by the expatriate British community in St Petersburg. As the newspaper reports all recognised, she had displayed extraordinary resilience in bringing up a child in a foreign land where she did not speak the language and her husband was in prison. While John Bellingham grappled hopelessly with the enemies who denied him justice, she had held the small family together through her work as a dressmaker.

Once back in England, she had gone to stay with her uncle, James Nevill, a Quaker who worked as a heel-maker for the shoe industry in Wigan, about twenty miles from Liverpool. There she met Mary Stevens, a young, unmarried friend of Mrs Nevill, and together they set up in business in Liverpool as dressmaker and milliner.

Ann Billett had been to visit them and could testify that the two Marys made a successful team, designing, making and selling clothes and hats. The Mrs Bellingham who came to join her husband in London in 1810, having left her two young children with Mary Stevens, was a woman of both courage and resource. She and Ann Billett accompanied Bellingham in his restless visits to government offices demanding redress for his wrongs, but they retained their own judgement about his chances of success.

Each quickly came to the conclusion it was a lost cause. That much was clear from the moment when the Foreign Office spokesman replied that 'his Majesty's government is precluded from interfering in the support of your case'. Not only were Britain and Russia nominally at war, but his imprisonment had been for debt, a civil matter between two businessmen, and thus not of government concern. Bellingham might have been blind to the difficulties, but both his wife and Ann Billett realised that his plan to get compensation was doomed. 'Neither she nor I gave any credit to it,' Ann commented briskly to Harmer.

In their exasperation, both women must have told Bellingham that they thought he was mad, because in a bizarre episode he took them back to the Foreign Office to ask the under-secretary for an opinion on his sanity. 'Sir, my friends say that I am out of my senses,' Bellingham said bluntly, 'is it your opinion, Mr Smith, that I am so?' With a nice display of Foreign Office tact, Mr Smith replied, 'It is a very delicate question for me to answer. I only know you upon this business, and I can assure you that you will never have what you are pursuing after.'

His negative should have been clear enough, but Bellingham appeared to be delighted by it. To Ann's incredulity, as she told Harmer, he turned to his wife as they were driving home in the coach, and patted her hand saying, 'Now I hope, my dear, you are well convinced all will happen well, and as I wished.'

For Mary Bellingham, it was the last straw. Ann Billett told Harmer that Mary had returned to Liverpool, determined to leave her husband, but the matter became less clear when she discussed it with her uncle and aunt, and Mary Stevens. All of them felt she should give the marriage another chance. Her uncle James admitted that 'I was one that advised her to live with him "as she had taken him for better or for worse".' In the end Mary let herself be talked into keeping the marriage alive. But even so she was determined that, as the newspapers reported, 'she would not live with him until he made a Solemn promise to give up wrong thoughts of his wild goose schemes & expectations'.

Her husband delayed his answer while he applied unsuccessfully twice more for compensation, first to the Treasury, then the Privy Council.

In May 1810 Bellingham made one last, desperate effort, going in person to 10 Downing Street where he gave Michael Herries, private secretary to Spencer Perceval, a document for the Prime Minister. Herries asked him to return later when he had read its contents. The author described himself as a frustrated petitioner who, 'having suffered a long and improper detention in Russia, has applied to His Majesty's Privy Council for redress, and it appears by their lordships' answer to be of a nature not their power to grant'. Consequently he wished the Prime Minister to allow him to present the same petition to Parliament. Still docketed with the paper is the brief reply that Herries gave Bellingham when he returned: 'Answered him verbally the 22nd May that Mr Perceval could not give permission for the introduction of his petition.'

Rebuffed by the Prime Minister himself, Bellingham at last accepted defeat. He returned to Liverpool, and agreed to his wife's condition that he must abandon his plans for compensation. 'This he did most solemnly promise,' James Nevill explained, 'and even burnt a parcell of papers which he stated was those relating to the affair.' Trustingly Mary welcomed him back, and was soon pregnant with baby Henry.

Even in his most deranged ravings in 1810, John Bellingham never hinted at any thought of taking violent retribution. Two years later, he returned to London with the calm intention of executing Spencer Perceval as a matter of justice. During that time, something evidently happened to change his mind. If any rational motive did exist for the killing, it had to be found in Liverpool. As part of his investigations, John Vickery, the Bow Street Runner, would routinely have asked for further information from the magistrate's officer responsible for carrying out investigations in Liverpool. But time ran out before any reply arrived. On Friday, 15 May 1812, Bellingham stood trial at the Old Bailey for the murder of the Prime Minister.

# The Prosecution Presents its Case

The only question you have to try, is, whether the prisoner did wilfully and maliciously murder Mr. Spencer Perceval or not.
Lord Chief Justice Mansfield's instruction to the jury, 15 May 1812

In the four days since the murder, John Bellingham had emerged from anonymity to become a celebrity. From daybreak on the day of his trial, crowds thronged into the streets around the Old Bailey. Windows in the houses overlooking Newgate Prison and the court-house filled with spectators, many of them women, and it was noted that fashionably dressed ladies were conspicuous amongst those attempting to gain entry to the Old Bailey itself. Ever since the initial reports of his resemblance to the radical MP Sir Francis Burdett, whose saturnine good looks were well-known, rumours had spread about Bellingham's dark complexion and tall frame. 'Women were struck by his fine and manly person,' ran the gossip. 'Strange tales of his amorous complexion, whispered abroad, did not weaken that favourable impression.'

Admission was supposed to be by ticket only, but bribery proved just as effective, although the price quickly rose from one to three guineas before the trial opened. 'So great was the press,' a horrified *Courier* reported, 'that a great number of eminent persons of both Houses of Parliament were compelled to intermix indiscriminately with the multitude in the body of the Court.' The sweaty odour of rarely washed bodies must have mingled with the scent of herbs and flowers that were placed along the window ledges, in the dock and in front of the judges' bench to counteract the muddy, sewage-flavoured air that floated up from the underground passageways connecting the court to Newgate prison. No one, however, appears to have left.

At ten o'clock, the trial began with the arrival of the seventy-nine-year-old judge, the Lord Chief Justice of the Common Pleas, Sir James Mansfield. The Lord Mayor of London, two other judges, and various peers of the realm, including the royal duke of Clarence, packed on to the bench on either side of him. John Bellingham, standing alone at the bar of the court, was almost the only person not rubbing elbows with his neighbours. He was wearing the same clothes as in the House of Commons, though the brown coat, torn in the struggle, and the waspish yellow and black-striped waistcoat were now the worse for wear. A sketch of him in profile showed a long face, whose pronounced nose and slightly undershot jaw were striking although too stretched to be handsome. With his dark hair cut short by a prison barber, he appeared respectable but, as events were to show, he would have done better to appear in rags, unshaven and gibbering nonsense.

There could be no doubt that he had killed Perceval. He had admitted it at the committal proceedings, and many times subsequently, and eyewitnesses had sworn to it at the coroner's inquest. From the legal point of view, the only question was whether he had committed the murder while mad. Bellingham's fate depended upon Harmer's ability to assemble convincing evidence of insanity.

The previous night the solicitor had taken a long affidavit from Ann Billett testifying to his derangement. At her suggestion, Harmer had then taken a shorter statement from her friend, Mary Clarke, who had also witnessed Bellingham's behaviour in 1810 after his return from Russia. But in a setting that placed the greatest reliance on 'the masculine intelligence', they needed reinforcement from male witnesses. These were conspicuously lacking. The mail coach took twenty-two hours to reach Liverpool, so there had been no chance to get anyone from Bellingham's home city to give testimony, although Harmer had hopes that witnesses might arrive before the end of the day. Of the two experts on insanity he had asked to testify, only Samuel Simmons had replied, excusing himself on the grounds that he was seriously ill – and indeed he died a few months later. No word had come from Thomas Munro, the man who had helped secure Hadfield's acquittal. As the trial opened, Harmer's greatest need was for time. A postponement until after the weekend would be enough.

The calibre of the defence team he had assembled offered at least a glimmer of hope. Peter Alley, later famous for his eloquent defence of the Manchester demonstrators caught up in the Peterloo massacre of 1819, already had a reputation as an abrasive cross-examiner. Charles Phillips, the ultimate authority on his fellow attorneys, judged him to be 'zealous, industrious, bold and impassioned', but if anything, Alley was too volatile, too liable to anger at judicial interference, for such a political trial. His junior, Henry Revell Reynolds, who would epitomise the new breed of careful, professional Victorian lawyers, might have been better suited to the circumstances. But he too could barely contain his contempt for the lynch mentality that gripped both prosecution and bench. The conduct of the trial was, he said later, 'the greatest disgrace to English justice'.

Until 1836, legal procedure did not permit professional counsel to plead on behalf of murderers, only to cross-examine witnesses and to offer advice. Within those limits, Alley fully intended to test the sanity argument in court. When Mansfield asked how the prisoner pleaded to the charge of murder, Alley promptly stood up and asked for a postponement 'to shew that the prisoner could be proved to be insane'. He must have guessed he would get nowhere. The Old Bailey sat for eight sessions a year, each lasting about ten days. The trial had been rushed into the first days of the May session, forcing already scheduled cases to be postponed until the next session in July. The judge was not likely to let the case drag on.

Stonily, Mansfield swept away Alley's interruption, repeating that the accused must first plead guilty or not guilty before evidence of insanity could be addressed. At that, Bellingham himself protested that he could not plead until he had the papers that had been taken from him in the struggle after he had shot Perceval. His objection received the same treatment. For the third time the accused was asked how he pleaded. 'Not guilty,' Bellingham replied at last. 'I place myself upon God and my country.'

Alley returned to the attack, asking how he could defend the prisoner without his papers and without witnesses. He cited the affidavits given by Ann Billett and Mary Clarke stating that John Bellingham had been deranged since his return from Russia. Their important evidence could be corroborated by his friends in Liverpool. But the government had allowed no time for these witnesses to be presented. As a matter not simply of justice but of humanity, a postponement was essential.

'It was only on Monday that the alleged act was said to have been perpetrated,' Alley declared, working up his temper. 'A letter could not have been sent until the next day. It is impossible that any answer could have been received by today. Even where a person is tried in the town in which he resides,' he ended in exasperation, 'some time must be necessary to enable him to provide evidence for his trial.'

The Attorney General, Sir Vicary Gibbs, who was leading the prosecution, dismissed Alley's plea contemptuously. It was, he declared, nothing more than 'a contrivance to delay the administration of justice'. Whatever the women's affidavits maintained about the past, the fact was that while Bellingham was in London, he had been leading a perfectly normal life. There was no need to wait for Liverpool witnesses. The Attorney General had an acid manner that earned him the nickname of Vinegar Gibbs. 'Where has the Prisoner been for these four months?' he demanded. 'He has been resident in this town, in the midst of a family in this town, known to multitudes of persons in this town, transacting business in this town, and with as much sagacity and as perfect and masculine an understanding as any man who now hears me.'

Rubbing salt in the wound, he blamed the defence for not secur-ing evidence from experts 'whose statement your Lordship would have regarded as of deep importance'. Angrily Alley corrected him, but the Lord Chief Justice was as anxious to hurry on as the pros-ecution, and he brushed the objection aside. The defence application for a postponement had to be dismissed, Mansfield announced, because the affidavits of the two women were not enough to suggest he was insane. Carefully misreading their import, he said the testi-mony related to his behaviour in Russia. 'Now could it be supposed,' he asked, 'that [Bellingham] went, or would be permitted to go, to Russia if he were in a disordered state of mind?' There were, there-fore, no grounds for postponement, and the trial could continue.

The jury was sworn and Gibbs began to set out the case against John Bellingham in all its stark detail. The victim, he reminded the jury, was the sort of man who, given the chance, would have used his last conscious moments praying for forgiveness for his murderer. But Bellingham had denied him that Christian consolation. He had prepared carefully for the crime, planning and practising for weeks beforehand. He had waited by the door of the lobby until the prime minister appeared, then coldly murdered him.

There could be no question of insanity. Even someone incapable of looking after his own affairs would be 'criminally liable', the

Attorney General insisted, 'provided he had a mind capable of distinguishing between right and wrong'. Bellingham not only managed his own affairs in London, but his wife's as well. Finally, Gibbs pointed out, it was beyond question that this sane, strong-minded man had acted alone. Having outlined the prosecution case, the Attorney General then began to call witnesses to the murder itself and to the prisoner's meticulous planning.

To spectators in the courtroom, Bellingham remained an object of fascination. Whatever James Harmer believed, it was apparent to them that the prisoner himself agreed completely with both the judge and prosecution about his own sanity. What struck everyone was his composure. Undisturbed by their gaze, he himself 'frequently looked round and appeared to contemplate the crowd with a curious eye'. At one point, he refreshed himself by eating an orange taken from his pocket, then he asked for a chair and sat down 'very much at his ease', according to *The Globe*. While witnesses were being questioned, he distracted himself by rubbing in his hand the herbs that were scattered around the dock, and smelling their scent on his fingers.

The evidence should have concerned him more. Its purpose was to convince the jury not only of his sanity, but of his premeditation. Like a film run backwards, it began with the pistol shot, the dying prime minister falling to the ground, and the arrest of his murderer. The witnesses who had given evidence at the committal proceedings described the scene once more, and the only new detail came from the enigmatic General Isaac Gascoyne. He revealed that when the murder took place he had been writing in a committee room upstairs whose door opened onto a balcony overlooking the lobby. 'It was nearly the same thing, as to hearing, as to being in the lobby of the House,' he testified. 'I heard the loud report of a pistol shot, and almost instantaneously the cry of "Close the doors." I rushed downstairs, through the House, and into the lobby.'

Having established that Bellingham was in the general's grasp, the Attorney General called John Norris, the House of Commons servant, as a witness. He pushed the clock back to about five minutes past five o'clock, the last moments before the living prime minister arrived in the House of Commons. As Norris passed through the door on his way to walk upstairs from the lobby to the passage to the Strangers' Gallery, he noticed the tall man in the dark coat by the door. 'I observed him, as if watching for somebody that was coming,' he said, adding that the man seemed anxious and had his hand inside his coat. 'Perhaps the impression is stronger on my mind now than it was then,' Norris went on, as though conscious that he might have asked Bellingham what he was doing, and thereby changed history. But, as he told the court, it was not the first time he had encountered the stranger. 'I had seen him frequently in the gallery of the House of Commons, and about the passages of the House.' Saying nothing to Bellingham, Norris had left the lobby, toiled up the stairs and was nearing the gallery when he heard the shot.

The evidence of Vincent Dowling, *The Day's* reporter, turned the calendar back another week. He told of his encounters with Bellingham in the Strangers' Gallery when the tall man had come in and asked to have Perceval and other members of the government identified. 'On one occasion I sat immediately next to him, while the House was in debate,' Dowling said. 'I sat next to him about half an hour; I cannot say the precise time; there was a sort of general conversation between him and myself, and some other person that was sitting near me.'

Three more weeks dissolved away with the testimony of William Taylor, the aptly named tailor. On 25 April Taylor had been walking down Guilford Street, the commercial thoroughfare that cut across the end of New Millman Street. There he bumped into Bellingham, who 'informed me that he had a small job to do, and if I would step back with him he would give it me immediately'. At his lodgings, Bellingham produced a dark brown coat, and asked Taylor 'to make him an inside pocket on the left side, so as he could get at it conveniently; he wished to have it a particular depth; he accordingly gave me a bit of paper about the length of nine inches'.

At this point, the Attorney General paused, evidently to let the jury appreciate the significance of Taylor's evidence because he repeated the phrase, no doubt with slow import, 'He gave you a bit of paper about nine inches in length.' Using the paper as a pattern, Taylor sewed the pocket in place the same day, 'he was very particular to have it home that evening,' the witness confirmed.

The precise size of the pocket was significant because just four days earlier, on 21 April, Bellingham had gone to the well-known City of London gunsmith, William Beckwith, and purchased a pair of steel pistols. They were designed to be concealed, and used only at close quarters. The length of the grip and firing mechanism was seven inches, and each had a detachable screw barrel that added another two inches. Beckwith told the court he had charged Bellingham four guineas for the two pistols, together with bullets, gunpowder, a key for screwing the barrel into place, and a kit for casting more ammunition. He also advised him to practise with the weapon, since the short barrel and large half-inch calibre would be hopelessly inaccurate over any distance of more than a few feet.

The Attorney General was careful to draw the attention of the jury to the implications of the two witnesses' evidence. During the next few days, he pointed out, Bellingham had gone to the wooded land around Primrose Hill, and practised shooting at trees with Beckwith's pistols. The experience convinced him that he needed to hold the muzzle virtually against his victim to be sure of hitting him. It also demonstrated that precious minutes would be lost in screwing the barrel into place. The weapon would have to be prepared before he left home, and he would need a pocket exactly nine inches deep to hold it. In case of a misfire, he decided to carry the back-up pistol, loaded and cocked, in the pocket of his nankeen trousers, but the murder weapon would be concealed in his secret pocket, from which it could be drawn at the last moment.

With attention concentrated on the pistol, events were brought abruptly up to date by testimony from the Bow Street Runner, John Vickery. He confirmed that while searching Bellingham's rooms he had found in a drawer the gunpowder, ammunition and bullet moulds purchased from Beckwith. In court the murder weapon was now produced and, in a moment of theatre, one of the bullets was inserted into the barrel. 'This ball fits the barrel exactly,' Vickery announced. 'And it was made in this mould, I have no doubt.'

Finally, the prosecution demonstrated with elaborate care that the coat Bellingham was wearing in the dock was the one that Taylor had altered. None of the evidence was in question. Alley had only found it possible to intervene once, when by questioning one of the MPs at the scene of the murder, he tried to point out Bellingham's irrationality. He drew out the fact that Bellingham had expressed no personal dislike of Perceval, and that the only motive he had offered for his action was the lack of compensation for his losses in Russia. 'That is the reason he gave you?' Alley demanded, 'mere want of redress of grievance on the part of the government?'

It was a tiny pebble to rescue from the avalanche of evidence produced by the Attorney General. By launching it in such detail, the prosecution had illustrated how carefully, logically and cold-bloodedly the prisoner had planned his crime. When the Attorney General sat down, no one could seriously believe Bellingham to be a lunatic, or that for at least four months he had acted with anything but conscious intent to murder.

* * *

There was, however, a serious gap in the prosecution case, and one of its own making. The testimony of Ann Billett and Mary Clarke carried genuine significance. No one could have mistaken the frenzy of John Bellingham's behaviour two years earlier, in 1810. When the women described him as deranged at that time, they were undoubtedly using the word accurately. Had he determined to assassinate the prime minister when he first returned from Russia, or Lord Leveson-Gower, or anyone else he blamed for his misfortune, it would certainly have been the work of someone out of his mind.

The Attorney General, however, had equally good justification for stressing the normality of Bellingham's conduct in 1812. No one who met him in London during that time – including one crucial witness who knew him well in Liverpool, but was not called to testify – supposed that Bellingham was anything but sane. Everything he did up to the final moment appeared to be planned, self-contained and, in the way of life he established with Rebecca Robarts, comfortably civilised. Only at the very last did the beautiful plan begin to become so sublimely terrifying that, as he confessed to Sir William Curtis MP, 'I have been fourteen days in making up my mind to the deed.' Not until forty-eight hours before the murder did he finally screw up his courage to kill Spencer Perceval.

In other words, the pattern of John Bellingham's behaviour changed utterly between 1810 and 1812 – wild, excitable and deranged on his return from Russia, but calm, organised and sane while staying with Mrs Robarts. The anxieties that propelled him towards madness in the spring of 1810 were clear enough. But no one wondered why he behaved so differently in the spring of 1812. His goal had not altered – he still wanted compensation for his losses, although only £8,000 instead of the 'hundred thousand pounds' he had expected in 1810. And he still followed the same strategy of petitioning and interviewing ministers and their staff.

But his emotional state was transformed. Clearly something had happened to him.

What it was did not matter to Sir Vicary Gibbs or to Sir James Mansfield. They were intent on hanging Bellingham. The only motivation they suggested for his action was his wicked character. But to anyone interested in the truth, in how the Prime Minister really came to be killed, there had to be some reason for the murder – unless the prisoner really were insane. Even the spectators in court expected something more. When John Bellingham stood up to defend himself, there was a hushed air of expectancy.

The argument they heard from him was so bizarre that most of those present were left bewildered. The majority suspected that he might be mad after all, and a few thought he might be lying. No one could believe that he was being both rational and truthful.

# Bellingham and the Absence of *malice prepense*

When a Minister is so unprincipled and presumptuous at any time, but especially in a case of such urgent necessity to set himself above both the sovereign and the law, as has been the case with Mr Perceval, he must do so at his personal risk, for by the law he cannot be protected. Gentlemen, if this is not fact, then the mere will of the Minister would be law, it would be this thing today and the other tomorrow. What would become of our liberties?

John Bellingham addressing the jury, 15 May 1812

Sprinkled among the spectators in court were five or six shorthand writers busily preparing records of the trial for immediate publication. As John Bellingham began his defence, they noted not just his words but his manner. They described his patched coat and short hair, his quiet, reasonable voice, his fluent delivery, broken by occasional tears and sudden flurries of emotion. They were trying to supply an answer to the question that their readers would certainly ask themselves – Was he sane? Whatever Vinegar Gibbs might assert, ordinary people wanted to come to their own conclusion.

The accused started by politely insisting on having back the papers that had been taken from him in the House of Commons. Without them he could not defend himself. These were his petitions to ministers and the answers he had received. They were duly handed over, although he only once consulted them. But with the papers in his hand he felt able to begin his defence. He did so by thanking the Attorney General for insisting on his sanity. 'That I am insane I certainly am perfectly ignorant, and I assure you that I never had an idea of it.' The only occasion when he thought he might have gone mad was when he lost control of himself in front of Archangel's military governor. As he said this, the shorthand writers noted that he choked up. 'Gentlemen, I beg pardon,' he said when he had wiped his eyes. 'This is the first time I ever was in public in this kind of way.'

So far from pleading insanity, he told the jury, his defence would be based on the proposition that the killing of Spencer Perceval was entirely lawful. 'Had I murdered him in cold blood, I should consider myself a monster, not only unfit to live in this world but too wicked for all the torments that may be inflicted in the next.' Not even Perceval's family could regret 'this catastrophe' more than Bellingham himself. From the start, he wanted to dispel any suspicion that he had some private motive for the killing. 'I had no personal or premeditated malice towards that gentleman; the unfortunate lot had fallen upon him as the leading member of that administration which had repeatedly refused me any reparation for the unparalleled injuries I had sustained in Russia.'

Unlike the backward pattern of the prosecution, his defence moved forward from the moment in 1804 when he arrived in Archangel. Step by step, he took the jury through the repeated imprisonments in Russia, through the barrage of appeals for justice in 1810 and 1812, to the point where Perceval denied him the chance to present his petition to the Commons.

Nothing the jury had heard from the prosecution could have illustrated Bellingham's self-possession more convincingly than the two-hour speech he delivered in his defence. His only aid was the bundle of papers that had been returned to him minutes before he began to speak. It was, however, a story he had told many times before, the epic narrative of his Russian venture. The detail of debts, and lawsuits, and petitions, and hearings, might confuse his listeners, but to Bellingham the thread of his argument was clear. He was being stitched up by the Dutch and Russians, 'and Lord Gower refused to interfere in the business, and the Consul [Sir Stephen Shairpe] told me I must pay the money'. Occasionally he broke down, overcome by his own descriptions of his suffering in St Petersburg. 'I had been but recently married to a wife, then only twenty years of age, with an infant at her breast, and pregnant with a second child,' he declared. 'Yet I was doomed to continue immured in a dungeon.' At such moments, he wept with self-pity while the court silently watched and the shorthand writers scribbled, but invariably he gathered himself together and continued his narrative.

His betrayal by Leveson-Gower – the refusal to come to his aid in Archangel, the decision in St Petersburg to hand him back to the Russian authorities, the indifference to his suffering – was what he kept coming back to. 'What must his heart be made of?' Bellingham exclaimed, once more on the edge of tears. 'Gentlemen, I appeal to you as men, as fathers, as Christians, if I had not cause of complaint.' As he neared the end of his speech, he gave vent to a damaging exclamation: 'If I had met Lord Gower, he would have received the ball, and not Mr. Perceval.' It was symptomatic of Bellingham's self-absorption that he should have looked round with surprise at the murmur of disapproval in the court. In his mind, his dispassionate execution of the prime minister was quite distinct from his passionate resentment against Leveson-Gower.

Finally he turned to the papers in his hand. In laborious detail, he read out the petitions he had presented in 1810 and 1812 to the Prince Regent and to the Privy Council, and the appeals he had then made to the Prime Minister and other members of the government to be allowed to petition Parliament, and the stone-walling replies sent by a succession of civil servants – 'I am to inform you that his Majesty's Government is precluded from interfering . . .', 'their Lordships do not find that it is a matter in which they can interfere . . .', 'the time for presenting petitions having elapsed . . .' The last of his letters was to the magistrates at Bow Street reminding them that the right to petition Parliament for redress 'is the birth-right of every individual'. It was to them that he made his intentions most obvious. The government had denied his natural rights, and denied him justice. He appealed to the magistrates to persuade ministers to grant what they had so far refused him. 'Should this reasonable request be finally denied,' he wrote, 'I shall then feel justified in executing justice myself – in which case I shall be ready to argue the merits of so reluctant a measure with his Majesty's Attorney-General, wherever and whenever I may be called upon so to do.'

The case he made explained why he felt so relaxed. In his view, everything was going to plan. He had executed justice, and here he was arguing the merits of the killing with the Attorney General. However skewed the steps of his argument, they followed a clear pattern. The failure of the government's representative in Russia to help him had cost him money. The refusal of the government in 1810 to compensate him for Leveson-Gower's failure to help was an injustice. By denying him the right to appeal against this injustice through a petition to Parliament in 1812, the government had prevented him exercising a basic civil right. 'Justice is a matter of right, and not of favour; and as such, I think it should be dispensed at all times . . . . Where can an injured subject appeal so justly as to Parliament? and if that constitutional door be shut against him, where is his redress?'

This was the very heart of his argument. It was for an abstract right rather than for a commercial loss that Perceval, the representative of unjust government, had to be killed. The difference constituted the core of Bellingham's defence. Because he was acting in the interests of natural justice rather than of personal revenge, the killing could not legally constitute murder. 'That my arm destroyed him, I allow,' ran the most eloquent recorded version of Bellingham's speech. 'That he perished by my hand, I admit; but to constitute felony, there must be *malice prepense*, there must be the wilful intention, and I deny that it has been proved. Unless proved, however, the felony cannot be made out; this you will shortly hear from the Bench, and in that case you must acquit me.'

He sat down, flushed, breathing hard, and once more on the verge of tears. Yet within minutes he had regained his calm self-control. Nothing else that happened in the trial shook his confidence in his line of defence. Up to the very moment that the foreman of the jury delivered his verdict, Bellingham was convinced that he would be found innocent. As the judge was summing up, Bellingham leant over to his solicitor, and whispered that Harmer should be sure to send a note in time for the evening mail coach to Liverpool to tell his wife, Mary, that he had been set free.

After Bellingham finished his long speech, Peter Alley attempted to repair the damage by demonstrating that despite his client's apparent coherence, his behaviour was indeed that of a madman. Although not allowed to plead, a barrister could examine witnesses. He called Ann Billett into the witness box. She was, the shorthand writers noted, 'very moved'. Since Alley's one convincing witness was evidently close to breaking down, he restricted himself to establishing that she had known Bellingham since childhood, thus giving weight to her opinion that he was deranged. He got her to say that Bellingham's father had died insane, then he sat down.

In cross-examination, however, Gibbs lured Ann Billett into asserting that '[Bellingham] has been more than three years in a state of derangement', then forced her to admit that she had not seen him for more than a year. Defiantly she recalled his wild behaviour in 1810, and the embarrassing encounter with Mr Smith of the Foreign Office who had implicitly confirmed her impression that he was out of his mind. But whatever might have been true about his traumatised state of mind at the time, she could offer no evidence about his behaviour in 1812. Step by step Gibbs chipped away at the picture of 'perfect derangement'. Had Bellingham ever been confined? Had someone else been put in charge of his affairs? Had his friends been forced to take care of him? Had Mrs Billett warned the government that he was mad? To all of which she answered with a monosyllabic 'No'.

Mary Clarke's evidence received the same treatment. She agreed that Bellingham had conducted business by himself in London. No doctor had been consulted about his state of mind, no restrictions had been placed on his movements, and when she unexpectedly met him in January 1812 he had behaved reasonably and appeared capable of looking after himself. In the absence of his two mental-health experts, Alley turned to his last witness. This should have been Rebecca Robarts. Calling her was a sign of desperation – she had already told Vickery of Bellingham's considerate, civilised behaviour – but there was no one else in London in a position to give evidence that the accused was prone at least to delusion. Even this forlorn hope evaporated when her chambermaid, a young girl called Catherine Figgins, stepped into the witness box instead. Mrs Robarts was too ill to attend, she explained, and so she had been sent in her place. Beyond being able to say that over the weekend Bellingham 'seemed confused' and 'not so well as he had been', the chambermaid's testimony shed no new light on his sanity, and in cross-examination she readily admitted that he was 'a remarkable, regular man'.

By the time the elderly chief justice came to sum up, there could not have been much doubt as to the outcome. But Sir James

Mansfield managed to screw down the lid of Bellingham's coffin with the way he delivered his opening sentence. 'Gentlemen of the jury,' ran the otherwise dry report of his performance in the *Old Bailey Sessions Papers*:

> you are now to try an indictment which charges the prisoner at the bar with the wilful murder (here the learned judge was so hurt by his feelings, that he could not proceed for several seconds) of Mr. Spencer Perceval, (in a faint voice) who was murdered with a pistol loaded with a bullet; when the prisoner mentioned the name of (here again his lordship was sincerely affected, and burst into tears, in which he was joined by the greatest portion of the persons in court) a man so dear, and so revered as that of Mr. Spencer Perceval, I find it difficult to suppress my feelings.

In this emotional atmosphere, it was surprising only that the jury should have taken as long as fourteen minutes to find the prisoner guilty of murder. Seven hours after his trial had begun, Bellingham was sentenced to be taken 'to a place of execution, where you shall be hanged by the neck until you be dead; your body to be dissected and anatomized.'

When asked whether he had anything to say, the prisoner remained silent, showing no apparent response. Disappointment was an emotion that he must have been used to, and he accepted the outcome stoically, as though he expected no less of a world that had always proved hostile. The only regret he ever expressed was that Alley had not called any of the witnesses, including Shairpe and Leveson-Gower, who Bellingham had hoped would testify to the injustice of his Russian treatment.

The kangaroo nature of the trial had made it obvious that the government intended to have Bellingham executed as quickly as possible. Yet the speed with which the foregone conclusion was reached not only left unexplored the problem of his motivation and passed over the transformation in his behaviour, it created a mystery of its own.

As Catherine Figgins concluded her evidence, Peter Alley made one final effort to win more time, and sent an urgent message to the doorkeeper asking whether any witnesses had arrived from Liverpool. Amazingly, Sheriff William Heygate returned to announce in open court that indeed two people from Liverpool had just turned up in a post-chaise and four 'to give evidence in favour of the prisoner'. They knew someone who matched Bellingham's description 'in whose conduct they had seen frequent marks of derangement'. Alley's hopes, however, were instantly dashed by Heygate's next words. Instead of producing the potential witnesses for examination in the witness box, the sheriff went on to say that having been shown into the court, they had decided that Bellingham was not the person they were expecting to see, and had left.

There was no quicker way to travel, and none more expensive, than in a speedy post-chaise, painted a distinctive yellow and drawn by teams of hired horses that were changed every twenty or thirty miles. The two potential witnesses probably took as little as twelve hours to come from Liverpool, fifteen hours faster than the mail-coach. The speed and the huge cost they had incurred showed how vital they believed their testimony to be. That they should have gone to such trouble and expense simply on a whim to help a stranger they only knew by sight is hardly credible. They must have come specifically to help Bellingham. His name appeared in Wednesday's *Liverpool Courier*, and his description was in the Thursday edition of the *Liverpool Mercury*. Alley's appeal for witnesses would have reached the mayor by Thursday afternoon, well before the pair left. Either they lost their nerve when confronted by the crowded courtroom or they were actively dissuaded by Heygate and the Attorney General from holding up the rushed trial.

As though their arrival were not dramatic enough, barely twenty minutes later the town clerk of Liverpool, Richard Statham, galloped up with three more witnesses, carrying 'papers which the Mayor of L[iverpool] thought would be material in the trial of Bellingham'. They too had come 'express' from Liverpool in order to give their testimony, and the expense was so great that Statham later asked the government to contribute towards the costs. Unfortunately their journey was also in vain. Despite the furious pace of their journey south, they arrived minutes too late to take part in the proceedings. By the time Statham hurried into the Old Bailey, the judge had completed his summing-up and the jury had retired to consider its verdict.

Nevertheless, the appearance of no fewer than six unexpected witnesses from Liverpool, all ready to testify at John Bellingham's trial, could not have been a coincidence. The Prime Minister's former colleagues might only have been interested in executing his murderer, but Perceval's friends, eager to understand *why* he had been killed, must have had an inkling that the answer was to be found in Liverpool rather than in a courtroom in London.

# The Compelling Evidence of Miss Stevens

As a general minister Mr Perceval inflicted all the evils on the country which can result from the combined effects of boldness, ignorance and tenacity. Of the philosophical principles of law, civil policy or political economy, he knew very little, and rather piqued himself indeed upon despising them.

*Edinburgh Review*, June 1812

On the afternoon of Friday, 15 May, the day of the trial, Mary Stevens, Mrs Bellingham's business partner and closest friend, returned to Liverpool by the mail-coach from London. She went straight from 'The Golden Lion' inn, where the London coach terminated, to the Bellinghams' home at 46 Duke Street. Twenty-four hours earlier she had been with John Bellingham in his cell as he awaited his trial. Mary Stevens carried with her back to Liverpool two letters he had written, one for his business colleague, John Parton, and the other for his wife. She also brought a message from Bellingham telling his wife that he would be released the following day, and she could expect him home shortly, a free and wealthy man. The ensuing conversation between the two women must have been unimaginably fraught.

The first rumours of the murder might have reached Mary Bellingham as early as Wednesday as the brief notice in the *Courier* filtered through its readers to the wider public. But on Thursday both of Liverpool's papers carried detailed reports, and when the town clerk, Richard Statham, paid her a visit, she learned the full truth. Statham may not have told her directly of James Harmer's request for evidence of insanity, but he certainly let her understand that it was desirable to have evidence that his behaviour was irrational, obsessive, and had nothing to do with sentiment in Liverpool. The papers he subsequently carried south to Bellingham's trial were Mary Bellingham's statement, probably supported by written testimony from two further witnesses whose addresses she knew, Bellingham's business partner, John Parton, and his solicitor, Thomas Avison. Until Friday afternoon, however, Mary Bellingham had heard nothing that might have suggested why her husband had committed such a terrible deed. No one, however, was better placed to explain than Mary Stevens.

Between the two women, there was a bond closer than that of a business partnership. Together they rented the Duke Street house that served as both home and shop, and although Mary Stevens was the less well-educated, it was her unshakeable commonsense that anchored the pair. Perhaps most importantly, she helped look after the three Bellingham children with a fund of affection that made her, as even Bellingham himself recognised, a natural second mother to them. While Mrs Bellingham concentrated on hats, Miss Stevens clearly had a flair for designing dresses, and from the beginning of their partnership in 1806, the firm of Bellingham & Stevens, as they were listed in *Gore's Trade Directory*, had quickly found customers among Liverpool's wealthy inhabitants. Indeed Liverpool's love of fashion would soon earn it a reputation as the best-dressed city in England.

The arrival of John Bellingham two years after they started work together could only have appeared as an intrusion. In law, he owned his wife's share of the business, and although he evidently made himself agreeable, as he always did to women, and kept the accounts in order, Mary Stevens made it plain that her loyalty was always to his wife and children. Nothing he did ever quite won her over. That he appeared to contribute little financially to the household could not have helped his cause.

The Archangel disaster had, by his own account, left Bellingham almost penniless. As he explained to the jury, 'My affairs [were] ruined by my long imprisonment in Russia through the fault of the British minister, my property all dispersed for want of my own attention, my family driven into tribulation and want, my wife and child claiming support, which I was unable to give them, myself involved in difficulties, and pressed on all sides by claims I could not answer.'

His return to Liverpool in May 1810, six years after he had left, could not have been easy. His Irish business had disappeared and the city had undergone a radical change. The slave trade that had been the source of all its wealth for almost three generations had been made illegal, and the old financial and political networks were struggling to readjust. A sense of disorder was in the air. For lack of an alternative, Bellingham had set about resurrecting his former trade, and, according to Mary Stevens, 'he went over to Ireland for the purpose of re-establishing his connexions in Business'. Among those Bellingham met would have been John Neville, but his reprobate father-in-law had gone bankrupt again and, having moved from northern Ireland to Dublin, was no longer in the linen trade. Clearly Bellingham did find some customers – Mary Stevens referred to him as a merchant, and said that John Parton 'transacted business for Mr B in Liverpool' – but everything was on a small scale.

In Liverpool circles, John Bellingham was known mostly as an insurance broker, suggesting that he and Parton also acted as agents insuring the almost risk-free Irish trade where profits were pared to the bone. When Ann Billett visited the Bellinghams in 1811, she did not see him do any business during the week she was there. And he certainly did not earn enough to sustain the family, because his wife had to keep working at a business she found 'very uncongenial to my feelings'.

In the last half of 1811, their situation was made worse as the already wounded city was gripped by a national economic recession. By December 1811, half of all skilled workers in Liverpool – shipwrights, sailmakers, riggers and brassfounders – were out of work, and four out of five casual labourers such as dockers and porters had lost their jobs.

The Bellinghams were not immune. The Irish business suffered as people patched their own shirts, turned their own collars, and ate more bread in place of beef. At the Chester Fair, the great showcase for Ireland's exports, 'a vast deal of Irish linens' were left on the shelves, and there was 'little demand for cattle'. With the English market contracting, Irish demand for goods manufactured in the Midlands faded.

The pinch affected the fashion industry too, and fewer orders were placed for hats and dresses that winter. When Phillips & Davison, a London silk supplier, inadvertently delivered more ribbon than Mary Bellingham's hat-making business could use, and insisted on payment, she was distraught. 'It is their Traveller's mistake, and not any fault of ours,' she insisted. 'Miss Stevens merely ordered 6 or 8 yards for millinery as we had none in the house and they have sent a large quantity, we do not know how much as we never opened the parcel as we saw by the size of it it was not the order given.'

The mistake had a fateful consequence. Bellingham promptly seized on the need to sort out the problem as an excuse for travelling to London. At the same time, he intended to carry out a private business deal of his own. Before the trial, the London newspapers reported the interesting discovery, presumably made by John Vickery, that when Bellingham came to the capital it was to buy iron. This was an expensive commodity to purchase in trade quantities, and since he had no money he must have been acting on commission for another Liverpool merchant. But when he left Duke Street at the end of December 1809, his wife had every reason to believe that it was solely to sort out the family's financial problems.

Anxiety about their lack of money never left Mary Bellingham's mind. 'I think I need not intreat you to act with economy,' she wrote to him on 18 January 1812, more than a fortnight after he had left Liverpool, 'your feelings for your familly will induce you to keep to it.' But she could not help pointing out that their tiny business could not afford his absence. 'You will be there three weeks on Thursday, and you know I cannot do anything with regard to this business until your return. We have got in very little money since you left.' Although 'extremely surprized' that he had not come back, she was not yet alarmed. She could still persuade herself that he only had to be reminded how vital he was to the household – 'Pray let us know when you intend to return' – and he would hurry home.

Whatever their disagreements, John and Mary Bellingham were completely united in their love of Henry, the youngest of their three sons. His birth in the autumn of 1811 had set the seal on their reconciliation, and both doted on him. When Bellingham left for London, the baby was uncomfortable and crying, and the most urgent concern in his first letter home in early January 1812 was for Henry's health. Mary understood his feelings and her reply had begun, 'I am glad to relieve you immediately regarding darling Henry who is wonderfully recovered and has cut two teeth.' She ended it, 'The children send dear Papa each an affectionate kiss with one from Mamma' and a final 'yours very affectionately'.

Either his reply, which has not survived, or his failure to respond drove her to search his room. There, according to an affidavit from Mary Stevens, she 'accidentally discovered' a note referring to a petition asking for compensation for his Russian losses that he intended to present to the Prince Regent. The note also revealed that he had given the document to his lawyer, Thomas Avison, presumably for his expert advice since formal petitions had to be drawn up according to a specific formula. When Mary Stevens confronted John Parton, he confirmed that Bellingham had 'meditated such application [for compensation] for some time'. The solemn promise made to his wife had been deliberately broken, and his trip to London had been deceitfully planned for something other than business reasons.

The news had thrown Mary Bellingham into despair. She became physically ill and lost weight. Her letters blaming Bellingham for his bad faith no longer exist, but in reply he must have insisted he had a plan that made payment of the compensation a certainty. She did not attempt to believe him. Then in mid-April, when he was about to buy the pistol with which he would kill Spencer Perceval, he sent an extraordinary message addressed to the two Marys in Duke Street.

The covering note to his wife was brief, and mostly concerned business matters and the welfare of baby Henry: 'I could have wished when you had written, you had mentioned where and with whom Henry is, and let me know how the dear boy goes on.' But it enclosed a second, longer letter that began, 'My dear Miss Stevens, As my affairs in London are terminating according to wish, you may easily imagine it's my desire for Mrs B- to quit the Business as soon as possible and for you to come into full possession of it.' In other words, he was so certain of being paid a large sum in compensation that his wife could afford to retire, and he had decided to make over her share in the dress-making business to her partner. His proposal was as detailed and business-like as an accountant could make it. Mary Stevens was to have his wife's share debt-free; she was to come to London so that he could personally introduce her to 'the respective Trades people for the arrangements';

and finally she was to 'Bring the Books and [have confidence] in me to do what is right and proper – you will not be deceived.'

His announcement drove his wife to a new pitch of desperation. 'If I could think that the prospects held out in your letter receved yesterday were to be realized,' she wrote bitterly, 'I would be the happiest creature existing, but I have been so often disappointed that I am hard of belief.' Her husband's wild optimism must have brought back memories of her theatrical, self-deluding, twice-bankrupted father. Bleakly she reminded Bellingham of the financial reality of their situation. 'Be certain you can make good your intentions, for should you not ultimately be enabled to fulfill them, we would be sunk in ruin from not having sufficient means to meet the tradespeople.'

Poverty had forced her to send Henry and his middle brother out to an infants' nurse so that she and Mary Stevens could work undisturbed. James, the eldest, aged nine, should have been going to school but had to be kept at home because, in Bellingham's absence, she could no longer afford to pay the fees. But the house at 46 Duke Street doubled up as workplace and shop, and she confessed to being 'very uneasy at James being at home, having so much valuable Linen in a work room'.

Briefly she allowed herself to cling to a tiny sliver of hope that Bellingham's prospects were not entirely an illusion. Her first impulse was not to let Mary Stevens know of his offer because, as she told her husband, she wanted to allocate her share to her cousin, Eliza, who had helped her look after James when she first arrived back from St Petersburg in 1808. Then, as though her husband's attempt to take this decision for her was the last straw, she burst out:

I cannot help remarking that in writing to Miss Stevens you address her in the same manner as me, 'Oh my dear Miss Stevens & yours truly John Bellingham'. Now I cannot help feeling hurt that there is no distinction made between an indifferent person and an affectionate wife who has suffered so much for you and your children – it appears as if I was no more to you than any woman that you were obliged to write a letter to . . . . [To] a delicate & feeling mind: these are insults, more particularly as my indisposition seems to have been forgotten . . . . The change in my appearance will convince you that I have been very ill, as I am now as thin as I ever was. If I was to follow your example, six lines might fill my letter – but perhaps I am not worthy of more.

This time there was no 'very affectionately', only a cold 'yours truly'.

Almost certainly, she had no cause for sexual jealousy. Bellingham was too orderly in his ways to enjoy the messiness of an affair, but he liked to win affection. With the young widow, Rebecca Robarts, he presented himself as the ideal tenant, respectful, attentive, and always ready to take her to church services and museums. Mrs Robarts admired him enough to allow him more than two months' credit on his rent but, whatever warmer feelings she might have had and he might have encouraged, there was no indication that they led to any unbuttoned intimacy.

Equally with Mary Stevens, he acted the competent, masterful male, who examined the books of the women's business and kept them in order. He undoubtedly expected gratitude, even a certain tenderness, in return for giving her half the business free of charge, but by enclosing the letter to her in one to his wife he showed clearly enough that he wanted no more. However, he was to be disappointed even in that modest ambition. Mary Stevens, who probably saw him more clearly than any other woman close to him, refused to believe in his act of generosity. Her scepticism gave rise to a uniquely clear-eyed account, recorded later under oath, of his behaviour immediately before the murder.

\* \* \*

Evidently both women must have discussed among themselves the contents of his letters to them, because on Tuesday, 5 May Mary Stevens travelled south on the overnight coach to London. The next morning, five days before the murder, she took lodgings with a Mrs Barker close to Hatton Garden. Bellingham had promised to meet her at the coaching inn, but failed to turn up. She sent a note for him at New Millman Street, and on Friday, 8 May he called round to see her. In evident irritation, she declared bluntly that 'she and Mrs B were very much hurt to find one of the Objects of his Journey was to continue his application to Government for redress. That she represented to him how he was [wasting] his time, and the loss his Children were sustaining in their education in consequence of [his] absence.'

Her accusation must have cut him to the quick. It precipitated an angry argument that he concluded by saying 'he would be undeserving the name of a parent if he did not endeavour to make some provision for his Children'. It was too late then to go through the accounts, but he promised to return the next day.

When she saw him for the second time, on the Saturday before the murder, Mary Stevens made her disbelief plain by asking about his plan on which the handover of the business depended. 'I suppose,' she said sceptically, 'nothing further has transpired?' He replied, with complete accuracy as it turned out, 'Nothing, for he had been rather dilatory that week in consequence of [her] arrival, but he determined to set about it vigorously on Monday.'

Bellingham then took her and Mrs Barker to see an exhibition of watercolours in Piccadilly. Afterwards he went away with the books of the millinery business, which he as an accountant had kept and, as even Miss Stevens admitted, 'with which he was very conversant'. On Sunday morning, one day before the assassination, he returned with them together with letters for her to take back to his wife and John Parton, his business partner. This time Mary Stevens was struck by the look of nervous strain on his face. She did her best to persuade him to return with her to Liverpool, and thereby came within a hair's breadth of uncovering what he intended to do the next day.

It was clear, she said, that Perceval's government would not give him what he wanted, to which Bellingham immediately replied there would soon be a new ministry. Not realising what he meant, she objected that the appointment of a new administration would 'retard your concerns. Would it not be better to relinquish it than try to oppose the powerful so much?'

Clearly stung, he snapped, 'I will not. If Ministers refuse to do me justice, I will do it myself.'

Mary Stevens refused to back off. 'How are you to obtain this?' she demanded. When he replied, 'I will bring it into a Criminal Court,' she pushed him harder, 'What do you mean? Is that the Court of King's Bench?' By now she had reached the homicidal heart of his plan, but at that point Bellingham clammed up. When she asked again, he refused to explain, only repeating that he would 'compel the Minister to do him justice'.

In her sensible fashion, Mary Stevens then ended the conversation by saying firmly that she hoped it would be over soon so that he could return to his family. She intended catching the evening coach back to Liverpool after a day in the country, and with what must have been frigid politeness he wished her good morning and a pleasant journey.

However foolish she judged him to be, Mary Stevens never thought he was mad. While making her affidavit, she was asked about his mental state on this last day before the assassination, and declared that he did not betray 'any symptoms of derangement nor has he done so during the time of [her] knowledge of him, but when speaking of his application to government he was very violent'.

It was probably as good a judgement as could be made. However deep-seated his obsession about the injustices he had suffered, the clearest indications of Bellingham's underlying sanity were the unmistakable symptoms of stress that he betrayed. At one point in their conversation, he placed his hand on his heart, and said, 'You do not know Miss Stevens, what I have endured the last 6 months. I would rather commit suicide than undergo it again.' For the first time, she believed what he said and was deeply alarmed. 'God forbid that you should come to such an act,' she had exclaimed. 'But your countenance shews what you must have suffered.'

A psychopath would have had no qualms about the murder. But it appalled John Bellingham. If there is a key to unlocking the mystery of the Prime Minister's murder, it lies here.

What struck all observers at the trial, and ensured that Bellingham would be condemned to death, was the coherence of his defence. However misplaced, his argument possessed a logic of its own. It hinged upon the legal understanding of what constituted murder. The vital ingredient that turned a killing into a murder was premed-itated malice or, in the lawyer's Norman French used by William Blackstone in his classic definition of the crime in his *Commentaries on the Laws of England*, '*Malice prepense* is necessary to constitute murder.' Bellingham referred to this concept several times and in different ways during the trial. His last words to the jury were, 'I disclaim all personal or intentional malice against Mr Perceval.' He assured them that the judge would tell them 'you must acquit me' because there was no evidence of *malice prepense*. And in a phrase he had repeatedly used before, he told them that 'a refusal of justice was the sole cause of this fatal catastrophe'. It was an oddly legalis-tic argument, and even his use of the phrase *malice prepense* rather than the common English version, malice aforethought, was the wording that a lawyer would have chosen.

The *malice prepense* argument, as Bellingham understood it, depended on showing that there was no personal ill-will in what he had done. Justice was all he sought. Every level of government, from the Prince Regent to the Bow Street magistrates, had been tested to see whether the door of justice would be opened. Only when none of them responded did he proceed to his final option. It was there, clearly stated, in his letter to the magistrates, 'Should this reasonable request be finally denied, I shall feel justified in executing justice myself.'

There was a fundamental flaw in his reasoning. The requirement of *malice prepense* was designed to exclude an accidental or unintended killing from the definition of murder, rather than a judicial execution. As Mansfield pointed out in his summing up, 'If a man fancied he was right and, in consequence, conceived that . . . he had a right to obtain justice by any means which his physical strength gave him, there is no knowing where so pernicious a doctrine might end.' What Bellingham overlooked was that the mere act of planning someone's death was enough to constitute malice aforethought.

Nevertheless, his strangely formal defence points to the nature of the difference between his frenzied appeals for compensation in 1810 and his methodical behaviour in 1812. When he first returned from Russia, it is clear that, in his traumatised state, he was driven by demons. In 1812, as his argument in court revealed, he had a plan whose endgame was the execution of Spencer Perceval. Everything he did during his months in London, from the petition sent to the Prince Regent in January to the assassination in May, constituted a single process.

The killing would force the government to bring him into court where the jury would have no option but to acquit him of murder. Their verdict, the judgment of the ordinary people, would at last drive an unjust government to pay him proper compensation. In contrast to the wild demands made in 1810, the sequence of events he undertook in 1812 amounted to a business plan designed to bring a financial return. And instead of the hundred thousand pounds he had talked of to Ann Billett, he soberly estimated he would receive a sum of about £8,000.

Although her affidavit did not mention it, Mary Stevens had seen Bellingham once more. When she heard of his arrest, she went to visit him in his cell just before she caught the coach to Liverpool. It was there that he assured her that his plan had succeeded, and that he would be released the following day. In her anguished discussion with Mary Bellingham, this assurance must have had a hollow ring. Neither woman could have been unaware that his plan was about to leave his wife a widow, his children fatherless, and all of them in penury.

Yet as they agonised over the idiocy of his reasoning, both of them must have kept stumbling over a problem.

To show that every avenue to justice had been tried was not a quick process. Bellingham's plan of campaign had taken months to carry out. Somehow he had been able to afford to live in London all that time. Yet he had no money.

# The Search for the Truth behind the Murder

In its magnitude, and its cruel effects, the slave trade stands alone among our national offences; defying, like Satan, in the foremost rank, the wrath of the Almighty.

James Stephen, *The Dangers of the Country*, 1807

In place of the comfortable room where he had been held before the trial, John Bellingham was taken back to a narrow, vaulted cell reserved for condemned prisoners awaiting execution. Barely nine feet long by six feet wide and lit by a small barred window high in the wall, it enclosed the prisoner like a stone coffin. As a good journalist, William Jerdan had once asked to be locked up there simply to experience the effect, but he was almost immediately suffocated by claustrophobia. 'I screamed for the gaoler,' he recounted, 'but no one answered my call; reason had not time to exercise its influence, and after another fruitless effort with hand and voice I fell insensible upon the pavement.'

According to the account fed to the press by the keeper, however, Bellingham never lost his sense of self-possession in this bleak hole. Newman also revealed that in the brief period between the sentence and execution, a series of visitors arrived attempting to understand what lay behind his crime. Although physically weighed down by chains, and destined for hanging on Monday morning, the prisoner greeted each newcomer respectfully, expressed sympathy for the children of the murdered Prime Minister, but remained obstinately convinced of the rightness of his action. 'Yet with all his expressions of sorrow for the fate of Mr. Perceval, and the misery of his family,' the *Annual Register* exclaimed in exasperation, 'neither Priest nor Layman, Churchman nor Dissenter could obtain from him any acknowledgement of guilt on his own part in the premeditated assassination by which he had produced so much and such wide-spread grief.'

Among the most persistent was the clergyman who would attend him on the scaffold, the Ordinary of Newgate, Dr Samuel Forde. As a priest he anted a confession for the sake of Bellingham's soul, but on Saturday morning he had to give way to magistrates from the City of London. The responsibilities once resting on Harvey Combe had passed to the City authorities, and they now pressed the murderer to explain what had really driven him to his crime. The attempt was fruitless. Bellingham refused even to admit that he had done anything wrong.

'Government think to intimidate me,' he replied when one of the magistrates tried to bully him into giving up his supposed secret. 'But they are mistaken. I have been guilty of no offence, having only done an act of justice.'

To the eminently rational Samuel Romilly, such an attitude was one further symptom of Bellingham's insanity. 'No person can have heard what the conduct and demeanour of this man have been since he committed the crime,' he wrote in his diary, 'without being satisfied that he is mad.' William Cobbett, whose conviction for libel made him a fellow inmate of Newgate with Bellingham, decided that 'he was one of those unhappy men who are driven to a state of insanity by not being able to bear misfortunes, and especially misfortunes proceeding from what they deem wrong'. In the views of these people, and probably of the majority of people who read the shorthand writers' accounts of his trial published in pamphlets and the weekend newspapers, the murder was simply the act of a lunatic in the grip of a delusion. It was a senseless accident, without purpose or wider significance.

For the Prime Minister's grieving family and friends, Bellingham's refusal to reveal some deeper motive was as frustrating as the public assumption of his insanity. Sharing Spencer Perceval's Evangelical belief that his career was the working out of Providence, they needed to understand the real purpose behind his assassination. At the time of his death, the Prime Minister headed the most powerful democracy in the world, and, should Napoleon be defeated as Daniel had prophesied, quite simply the most powerful nation on the globe. Still more importantly in Evangelical eyes, his government directed the most powerful Protestant state in creation, capable of putting an end to Catholicism, sending missionaries to every corner of the world, and bringing forward the arrival of the new millennium.

The Prime Minister had transformed these tenets into government policy, and the growing might of the British empire was proof that it was indeed acting as an agent of Providence. 'And whither can the fainting eye of human misery turn,' demanded the egregious Reverend Daniel Wilson, soon to become bishop of Calcutta, 'but to this great Protestant Empire, which God appears to have aggrandized, at the present momentous period, with the design of employing her as the herald of mercy to mankind?' At the head of such a nation, Spencer Perceval could have done more to improve the condition of humanity than anyone else on earth. That God should have brought him to such a powerful position, then used Bellingham to cut short his life when there was so much left to do, challenged one of the deepest tenets of their faith.

To one friend and ally, it was especially difficult. None of Perceval's political colleagues understood better than James Stephen the Prime Minister's unshakable conviction that he was both the instrument of Providence and a politician who needed guile to do God's work. Stephen was the master strategist of the campaign to abolish the slave trade, but he owed his greatest victories to collaboration with the murdered Prime Minister.

James Stephen was William Wilberforce's brother-in-law, and his renowned fierceness of character caused the great abolitionist deep anxiety when he learned who his widowed sister, Sarah, was about to marry. Stephen was, Wilberforce wrote, 'an improved and improving character, one of those whom religion has transformed and in whom it has triumphed by conquering some strong natural infirmities'. However, Stephen's chief infirmity, his feral temper, had clearly not been entirely defeated because Wilberforce forecast gloomily that this, his sister's second marriage, would be like 'going to sea once more in a crazy vessel'.

Fortunately Sarah turned out to be just as fierce as her husband. To save money for charitable purposes, she wore her clothes until they were patched and darned beyond further repair, and felt it dishonest not to express her opinions as directly as possible. Thus the marriage proved a surprising, if volcanic, success. In a paroxysm of grief after her death almost twenty years later, Stephen blurted out to Wilberforce, 'O she was a friend of my soul! She told me frankly all my faults.'

Since a single soul was worth more than an empire, the only conceivable explanation that Stephen could find for Perceval's murder was that Providence intended it to be the means of saving his murderer's soul. On Saturday morning, therefore, he also visited Bellingham in the condemned cell to persuade him that he had sinned. According to keeper Newman's report, the condemned man was 'composed, and even cheerful, but rather taciturn' that morning. He had asked for his usual basin of tea, but was told that, according to regulations, he would receive only bread and water until his execution. He received this news as stoically as he had the verdict in court. But to Stephen's suggestion that his killing of the Prime Minister was a sin, he flared up, exclaiming yet again that it was no more than an act of justice.

Frustrated by Bellingham's refusal to accept that he had done anything wrong, Stephen returned the next day with none other than the evangelical Reverend Daniel Wilson. For two hours, Wilson harangued Bellingham: 'O! what will be the misery you will endure, if you rush into [God's] presence in an impenitent state! How unspeakably solemn is eternity! Never-ending duration! And how soon will this overwhelming scene burst upon you!' Loaded down with heavy iron chains, Bellingham listened politely but remained obdurate. 'I confess my sins,' he answered calmly, 'but I cannot say I feel the sorrow you describe.' But Wilson wanted something more. Bellingham's action only made sense in a wider context, as a force of evil. Deep down in him there had to be some revelation that explained why the catastrophe had occurred. Wilson continued hammering away until he was exhausted, 'Let me again and again entreat you to confess and forsake your sins.'

The only concession Bellingham made was in response to Wilson's emotional description of the pale-faced widow, Jane Perceval, and her weeping children kneeling around the coffin of her dead husband. 'She must be a good woman,' he murmured, hanging his head. 'Her conduct was more like a Christian's than my own, certainly.' But beyond that he would not go. When the keeper at last entered the cell to break up the interview, Wilson had got no nearer to convincing Bellingham to say the one word, to confess the vital link, that proved him to be acting on behalf of the forces of evil.

The list of visitors did not end with Stephen and Wilson. Just before eleven o'clock on the last night of Bellingham's life, Joseph Butterworth, a government-subsidised bookseller in Fleet Street

The Right Honourable Spencer Perceval, Prime Minister, Chancellor of the Exchequer. According to his friends, 'a man more highly blest by nature was never known,' but in the view of his critics he was 'the most mischievous of all the bad ministers.' NATIONAL PORTRAIT GALLERY, LONDON

John Bellingham. Attested as a 'most correct likeness' by Newgate's priest or 'Ordinary,' the Reverend Samuel Forde, who knew the sitter well.

© TOPFOTO/THE IMAGE WORKS

The assassination of Spencer Perceval in the lobby leading to the House of Commons. This contemporary print accurately conveys Bellingham's fashionable clothing.

© TOPFOTO/THE IMAGE WORKS

## ASSASSINATION OF MR. PERCEVAL.

We have the painful duty of communicating to our readers a most atrocious and afflicting event—the Assassination of the Right Honourable Spencer Perceval, under circumstances that find no parallel in history. Whether the horrid perpetrator were really insane, does not distinctly appear, but we are informed that he has been confined for some time in a receptacle for lunatics. The circumstances that have reached us are the following :—

Yesterday afternoon, at about a quarter past five, as Mr. Perceval was entering the Lobby of the House of Commons, he was shot by a person of the name of Bellingham, who had placed himself for that purpose at the side of the door leading from the stone staircase. Mr. Perceval was in company with Lord F. Osborne, and immediately on receiving the ball, which entered the left breast, he staggered and fell at the feet of Mr. W. Smith, who was standing near the second pillar. The only words he uttered were, " Oh! I am murdered," and the latter was inarticulate, the sound dying between his lips. He was instantly taken up by Mr. Smith, who did not recognize him until he had looked in his face. The report of the pistol immediately drew great numbers to the spot, who assisted Mr. Smith in conveying the body of Mr. Perceval into the Speaker's apartments, but before he reached them, all signs of life had departed. Mr. Perceval's corpse was placed upon a bed, and Mr. Lynn, of Great George Street, who had been sent for, arrived, but too late even to witness the last symptoms of expiring existence. He found that the ball, which was of an unusually large size, had penetrated the heart near its centre, and had passed completely through it. From thence the body was removed to the Speaker's drawing-room, by Mr. Lynn and several members, and it was laid on a sopha.

Headline and article in the *Morning Chronicle* the day after the assassination.

William Wilberforce MP, responsible for the 1807 law making the slave trade illegal, and an ardent supporter of Perceval's efforts to put the law into effect.
LIBRARY OF CONGRESS

James Stephen MP, architect of the anti-slavery campaign, who avowedly 'would rather be on friendly terms with a man who had strangled my infant son than support an administration guilty of slackness in suppressing the Slave Trade.'
NATIONAL PORTRAIT GALLERY, LONDON

Lord Granville Leveson-Gower, ambassador to Russia and, by coincidence, both the cause of Bellingham's sense of injustice and the object of Maria Perceval's dismissive judgement that he was 'handsome enough, but his features are too pretty for a man and he is rather silly looking.' NATIONAL PORTRAIT GALLERY, LONDON

General Isaac Gascoyne, MP for Liverpool, who 'considered the slave trade so great a blessing that if it were not in existence at present, he should propose to establish it.'

The Old Bailey, the central criminal law court where all important cases were tried. Newly modernised in 1774, it was designed to allow better reporting of proceedings, as the number of pamphlets on Bellingham's trial testified. NATIONAL PORTRAIT GALLERY, LONDON

The House of Commons as it was before being burned down in 1834: an airless, candle-lit cockpit where force of personality counted for more than reasoned argument. NATIONAL PORTRAIT GALLERY, LONDON

James Harmer, who undertook John Bellingham's defence, was the prototype of the new breed of professional lawyer, 'a worthy and a clever man' in the opinion of his colleagues.

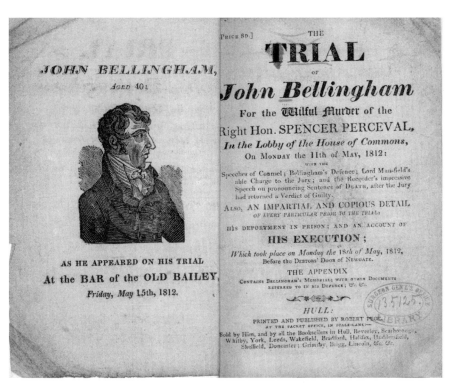

One of the many pamphlets printed immediately following John Bellingham's execution, evidence of the popular interest in the mysterious motives that had driven him to murder the Prime Minister.

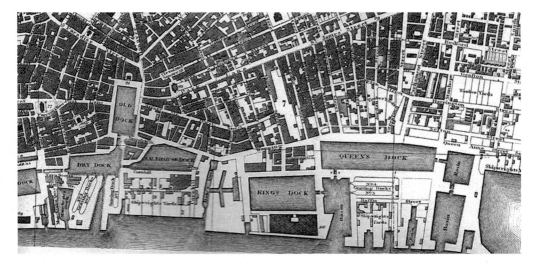

Aerial view of Liverpool and its numerous docks.

Liverpool from the River Mersey around the time of Perceval's assassination.

and a firm supporter of Perceval's anti-slavery policy, was allowed into Newgate prison with a pass from the City of London sheriffs. Like Stephen and Wilson, he too was an Evangelical, and he too prayed with Bellingham. With more sympathy than his predecessors, he recorded the condemned man's belief 'that in a few hours more he should be in a better country than this – for it was a miserable place'.

Butterworth, however, was not simply interested in the state of Bellingham's soul. He had a question to put on behalf of the government. Reminding Bellingham that he would soon have to answer for any untruths before God, he asked, 'Had you or had you not, some other person or persons concerned with you in the murder of Mr Perceval?'

'No,' Bellingham replied, 'I do most solemnly declare I had not.'

It was the answer the government wanted to hear. The lingering suspicion that Bellingham must have had someone to help him persisted right up to the moment the rope was placed around his neck, but this was the most convincing denial he ever issued. Once he had heard it, Butterworth slipped away into the night.

There is no reason to suppose that Bellingham was lying. Indeed in his adamant refusal to cave in to the pressure to 'confess' that he sinned in killing Perceval, he demonstrated his commitment to telling what he saw as the truth. Yet it is also apparent that his grasp of reality had a particular flaw. However his state of mind is categorised, as deranged, obsessive, or sinful, he had a remarkable capacity to see only that part of the world that made sense to him. The question of how he had financed his long stay in London lay outside its narrow scope, and in the haste to hang him, it escaped the attention of the authorities as well. The records, however, showed that he was not short of money.

Among the items that the Bow Street Runner, John Vickery, removed from the rooms in 9 New Millman Street was the murderer's blue-backed 'Washing book'. In it Bellingham recorded in typically neat detail his weekly laundry lists, and the prices he had paid for having his shirts, drawers, cravats, stockings and dressing gowns washed. His cravats were changed daily, his shirts at worst every other day, as were his stockings and handkerchiefs, and he often paid more than half a crown a week in laundry bills for the pleasure of being clean and well-dressed.

He took similar care in making himself comfortable. Mrs Robarts's lodging house was on the corner of Ormond Street – the modern Children's Hospital is barely three streets away – and his rooms on the first floor received light from two sides. The area was unfashionable, but quiet and respectable, a convenient place to stay for visitors consulting the high-priced lawyers in nearby Lincoln's Inn and Gray's Inn, and less than an hour's walk from the palace of Westminster. Rebecca Robarts charged half a guinea a week for her rooms, with luxuries such as a fire costing another 5s a week. Even when the weather grew warmer in April, Bellingham still chose to keep the expensive fire in his room rather than suffer from cold.

There were other receipts in the bundle of papers that Vickery took away. The printer who had produced Bellingham's pamphlet containing his petition and correspondence with the Privy Council and other government departments had charged almost £10 to run off no fewer than 660 copies. The two pistols from William Beckwith had cost four guineas. A new suit of clothes ran to £7 10s. On his last Saturday and Monday of freedom, Bellingham had taken Mary Stevens and Mrs Robarts to exhibitions where the entrance fee was not less than one shilling each. And, as the chambermaid, Catherine Figgins, explained, twice on the last Sunday he and his landlady went to the fashionable Foundlings' Hospital church in nearby Coram Fields where collections were taken up for the support of the foundlings, and worshippers were expected to give generously. Finally, Vickery noted that in Mrs Robarts's keeping was a pledge of £20 to Bellingham from a Mr Wilson.

Whatever else might be mysterious about Spencer Perceval's assassin, it was clear that he did not stint himself. While he was in London, at least £85 passed through his hands, and those who arrested him at the scene of the crime found another £2 9s 6d in his pockets. As a yardstick, £50 was the annual salary of the government law clerks who lived in the neighbourhood. The amount that Bellingham spent in less than five months would have paid the wages of a grammar-school headmaster for a year and a half.

It was not unthinking expenditure. On the very morning of the murder, the washerwoman had returned a dressing gown for which she had charged a shilling, a sum he had questioned, saying 'If he had known the price would be more than eight pence he would have washed the gown himself.' But Bellingham appreciated comfort, he had cultivated tastes, and he enjoyed the more refined pleasures of the capital. The real mystery was how he afforded them.

Although some newspaper reports alleged that he had received 'remittances' from his wife, they were almost certainly untrue. Mary was too hard pressed to find anything extra for him, not even earning enough to keep their eldest child in school. By April she was, as she told her husband, 'greatly distressed for money', and a few weeks later she was 'totally destitute'. Yet in London, her husband was living on an income equivalent to around £200 a year.

It is possible that only the highly experienced John Vickery saw all the receipts and thus had the chance to assess their significance against the widespread reports of the Bellinghams' poverty. With barely a week before the execution, he had no time to undertake the necessary enquiries, but the pattern of Bellingham's behaviour in the months before the murder would surely have aroused his suspicions. In the sixty or so Old Bailey cases in which he appeared as the arresting officer, Vickery showed himself to be an exceptional detective. He had a policeman's eye for the detail that did not fit – a badly loaded basket that turned out to contain stolen furs, the furtive behaviour of two men who were sharing out money after a robbery – and in a service often accused of corruption he was rare in being trusted by criminals not to plant evidence.

The salaried Metropolitan Police, who supplanted the Bow Street Runners in the 1840s, always disparaged their predecessors on the grounds that their income depended largely on the rewards paid for apprehending criminals and returning property, a practice that encouraged corruption. But it was also true that among their contemporaries the Runners enjoyed a high reputation for their professional expertise. They had contacts with magistrates' courts around the country, they were called in to help on cases far from the capital – Vickery himself went to Wiltshire to help in apprehending a murderer there, others travelled to Yorkshire and Scotland – and, as he himself told a parliamentary select committee in 1816, 'at Liverpool, Birmingham and Manchester, there was a Police office, and regular communication [was maintained] between the offices and Bow street'. With time, an officer like Vickery could certainly have tracked down the source of the assassin's funds.

From the evidence found in John Bellingham's rooms and from questioning witnesses, Vickery would have learned that the murderer arrived in London off the Liverpool coach on 27 December 1811 and paid for a week's lodging with Mrs Robarts. On 2 January he told her he was staying on, but without specifying for how long. Nor did he pay her any more rent. Soon afterwards in Red Lion Square he bumped into Mary Clarke, the friend of his cousin, Ann Billett, whom he had last seen in 1810. Their conversation was brief, but, according to her testimony, when she asked what he was doing in London, 'He said he came upon business, and he might not stay above ten days or a week.'

Up to that point, there was nothing extraordinary about Bellingham's behaviour. He visited General Gascoyne in his Mayfair home to discuss having his petition presented to Parliament, and was told that only a minister could introduce a petition concerning money. Some of his time must also have been devoted to meeting the appropriate brokers in the Baltic Coffee House to arrange the purchase of iron and its shipment to Liverpool. On 21 January he sent the Prince Regent his petition for compensation, and asked for royal permission to present it to Parliament. By rights the document should have been passed on to the Privy Council for its advice. But somewhere in the bureaucratic process his petition was mislaid. Bellingham did not learn what had happened until late in February. By then the fee for the purchase of iron and whatever other money he had been able to bring with him from Liverpool had run out. Significantly, he owed Rebecca Robarts more than two months' rent, and, as he told the jury, 'under these circumstances, I was plunged into ruin, and involved in debt'.

But at the very moment when poverty should have forced him to cut his losses and go home, Bellingham began to spend freely. He commissioned the expensive printing of his pamphlet on 28 February, and paid a substantial deposit. On 5 March he was suddenly able to pay nine weeks' arrears of rent in full. Soon afterwards he ordered a new pair of pantaloons and a fashionable toilinet waistcoat from a tailor. On 12 March he completed payment on the printing order. Altogether, in the fortnight after he was plunged into ruin, he spent about £25, six months' salary for a government employee.

From the same date in February, he began again his attempt to petition Parliament. The Prince Regent was sent another memorial and when he refused permission on the advice of the Privy Council, Bellingham methodically set about approaching the ministers of all the relevant government departments – Home Office, Treasury, Chancellor of the Exchequer and Prime Minister – and making personal visits to each. He spoke to the clerk of the Privy Council, the solicitor for the Treasury, and to Spencer Perceval's secretary whose written reply summed up all the others, 'Mr Perceval thinks [the petition] is not of a nature for the consideration of Parliament.'

Having exhausted the executive branches of government, Bellingham appealed to the legislature by distributing the pamphlet to every Member of Parliament. When that achieved nothing, he turned to the judiciary in the shape of the magistrates at the Public Office in Bow Street. On 23 March he sent them a bundle of papers – the petition accompanied by copies of all the ministerial rejections, together with a letter explaining that by refusing 'to permit my grievances to be brought before Parliament for redress' the government was closing 'the door of justice'. But this time, because he had by now completed his appeals to each branch of government, he outlined the shape of his plan. 'Should this reasonable request be finally denied, I shall then feel justified in executing justice myself.' Such an outcome would be, he said, an 'abhorrent but compulsive alternative'.

In a sense his plan was mad. To channel his desire for justice into a yes/no choice, with death as the penalty for a wrong answer, was crazy. But it was also beautiful in the sense that Goethe's Werner found beauty in double-entry bookkeeping. At the heart of Bellingham's plan lay an accountancy system that set his sufferings in a Russian prison where the bedbugs clustered as thick as bees in a hive against an ambassador's refusal to intervene, and a Prime Minister's denial of his right to petition for redress. The system was called justice. When the columns were totalled up, there was an imbalance between personal pain on one side and government indifference on the other. The deficit could be cancelled out by £8,000 in compensation – or by death.

In Bellingham's mind, this automatic outcome ensured the absence of *malice prepense*. Because payment or execution were simply consequences of the system, devoid of human emotion, the assassination could not be termed murder. But first the injustice of the government had to be made clear. Hence the need to approach every branch of government, and to demonstrate its refusal to do him justice. That took time, and Bellingham needed money to live. To be precise, to live by his standards, he needed £20 a month.

In his April letter to Mary Stevens promising to give her half the business free of charge, Bellingham offered a curiously phrased reason for his generosity. He could afford to do so because 'my family has had the benefit of a maintenance'. Bellingham liked to use precise, technical terms – *malice prepense* rather than 'malice aforethought' – and the *Oxford English Dictionary* defines a maintenance first as 'the amount provided for a person's livelihood', but this is followed by a secondary meaning: 'aiding and abetting litigation . . . undertaking to indemnify the Plaintiff against the costs in the case'. An investment in a plan that depended, as Bellingham himself put it, on a 'point of law', would have exactly fitted such a definition.

Vickery had one real lead to the source of the money, the £20 that Mr Wilson had promised to pay Bellingham. Although his report gave no further details, circumstantial evidence suggested that it was drawn on Thomas Wilson & Co., a London company with a particular expertise in providing finance for the Baltic trade. Wilson's services were used by many Liverpool merchants, but especially by the agents of United States exporters who wanted to trade with Russia. It need not have taken Vickery long to find out on whose behalf the letter was issued. But lack of time crippled his investigation. The discovery of the £20 promissory note was made on the evening of the assassination. He and the two other Runners assigned to the case had just three days before Bellingham's trial opened. The Attorney General, Sir Vicary Gibbs, required evidence that showed premeditation and sanity, and the officers had concentrated on assembling a picture of the accused, and tracking down and questioning witnesses who would substantiate the government's case.

The rush would have unsettled Vickery. The hallmark of his detective work was a slow, methodical approach. At the start of his career, he once let a man escape from a yard by rushing in to arrest him before a back-gate had been secured, and the lesson was not forgotten. The evidence suggests he was a big man – he was the one posted at the rear of a house when the Bow Street officers were making a raid, and criminals did not resist once he had his hands on them – but with his size went patience. He would note every detail at a crime scene; it was his habit to tag the evidence carefully or to mark it with a knife so that it could be identified in court; and he checked every alibi in person. It was typical of Vickery that he should have made a physical test to ensure that the ammunition in Bellingham's rooms fitted his pistol. And his unhurried manner encouraged suspects to trust him. When he arrested Robert Watkins, who turned out to be the Wiltshire murderer, Vickery noted that he 'seemed disposed to talk', and in relaxed conversation coaxed from him a full if inadvertent confession.

No doubt he sent a request for information to the Liverpool magistrates and to the police office attached to the court but, like James Harmer, Vickery would have been frustrated by the slowness of communication. The annual government grant of £600 that covered the cost of the Bow Street Public Office did not run to hiring post-chaises. When Sir Vicary Gibbs stood up in the Old Bailey on Friday morning, he had the evidence he wanted – the premeditated purchase of a weapon, the intent to conceal it, and proof that Bellingham 'was a man of sense, capable not only of carrying on his own business, but that he was entrusted with the business of others'. In the rush, however, Wilson's name had clearly dropped off the list.

The evidence from Bellingham's room that his sudden expenditure began in late February might have prompted Vickery to consider the wider significance of the date. Given the identity of the victim, he could hardly have avoided being aware of the political context. In February all the London newspapers, from the Whig *Morning Chronicle* to the Tory *Morning Post*, had chronicled the outcome of a power struggle between the Prime Minister and the Prince Regent. A month earlier, the doddery old king, George III, had finally gone irredeemably mad, and the prince seized the chance to try to remove from office the man who had humiliatingly forced him to take back Princess Caroline as his wife. Acting in concert, Lord Wellesley, the Foreign Secretary, resigned from the government, on the grounds that Perceval had unconstitutionally taken over 'the Supreme Command of the Cabinet', while the Prince Regent appealed to the Whigs to support a new, coalition ministry with Wellesley as Prime Minister.

The attack rebounded badly. First the Whig grandees, Grenville and Holland, refused the prince's offer because they recognised that without Perceval they had no hope of commanding a majority in the Commons. Next, the entire cabinet, at Perceval's suggestion, promised a mass resignation rather than serve under Wellesley. To establish his mastery beyond doubt, the Prime Minister then drafted what amounted to a surrender document for the Prince Regent to sign. It publicly declared that the prince was 'well satisfied with the principles upon which my present servants have acted, and with the success which has attended their measures'.

From late February 1812 Perceval's position as supreme commander of the government could no longer be doubted. He appointed the cold and serpentine Castlereagh in Wellesley's place, and recruited to the cabinet two of the nation's most efficient vote-gatherers – in England, Henry Addington, now Lord Sidmouth, and in Scotland, Henry Dundas, now Lord Melville – tossing offices and sinecures to their hangers-on to secure their loyalty. That was the only way in which contemporaries could see the unreformed constitution working, as a spoils system – 'without corruption,' observed Alexander Hamilton, secretary of the United States Treasury, 'it would fall apart'. With the king mad, the Prince Regent neutered, the country gentlemen loyal, Spencer Perceval's position as Prime Minister was not just impregnable, but he was close to exercising a parliamentary despotism.

His dominance should have given an investigator pause for thought. William Pitt had used the system to hold office for fourteen years, and the next Prime Minister, Lord Liverpool, would last for seventeen. At the age of forty-nine, Spencer Perceval could expect a similar span in office. Anyone hoping for a quick change of government policy could abandon the thought as unrealistic. In his memoirs, Henry Hunt suggested that this political shift was what lay behind the assassination – Bellingham realised that his petition would never be accepted while Perceval was alive. Hunt was wrong. But February's events might have provided a motive for the person paying the killer's maintenance.

## Choking to Death the Illegal Slave Trade

The boxes in the front room and in the back room I have no doubt but they were broke open by these tools, we fitted them; this tool has a jagged edge, there is the impression of this tool on the box exactly, this tool was rusty, and on the box the rust was left, and it fitted the impression exactly, it was a strong elm box, it took some force to open it.

Evidence of John Vickery, Bow Street officer, in the trial of
William Askew for burglary, 1806, *Old Bailey Sessions Papers*

Had John Vickery been given more time to consider the source of the assassin's money, he would have begun his investigation with the classic question asked in the investigation of every crime with no obvious suspect: *Cui bono?* – Who benefits? Once posed, the question would have thrown up a surfeit of possible suspects. The *Morning Chronicle* named only the most obvious when it declared just before Bellingham's trial opened, 'It indeed afforded some relief to the agitated feelings of the community to find that the assassin was neither a Roman Catholic nor a Manufacturer – that he had nothing to do with the Orders in Council – and was not a Reformer of Political Abuses.'

Its readers might have expected the list of those with a motive for murder to be longer still. Wherever little Perceval had turned the paralysing beam of his boundless energy and narrow mind, he had made enemies. His indifference to the suffering of those he opposed ensured that their hatred took on a murderous quality, observable in the wild jubilation that greeted his assassination. 'He was a bitter persecutor,' judged the Whig magnate, Lord Holland, 'of such political and religious principles as he, without much painful inquiry or dispassionate reflection, disapproved.'

Two groups could be eliminated at once. Whoever backed Bellingham had money, and this took out of the reckoning both the Luddites who had publicly proclaimed their desire to see Perceval shot, and the London radicals who wanted his ribs to be broiled with the lardy flesh of the Prince Regent. Catholics could also be excluded from the list of suspects. However much they might want to see Perceval replaced by someone like George Canning who was sympathetic to their cause, there was no guarantee that a new government would enact any measure of religious emancipation – in fact the Prince Regent's opposition frustrated all attempts at toleration.

A detective who examined the scene of a crime closely enough to note how the rust on a jagged tool matched the rust and jagged marks on a broken box would surely have paid particular attention to the setting of the House of Commons at the moment when Perceval was shot. At first glance there might appear to be no great significance to the bad-tempered crowd of strangers who milled around the lobby and filled the gallery, but most were there for the same purpose, the inquiry into the Orders in Council. And it was remarkable how many of them were prominent in the abolition of the slave trade – Francis Phillips and William Smith in the lobby, Thomas Babington chairing the committee in the chamber, and Spencer Perceval himself. But perhaps Vickery might have been most interested in the man selected to lead the government's defence of the Orders, James Stephen, widely praised and reviled as the master strategist who had made the Abolition Act of 1807 possible. There was something about his character that would have attracted the sharp attention of anyone concerned with law and order.

Unlike his morally upright companions in the Saints, James Stephen was, as he himself confessed, a torn soul. Born in 1758, he grew up tall and good-looking, with dark, sensual eyes, attributes which allowed him to become a serial seducer in early life. Although he attended various schools, including Winchester College, his most important education came from Fleet prison, where his father was held as a debtor after his business collapsed. His experience in that unforgiving environment, including a daring jail break that his father organised, taught Stephen a bandit's view of conventional society that he never entirely lost.

He chose to practise law, motivated by a desire to avoid becoming its victim, and he first became interested in the abolition cause as a way of meeting girls. Having delivered a bravura speech as a teenager at a public debate in order to impress Maria, his best friend's girlfriend, he seduced her and made her pregnant, then set up house with her and his own girlfriend Anna Stent, while also having a child by someone else's wife. 'I have been told,' he said at the time, 'that no man can love two women at once, but I am confident that this is an error.'

The cost in lies and deceit, and other people's pain, caught up with him, however. 'I was in consequence plunged into a labyrinth of guilt and misery, from which my extrication was to human eyes almost impossible,' Stephen wrote in an uncompleted autobiography; 'and but for the infinite mercy of God, I should at this moment have been the Author of the destruction, the temporal destruction at least, if not the eternal, of more than one fellow being who fondly loved me, and whom I fondly loved.' This referred to a suicide attempt by Anna Stent, who had loved him since he was fourteen, and the nearness of her death was a turning point for Stephen. 'A sense of dependency on Providence for averting those dreadful consequences with which others were imminently threatened brought me to true repentance,' he confessed, 'and gave me a victory over those guilty passions by which I had been so long enslaved.' His transformation also awakened in him an awareness of other people's suffering that became remarkable in its passion.

Bringing his tangled love life to an end, he married Anna and in 1783 left London to practise as a lawyer in St Kitts in the West Indies. On the way the ship called in at Barbados, and he took the opportunity to visit the local court. There he found two slaves being tried for assaulting an overseer. Stephen watched the mockery of justice as they were found guilty after a brief hearing. Then, with a horror he never forgot, he heard them sentenced to be burnt alive. As he later learned, the verdict might either mean that they were consumed in flames or more probably baked on a red-hot sheet of iron laid over an open fire. During the eleven years he worked in the West Indies, he realised that there was nothing extraordinary about the barbarity of the sentence. It sprang naturally from the routine cruelty that was meted out every day to slaves wherever they were held.

Little had changed since Sir Hans Sloane's visit to Jamaica in the early eighteenth century when he observed that a rebellious slave was punished by 'applying the Fire by degrees from the feet and hands, burning them gradually up to the head, whereby their pains are extravagant . . . For crimes of lesser nature, Gelding, or chopping off halve of the foot with an Ax . . . . For Negligence, they are usually whipt by the overseer with Lance-wood Switches, till they be bloody . . . . After they are whip'd till they are Raw, some put on their Skins Pepper and Salt to make them smart.' In 1756 Thomas Thistlewood, a Jamaican slave owner, boasted in his diary of the refinement he added to the usual punishment: 'Derby catched by

Port Royal eating canes. Had him well flogged and pickled, then made Hector shit in his mouth.'

By the time James Stephen and Anna returned to Britain in 1794, his hatred of the planters and slavers had reached such a pitch that, as he confided in his autobiography, 'I would rather be on friendly terms with a man who had strangled my infant son than support an administration guilty of slackness in suppressing the Slave Trade.'

Back in London, he chose to specialise in marine law, and in particular the abstruse law that governed privateering. The rules that decided whether a vessel taken by a privateer could be treated as a prize or had in fact been seized illegally were arcane. But with the disposal of cargoes worth £10,000 or more riding on the result, tempers ran high, and the furious atmosphere gave the court its nickname, the Cockpit. Within its precincts, there was a general recognition, however, that Stephen's mastery of detail and savage determination to win at all costs made him cock of the walk.

He naturally gravitated towards the Clapham Sect and, after Anna's death in 1797, his marriage to William Wilberforce's sister, Sarah, cemented his position at the heart of the abolitionist cause. With this ferocious, driven man, Spencer Perceval developed a political partnership that was in many ways closer than a friendship. They were bound together by a passionate detestation of slavery, a conviction that their lives served a higher purpose, a background in the law, and a readiness to use any means to achieve their ends. Yet their collaboration lacked personal warmth.

Perceval shared the values of the Clapham Sect, but never belonged to their social circle. It was partly because the Percevals divided their time between Downing Street and their Ealing home west of London, but it was also a matter of temperament. The Saints were wealthy, convivial, and at the tolerant end of the Evangelical spectrum. Spencer Perceval had had to work for his money, he lacked time for partying, and he was unrelenting in his hostility to any form of Christianity that differed from his own. Soon after her father became Prime Minister, Fanny Perceval conveyed the underlying irritation the Percevals felt about Wilberforce's unpredictable views: 'Mr Wilberforce I do not think has behaved at all well,' she wrote to her eldest brother. 'Papa has hardly proposed a single thing that he has not objected to, and all for the pleasure of contradicting . . . I wish he would not "Friend" Papa any more, and go over [to the opposition] at once.' Yet where slavery and the trade in captive Africans were concerned, those doubts vanished, and, in Stephen, Perceval found a Saint whose outlook was even harder and more urgent than his.

Their first success had been to push William Pitt into stopping the importation of slaves to Guiana, but their mission to make the Act abolishing the slave trade effective united them till the day that Perceval was shot. Initially both men, in common with other abolitionists, imagined that the measures contained in the Abolition Act would in themselves bring the slave trade to a halt. At the moment of victory in Parliament, Wilberforce had turned to his fellow Saint, Henry Thornton, and gleefully exclaimed, 'What shall we abolish next?' His mistake was understandable. No one had tried to abolish the trade in slaves before. It was a skill that could only be learned from experience.

The Act had made it a crime punishable by confiscation of goods or a fine of £100 to engage in any activity concerned with the purchase, transport or sale of slaves. To enforce the law abroad, a garrison and a court were established in the British colony of Sierra Leone in west Africa to capture and convict traders who entered that corner of the empire.

Optimistically the abolitionists at once moved on to the next stage, building an African society that would resemble Europe's. In

1807 Perceval and Stephen became co-founders, with Wilberforce and others, of the African Institution whose goal was to 'introduce the blessings of civilization' to Africa by fostering the spread of education, of smallpox immunisation and of trade. It took time to realise that slaving had not gone away, only underground.

Hints of what was happening appeared in the 1809 report of the African Institution, but the following year the grim reality became unmistakable. 'It has been discovered, that in defiance of all the penalties imposed by Act of Parliament,' the report commented, 'vessels under foreign flags have been fitted out in the ports of Liverpool and London, for the purpose of carrying Slaves from the Coast of Africa to the Spanish and Portuguese Settlements in America.'

Under the laws of Spain and Portugal, the trade in captive Africans remained legal. It was easy for a Liverpool shipper to recruit a partner from one of these nations to become the nominal owner of a slave cargo ostensibly destined for Spanish and Portuguese colonies, in particular Cuba and Brazil. But the illegal trade took many forms. It registered Liverpool ships under foreign flags. It provided crews and skippers for genuinely foreign ships in exchange for a share of the profits. It dealt in equipment, such as that carried by a ship stopped in the Thames in 1810 whose cargo included 660 padlocks, 93 pairs of handcuffs, 197 shackles, almost six tons of chains and 'one box of religious implements'. But the most pervasive aspect of the illegal trade was participation through investment.

Bankers in London and Liverpool made credit or cash available to equip slaving voyages originating outside the British empire, or furnished vessels with papers identifying them as foreign-registered. Once the ship had taken on its human cargo, it might land them anywhere, not just in Spanish Havana or Portuguese Rio de Janeiro, but in American New Orleans or British Trinidad. So long as

Britain's financial web reached there, any port could be a market, and any investor could be sure of a return.

To abolish such a deeply established, highly profitable trade called for prolonged government commitment. Legislation turned out to be no more than the overture. From the day of his appointment in 1807 as Chancellor of the Exchequer in the duke of Portland's ministry, Spencer Perceval threw his growing political authority behind the persistent, aggressive policy needed to kill slave trading. The Bible-driven persistence that kept Wellington in Portugal, the blackmailing ruthlessness that forced the Prince of Wales to take back his wife, the bigoted contempt that swept Catholics to the margins of society and William Cobbett into prison – all were focused against illegal slavers. He began by persuading the cabinet to authorise the Sierra Leone court to pay a bounty of £40 to privateers and ships' captains for each slave they liberated. In 1809, again at his urging, a deeply reluctant Admiralty agreed to send two Royal Navy vessels, regarded as superfluous to other requirements, on a permanent patrol of the west African coast. Then the cabinet issued an Order in Council requiring the administrators of recently acquired colonies in the West Indies, still under direct control from London, to begin registering their existing populations of slaves in order to make it more difficult to smuggle in more. The legal and financial arguments needed to win the support of other ministers for these measures were supplied by James Stephen. The remorseless Perceval hammered them home, but Stephen dug out the facts, and in return the Chancellor of the Exchequer used his powers of patronage to find his colleague a safe Irish constituency so that he could become an MP. To give Stephen more time for his anti-slavery research, Perceval also appointed him to a well-paid job as a master in Chancery.

*  *  *

The partnership acquired greater momentum with Perceval's appointment as Prime Minister. His first step was to force the Admiralty to provide a beefed-up squadron of five ships including frigates to patrol the African coastline constantly. This was the true beginning of what became known as the 'West Africa squadron', a unit periodically riddled by disease and despair, but one that grew into the emblem of the British empire's ideological commitment to the eradication of slavery.

At home, Perceval's government drastically strengthened the penalties for breaking the law. In 1811 any connection to the slave trade, including financing and equipping a ship, became a felony punishable by imprisonment and up to fourteen years' transportation to penal colonies in Australia. In place of the voluntary register of slaves, his cabinet passed Orders in Council imposing a mandatory registration of all existing slaves in Trinidad, followed by similar orders for other new colonies such as St Lucia, and Mauritius in the Indian Ocean. Step by step these measures squeezed each aspect of the trade and reduced its profit. Yet as significant as any legislation was the unremitting political support the Perceval government gave to the remarkable judge in charge of the Sierra Leone court.

What Oskar Schindler did for Jews in Nazi Germany, Judge Robert Thorpe accomplished for slaves in west Africa. Using his small base of power in Sierra Leone, he confiscated the ships of slavers found on the high seas, regardless of their nationality, and released their captives. Then he went further, actively encouraging Royal Navy squadrons and privateers to mount raids on slave stations along the African coast far outside his jurisdiction. At Goree and on the Pongus river hundreds of miles away, ships' captains used Thorpe's written authorisation to free slaves who were being assembled for transportation across the ocean, and to seize the ships in which they were about to be carried to the Americas.

Thorpe had a tiny legal justification for this flagrant abuse of international law. When slavery was made illegal in Britain in 1772 by the *Somerset* case, the judge, an earlier, better Mansfield, declared that the natural right to liberty made slavery 'so odious, that nothing can be suffered to support it, but positive law'. The lack of any such explicit statute making slavery legal under Spanish or Portuguese law was Thorpe's excuse for freeing their slaves. Only while he had the backing of the government could he make this vestigial argument stick. But during Perceval's lifetime he had that unconditional support, and Thorpe's unilateral action along the west African coast resulted in the release of almost four thousand Africans destined for slavery.

In this unremitting struggle against the illegal trade, the partnership between Perceval and Stephen was so close that it became impossible to say who took the lead. The Whig, Henry Brougham, asserted that 'the influence of his friend, Mr Stephen, over [Perceval's] mind was unbounded'; and in terms of intellect and intensity, he was undeniably Perceval's superior. On the other hand, Stephen lacked the confident charm, ambition and inborn political instinct that made Perceval so formidable. Certainly John Quincy Adams, the well-informed American Minister in St Petersburg who kept a close eye on London politics, thought that 'Mr. Stephen echoed back the word of Mr. Perceval', and did not hesitate to hold the latter responsible for the consequences of their alliance. In ruthlessness, however, they were almost a match. To choke the hydra-headed trade to death, they were even prepared to use what turned out to be a doomsday weapon.

The weapon was designed by James Stephen, and was originally intended for use against the French. Its purpose was outlined in a pamphlet published late in 1805 called *The War in Disguise*. Drawing on his experience as a maritime lawyer, Stephen showed that from the outbreak of the war with France in 1793, the enemy had gradually transferred all its trade from its own vessels to ships flying a neutral flag, predominantly that of the United States. Because neutral shipping was allowed free passage, this had rendered the existing blockade maintained by the Royal Navy round the coast of France utterly ineffective. Sugar from French Martinique and cotton from Guadaloupe were exported to the United States, then carried as American produce under the Stars and Stripes across the Atlantic to European ports. On the return voyage, their cargoes consisted of French weapons, pottery and wheat, carried in American-flagged ships ostensibly to the United States but in reality to French colonies.

When Holland and Spain fell under French control, those two countries adopted the same policy. 'Spain and Holland have totally ceased to trade under their own flags, to or from the ports of any of their colonies,' Stephen claimed. 'In short, all the hostile colonies . . . derive from the enmity of Great Britain, their ancient scourge and terror, not inconvenience but advantage; far from being impoverished or distressed by our hostilities, as formerly, they find in war the best sources of supply, and new means of agricultural as well as commercial prosperity.' It was time, he argued, for the Royal Navy to stop and search neutral vessels in order to control the trade of Britain's enemies. And the news of Admiral Horatio Nelson's crushing victory at Trafalgar, which arrived as Stephen was correcting the proofs of *The War in Disguise*, showed that Britain had the overwhelming naval supremacy to make such a policy work.

In 1807 the Chancellor of the Exchequer presented Stephen's theory to the cabinet, and asked for a more stringent blockade that required all neutral ships carrying cargoes to Europe to register them at a British port. Since Napoleon had proclaimed a blockade on Britain in 1806 with a decree from Berlin, the cabinet welcomed the chance to retaliate. The president of the Board of Trade, Lord Bathurst, presciently warned that the hostility created in the United States might lead to war, and 'an American war would be severely felt by our manufacturers'. But no other minister anticipated the ramifications, both intended and unintended, of a trade war.

Certainly Perceval himself did not understand the gigantic market forces that were beginning to drive international commerce. The purpose of the blockade, he told his colleagues, was not to stop trade with Europe but to force it to go through British ports: 'either these countries will have no trade, or they must be content to accept it through us,' he said. During November 1807 no fewer than nine Orders in Council were issued requiring a neutral ship with a cargo for the European mainland to register it first at a British port, paying a British tax of up to 15 per cent. To put this policy into effect, the Royal Navy was authorised to board any vessel under any flag that was encountered on the high seas to check its cargo and its papers.

The blockade against France was the weapon that Stephen wanted to use against the illegal slave traders. William Wilberforce, who knew him better than most, believed that he had always intended to employ the Royal Navy to prevent slaving. But it was the Prime Minister who wielded the weapon. Under Spencer Perceval's direction the Royal Navy was transformed into an international police force to combat an international crime. In his diary Wilberforce recorded tersely that Stephen 'agrees with Perceval *passim*, and with the government as to their grand scheme of policy – Order in Council; indeed it is his measure.'

Yet there was a difference between them. Whereas Perceval understood that success depended upon nurturing political loyalties and keeping personal ambitions well-regulated, the ferocious Stephen was ready to sacrifice everything to demolish the slave trade, 'and in its associated iniquity, the dreadful slavery of our colonies'. Not to do so was to risk God's goodness being withdrawn from the British. 'Who are the people that have provoked God thus heinously,' he demanded, 'but the same who are among all the nations of the earth, the most eminently indebted to his bounty?' Together, politician and firebrand made the extermination of the slave trade a crusade.

No other place suffered more grievously from their onslaught than Liverpool. For fifty years, most of its wealth had come from the West Indies trade – the profitable triangle that carried leg-irons, jewellery and axes to Africa, humans to the West Indies and sugar or cotton to Liverpool, and the less profitable but healthier triangle that took Cheshire salt to Newfoundland, salted cod to feed the West Indies slaves and Caribbean produce to Britain. For almost as long, these merchants had run the city's government, its common council, and used it to finance the massive public works – the docks, warehouses and canals – that had made it the second largest port in the country. But the West India group also represented the slave trade. Until 1807, the most prosperous, most respectable members of the oligarchy that ruled Liverpool had been the merchants who sent almost two hundred ships a year to the African coast, the Gascoynes, Gladstones, Pennys, Leylands and Aspinalls. Until 1807, they had invested about £1 million a year in the business of buying and transporting captured Africans to the West Indies and to north and south America.

In the last eighteen months before the legal ending of the trade on 31 December 1807, Liverpool's slave traders had shipped across the Atlantic 49,213 captive Africans for a return of more than £2 million. George Case, a former mayor, sent out no fewer than eight slaving expeditions in that time; others managed five or six. The chance of a final profit produced a kind of feeding frenzy that brought in outsiders such as James Bibby from the Irish trade and

Atlantic traders like Joseph McViccar, whose vessels were usually bound for the United States. No one quite knew what so many shipowners would do when this lucrative business became illegal.

John Aspinall, a former mayor of Liverpool, its deputy mayor in 1812 and a member of the West India group's inner circle, represented the respectable choice. In the wake of the Abolition Act, he changed the cargo of his two ships. West Africa remained their destination, but instead of loading slaves they brought back palm oil for the rows of lamps that lit Liverpool's grand mansions. Of twenty-two ships carrying palm oil in 1809, seventeen were former slave ships. Other slavers who decided to go straight after 1807 turned to the Baltic trade, importing Russian products through St Petersburg or Archangel. This was where John Gladstone, another former slaver and owner of a reputed one thousand slaves in the West Indies, sent three of his ships. But the movements of at least fifty former slave vessels, and as many as one-third of the original two hundred-strong fleet, were unaccounted for.

Some, if not most, had gone illegal. Although the participants concealed their identities, clues could be found in the blue pages of the Liverpool ships' registry where the fate and changing ownership of each one had to be recorded. It was striking how many left the registry in the years of Perceval's premiership, and astonishing what bad luck suddenly afflicted Liverpool's shippers in places where slaves might be traded. Vessel after vessel was reported 'lost off the coast of Africa', 'lost off Cuba', 'lost off Brazil', but whether in storms or by transfer to a more slave-friendly flag could not be established.

No fewer than four vessels belonging to William and James Taylor were reported as being 'lost off the coast of west Africa' between 1809 and 1812. Despite losses that should have driven them into bankruptcy, the Taylor brothers continued to prosper, almost certainly from slaving profits made under another flag. Just months after buying out the partner of his new vessel, the *Nile*, James

Penny, the millionaire slave trader who gave his name to a lane and a Beatles hit, found it necessary to remove *Nile* from the registry in 1811 because it was discovered to be 'unserviceable' while in the West Indies. Either the shrewd Penny had been duped by his partner or he found it more convenient to register the ship under a more tolerant regime. In transferring the *Amelia* to a Brazilian owner in 1811, Samuel Holland hardly bothered to conceal the fact that he was continuing to conduct his business under the flag of the most slave-friendly nation in the Americas. Suspicions even hovered around John Gladstone, father of the upright W. E. Gladstone, who supposedly had transferred all his ships to the Baltic trade but reported that his ship *Blanchard*, a well-known slaver, had been 'lost off the coast of Brazil' in 1811.

Driven out of a formerly respectable trade by Spencer Perceval's zeal, these owners, together with their investors and crew, had been transformed into felons liable to fines and confiscation, even transportation to Van Diemen's Land. The illegals had every motive to hate the Prime Minister who persecuted them so vengefully. It was Perceval who had championed the cause of abolition, introduced punitive measures for infringements of the Act, and ordered the Royal Navy to hunt down their vessels like terriers after rats. In February 1812 they must have feared that his basilisk hatred would pursue them for decades.

For such people, any Prime Minister would have been better than Perceval, but when Lord Liverpool was appointed to succeed him in June 1812, the illegal slavers must have felt themselves blessed. Until 1807, the new Prime Minister had been a staunch advocate of the slave trade, to the point of receiving a vote of thanks from the Liverpool council for his support. Although declaring himself opposed to the trade following its formal abolition, his government's lax policy contrasted sharply with Perceval's moral fervour.

It immediately dropped the compulsory registration of existing slaves in the West Indies that Perceval and Stephen were preparing to push through against the wishes of planters. The measure was not needed, Lord Liverpool blandly assured the abolitionists, because 'there was no evidence of smuggling [slaves]'. The voluntary code that was substituted became, as James Stephen angrily predicted, a dead letter. At the same time as the market in the West Indies was being relaxed, Judge Richard Thorpe in Sierra Leone was crippled by a withdrawal of political support for his extra-legal onslaught on international slavers. Far from urging the lords of the Admiralty to greater efforts, Foreign Secretary Castlereagh asked them in 1813 'to instruct His Majesty's cruizers not to molest Portuguese ships carrying Slaves *bona fide*'. And Thorpe's campaign was finally halted in 1815 when Spanish claims against his arrest of two hundred of their slave ships were upheld by the Privy Council.

By no coincidence, the number of slaves shipped across the Atlantic in that year jumped by almost twelve thousand to more than forty-eight thousand souls. This represented an increased return of about £600,000 for the illegal slavers, or very approximately £60 million in purchasing power today. Murder has been committed for less.

But the slave trade was not the only business in Liverpool to be hit by the Orders in Council.

Richard Statham, the town clerk, had impressed on Mary Bellingham the importance of distancing her husband's action from Liverpool affairs. Accordingly, soon after her return to Liverpool, Mary Stevens went to the council chambers to pass on her own information about Bellingham's behaviour. Her testimony was deemed of such importance that in Statham's absence her affidavit was taken personally by the deputy mayor, John Aspinall. Apart from the general desire to protect Liverpool's reputation,

Aspinall's particular interest was the West India trade. It was important to know whether there was any connection between the assassin and the disgruntled slavers.

Mary Stevens's commonsense and tone of unremitting scepticism about Bellingham's plans showed her to be a reliable witness. Aspinall would have been alert to any hint of collaboration, and relieved that nothing in her affidavit implicated the West India trade. That, however, was not the sum of Miss Stevens's information. She also had Bellingham's letter to his business partner, John Parton. What it revealed was the scope of his interests during his time in London. He had not simply expected to buy iron while he was there, he had hopes of returning to the Russian trade.

To a Liverpool insider like Aspinall, the implications would have been immediately apparent. Although Gladstone and other former slavers were involved with the Baltic trade, they all used their own, British-flagged vessels, and thus were unaffected by the Orders in Council, indeed they benefited from the restrictions put on neutral shippers. However the huge bulk of Russian iron, hemp and tallow shipped through Liverpool was destined for the United States. Almost certainly, whoever commissioned John Bellingham to buy iron in London was not a slaver, but someone engaged in the American trade.

Since the beginning of the war with France in 1793, American business had grown phenomenally, until it was worth £18,000,000 a year to Liverpool shippers. In effect Liverpool had become the hub of a trade that involved not just Britain, but every part of Europe, with the Russian portion growing faster than any other. The interests of traders shipping goods to and from the United States made them bitter rivals of the West India group. What the former wanted was free trade, and an end to the special privileges and monopolies of colonial trade that every sugar dealer and slave dealer had depended upon.

Generating more profits and attracting more participants, Liverpool's United States traders were already challenging the West India group for control of the city's council in 1809 when Spencer Perceval became Prime Minister. That challenge abruptly ended with the detonation of the doomsday weapon that he and James Stephen had devised against the illegal slave trade. Paradoxically, it hit no one harder than the merchants trading with the United States.

In February 1812, their own spokesman had publicly estimated their losses from the Orders in Council to be more than £1 million, or roughly £100 million in modern money. It dwarfed any motive for murder the illegal slavers might have had.

# How to Kill an Economy

He never knew trade to be so bad, that he had never known so
many failures in the same space of time, nor so many capitalists
decline business, or fall off in their capital. The failures, he said,
had arisen principally from the non-intercourse of the United
States of America.

> Evidence of Joseph Yates, Liverpool merchant, to the
> House of Commons, June 1812

At 11 o'clock on Sunday night, 17 May, after James Stephen and the
Reverend Daniel Wilson had left the condemned cell, John
Bellingham set himself to write a last letter to his wife. His mood
was curiously serene. His only real concern was for her financial
security after his death, but Newman, the keeper, must have told
him of the widespread sympathy for him, and of plans to raise
money for her. 'My Blessed Mary,' he began, 'It rejoiced me beyond
measure to hear you are likely to be well provided for, I am sure the
public at large will participate in, and mitigate your sorrows.'

Money had always been his anxiety. He had been brought up to
expect a standard of living that he could rarely afford. Temperamentally,
he enjoyed being neat, fashionable and having women admire him.
His clothes and his preferred way of life were those of a gentleman.
But in Liverpool, where status was determined by how far above the

River Mersey you lived, the Bellinghams' home was rather too close to the squalid houses jumbled round the docks, rather too far from the substantial dwellings at the top of Mount Pleasant.

His taste in entertainment, as Rebecca Robarts could testify, ran to theatres, exhibitions and concerts. But his preferences were all expensive, and with three young sons to provide for, the struggle to climb further up the hill, away from the Mersey and towards the respectability of Mount Pleasant, cost more than he could afford. It was his desire for the security that money could bring that had driven him to take the gamble in Archangel.

'I assure you, my love,' he went on, 'my sincerest endeavours have ever been directed to your welfare. As we shall not meet any more in this world, I sincerely hope we shall do so in the world to come.'

The sentiments and loving tone were at variance with rumours of a rift in their marriage. Several newspapers had claimed that before the assassination the Bellinghams were about to separate. Undeniably tensions existed between the two. Ever since Bellingham had returned to Liverpool in May 1810 and won his way back into the family by promising to give up any further attempt to get compensation from the government, his Russian experience had haunted the couple like an infidelity. It was something both knew of but dared not mention. 'It is always a matter of dissension between me and Mrs B,' Bellingham admitted to Mary Stevens, 'and we never shall be happy until it's settled.' Ann Billett who visited the Bellinghams in Liverpool in 1811 went so far as to say that he became 'violent' whenever the matter came up. And anxious to preserve the peace, Mary Bellingham remarked that 'she had decided never to raise the subject of Russia because it so clearly upset him'.

Yet the tenderness in his final letter was not invented. Friends in Liverpool described him as 'a most affectionate husband and father,

particularly fond of his children'. And Bellingham himself, in a rare
moment of revelation, declared that 'no person was more inclined
to be domestically happy than himself'. Even James Nevill, Mary's
uncle and rescuer after her return from St Petersburg, who publicly
declared him to be 'uniformly cruel' in failing to look after his wife
properly, admitted that 'In his manners he was kind to his family.'

Of all his children, it was baby Henry to whom Bellingham was
most devoted. And his love for the boy must have starkly empha-
sised his own incapacity to provide adequately for the family. The
timing of his son's birth made it worse. The arrival of a new mouth
to feed in the late summer of 1811 coincided with the dramatic
collapse of Liverpool's trade. Throughout Henry's first months of
life, the economy of the city was in free-fall. By the end of the year
so many people had been thrown out of work that more than
sixteen thousand people, a fifth of Liverpool's population, were
dependent on free food and clothing handed out by the churches.
Holding baby Henry in his arms that winter may well have been
the trigger that prompted John Bellingham to think once more of
the riches he had lost in Archangel, and the injustice of being
denied compensation for what had been taken from him.

The recession was a direct consequence of the Orders in Council.
Every kind of trade suffered, but none more heavily than that with
the United States. In part this was an inescapable consequence of
the size of the United States merchant fleet, which had captured
the bulk of trade in the northern hemisphere since war broke out
between Britain and France in 1793. From about £9 million in that
year, the value of goods carried by US-registered vessels had multi-
plied phenomenally to more than £60 million by 1807.

As Stephen's *The War in Disguise* had revealed, much of that
growth came from carrying the produce of French, Spanish and
Dutch colonies to their home countries, and returning with cargoes

of European goods needed in the Caribbean and South America. But close to £40 million came from a rocketing growth in trade between Britain and its former colonies, with almost half passing through the port of Liverpool.

The two countries made a perfect match. On one side of the ocean, the first industrialised nation in the world, on the other a gigantic, undeveloped, rural economy with a limitless appetite for manufactured goods of every kind – metal, machinery, glass, pottery, jewellery, even toys – and producing an infinite supply of raw cotton, tobacco and wheat for trade in return. As early as 1790, just seven years after the United States won its independence, the importance of Liverpool to its trade led to the appointment of James Maury as American consul there, the first time the young republic had created such a post.

Unlike the West India merchants who shipped cargoes in their own vessels, those engaged in the United States trade acted primarily as agents, arranging ships, cargoes, and warehouses for importers and exporters. They warehoused wool from the West Riding, textiles from Manchester, ironwork from Birmingham, linen from Ireland, until they could be loaded on a ship bound for the United States. Other warehouses held Massachusetts timber, cotton from the Carolinas, and Pennsylvania wheat for British customers. And from 1803, the traders had increasingly begun to arrange the import of consignments of iron and hemp from Russia for onward sale to American merchants. Each ton of goods sweated money into Liverpool pockets. Fees were charged for storage, for finding a vessel, for letting it enter the port, for loading, for shipping, for insuring, for extending credit, and – if necessary – for forging the appropriate papers. And the fees were high enough to bring complaints from the future president, Andrew Jackson, then exporting cotton from deep in Tennessee on the far side of the Appalachian mountains.

As early as 1801, an American Chamber of Commerce was set up in Liverpool, the first to be established abroad. Most of its members were British traders engaged in the usual two-way exchange of goods with the United States. But as the trade developed, a growing colony of American citizens came to do business in Liverpool, either trading on their own account or more often acting as agents for merchants and shippers in the United States. Many of these agents, such as Richard F. Breed from Massachusetts, William Brown from Baltimore, Elisha Peck from Connecticut, and Thomas Hazard were also involved in a complex three-way trade including Russia.

In 1800, when Tsar Paul officially banned trade with Britain, American-flagged ships exploited the opportunity to move into the Baltic trade carrying the iron, hemp and tallow that was so desperately wanted in Britain. After the tsar's assassination in 1801, British traders, including John Bellingham, returned in force, but American ships continued to carry Russian goods, only now they took them across the Atlantic for their own home market. For the agents of United States companies in Liverpool, it offered a third opportunity to make a profit – raw cotton or tobacco to Liverpool, then woven textiles, processed tobacco, or refined sugar for Russia, where the commodity could be exchanged for iron and hemp in St Petersburg or Archangel for shipment back to the United States. So rapid was the growth of Russian business that in addition to its St Petersburg embassy, the United States had to appoint a consul in Archangel, who happened to be Sam Hazard, Thomas's brother.

This mushrooming activity signalled the arrival of a modern way of conducting trade. Instead of the mercantile model, followed by the West India group, that prized trade between the home country and its colonies as the main source of a nation's wealth, the Atlantic trade responded simply to supply and demand. As Adam Smith explained in *The Wealth of Nations*, mercantile trade not only

created an inefficient market because it restricted trade to the colonial power and its dependencies, but it also fundamentally
misunderstood the nature of wealth, imagining it as a static value
that could be accumulated behind trade barriers. The Atlantic business, by contrast, was virtually free of restraint, a marketplace for
goods of all kinds, open to merchants, bankers and shippers of
every nationality. In this context, wealth was made up not just of
the capital value of the goods, but of the accompanying investment
and income that flowed between customers, suppliers, shippers
and financiers in pursuit of greater returns. This market-driven
trade behaved in ways that few anticipated.

One surprising characteristic was pointed out in a petition
protesting against the Orders in Council that was presented to
Parliament by the manufacturers of Birmingham in 1808. Despite
the war with France, the petition explained, Britain's exports to
French-dominated Europe were worth £10 million a year.
Napoleon's blockade made it difficult for the manufacturers to send
these British goods directly to Europe, so instead they were first
despatched to the United States, then carried in American-flagged
ships to France. In the words of the petition, 'the neutrality of
America has been the means of circulating, to a large amount,
articles of the produce and manufactures of this country in the
dominions of our enemies'. In the more vivid language of the law
lord, Thomas Erskine, 'America . . . continued to smuggle [our]
goods into France, for her own interest, and France contrived to
buy them for hers. The people huzzaed their emperor in the
Tuilleries every day, but they broke his laws every night.' Clearly, if
the Royal Navy prevented American vessels reaching Europe, the
damage would not be confined to the United States and Europe.

In response, Perceval's government reshaped the economic blockade in April 1809. New Orders allowed United States vessels to trade
in the Baltic without registering at a British port, and, at the same

time, made it simpler for individual traders to apply for special licences to trade with Europe. During 1810, more than eighteen thousand legitimate permits were issued for voyages to Europe, enough to meet the needs of the manufacturers. Napoleon's troops in Spain were largely clothed in uniforms made of British cloth and fed on American wheat carried by licensed vessels, while two million boots made of English leather were exported to Poland so that his army could march into Russia. Meanwhile eight thousand tons of wheat from northern France came through British ports, including Liverpool, to feed British soldiers preparing to sail for Spain. But as well as the official licences that made this trade legitimate, an uncountable amount of forged paperwork was also in circulation.

When John Bellingham returned to Liverpool in early 1810, the city, although still prosperous, had begun to be infected by a dangerously anarchic mood. Significantly, but not surprisingly given the example set by illegal slavers, the Atlantic traders decided to break the law en masse rather than observe the Orders in Council. False papers were routinely provided for American vessels bringing in cotton and tobacco, so that if stopped by the Royal Navy when sailing to Europe, they could show that their ship was British, or had called at a British port and paid British taxes, and was thus free to pass.

By the summer of 1811, about the time baby Henry Bellingham was born, the policies of Spencer Perceval's government had driven a large number of otherwise respectable Liverpool merchants to break the law and use false papers, false registration documents, false inventories, false bills of consignment. 'Not only are the names forged,' Henry Brougham told the House of Commons in 1812, 'but the seal is also forged, and the wax imitated. But this is not enough. A regular set of letters is also forged, containing a good deal of fictitious material.' As evidence, he quoted the advertisement of a Liverpool company which announced that 'we have established ourselves in this town, for the sole purpose of making simulated papers'. They promised to provide perfectly forged ships' papers and licences needed to carry goods to twenty different ports, based on 'the original documents'.

Yet despite Liverpool's best efforts, almost one thousand United States vessels were seized by the British between 1807 and 1812 to be sold as prizes, and countless more were stopped and searched. Although the French, Dutch and Danish navies subjected American ships to similar searches and took more than five hundred as prizes, it was the actions of the Royal Navy that rubbed rawest on American nerves. Influential voices in the United States soon began to talk of war as the proper response.

Whenever a Royal Navy boarding party inspected the cargo and papers of a United States vessel, it took the opportunity to press-gang into its service any seamen regarded as British subjects. The practice had begun in June 1807, when the British warship HMS *Leopard* on patrol in the waters off Norfolk, Virginia, battered the United States frigate *Chesapeake* into submission so that the crew list could be inspected for possible deserters. Three of the four sail-ors arrested by *Leopard*'s boarders turned out to be American citizens. The fury caused by the incident was rekindled every time another seaman was taken off an American ship.

Both President Thomas Jefferson and his successor in 1809, James Madison, tried to retaliate by imposing a trade embargo on Britain. Faced by the prospect of bankruptcy if they obeyed the law, most United States merchants preferred to turn smuggler, and the embargoes failed. But in the 1810 Congressional elections, the repeated humiliations produced an upsurge of political fury. Led by two of the giants of nineteenth-century American politics, James Calhoun of South Carolina and Henry Clay of Kentucky, a lobby demanding an armed response to what Clay called 'British slavery

upon the water' began to influence the new Congress. The mani-
festo of the War Hawks, as they were dubbed, was summed up by
Tennessee congressman, Felix Grundy: 'we will resist by force the
attempt made by [the British] Government to subject our maritime rights to the arbitrary and capricious rule of her will'.

In May 1810 Congress gave the president what turned out to be
an effective weapon against the two European predators, France
and Britain. Under the Macon Act, complete freedom of trade
with Europe would be permitted, but Madison could impose a
total ban on one European power, if the other lifted its blockade
before March 1811. In response Napoleon publicly announced
that France intended to comply – covertly he instructed officials
to continue to seize American vessels bound for Britain – but in
London the United States ambassador, William Pinkney, found
Perceval intractable. The Prime Minister declared point-blank
that he was utterly opposed to 'courting of negotiations or expla-
nations with Mr Pinckney [sic] of what England will do if America
shall do this or do that'.

Henry Brougham blamed Perceval's attitude on his 'scorn of
the Americans, whom he disliked with the animosity peculiar to
all the courtiers of George III'. But the roots went deeper than
snobbery. Intelligence gathered by the African Institution had
identified the nationality of the ships, owners and crews that had
taken over Britain's leading role in the slave trade. From agents on
the ground in Africa and from the courts where privateers took
slave ships they had captured to be condemned as prizes, the
Institution concluded in 1810 that 'The persons who are by far the
most deeply engaged in this nefarious traffic appear to be citizens
of the United States of America.'

It had become illegal to import slaves into the United States in
January 1808, but without a navy capable of enforcing the law
American slavers operated without fear of the consequences. James

Stephen had already suspected they were proliferating from the number of cases in the Cockpit that involved American slavers sailing under false colours. And he had powerful support from Judge Robert Thorpe in Sierra Leone. 'The Americans swarm on the Coast,' he wrote, 'their Factors and Agents are evidently spread, and with Spanish or Portuguese Flags, papers and citizenships they still carry on the Slave Trade extensively.'

Whatever papers it carried, there was no disguising a slave ship, with its fast, narrow lines, foul smell and rows of shallow decks, like a chest of drawers, suitable for shipping humans lying prone. Unpredictable though the effects of the blockade might be on international trade, it was undoubtedly having the intended impact on the slave trade. From 1807, the court in Sierra Leone had dealt with several hundred slave ships boarded by British warships and privateers. Although some were captured by the West Africa squadron near to the coast, many were taken on the high seas, often close to Cuba or Brazil. No fewer than two hundred were flying the Spanish flag, although many were owned and crewed by Americans, and probably financed by British money. The mounting losses not only hit the illegal slavers hard, but undoubtedly deterred other shippers and financiers from fitting out ships for the trade. The impact of this onslaught was evident in the dramatic reduction in the number of slaves taken from Africa. From a peak of about eighty thousand slaves transported in 1807, the number had fallen to around forty-two thousand in 1810.

Perceval's obstinacy in the face of United States pressure to withdraw the Orders in Council was grounded in the belief, fostered by James Stephen, that the illegal slave trade was covertly dictating American policy. The War Hawks, it was noted, were dominated by representatives from the slave-owning states of South Carolina, Kentucky and Tennessee. All had a direct interest in relaxing restrictions on the illegal trade. To emphasise the hard line the British government intended to take, Stephen published a pamphlet in 1810 with the belligerent title, *Coup d'oeil on an American War*, arguing that hostilities with the United States would be in the national interest because it would leave trade routes free for British vessels.

Nevertheless, in their combined zeal, Perceval and Stephen were creating the conditions for the first worldwide economic depression of the industrial era.

In March 1811 the United States prohibited all trade with Britain. This time the ban held. In Liverpool the effects were immediate. Over the first six months of the year, the revenue from harbour dues dropped by a third. In September the United States consul, James Maury, could count no more than seventeen American vessels in port compared with nearly a hundred the year before. By the end of 1811, exports formerly running at close to £10 million had been cut to £1.4 million. The *Liverpool Mercury*, newly launched that year to represent the voice of reform and the interests of the Atlantic trade, warned that 'the distress in this town has been excessive, and it seems impossible to impute this to any other cause but the great reduction of trade with America'.

Those engaged in the Atlantic trade could not afford hold-ups in the flow of business. As agents, they depended on high volumes and long lines of credit from London banks so that they in turn could extend up to eighteen months' credit to their clients. The speculator Richard Breed, for example, could get immediate credit of £16,000 from Hughes & Duncan, Liverpool financiers, but his wish to make a long-term speculation in wheat for twice that sum required approval from Barings in London. These characteristics made the Atlantic trade uniquely vulnerable.

Suddenly, like a sub-prime housing crisis, confidence in United States business evaporated, and credit from the London banks dried up. Liverpool's warehouses were quickly crammed with exports that could find no ships, and imports that no one could buy for want of money. On the west African coast, the incidence of illicit slaving was falling, but in Liverpool the American trade was dying. In September the *Mercury* called for a mass petition to the Prince Regent demanding that the Orders in Council be lifted. But when the matter was raised in Parliament, Perceval's government swept aside the objections.

Significantly, the government spokesman was James Stephen, who defended the Orders as an essential weapon in the war against Napoleon. The *Mercury* angrily noted that he had 'the temerity in a moment of premature triumph to boast that the Orders in Council were the production of his brain . . . many a poor, starving family may lay their distress at the door of that gentleman'.

As it spread, the credit crunch hit trades that had nothing to do with exports to the United States. Organisers of the Chester fair where there was normally brisk demand for Irish goods like linen, beef and butter reported that 'the general stagnation of every species of trade was never more severely felt than at our present Fair'. Even the Baltic and West India merchants began to feel the pinch. And looming over the depression was the growing threat that the trade dispute with the United States would escalate into war.

When Congress reassembled in November 1811, the War Hawks immediately pressed for a rearmaments programme, including the building of new frigates and the recruitment of an army of twenty-five thousand men. The report of the Foreign Affairs committee, packed with hawks, recommended that 'the Orders in Council, so far as they interrupt our direct trade . . . ought to be resisted by war'. Summing up the political mood, Felix Grundy declared to his fellow slave owner, Andrew Jackson, 'Rely on one thing, we have War or Honorable Peace before we adjourn.'

There was little popular enthusiasm, and none in New England, for fighting what was generally thought to be a southern planters' war. Thus the New York and New England merchants, whose sufferings were being used as the excuse for belligerence, were the most vociferous in opposing the hawks. A writer to the New York *Evening News* declared that out of $45 million worth of United States exports, $37 million went to Britain. 'Now, after this,' he concluded, 'let me ask you what you think of making war upon Great Britain and her allies, for the purpose of benefiting commerce?' As the War Hawks gained influence in Congress, American business sent increasingly anxious messages to its agents in Liverpool urging them to find a way of having the Orders in Council removed.

To traders in Liverpool who could see the economic devastation before their eyes and at the same time heard from their partners in Boston, New York and Philadelphia of the rising threat of conflict between Britain and the United States, it was peculiarly obvious that Spencer Perceval had to be made to change his mind. And if he refused, to some of them at least his removal appeared preferable to war.

The *Mercury* columnist who described Perceval as 'the cadaverous looking, little gentleman on the green benches' was not alone in blaming the Prime Minister for the economic crisis that engulfed the town. The belief was shared by almost everyone engaged in the United States trade. Bankers such as William Roscoe and Hughes & Duncan had seen their profits slashed – the latter slumping from £32,000 to £13,000. The value of imports and exports tied up in Liverpool's warehouses was estimated in 'millions'. A single cargo of Virginia tobacco was worth up to £5,000, and a speculator like Richard Breed was ready to invest £35,000, or almost $200,000, in American wheat on the expectation that trade would be resumed. For such merchants, it was becoming obvious that the riches they might make or lose depended solely upon the will of Spencer Perceval.

When Bellingham began to plan how to force the government to pay him what he deserved, he found himself in the company of people whose ideas were running in the same direction. The focus of all their frustrations was the unyielding intransigence of one man.

In this bitter, desperate atmosphere, many Liverpool merchants, accustomed to breaking the law to make a profit, must have talked of the simplest solution to their troubles, the elimination of the man responsible for all the town's woes. The idea of political assassination was certainly current. A columnist claimed in the *Mercury* that 'we have ourselves heard persons who did not hesitate to declare that the assassination of a tyrant may on some occasions be a meritorious action'. The argument had originally been put forward by a government-financed newspaper, with Napoleon as the proposed victim. But, the *Mercury* pointed out, the principle could equally well be applied to other targets closer to home.

No doubt in Liverpool's salty fashion, loud voices declared that killing Spencer Perceval would be for the good of the country, and whoever did it would be a hero. And in the heat of the discussion, someone with a smattering of legal knowledge could have claimed that in the circumstances it would not even constitute murder, because it would be a patriotic act, committed without *malice prepense*. Whether he heard it casually, or someone deliberately suggested it to him, the idea remained firmly in Bellingham's mind.

That winter he broke the promise to his wife, Mary, to give up all thought of compensation. But when he returned to thinking about it in 1811, he did so less like a refugee from Russia, and more like the man he was, a hard-pressed merchant of Liverpool. He had a realistic target of £8,000 compensation, and a plan that would force the government to pay it. The process would involve approaching ministers as he had in 1810, but this time he intended to work his way methodically through each arm of government. If at the end he was still refused what he wanted, the injustice of it would be obvious to everyone. Out of Liverpool's fury and his renewed desire for compensation, a plan evolved whose endgame was assassination.

Even at that early stage, he probably voiced something about it in public. 'I was very well known in Liverpool,' Bellingham assured the jury, 'I could have got the signatures of the whole town [for my petition].' It may have been an exaggeration, but his obsession was certainly familiar to many people. The witnesses who rushed down to testify at his trial to his derangement had clearly heard some of his contributions to the wild discussions. Unfortunately, they realised too late that while others had given vent to pure rage, Bellingham had expressed serious resolve.

# The Russian Connection Returns

He has not been shaved. He complains seriously of this last
prohibition, as he thus will not be able to appear as a Gentleman!
Report in *The Times* referring to Bellingham's protest against
prison regulations forbidding condemned prisoners the
use of a razor, 18 May 1812

In his memoirs, Lord Holland recorded his distasteful encounter
with a Birmingham manufacturer a few days after the Prime
Minister's murder. 'With a demure countenance and a subdued
voice,' Holland wrote, the Birmingham man condemned the public
displays of joy at Perceval's death. '"It is indeed disgusting, and
yet," added he with an arch, puritanical smile, "it proves the sad
condition of the poor manufacturers, and it cannot be denied that,
in the present critical state of the question on the Orders-in-
Council, the finger of a benevolent Providence is visible in this
horrible event."'

Leaving Providence out of it, the manufacturer was undeniably
right about a sense of popular relief, amounting almost to achievement, among wholly respectable people at Spencer Perceval's
elimination. Everyone had suspected that he alone was responsible
for keeping in place the Orders in Council, and his murder supplied
the proof. So long as he existed, the Orders were invulnerable;

without him they simply evaporated, and almost at once the recession began to lift. An investigator like John Vickery, doggedly determined to understand why the Prime Minister was murdered, would have been intrigued by the widespread schizophrenia, deploring the murder but rejoicing that it had happened.

In June Lord Liverpool was appointed to succeed Perceval as Prime Minister, and at the first opportunity Henry Brougham then tabled a motion in the House of Commons calling for the Orders' repeal. Twice before while Perceval was alive, Brougham's attacks on the Orders had been defeated by large majorities. This time, despite vehement opposition from Stephen and Wilberforce, he found himself pushing at an open door. Perceval's former cabinet colleagues had already decided the Orders were to be withdrawn.

During the debate Castlereagh tried to justify this abrupt reversal of policy by pointing to Napoleon's announcement in April of a second decree withdrawing the French blockade. But in private he agreed with Wilberforce when the veteran abolitionist objected that the decree was spurious and French policy was unchanged. 'Aye,' Castlereagh admitted, 'but one does not like to own that we are forced to give way to our manufacturers.'

Had Vickery travelled to Liverpool in June 1812, he would have found its most civilised Mount Pleasant citizens caught up in celebrations at the withdrawal of the Orders in Council. 'The town,' declared the polymathic banker, William Roscoe, 'had arisen from the dead.' Anticipating the restoration of the multi-million pound, American trade, and a general slackening of controls on shipping everywhere, Roscoe and his wealthy friends raised enough money to present a solid silver plate to Henry Brougham.

Attempting to justify what looked uncomfortably like pleasure at the Prime Minister's death, the Atlantic trade's own newspaper, the *Mercury*, went out of its way to insist that Bellingham's action played no part in this triumphant outcome – 'the petitioners [against the

Orders],' it editorialised soon after the Prime Minister was shot, 'must [have] be[en] ultimately successful whether Mr Perceval be minister or not.' The *Mercury*'s denial of the obvious demonstrated how the national schizophrenia could be resolved – by presuming that the Prime Minister's personality and policies had really been irrelevant to the grand sweep of events, and that his murder was therefore no more than an aberration. It marked the beginning of what became a national amnesia about Spencer Perceval's premiership until his very name slipped out of history. In fact, the reverse was true. Spencer Perceval's central position in the grand sweep of events – the war with Napoleon, the fight against the slave trade, the arrival of industrialism and the emergence of a trading pattern driven by market forces – explained why he had to die.

Amongst the citywide euphoria, Vickery, that careful detective, would surely have noted the exceptional satisfaction felt by the American trade. At a special session of the American Chamber of Commerce, convened on 25 June to hear about the withdrawal of the Orders, no fewer than thirty-seven members turned up, and in their relief they voted the generous sum of £500 towards the expenses of those engaged in lobbying against the Orders.

The minute books of the chamber, a volume the size of a small suitcase, showed how desperate conditions had become before the assassination. So few of the fifty or more members turned up for meetings that most had to be cancelled for lack of a quorum. Its chairman, John Richardson, estimated that his members had goods worth 'about a million in money' held in warehouses awaiting import or export. He had personally lost £20,000 when two cargoes he had tried to smuggle into the United States were confiscated. By contrast, in the summer after Perceval's murder members of the chamber shipped out more than £1.5 million of goods, worth roughly £150 million in today's prices.

THE NEW SHET

# THE NEW

# Shetland Sheepdog

by MAXWELL RIDDLE

*ILLUSTRATED*

*Drawings by JEAN SIMMONDS*

FIRST EDITION . . . Thirteenth Printing

1989
HOWELL BOOK HOUSE INC.
230 PARK AVENUE
NEW YORK, N.Y. 10169

A. Raymond Miller

# Contents

| | | |
|---|---|---|
| Preface | | 9 |
| Foreword | | 11 |
| 1. | The Makeup of a Sheepdog | 13 |
| 2. | Original Home of the Shetland Sheepdog | 17 |
| 3. | Ancestors of the Shetland Sheepdog | 21 |
| 4. | Establishment of the Breed | 23 |
| 5. | First Standards of the Breed | 31 |
| 6. | Modern Breed Standards | 37 |
| 7. | Recognition of the Breed | 51 |
| 8. | The Shetland Sheepdog Comes to America | 57 |
| 9. | Renewal of American Interest in Shetland Sheepdogs | 63 |
| 10. | American Shetland Sheepdog Association | 77 |
| 11. | The National Specialty Show | 81 |
| 12. | The Shetland Sheepdog Futurity Stakes | 89 |
| 13. | Canadian Shetland Sheepdog Pioneers | 93 |
| 14. | Modern Shelties in Canada | 97 |
| 15. | The Modern Shetland Sheepdog in Great Britain | 103 |
| 16. | Shetland Sheepdog Litters | 111 |
| 17. | Color and Coat in the Shetland Sheepdog | 113 |
| 18. | Eye Color in the Shetland Sheepdog | 123 |
| 19. | Character of the Shetland Sheepdog | 127 |
| 20. | About Measuring Shetland Sheepdogs | 135 |
| 21. | How to Groom Your Shetland Sheepdog, by Barbara Curry | 139 |
| 22. | How to Show Your Shetland Sheepdog | 143 |
| 23. | Shetland Sheepdog Working Trials on Sheep | 151 |

24. Shetland Sheepdog in Obedience    159
25. Great Shetland Sheepdog Sires    165
26. Great Shetland Sheepdog Dams    181
27. The Great Shetland Sheepdog Winners    189
28. Birkie, the Shetland Sheepdog Film Star    197
29. Great Canadian Kennels, Sires, and Dams    201
30. Shetland Sheepdog Eye Disease    215
31. Shetland Sheepdog Pedigrees    219
    Bibliography    224

There are 168 Illustrations
in this book. Pictures taken
by the finest photographers
in America, Canada, England
and Scotland are included.

Carmylie As If Bi Chance, pointed
black and white bitch, owned by Jean
D. Simmonds.

# Preface

MAXWELL RIDDLE is a giant in mental capacity, a dynamo in physical energy—and virtually omniscient in dog lore. In quality and number, his accomplishments as an authority on dogs are unparalleled among his contemporaries in the field.

He has owned, bred and shown many breeds. His judging assignments, covering all breeds, have taken him to five world areas; America, Canada, Australia, Africa and South America. His weekly column was syndicated for many years in the *New York Post* and other newspapers in the U.S.A.; he has written several dog books; he contributed more than half the articles in *The International Encyclopedia of Dogs;* and he is an associate editor of *Dog World* and contributor to other magazines.

Past President of the Dog Writers' Association of America, he has won *all* of the Association's journalism awards, to which he is eligible, for excellence in writing—many of them two and even three times. In 1973, after many terms of office, he retired as President of the Ravenna Kennel Club which he has also served as show chairman for 34 years. He has also served as President and show chairman of the Western Reserve Kennel Club of Cleveland.

When appeals to leading Shetland Sheepdog fanciers for a new book on the breed failed to bear fruit, I turned to Max Riddle because of his long-time knowledge of and fondness for the breed. Possibly he has learned more about Shelties than most of their fanciers can recite today. What he did not know when he undertook this assignment, he took the trouble to find out—as his excellent chapter, "Establishment of the Breed," attests. He visited the Shetland Islands in 1972 expressly for the purpose of docu-

9

menting the breed's early history in the land of its origin. Greater dedication hath no man!

It is an honor and privilege to present this useful, fascinating and wholly splendid work to friends of the Shetland Sheepdog. Assuredly, they will share our gratitude to Maxwell Riddle for it.

—*Elsworth Howell*

The author, Maxwell Riddle.

# Foreword

THIS book would have been impossible without the aid of many dedicated and unselfish Shetland Sheepdog fanciers who have aided so much in gathering information. They include Mrs. June Korenko, Mrs. Barbara Curry, Mrs. Dona Hausman, Mrs. Beverley Muhlenhaupt and many others in the United States. In Canada, I am indebted to Mrs. Frances Clark and Mrs. Pat Ristau. Both the American and Canadian Kennel Clubs have been most helpful. In England, my thanks go to Miss Felicity Rogers; and in Shetland itself, to James Thomson and to the Lerwick Library. Jean D. Simmonds gave permission to use some of the illustrations from her own *The Illustrated Shetland Sheepdog Standard*. And finally, to the Cleveland Public Library, whose facilities are almost unexcelled anywhere for canine research.

—*Maxwell Riddle*

# 1

# The Makeup of a Sheepdog

WHAT is a sheepdog? One can answer the question superficially in two sentences. A shepherd is one who tends sheep. And a sheepdog is a shepherd's dog. Some sheepdogs, notably the German Shepherd, are called shepherd dogs. But most shepherds' dogs are called sheepdogs. However, this tells you virtually nothing about a sheepdog. One might paraphrase Gertrude Stein's famous phrase about a rose: A dog is a dog is a dog. But a sheepdog is something more than just the physical being we call a dog. It is a marvelous combination of instincts and aptitudes, conscience, responsibility, and intelligence.

To understand how the sheepdog developed—or at least why—you must start at a point long before the beginnings of recorded history. Early men had been food gatherers and vegetarians. Evidence indicates that, during the Paleolithic Age—the Stone Age—only the dog was domesticated. This may have come 100,000 years ago.

But man became a hunter, a meat eater. During a period, which has sometimes been called the Mesolithic Age—the transitional age—domestication of almost all the plants and animals which we have today was accomplished. At least when the Neolithic Age—New Stone Age—arrived, it began with the triumph of agriculture.

Men had discovered that they need no longer hunt for all their food. They could keep domestic animals for food and clothing, and they could grow annual crops. Sheep were the first of the food animals to be domesticated. The time was 8,000 to 10,000 years ago. Cattle and horses came later. Solving some problems for people, they also created other problems.

13

The sheep of those far off days must have been far more difficult to handle than are the gentle animals of today. For one thing, they were closer to their wild relatives. For another, they were constantly in danger of death from the attacks by wolves, lions, and other carnivorous predators. There were an abundance of these in the forests, in mountain lairs, on the plains, and on what we would call "grazing land." Even if domestic to a point, the sheep would remember their past. Safety lay in the stampede. Let a few die that the rest might live.

Probably the dogs of the time were both large and ferocious. They were too close to their own wild state not to have been so. We can assume that they had weather resistant coats; which would be double—an outer coat of guard hairs, and a soft, dense under coat. Since sheep raising was done in temperate and northerly climates, rather than in the tropics, we can suppose that the dogs were of northern, Spitz Family type. But these qualities do not make a sheepdog. They were—and are—important. More important still is the character of the dog.

Their owners must have noted variances in behavior. They watched and studied their dogs. A dog would act in a certain way. Its owner, with the remarkable understanding he had of animals, would recognize the unconscious act of the dog. It would be useful. So he would train the dog to perform consciously that act which it had done automatically. He would search for other dogs with similar traits. And he would breed the best of these dogs together.

Some dogs fight silently. Others growl, roar, and make a terrible noise. The first dog might attack a predator and drive it off without scaring the sheep over which it guarded. But the battle noise of the second dog might frighten the sheep into a stampede.

Perhaps the ancient shepherd noted that some dogs liked to show their dominance by driving the sheep, by making them move this way or that. Such a dog might be trained to herd sheep. The Swiss lake dwellers taught their dogs to drive the sheep into the lake huts at night. The bridge could then be lifted. Such driving dogs would be useful only if they did not get so excited that they attacked the sheep. Those with the necessary restraint would be used for breeding.

These unknown shepherds noted that some dogs seemed to have a natural instinct to guard—a property guarding instinct, it is called. They noted that dogs, as do wolves, mark out territories for themselves. Such dogs will chase out invading dogs. But then, the shepherds must have noticed that some dogs, having a guarding instinct, also insisted upon keeping the sheep inside the home territory. They bred for this characteristic also. So they developed dogs which seemed to claim ownership of the flock.

Shepherds have always claimed that their dogs could count and seem to know when one of the flock is missing, setting out to round it up.

Some dogs appeared to learn by themselves to keep a flock moving toward a water hole, or along a trail. All these traits observed by the prehistoric shepherds were bred to and strengthened.

It seems unlikely that these ancient breeders paid any attention to type. In the northern latitudes, a double weather resistant coat was necessary. This was a natural feature of the northern, Spitz Family dogs. A thick neck ruff was also important, since it protected the throat during battle. Northern dogs also had erect or semi-erect ears. Dogs with erect ears probably hear better and can locate the direction of sound better and quicker than drop eared dogs. This trait also would be kept. So would the speed and the ability to stop quickly and to turn sharply.

But type, as we know it today, was probably ignored. Such type as did develop came through other factors. Villages were often isolated. Village dogs were bred to village dogs, and a sort of vague local type did develop. The dogs had a common heritage. An occasional cross breeding hardly disturbed this. Unless the cross produced some factor which the shepherds considered to be of value, it quickly disappeared from the line.

Even today, if one goes into the farming areas of America, older people are likely to ask: "What has become of the old fashioned 'farm shepherd dog'?" These were not purebreds. They were bred for performance and not for type. But they belonged to an ancestral type just the same. Vaguely, they resembled the northern dogs. They had prick or semi-prick ears, fairly long outer guard coats, and soft, dense undercoats. They had a neck ruff and a curving tail with a thick brush. It is not hard to believe that the genes of those dogs still exist in the Shetland Sheepdog.

LERWICK FROM THE STONY HILL.

Copy of engraving by John Irvine, Lerwick.

16

# 2

# Original Home
# of the Shetland Sheepdog

---

THE Shetland Sheepdog was first developed in the Shetland Islands. It is necessary, therefore, to consider the breed's original home. The Shetland Islands stretch northward from a point about 130 miles north of the northernmost point of the Scottish mainland. There are about 100 islands large enough to be called islands, and perhaps 100 more which are not.

The largest island is called Mainland. It is 50 miles long, but is quite narrow. About one third of the way up the island is the village of Lerwick. It is the county seat. Lying on the east side of the island, Lerwick has a good harbor protected by a smaller island, called Bressay.

Aside from Mainland, the major islands are Yell and Unst. Unst is the northernmost, and Muckle Flugga Lighthouse is the northernmost point in the United Kingdom. It was on Unst that the finest scarves were knitted. They were so fine that an island boast is that they can be drawn through an average sized wedding ring.

The islands cover a land area of 549 square miles. Northmaven, on the northern part of Mainland has Ronas Hill. It is 1,475 feet above sea level and is the highest point on any of the islands. The scenery on most of the islands is ruggedly beautiful. The coast is indented with sea lochs or voes which are often enclosed by steep walls, or hills. There are very few trees, and in many places, the soil is thin and of poor quality.

These pictures are of Mrs. Lorna Irvine Burgess, granddaughter of Alexander Irvine, a founder of the breed. Mrs. Burgess's Hjatland Kennels, Robinsrae, Dunrossness, in Shetland, Scotland, is the oldest Sheltie kennel in existence.

*H. Peace*

18

Only a small part of the islands lie below latitude 60 degrees. That means that they are in roughly the same latitude as Bergen, Norway, or even farther north. Yet the climate is not as cold as might be expected. The reason lies in the American Gulf Stream. As it breaks away from the American coast, the Gulf Stream breaks up into several branches. Sometimes these are lumped together as the North Atlantic Current. One branch enters the Norwegian Sea to the north of Scotland. Another turns southward into the North Sea.

The current warms the Shetland Islands. But it also helps to set up ceaseless winds. These winds are so strong and so steady that few trees can exist. As at Punta Arenas at the southern tip of South America, vegetable gardens must be sheltered from these winds. Mighty storms rage across the islands. Yet there are pleasant days in the summer, and daylight lasts nearly 24 hours. Tennis and golf games are held annually at midnight.

The population of the islands has steadily declined during the last 100 years. Wool growing no longer supplies sufficient income for the islanders, most of whom still there fish during a part of the year. In recent years, the development of synthetic fabrics has further cut the demand for wool. And modern fishing fleets, which roam the world and use highly sophisticated means for locating fish, have severely cut down fish populations. Refrigeration and world population increases have helped to make commercial fishing a world wide industry. For these reasons, fishing off the islands has declined as a source of local income. There are, however, quick freezing and fish meal plants.

The Shetland Islands are sometimes called Zetland. Both names come from the Norwegian, Hjaltland. The Norsemen have left a heavy influence on the islands. They were, in fact, Norwegian until 1468 when the Shetland and Orkney Islands were pledged for the dowry of Princess Margaret of Norway, who married James III of Scotland. Since the pledge was never redeemed, the islands became the property of Scotland.

The wool from the Shetland sheep is very fine. It is also light. The crofters, or their wives and daughters, made loosely woven scarves, gloves, socks, and sweaters in patterns known for centuries as "Shetland" or "Fair Isle." But in our time the term has come to mean a fine wool. Today, most fine wool garments titled "Shetland" probably come from mainland Scotland.

A simple way to describe a crofter is to say that he is a tenant farmer. Crofting is an ancient way of life in Scotland and in the Orkney and Shetland Islands. A crofter lives with his family in a small home on the land he rents. He pays an annual rental, cultivates what land is arable, and raises sheep, cattle and ponies. In former times, the cattle were light and rather small, but they gave comparatively large amounts of milk. The Shetland pony has spread all over the world. It is not, as sometimes

19

stated, a miniature horse since it differs from the horse in many respects, apart from size. Unlike the horse, it does not require grains. It can live all winter on hay alone, or upon hay and such grasses as it can find. Nor does it require shelter. Those ponies bred in the islands are able to stand both the raging storms and the ceaseless winds.

Wolves and other carnivorous predators disappeared from the islands centuries ago. But sheepdogs were needed. They could take the sheep out to the downs without human help, and they could bring them back to shelter. They knew the sheep in their own flocks, and could distinguish them from the sheep in other flocks. As with the Iceland Dog, they could also herd the ponies. This was necessary at times. Moreover, in times of food scarcity, the ponies would tend to come down to the gardens; the sheepdogs kept them out and sent them back to the grazing lands.

Life in the Shetland Islands has never been easy. Food has never been plentiful, and income has been low. The crofters had ponies instead of horses. And they had their small cattle (of which, today, not more than 50 exist.) They could not afford large sheepdogs. And indeed, since the predators were gone, there was no need for a large dog. Enter then, the ancestors of the Shetland Sheepdog.

James Thomsen, far left, at Shetland Sheepdog Trials in Shetland.

This is a cross down from "Yakki" Dog
which would be crossed again with a smaller
dog. The little girl is James Thomsen's
daughter.

# 3

# Ancestors of the Shetland Sheepdog

THE era of the purebred dog began about 1870. But most modern breeds can trace their exact ancestry no farther back than 1890 to 1910. In the years since 1870, enthusiastic breed specialists have been trying to trace their breeds back to the time of ancient Egypt. For the most part, they have simply stretched, bent, and tortured facts and history in an effort to prove an ancient origin for their breeds. They have simply manufactured romantic lies about the origin of their dogs. It will not be the function of this book to concoct or perpetuate such lies.

We did make certain points in both Chapters 1 and 2. We pointed out that, so far its mental capacity, its inherited instincts, aptitudes and its trainability go, the sheepdog is older than recorded history. Although many of the northern, or temperate zone, sheepdogs conform vaguely to type, type breeding did not develop until the recent past. And in Chapter 2 we showed that the difficult life in the Shetland Islands made a small working sheepdog a necessity.

That difficult life caused conformation breeding to arrive in the Shetland Islands very late. Still, since type or conformation breeding did begin, we need to ask ourselves what the Shetland Islanders had to work with. What was their basic stock?

More than 200 years ago, naturalists such as the immortal Buffon considered that the shepherd's dog was the basic dog from which all others have sprung. The type of dog they had in mind, conformation wise, was a medium sized dog belonging to the Spitz family of northern dogs.

The Picts, who lived in Shetland during the seventh and eighth centuries, brought with them sheep and sheep dogs. The dogs were undoubtedly of Spitz type. The Iceland Dog also is of Spitz type, and so was the dog of the Greenland whalers, a breed called "Yakkie." Both the Iceland fishing fleets and the Greenland whalers stopped at Shetland, going and coming. Their dogs accompanied them. It is worth noting that the Iceland Dogs, as the Shetland Dogs, herd ponies as well as sheep.

During the early part of the 19th Century, the island dogs were called "Haad." They were much larger than the later dogs. And their purpose was to chase, throw, and hold the wild sheep until the herdsman could secure it. But by 1850, Scottish shepherds had developed both Scotch Collies and Border Collies, together with the present methods of working sheep. The new methods made it possible for the Shetlanders to develop a smaller herding dog.

Still, the type of the Scotch Collie was much admired, and Shetland and Collie crosses were certainly made. But the Collie of 1850, or even of 1900, was not the Collie of today. It was close to modern type, but it was smaller. The standard in 1900 called for males to be 21 to 24 inches at the shoulder. These dogs were slightly larger than those of 1850, just as the modern Collie is two to four inches taller than his ancestors of 1900.

There is no doubt that great herding dogs from Scotland were taken to the Shetland Islands. Because of the islanders' demand for a small herding dog, it is likely that dogs of 21 inches or less at the shoulder were used. Border Collies had a maximum shoulder height of 21 inches. These great little performers were competing in sheepdog trials a scant half dozen years after dog shows were established. By 1873, they had achieved national importance in Wales. The smallest of these may also have been taken to the Shetlands.

At any rate, by 1910 very small, Collie type dogs abounded in the Shetland Islands. They have been described as mongrels. They were not, as far as their abilities were concerned. All that was required was to improve their type.

All over the world, the need for the shepherd's dog was declining. Men everywhere were attempting to save the great herding dogs which they had developed. Population was declining in the Shetland Islands. Fewer of the crofters' wives and daughters were making yarn and weaving "Shetland" products. Breeders in Scotland and in England were developing very beautiful Collies. The Shetland Islanders could not do otherwise.

Enter then, the Shetland Sheepdog.

22

# 4

# Establishment of the Breed

---

THE Shetlanders could not escape the world wide ferment to save native breeds from extinction. Their little sheepdogs performed so marvelously well that they had also become very popular among herdsmen in the northern sections of the Scottish mainland, around Dundee, Inverness and Wick. As early as 1900, efforts to save and purify the breed had begun.

One of the earliest breeders was Alexander Irvine of Vatchley, Shetland. By 1902 he had firmly established a kennel. He called it Hjatland, after one of the Norse spellings of Shetland. It was history's first Shetland Sheepdog kennel, and it has remained continuously in operation ever since. Today it is operated by Mrs. Lorna Irvine Burgess, Alexander's granddaughter, at Robin's Brae, Dunrossness, Shetland.

In 1905, the Rev. H. B. Oddy arrived in Shetland to take over a parish near Lerwick. He traveled widely on Mainland and the other islands. English parsons had long played an important role in the preservation of hunting sports, and in writing upon dog subjects of all kinds. Rev. Oddy was one of them. He became acquainted with Alexander Irvine. And he watched the island dogs—called variously Toonie Dogs, Peerie Dogs, and sometimes Shetland Collies—herd sheep and ponies. He also watched the dogs work on the Scottish mainland.

In 1907 an effort was made to bring "Shetland Collies" to public notice by providing classes for them at agricultural shows. In August of that year, an advertisement appeared in the *Shetland Times*. It announced that classes would be held for Shetland Collies at the coming Lerwick

Fair. C. Lennie, Esq., of Scalloway, offered a prize of 10 shillings for the "best Shetland Collie dog or bitch."

*The Shetland Times* for Saturday, Oct. 31st, reports the judging of the Shetland Collies. There were 16 entered. The winner was a black and tan male named Sailor Bob. He was owned by A. Conley of Hill House. The name, Sailor Bob, may be significant. Many of the Shetland Collies went to sea on the fishing ships. And as we shall see later, a sea going Collie played an important part in the breed's conformation.

Let us return to the Rev. Oddy. He was so impressed by the work of the Shetland Collies that he wrote an article about them. This appeared in the English magazine, *Country Life. The Shetland Times* saw the article and reprinted it in full on April 25, 1908. We reprint it here.

> "Novelties of the canine world are continually appearing, and the latest is the arrival of the Shetland Collie. The breed is very little known outside Shetland, though during the last few years a number of small kennels have been formed in Scotland. Classes have been allotted to them at several Scottish shows. And at the Dundee show in March last, an effort was made to form a club, and if possible to obtain recognition from the Kennel Club.
>
> "Whether the breed has any real claim to be called the Shetland Collie is open to question, to my mind. I lived for nearly three years near Lerwick, and during that time went about a great deal, but never heard them spoken of as Collies. They were simply 'peerie dogs.' That they will do the work of the ordinary sheepdog is certain, and that they resemble the Collie in miniature cannot be denied. In coat, body, legs, feet, tail, and in fact in everything but the head and ears, they are a replica of the modern Collie.
>
> "The eye is larger, and the head shorter and thicker than that of the Collie today, but very much like the head of the Collie of 30 years ago. The ears are erect but this may be easily altered if those who are interesting themselves in the breed think it advisable. The colours are white and sable markings, sable, sable and white, tricolor, black and tan, and the blue marl. In weight they vary from six pounds to 10 pounds.
>
> "Where the breed is known, it is very popular and there is a brisk demand for good specimens. They are pretty, intelligent, and very hardy. I believe that, hitherto, they have been bred rather by accident than by design. When the proposed club is formed, and fanciers take up the breed in earnest, any objectionable points will doubtless be bred out."

The Rev. Oddy's article had an almost immediate effect. *The Shetland Times* for Nov. 21, 1908, carried this announcement:

> "For some considerable time now, the small class of dogs described as 'Shetland Collies' has been attracting attention, the dog being a general favourite. With a view toward preserving the purity of the breed, and

improving it, a meeting of those interested will be held in the County Hall on Monday evening for the purpose of forming a 'Shetland Collie Club.' "

The historic meeting was held on Monday, Nov. 23, 1908. Provost Porteus, chief magistrate of the county, acted as chairman. J. A. Loggie, who kept a public house or pub, announced that he was the person who had called the meeting. Here is the report, as it appeared in *The Shetland Times.*

"Mr. J. A. Loggie, Royal Bldg., said he was responsible for calling the meeting together . . . He stated he had been in communication with the secretaries of the Aberdeen Kennel Club, The Toy Dog Society, and the Scotland Canine Society, from whom he had gotten copies of rules and other information that would be useful to their club.

"It was moved by Loggie that a club be formed, and seconded by A. J. Jamieson of Scalloway. It was passed unanimously. The patronesses of the new club are Lady Marjory Sinclair, wife of the secretary for Scotland; Mrs. Alex Moffatt, Falkirk, wife of Sheriff Moffat, and formerly of Lerwick. The patrons are the Hon. J. Cathcart Waton, member of parliament for Zetland County; R. H. Bruce of Sumburgh; and Sir Arthur Nicholoson, Bart. (Bart. is the abbreviation for baronet, the lowest hereditary title. Author).

"The Honorable Presidents are Provost Porteus, Baillie Laing, and the Rev. A. J. Campbell. The committee is made up of A. J. Jamieson, Laurence Laurenson, Thomas Henderson Jr. of Spiggie, John Smith, Alexander Irvine of Vatchley, P. MacDougall, A. Nelson of Gott, J. W. Laurenson, Arthur Conley, William Manson, W. P. Harrison, and William Sinclair.

"It was announced that the demand for the dogs is greater than the supply. It is necessary to form a stud book. A membership fee of two shillings, six pence per annum will be charged."

On Dec. 12, 1908, *The Shetland Times* reported on the next meeting at which the studbook had been officially set up. Here is the report of that meeting.

"No dog shall be eligible for admission unless it complies with the standard laid down, and the owner's name, and the names of the sire and dam, date of birth, etc., be furnished. A charge of six pence shall be made for such registration.

"The next business was consideration of the standard, when it was agreed that the type and points of the Shetland Collie shall be similar to those of the rough Collie in miniature. That the height of the Shetland Collie shall not exceed 12 inches, nor the weight, 14 pounds.

"The following sub-committee was appointed to examine, measure, and weigh all dogs put forward for entry into the stud book. Thomas Henderson and Alexander Irvine for the south part of the islands; and John Smith, J. W. Laurenson, W. J. Greig, F. Hunter, and J. A. Loggie for the rest of the islands. There were 30 members enrolled."

Provost Porteus served as the first president and J. A. Loggie as the "Honourable Secretary." However, Collie breeders everywhere fought the new group and breed. They objected to the name Shetland Collie, and to the Shetland Collie Club. Finally, the name was changed to Shetland Sheepdog. It has kept this name ever since.

There now came agitation for recognition of a taller dog. First, Shelties were being bred and raised on the Scottish mainland, and even in England. And as a Shetland Islands' authority recently told the author: "Our cattle, dogs, and ponies seem to lose many of their native characteristics when bred away from Shetland. Perhaps removal to an easier climate is a factor. We only know that it happens."

Another factor was the undoubted crossing with small rough coated Collies. James Thomason, who joined the Shetland Sheepdog Trials Association upon its formation in 1923, and who served as its president for 20 years, tells the story of a small, good looking Collie which lived for some years on a fishing ship which traveled between Iceland and Shetland. The dog was named "Scott" after the master of the ship.

Scott was finally put ashore at Lerwick. But he always seemed to know when "his ship" was in. He would greet it joyously, and would stay on deck so long as it stayed in harbor. Since Scott had the freedom of Lerwick, he mated with many of the island bitches. Thomason, who remembers J. A. Loggie quite well, believes that this Collie is in the background of Loggie's famous early winner, Lerwick Jarl.

After the name of the club was changed to Shetland Sheepdog Club, T. & J. Manson of *The Shetland News* office published the constitution and "bye-laws" of the organization. To illustrate the seriousness of the members, we quote here several paragraphs from it.

"That the Hon. Secretary shall keep a Register known as the Shetland Sheepdog Stud Book, wherein all dogs belonging to members of the Club shall be registered. In such Register must be inserted, if known, the name of the dog, the breeder's name, date of birth, names of sire and dam, and of grand-sire and grand-dam. A charge of 1/- shall be made for such registration. No dog shall be eligible for registration unless it is certified to be roughcoated, and at least 10 months old, and not exceeding 15 inches in height, measured from the ground to top of shoulder at highest point.

"That all members of the Club entering dogs for prizes offered by the Club at any Show, must have their dogs registered in the Club Stud-book kept for registration. And for shows of Agricultural Societies in Shetland, the register certificate must be produced at the time of making entry, and that the registered number, along with the dog's name, shall be entered in the catalogue.

"If for any reason the Club ceases to exist, the Cups, Trophies, Assets and Records belonging to the Club shall be placed in the custody of the Kennel Club, London, with the least possible delay.

26

"THE KENNEL CLUB, London, is the final authority for interpreting the Rules and Regulations of the Club in all casts relative to Canine and Club matters.

"No alteration or addition may be made to the Rules, Constitution of the Club, or Standard of Points, unless by the sanction of a majority of members present at a Special General Meeting; the intimation of such proposed alteration must be made in writing to the Secretary at least one month before the date of the meeting, due notice of which shall be announced in the circular calling the meeting. Alterations shall not be brought into force until approved by the Kennel Club.

"The Club shall not join any Federation of Societies or Clubs."

It will be seen from all this that the Shetland Sheepdog Club had prepared itself for admission of its breed to championship classes at shows governed by the Kennel Club (England). And it had laid the ground work for the world wide popularity which was to come to the breed.

As was noted in Rev. Oddy's article, an effort had been made to form a Shetland Collie Club at Dundee. Nothing came of this at the time, although the project may have spurred the Shetland Islanders into forming their own club. But in 1909, the Scottish Shetland Collie Club was formed, with C. F. Thompson of Inverness as secretary. Thompson had founded his Inverness Kennels. Graham Clark had set up Ashbank. And Keith and Ramsay had founded Downfield. The club founded its own stud book.

Both clubs ran into immediate opposition at the Kennel Club, and by Collie fanciers. Both decided to retreat to the name Shetland Sheepdog. Thus, in 1910, the Kennel Club invited both clubs to send representatives to the Kennel Club council in London. They did so as the Shetland Sheepdog Club and the Scottish Shetland Sheepdog Club.

The breed was not at that time given official recognition. That came in 1914, the year in which the English Shetland Sheepdog Club was founded with A. C. Shove as secretary. In the meantime, the Kennel Club did accept registrations. There were 48 Shetland Sheepdogs registered in 1910. The breed was listed with such others in the miscellaneous class as Iceland Fox Dogs, Potsdam Greyhounds, Siberian Dogs, Roseneath Terriers, and Welsh Cockers. Maltese Poodles and Cairn Terriers were also listed. The former survives as the Maltese. But of the others, only the Shetland Sheepdog and the Cairn survive.

One of the great encyclopedias of the early part of the century was Sydney Turner's *Kennel Encyclopedia*. It was published in 1910, when Turner was chairman of the Kennel Club (England). James A. Loggie wrote an article for that encyclopedia. Since he was the first fancier of the breed to write about it, we close this chapter by quoting his article in full.

"That the Shetland Sheepdog is a distinct breed no one can deny. It was originally known as the Shetland Collie or Toonie Dog. The dog took its title from the fact of its being used to drive the sheep off the township croft, or what is known in Shetyand as the 'Toon.' Many years ago, when the large sheep farms were established in Shetland, shepherds from the mainland brought with them Scotch Collies, and gave the progeny to the crofters. But in-breeding and the want of keeping up fresh blood soon caused the breed to become diminutive. Few people (who have not visited Shetland) are aware of the conditions of these crofts; very few of them have fences or dykes to protect their crops, or to divide arable land from the hill pasture; and in seasons when the hills are scarce in pasturage, the sheep come down and feed off the stacks of hay and corn in the stockyard, and also eat the turnips and cabbage growing around the house. When this occurs, the dog has a duty to perform, and is used to drive the sheep back into the hills, and need not be accompanied by its master when once it gets the order to go.

"When the dipping season comes around the owners of sheep on hill scattold meet on a given date with their dogs and combine to drive the sheep to the dipping places appointed. This is known locally as 'caaing' or 'driving.'

"The Shetland sheep, although small, are very wild, and they require a good deal of handling to bring them together. They are very agile, and a five foot wall does not deter them from getting out, if they want to.

"The Shetland Crofter grudges keeping a large dog, principally on account of the food it requires, while the smaller one suits his purpose.

"Years ago when Greenland whalers called at Shetland, the men who belonging to those islands who formed a part of the crews, brought with them what was known as the 'Yakkie' dog, called after the natives of Greenland, who are known among the whalers as 'Yaks.' Distinct traces of this dog (which was found useful to the crofters) are still to be found among the Island dogs.

"These Yakkie dogs were bred with the Shetland dogs, and some of the strongest characteristics of the breed are often seen in the present Shetland dog, namely the black muzzle, large prick ears, and heavy brush of a tail, combined with a somewhat foxy appearance.

"The height of these dogs is usually 14 to 17 inches; but fashion, as in several other breeds, nowadays demands that these dogs should be bred smaller. This undoubtedly can be done; but like the building of Rome, cannot be expected in a day. In consequence of this desire for smallness, alien blood has been introduced, and with very unsatisfactory results, which have brought discredit on the native dogs. Fortunately, by the formation of two specialist clubs, the interests of the breed are now being more carefully looked after.

"In breeding, type is of the utmost importance, and Collie character must be kept carefully in view. Meantime, the best and most typical specimens exceed the standard of height which is being tried for; but once type is properly fixed, height and weight may be arrived at. The colours usually met with are Black and white and tan; Black, tan and white; Black, Sable, and Sable and white.

"They are very affectionate and faithful, and no kinder or more lovable dogs exist. They attach themselves readily to children and are never treacherous. They require little food and attention. They are hardy, and can live in outdoor kennels when required to. They are not prolific, having generally litters of about three or four; strange to say, females invariably predominate, being generally two to one. They are fleet and can stand a hard day's running well.

"In 1908, the Shetland Sheepdog Club was formed, followed by the Scottish Shetland Sheepdog Club in 1909. The combined membership is about 150. In 1909, the Kennel Club agreed to recognize the breed and registered the titles of both clubs. The Shetland Sheepdog Club standard of height was 12 inches and weight, 14 pounds, while the Scottish Shetland Sheepdog Club's standard of height was the same, but that of weight of 12 pounds. The clubs have done a great deal to popularize the breed and to stamp out alien blood. Any dog showing signs of Spaniel blood should be carefully barred.

"The Shetland sheep is a very small animal, only about half the size of the Scoth black-faced sheep. It is not, therefore, necessary to have so large a dog to herd and keep them in bounds as is required in the Highlands. The Shetland Sheepdog is purely a crofter's dog, and those who own 10 to 30 sheep will not have any other. Those shepherds, however, who have 30 to 700 black faced ewes have larger dogs."

*—James A. Loggie*

One will find much of a contradictory and confusing nature in this chapter. And one can smile a bit at Loggie's brave words at the beginning of his article. Perhaps he was anticipating a bit when he wrote "That the Shetland Sheepdog is a distinct breed no one can deny." And particularly since he, and other breeders were introducing Collie blood. But what is undeniable is that the breed was on its way. And Loggie and his 150 colleagues made it possible.

Ch. Chisterling Exquisite Dream, owned by Don Combee.

Amer. and Can. Ch. Ilemist Impossible Dream,
C.D.X., owned by Dr. and Mrs. John R. Frazier.

# 5

# First Standards of the Breed

JAMES THOMASON, who also spells his name Thomson, remembers James A. Loggie well. Loggie moved to Australia, but his influence on the Shetland Sheepdog was great. Thomason remembers that there was considerable opposition to some of the methods used by Loggie. Primarily, this involved his breeding methods. Loggie remembered the Rev. Oddy's criticism of the head. And he felt the head could be improved by crossing the Shetland dogs with small Collies.

This he did, and his dogs were improved in head. But they were also larger than the 12 inches at the shoulder mentioned by Rev. Oddy. Loggie's ideas prevailed. But here let us quote Thomason directly.

"Some of his dogs were the very foundation of the breed, such as Lerwick Hakon, Lerwick Jarl, Lerwick Olaf, and Zesta. The latter was a sable and white bitch which was a sensation at Cruft's Show in London in 1913. Had it not been for his efforts, backed by the Lerwick Club, I doubt that the breed as we know it today would have come into existence."

The Shetland Sheepdog Club at Lerwick set up the first full standard of the breed. It did this in 1910, at the time it had decided to yield and change the breed's name from Shetland Collie to Shetland Sheepdog. T. & J. Manson of *The Shetland News* office, printed the standard in booklet form. Through the courtesy of Lorna Irvine Burgess, we are able to print it here.

31

## Standard of Points of the Shetland Sheepdog

1. The SKULL should be as nearly as possible flat, moderately wide between the ears, and gradually tapering towards the eyes. There should only be a slight depression at top (stop? Author). The cheeks should not be full or prominent.

2. The MUZZLE should be of fair length, tapering to the nose, and should not show weakness, or be snippy or lippy. The nose must be black, whatever the colour of the dog may be.

3. The TEETH should be sound, and nearly as possible level. Very slight unevenness is permissible.

4. The JAWS clean cut and powerful.

5. The EYES should be of medium size, set somewhat obliquely and close together, of almond shape, and of brown colour—full of intelligence and expression.

6. The EARS should be small, and moderately wide at the base, and placed fairly close together on top of skull. When in repose they should be thrown back, but when on the alert brought forward and carried semi-erect, with the tips drooping forward.

7. The NECK should be of fair length, somewhat arched, and in proportion to the body.

8. The BODY should be moderately long and level with well-sprung ribs and strong loins; chest deep.

9. The FORELEGS should be straight and muscular, and with a fair amount of bone.

10. The HINDLEGS should be muscular at the thighs, with well-bent hocks.

11. The FEET should be oval in shape, soles well padded, and the toes arched and close together.

12. The TAIL should be moderately long, with abundant hair, carried low when the dog is quiet, with a slight upward swirl at the end, but gaily carried when the dog is excited, but not over the back.

13. The COAT must be double—the outer coat consists of hard hair; the under coat, which resembles fur, is short, soft, and close. The mane and frill should be abundant, the mask or face smooth, as also the tips of the ears. The forelegs well feathered, the hindlegs above the hocks profusely covered with hair, but below the hocks fairly smooth.

14. Any COLOUR except brindle is permissible.

15. The GENERAL APPEARANCE of the Shetland Sheep-Dog is that of the rough-coated Scotch Collie in miniature (Collie character and type must be adhered to). The height of the Shetland Sheep-Dog shall not exceed 15 inches at maturity, which is fixed at 10 months old.

*Faults*

Short nose; domed skull; large drooping ears; weak jaws, snippy muzzle; full or light eyes; crooked forelegs; cow hocks; tail carried over the back; under or over-shot mouth.

Head and Expression ..................................... 15
Ears ................................................... 15
Neck and Shoulders ....................................... 5
Legs and Feet .......................................... 10
Hind Quarters .......................................... 10
Back and Loins ........................................... 5
Tail ................................................... 10
Coat and Frill ......................................... 15
Size ................................................... 15
                                                        ———

                                                        100

Let us compare this with the Collie standard of 1907:

"Height of dogs, 21 to 24 inches; bitches, 19 to 21 inches; measured at the shoulder. Colors: sable; black and tan; black, tan and white; blue or red merle; other colors permitted provided the dog has Collie characteristics. General appearance: A strongly made dog with a fair amount of bone, built on racing lines, lithe and active. The expression highly intelligent, the eyes small (slightly almond shaped) and dark in color.

"The head rather long, without being exaggerated; flat on the skull; the muzzle fine, and tapering gradually to the nose, and well filled in—not falling away—under the eyes. The ears set on high, and should be very small. They should be carried semi-erect, with the tips inclining forward when the dog's attention is attracted and thrown back on the hair of the neck when running. The teeth should be sound and strong, and the mouth level. An over-shot or under-shot mouth is a bad fault.

"Some Collies are 'wall' or 'China' eyed. This is more often found in the blue merle dog; it is quite correct and gives a particularly pleasing expression." (Such dogs are often preferred by some old shepherds who hold to the superstition that a 'wall-eyed dog never loses its sight when he gets old). The body should be of moderate length, well ribbed up; back, strong; chest, deep; neck, long, and shoulders fine. The forelegs should be straight, with plenty of bone; the feet oval in shape with hard, strong pads; hind legs strong; the stifle joints should be well bent with the hocks let down.

"The coat is of the utmost importance as the dog has to endure all kinds of weather—snow storms, rain and gales, and the Scotch mists so prevalent in the Highlands. The outer coat should be of coarse hair, very abundant, dense, and straight. The under coat should be short, soft, and lie close to the skin. The frill around the neck should be very full and profuse, and extend to behind the shoulders. The back of the forelegs should be well feathered, but the hind legs should be free from feather. The brush should be shaped like that of a fox; but it is more fully coated. It should be carried down, reaching to within

33

a few inches of the ground, and never carried curled over the back. When the dog is excited, however, it may be carried slightly higher than usual."

The principal faults were listed as large ears, prick ears, ears set too low and carried down; thick, coarse head; large, full eyes; weakness in body properties generally; forelegs out at elbow; curly or soft coat, or a thin, open coat; lack of undercoat; over-shot mouth or under-shot; brush carried over the back, or possessing a kink; and cow hocks.

This, then, is a description of the dog which served as a model for the Shetland Sheepdog. It is noteworthy that, at least at that time, wall or blue eyes were permitted in all colors, and that some even preferred this color. The accent on coat was a major part of the Collie, which had to face the gales of the Scotch Highlands. And the little Shelties had to face even worse storms, and nearly constant gale winds. It is no wonder that the early standards thus specified a Collie coat.

Now let us return to the Scottish Shetland Sheepdog Club. Upon its organization in 1909, it had some 40 members. And they had their own ideas as to what a Shetland Collie should be. Their club standard called for a dog which is in appearance, an ordinary Collie in miniature; height about 12 inches; weight 10 to 14 pounds.

These were, of course, frustratingly vague requirements. They inevitably stimulated controversies. What is an ordinary Collie? Is it a run-of-the-mill farm dog, a moderately successful show winner, or a champion? Does "about 12 inches" permit a dog to be only fractions of an inch away from 12 inches? Could one be only 10 inches, or another 15? Moreover, the Scottish Club split the breed into rough coated and smooth coated varieties.

In 1913, the Scottish Club altered the standard to make "12 inches ideal." But this only added to the problem. How tall or how small should a dog be before it is penalized for being too far from the ideal? These questions are not lightly asked here, nor were they in 1913. And they continue to frustrate breeders and judges alike in other breeds. For example, the present Pug standard says: "Weight from 14 to 18 pounds (dog or bitch) desirable." One Pug champion was officially measured at 26 pounds.

In 1914, the English Shetland Sheepdog Club was founded with A. C. Shove as secretary. The following year, Miss J. Wilkinson, a great breed pioneer, became secretary. The English club also had the concept of a small Collie in mind. Its standard read:

"The general appearance of the Shetland Sheepdog is approximately that of the Show Collie in miniature." And again, 12 inches was given as the "ideal height."

That word "approximately" was to cause bitter argument for more

than a decade. It was one reason for the formation of a second English club, the British Shetland Sheepdog Breeders' Association. This club, though active and successful for a time, did not survive. Most of the members finally returned to the original club.

It was argued that "approximately" means only similar. But many breeders wanted an exact Collie in miniature. Others argued that an exact Collie in miniature was impossible. Still others argued against the fineness of the Collie head. Some wanted only a superior working dog which would resemble a Collie.

At the time the English Club was being formed, the Scottish Club altered its standard to make it more specific in some points. It now stated:

> "Appearance: That of the modern Show Collie in miniature (Collie type and character MUST BE ADHERED TO). Ideal height, 12 inches at maturity, which is fixed at 10 months of age."

The attempt to produce a smooth coated Shetland Sheepdog was also abandoned. Since 1914, there has been no such thing as a smooth coated Shetland Sheepdog.

Even as late as 1914, attempts were made to call the breed the Shetland Collie. The insistence of breeders that the Sheltie be a Collie in miniature was perhaps an adequate reason. And the dog really did do the work of the Collie. But all attempts failed. The breed was, at times, classified as a toy dog. But later it was placed where it belonged, in the working group. Today, Shetland Sheepdog breeders object just as strenuously to the still used "Toy Collie" as Collie breeders once did to "Shetland Collie."

SKULL flat, no prominence at occiput; cheeks flat merging smoothly into well-rounded muzzle; skull and muzzle of equal length (balance point inner corner of eye); topline of skull parallels topline of muzzle

EYES set somewhat obliquely; size medium; dark; almond-shaped rims; blue or merle eyes permissible in blue merles only

NOSE black

STOP slight but definite

FOREQUARTERS: shoulders slope 45-degree angle forward and downward to joint; at withers separated only by vertebra, sloping outward for rib spring; upper arm joins blade at approx. right angle; elbow joint equidistant from ground and from withers

CHEST deep; brisket reaches to point of elbow

FORELEGS straight from all angles, muscular, clean; bone strong; well-feathered

BODY moderately long, sturdy, all parts in proportion to whole

FEET oval, compact; toes well-arched, fitting tightly together; pads deep, tough; nails hard, strong

COLOR black, blue merle, sable (golden through mahogany): marked with varying amounts of white and/or tan

DISQUALIFICATIONS: Heights below or above specified range— 13 to 16″. Brindle color

HEAD refined: viewed from top or side, long, blunt-wedged tapering from ears to nose; jaws clean, powerful: underjaw deep, well-developed, rounded at chin and extending to base of nostril; lips tight-fitting all around; teeth level, evenly spaced; scissors bite

EARS small, flexible, placed high: carried ¾ths erect, tips breaking forward: in repose ears fold lengthwise, thrown back into frill

NECK muscular, arched, of sufficient length to carry head proudly

BACK short, level, strongly muscled

TAIL—last vertebra should reach hock joint; carriage at rest straight down or, slight upward curve: when alert, lifted but not over back: hair profuse

HINDQUARTERS slight arch at loins: croup—gradual slope to rear: hipbone (pelvis) set at 30-degree angle to spine; thighs broad, muscular; thighbone set at angle corresponding to shoulder blade and upper arm; hind legs heavily feathered

STIFLES distinctly angulated: length equals or exceeds thighbones

HOCK clean-cut, angular, sinewy; bone good; strong ligamentation: no feather below joint

METATARSUS short, straight viewed from all angles; dewclaws removed: hair smooth below joint

COAT: outer coat of long hair; straight, harsh; undercoat short, furry, so dense it gives "stand-off" quality; hair on face, ear tips and feet smooth; mane, frill abundant

RIBS well-sprung, flattened at lower half for free play of foreleg, shoulder

TUCK-UP moderate

PASTERNS strong, sinewy, flexible; dewclaws may be removed

SIZE—at Shoulder, 13 to 16″; neither under nor over

# 6

# Modern Breed Standards

---

IN the preceding chapter, we discussed the problems faced by breeders, both in establishing a breed and in developing a workable standard for it. Now the Shetland Sheepdog is well established as one of the world's most popular breeds. Since it has spread around the world, breeders have developed in each country. Conditions vary from country to country, and so do the ideas of the breeders. But the standards which they adopt are quite similar.

We are chiefly interested in the Shetland Sheepdog in North America— in the United States and Canada. Since the standards are almost identical, we are printing in full the American standard. But we are adding some information on those of England and Australia. The present American standard was approved by the American Kennel Club May 12, 1959; the Canadian standard in 1962.

When the Canadian standard was approved, it called for the disqualification of any male over 12 months of age which had neither, or only one, testicle descended into the scrotum. Canada later passed a general rule to conform to the American rule which disqualifies a monorchid or cryptorchid at any age.

Perhaps we should be more specific in this. Correct medical terminology calls a dog with only one testicle descended into the scrotum a unilateral cryptorchid. If neither has descended, the condition is called bilateral cryptorchid. But dog people usually speak of monorchid (one testicle descended) or cryptorchid (neither descended). The Australian standard does not mention the condition.

37

The English and Australian standards state that the ideal height for a male is 14½ inches, and for a bitch, 14 inches. The Australian standard adds that "anything more than one inch above these heights shall be considered a serious fault." The British standard also lists a weight of nine to 16 pounds. It is noteworthy that the Australian standard ignores seriously undersized dogs. It is considered only a serious fault for dogs to be over 15½ inches and bitches over 15.

In the United States and Canada, brindle color brings disqualification. It is permitted in England and Australia, even though serious breeders might frown upon it. The Americans and Canadians are also much opposed to the so-called degenerate colors, such as pale sable and faded blue, and self color in blue merles. They also severely penalize dogs with more than 50 per cent white body color. Other kennel clubs are less particular.

These points are worthy of note because Americans and Canadians import dogs from many parts of the world. They have always imported from the British Isles. But occasionally dogs are imported from Australia or New Zealand, or from continental Europe. It should also be remembered that Great Britain has now relaxed the rule which formerly disqualified monorchids. North Americans must, therefore, be very careful not to import such a dog. It might be a great winner in England, yet be disqualified and condemned for breeding in the United States and Canada.

Here is the American standard:

**Preamble**—The Shetland Sheepdog, like the Collie, traces to the Border Collie of Scotland, which, transported to the Shetland Islands and crossed with small, intelligent, longhaired breeds, was reduced to miniature proportions. Subsequently crosses were made from time to time with Collies. This breed now bears the same relationship in size and general appearance to the Rough Collie as the Shetland pony does to some of the larger breeds of horses. Although the resemblance between the Shetland Sheepdog and the Rough Collie is marked, there are differences which may be noted.

**General Description**—The Shetland Sheepdog is a small, alert, rough coated, longhaired working dog. He must be sound, agile and sturdy. The outline should be so symmetrical that no part appears out of proportion to the whole. Dogs should appear masculine; bitches feminine.

**Size**—The Shetland Sheepdog should stand between 13 and 16 inches at the shoulder. Note: Height is determined by a line perpendicular to the ground from the top of the shoulder blades, the dog standing naturally with forelegs parallel to line of measurement. **Disqualification**—Heights below or above the desired size range are to be disqualified from the show ring.

**Coat**—The coat should be double, the outer coat consisting of long, straight, harsh hair; the undercoat short, furry, and so dense as to give the entire coat its "stand-off" quality. The hair on face, tips of ears and feet should be smooth. Mane and frill should be abundant, and particularly impressive in males. The forelegs well feathered, the hind legs heavily so, but smooth below the hock joint. Hair on tail profuse. Note: Excess hair on ears, feet, and on hocks may be trimmed for the show ring. **Faults**—Coat short or flat, in whole or in part; wavy, curly, soft or silky. Lack of undercoat. Smooth coated specimens.

**Color**—Black, blue merle, and sable (ranging from golden through mahogany); marked with varying amounts of white and/or tan. **Faults**—Rustiness in a black or a blue coat. Washed out or degenerate colors, such as pale sable and faded blue. Self-color in the case of blue merle, that is, without any merling or mottling and generally appearing as a faded or dilute tri-color. Conspicuous white body spots. Specimens with more than 50 per cent white shall be severely penalized as to effectively eliminate them from competition. **Disqualification**—Brindle.

**Temperament**—The Shetland Sheepdog is intensely loyal, affectionate, and responsive to his owner. However, he may be reserved toward strangers but not to the point of showing fear or cringing in the ring. **Faults**—Shyness, timidity, or nervousness. Stubbornness, snappiness, or ill temper.

**Head**—The head should be refined and its shape, when viewed from top or side, be a long, blunt wedge tapering slightly from ears to nose, which must be black. **Skull and Muzzle**—Top of skull should be flat, showing no prominence at nuchal crest (the top of the occiput). Cheeks should be flat and should merge smoothly into a well-rounded muzzle. Skull and muzzle should be of equal length, balance point being inner corner of eye. In profile, the top line of skull should parallel the top line of muzzle, but on a higher plane due to the presence of a slight but definite stop. Jaws clean and powerful. The deep, well-developed under-jaw, rounded at chin, should extend to base of nostril. Lips, tight. Upper and lower lips must meet and fit smoothly together all the way around. Teeth level and evenly spaced. Scissors bite. **Faults**—Two angled head. Too prominent stop, or no stop. Overfill below, between, or above eyes. Prominent nuchal crest. Domed skull. Prominent cheekbones. Snipy muzzle. Short, receding, or shallow under-jaw, lacking breadth and depth. Overshot or undershot, missing or crooked teeth. Teeth visible when mouth is closed.

**Eyes**—Medium size with dark, almond-shaped rims, set somewhat obliquely in skull. Color must be dark, with blue or merle eyes permissible in blue merles only. **Faults**—Light, round, large or too small. Prominent haws.

**Ears**—Small and flexible, placed high, carried three-fourths erect, with tips breaking forward. When in repose the ears fold lengthwise and are

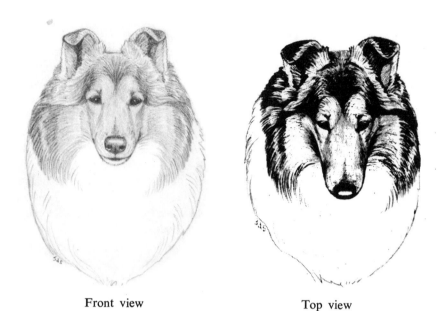

Front view              Top view

Profile

Drawings in this chapter—illustrating correct and poor heads, shoulder angulation, hindquarters, single-tracking and trot—are by the noted artist, Jean D. Simmonds.

Broad, round backskull combined with short muzzle, giving "Pomeranian" appearance. Ears set too wide on skull, eyes full. Lacking underjaw.

Snipey muzzle. Coarse, heavy cheekbones. Ears too large. Shallow underjaw.

High nuchal crest (occiput). Incorrect break to ears. Eye too small causing beady look.

thrown back into the frill. **Faults**—Set too low. Hound, prick, bat, twisted ears. Leather too thick or too thin.

**Expression**—Contours and chiseling of the head, the shape, set and use of ears, the placement, shape and color of the eyes, combine to produce expression. Normally the expression should be alert, gentle, intelligent and questioning. Toward strangers the eyes should show watchfulness and reserve, but no fear.

**Neck**—Neck should be muscular, arched, and of sufficient length to carry the head proudly. **Faults**—Too short and thick.

**Body**—In over-all appearance the body should appear moderately long as measured from shoulder joint to ischium (rearmost extremity of the pelvic bone), but much of this length is actually due to the proper angulation and breadth of the shoulder and hindquarter, as the back itself should be comparatively short. Back should be level and strongly muscled. Chest should be deep, the brisket reaching to the point of elbow. The ribs should be well sprung, but flattened at their lower half to allow free play of the foreleg and shoulder. Abdomen moderately tucked up. **Faults**—Back too long, too short, swayed or roached. Barrel ribs. Slab side. Chest narrow and/or too shallow.

**Forequarters**—From the withers the shoulder blades should slope at a 45-degree angle forward and downward to the shoulder joints. At the withers they are separated only by the vertebra, but they must slope outward sufficiently to accommodate the desired spring of rib. The upper arm should join the shoulder blade at as nearly as possible a right angle. Elbow joint should be equidistant from the ground or from the withers. Forelegs straight, viewed from all angles, muscular and clean, and of strong bone. Pasterns very strong, sinewy and flexible. Dewclaws may be removed. **Faults**—Insufficient angulation between shoulder and upper arm. Upper arm too short. Lack of outward slope of shoulders. Loose shoulders. Turning in or out of elbows. Crooked legs. Light bone.

**Feet (front and hind)**—Feet should be oval and compact with toes well arched and fitting tightly together. Pads deep and tough, nails hard and strong. **Faults**—Feet turning in or out. Splay-feet. Hare-feet. Cat-feet.

**Hindquarters**—There should be a slight arch at the loins, and the croup should slope gradually to the rear. The hipbone (pelvis) should be set at a 30-degree angle to the spine. The thigh should be broad and muscular. The thighbone should be set into the pelvis at a right angle corresponding to the angle of the shoulder blade and upper arm. Stifle bones join the thighbone and should be distinctly angled at the stifle joint. The over-all length of the stifle should at least equal the length of the thighbone, and preferably should slightly exceed it. Hock joint should be clean-cut, angular, sinewy, with good bone and strong ligamentation. The hock (metatarsus) should be short and straight, viewed from all angles. Dewclaws should be removed. Feet (see forequarters). **Faults**—Croup higher than

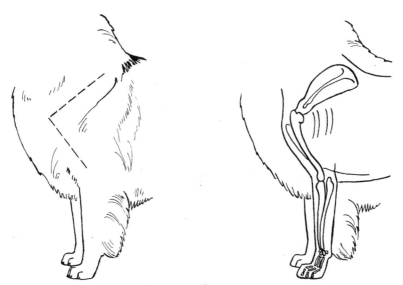

Correct: proper bone proportions and strong, straight legs.

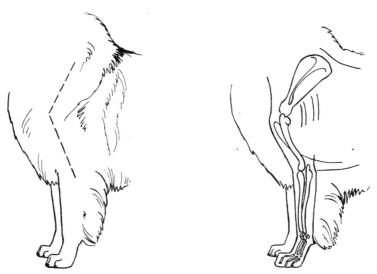

Poor: upper arm too short, shallow chest, weak pasterns.

withers. Croup too straight or too steep. Narrow thighs. Cowhocks. Hocks turning out. Poorly defined hock joint. Feet (*see* Forequarters).

**Tail**—The tail should be sufficiently long so that when it is laid along the back edge of the hind legs, the last vertebra will reach the hock joint. Carriage of tail at rest is straight down or in a slight upward curve. When the dog is alert the tail is normally lifted, but it should not be curved forward over the back. **Faults**—Too short. Twisted at end.

**Gait**—The trotting gait of the Shetland Sheepdog should denote effortless speed and smoothness. There should be no jerkiness, nor stiff, up-and-down movement. The drive should be from the rear, true and straight, dependent upon correct angulation, musculation and ligamentation of the entire hindquarter, thus allowing the dog to reach well under his body with his hind foot and propel himself forward. Reach of stride of the foreleg is dependent upon correct angulation, musculation, and ligamentation of the forequarters, together with correct width of chest and construction of rib cage. The foot should be lifted only enough to clear the ground as the leg swings forward. Viewed from the front, both forelegs and hind legs should move forward almost perpendicular to the ground at the walk, slanting a little inward at a slow trot, until at a swift trot the feet are brought so far inward toward center line of body that the tracks left show two parallel lines of footprints actually touching a center line at their inner edges. There should be no crossing of the feet nor throwing of the weight from side to side. **Faults**—Stiff, short steps, with a choppy, jerky movement. Mincing steps, with a hopping up and down, or a balancing of weight from side to side (often erroneously admired as a "dancing gait" but permissible in young puppies). Lifting of front feet in hackney-like action, resulting in loss of speed and energy. Pacing gait.

### SCALE OF POINTS

*General Appearance*
Symmetry . . . . . . . . . . . . . 10
Temperament . . . . . . . . . 10
Coat . . . . . . . . . . . . . . . . 5  25

*Head*
Skull and stop . . . . . . . . 5
Muzzle . . . . . . . . . . . . . . 5
Eyes, ears, expression . . . 10  20

*Body*
Neck and back . . . . . . . . 5
Chest, ribs, brisket . . . . . . 10
Loin, croup, tail . . . . . . . 5  20

*Forequarters*
Shoulder . . . . . . . . . . . . 10
Forelegs and feet . . . . . . 5  15

*Hindquarters*
Hip, thigh, stifle . . . . . . . . 10
Hocks and feet . . . . . . . 5  15

*Gait*
Gait—Smoothness and lack
of waste motion when
trotting . . . . . . . . . . . . . . 5  5
     TOTAL . . . . . . . . . 100

44

Correct hindquarters and tail. Proper leg angulation.

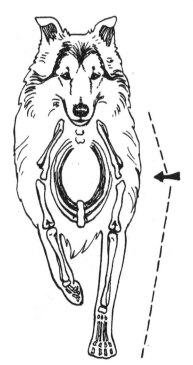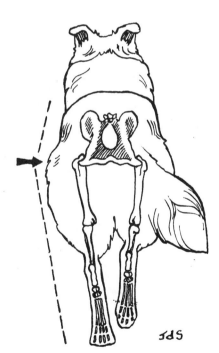

Correct position of singletracking, showing where proper break occurs. Legs are straight from breaking point to ground and are moving in direct line of travel.

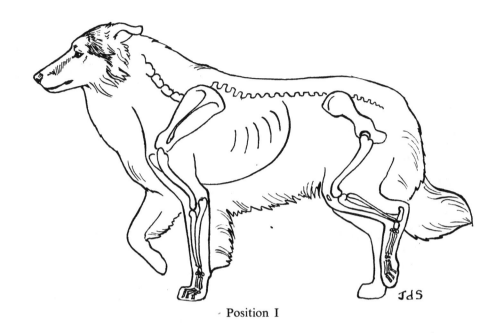

Position I

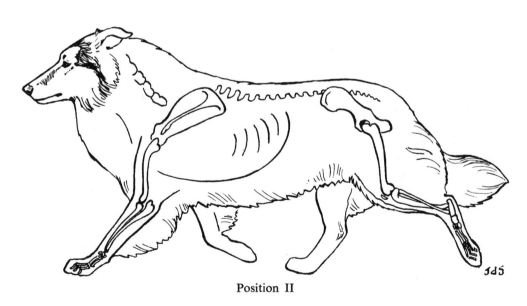

Position II

The correct trot: side view. Feet are lifted just enough to clear the ground. Free flowing movement, with no apparent effort. Full reach of front, strong drive to rear.

46

*Heights below or above the desired range, i.e., 13–16 inches. Brindle color.*

*Approved by the American Kennel Club May 12, 1959.*

Those who check this standard against the Collie standard of 1908 will note many similarities. Apart from size, the modern Shetland Sheepdog standard is vastly more complicated. It also includes a "scale of points." Most breed clubs seem unable to eliminate such scales of points.

Yet dogs cannot be judged by mathematics. Those who have tried have usually made such a mess of it that exhibitors have been left screaming. Some standards have included a scale, but have warned that this is meant only to be a guide to the importance of the various parts of the dogs. In 1907, William Stephens, a Collie author and judge, remarked: "The judging or selection of Collies, or, for a matter of that, any other breed, by points, is not satisfactory."

Whether the Shetland Sheepdog scale of points has any value is open to question. A common complaint is that some judges concentrate upon finding good heads, and ignore rear ends and gait. Such judges are called "head hunters." It can be argued that the scale allows only 20 points for the entire head, and only 10 for eyes, ears, and expression. If one divides the 10 into equal parts, then the ears would get three and a third points. Yet most judges would prefer to be shot rather than to give a winners ribbon to a prick eared dog.

On the other hand, the so-called head hunter might argue that only five points are allowed for hocks and hindfeet. A dog might have flat feet and cow hocks, and yet only five points could be taken off the score.

Temperament is a problem in Shetland Sheepdogs as it is in most breeds. The standard is reasonably clear on temperament, and states that the dog should not show fear or cringe in the ring. But the scale of points allows only 10 points for this. One wonders if such dogs should be given ribbons.

In the previous chapter, we noted that controversy has always accompanied the formation of breed standards, as well as their later interpretation. In the case of the Shetland Sheepdog, there has been more controversy than with most breeds. A major modern point of argument has concerned size.

In the Shetland Islands, small size was important. The islands are poor, and have had increasingly difficult economic problems since about 1925. Sheep raising has diminished, and has tended to show lesser profits. So

47

it was important to keep the dogs small. This was less true in other parts of Scotland and in England.

When brought to the United States and Canada, many dog breeds have tended to grow larger. Some have returned to parental size after a generation or two. Shetland Sheepdogs also tended to grow larger in North America. But because of the frequent early crosses with the larger Collies, they did not return to a smaller size.

The size controversy strongly erupted after World War II. The American Shetland Sheepdog Association wanted to alter the standard in many ways. It asked among other things for a height disqualification, both a minimum and a maximum. But at that time, the American Kennel Club opposed such disqualifications.

Moreover, Shetland Sheepdog breeders and owners were not unanimous on the issue. Naturally, breeders who had dogs which were over 16 inches, or under 13 inches, were opposed to any standard change which would disqualify their dogs. About 72 per cent of the members of the American Shetland Sheepdog Association favored the disqualifying clause.

At that time, the secretary of the association was A. R. (Ray) Miller of Scarsdale, N.Y. Robert W. Orr was president, and Dorothy Allen Foster was vice president. They led the battle for the disqualifying clause. So did Walter G. Miller of Bremerton, Wash.

Mr. A. Hamilton Rowan, secretary of the American Kennel Club, has supplied the writer with copies of the correspondence on the subject. The AKC had rejected the size disqualification in the proposed new standard. Walter Miller, acting as a private breeder, strongly protested. His arguments were among those which eventually brought approval.

On June 12, 1951, Walter Miller wrote to John C. Neff, executive vice president of the American Kennel Club, in response to an AKC decision disapproving the height disqualification clause in the proposed standard. Here are some pertinent quotes from Mr. Miller's letter:

"I will admit that it may be easier to get collie type in head and coat in the large Sheltie than in the small one. But who wants collie head type or runt collies? Or who wants all the collie weaknesses, including bad heads, weak jaws, cow hocks, and poor feet that our breed has inherited from the collie crosses, both declared and otherwise? These things all throw back in the large dog, as well as a lack of brains and working ability.

"We wish to breed a small dog 15 inches or under that can really work, and wish to have a standard of such a nature that we can breed this type for working and still enter the conformation shows with a chance of winning under judges who will consider soundness and type over lean skulls and draping coats of little practical value in bad weather.

"This is what we wish to get away from, the degeneration of our breed into a pretty toy that is useful only as a pet or bench show

48

dog. If we don't keep the size down and breed for soundness, that is what we will get.

"There is a little Sheltie down in Colorado, under 16 inches, who is the lifetime champion sheep dog of the state of Colorado. These are not AKC sponsored shows, but are contests promoted by sheep and livestock men who think their dogs are best and are willing to wager on them."

On June 28, 1951, Mr. Neff answered. We give excerpts from that letter.

"You present a very strong case for your contentions on size. This matter is never closed, Mr. Miller. If the American Shetland Sheepdog Association wishes to re-submit the Standard to us and support it with a presentation such as you make, I assure you that it would not be automatically disregarded on the theory that it was once examined . . .

"Our board would not quarrel with extremely emphatic language as to height, just so long as it did not require actual disqualification of the dog. I think I may have made that clear in the letter which I wrote to the club. The administration of disqualifying faults is an extremely difficult one and it is the judgment of our Board that a Standard which calls for extremely severe penalties is ever so much more desirable than one which calls for outright disqualification.

"That does not apply in all cases. That is to say, our Board would never say that there should be no such thing as a disqualification in a Breed standard. It does look with real disfavor on a Standard which includes disqualification for more than a certain percentage of a certain color in coat, and it looks with considerable disfavor on a disqualification for height or weight alone. It is their view that severe penalties prescribed for variations from the ideal height should do more for the improvement of a breed than a mandatory disqualification which could be applied to an outstanding specimen which was measured out of the breed by so little as one-half inch.

"If the parent club can convince our Board that its general viewpoint on this matter is erroneous, I assure you that nobody would be disposed to be adamant."

Controversy? There you have it. Collie breeders were joining the ranks of Sheltie breeders. They had their own ideas. They certainly would not agree on the question of Collie brains. But, as Mr. Miller indicates, there were "head hunters" among both Collie breeders and judges.

The proposed standard had asked for a disqualification for dogs with 50 per cent or more of white. This, along with the size disqualification, had been rejected by the American Kennel Club.

Following the Miller letter, the American Shetland Sheepdog Association conducted a winning battle for a size disqualification. In doing so, it paved the way for other breeds which have since placed height disqualifications in their standards.

But the battle against white color was at least partially lost. The AKC suggestion of a severe penalty was placed in the standard. This penalty has not only prevented predominantly white or heavily white spotted dogs from winning, it has also prevented the development of a white Shetland Sheepdog. The height and color provisions were included in the standard approved in March, 1952.

Ch. Apache of Karelane, owned by Shanteroo Shelties.

# 7

# Recognition of the Breed

As early as 1910, the Kennel Club of England accepted registrations of Shetland Sheepdogs even though formal breed status had not been granted. There were 48 registrations, but the pedigrees were not published. We find no registrations for 1911 and 1912. In 1913, Miss Beryle Thynne registered a black, tan, and white dog, Kilravock Laddie. He was whelped May 26, 1911 at C. F. Thompson's Inverness Kennel, a son of Inverness Yarrow and Inverness Topsy.

The English Shetland Sheepdog Club was founded in 1914, and in December of that year, the Kennel Club granted full breed status for Shelties. There were 64 dogs registered, and five were exhibited, although before any challenge classes were available. All five were owned by Miss Thynne. The English Shetland Sheepdog Club standard differed from those of the earlier clubs and this is discussed in a separate chapter. What is important here is that the breed was now sufficiently advanced for recognition by the English Kennel Club.

While recognition had not previously been granted, still the Kennel Club had registered a number of kennels of breeders of Shetland Sheepdogs. These included Lerwick, owned by J. A. Loggie of Shetland; Ashbank, registered by Graham Clark; Downfield, owned by Mrs. J. C. Ramsay of Dundee, Scotland; and C. F. Thompson's Inverness Kennels. Also, during 1914, Miss Beryl Thynne registered Kilravock, and the Misses Grey and Hill were given the name of Greyhill. The following year, Miss E. P. Humphries registered Mountfort. And in 1917, Miss D. Macdougal Currie registered Bonheur.

51

Miss Currie's kennel was the last to be registered before shows were halted until the end of World War I. During the remainder of the war, breeding was by special license only. Three kennels which did keep going were Kilravock, Greyhill, and Mountfort. That the breed survived is probably due to the dedication of these three kennels and their owners. When the war ended, the kennels had managed to save the foundation stock of the breed. They were able to augment their basic stock with dogs they discovered by scouring the Shetland Islands, Scotland and, to some extent, England.

If we could label a single dog as the foundation sire of the breed, it would have to be J. A. Loggie's Lerwick Jarl. He lived too early to have won a championship, but he was the grandsire of the breed's first two champions. Both won their titles just before shows were ended in 1917. Previous breed histories have credited Miss Beryl Thynne's Ch. Woodvold as being the first champion. Our own research indicates that the honor should belong to Ch. Clifford Pat.

During 1915, Clifford Pat, owned by the Misses E. Dawson and J. Wilkinson, won challenge certificates at Cruft's, Richmond and Kensington. Woodvold won challenge certificates at Ladies Kennel Association and Westminster in England. He did not win a third until Southend-on-Sea in 1916 when he again won at Cruft's.

Clifford Pat was born April 22, 1914. His breeder was W. Barnard. His sire was Clifford Sharper, a son of Lerwick Jarl. Woodvold's sire, Crichton Olaf, was also a son of Lerwick Jarl. Woodvold was bred by Keith and Ramsay, and he was whelped June 21, 1913. Frea, also a challenge certificate winner of 1915 owned by Mrs. B. Huband, was sired by Lerwick Jarl. Other challenge certificate winners of 1915 were Brittania of Kilravock, owned by Miss Thynne; Phoebe of Pix Hall, owned by the Misses Dawson and Wilkinson; Piggy, Misses Dawson and Wilkinson; and Shadforth Bretta, G. W. Hoggan.

Before shows ended in 1917, C. W. Higley's Taybank Uradale won a challenge certificate at Cruft's, as did Nada, The Lily of Kilravock. The latter was sired by Ch. Woodvold, but the former by an unregistered dog. That year, only 17 Shetland Sheepdogs were registered, and only three were in 1918. The following year, there were 22 registrations.

By 1920, shows were once again well established, and the Shetland Sheepdog had managed to survive. Still, their numbers were few. During that year, Walesby Select won challenge certificates at Kensington and Crystal Palace. Four others won one each. They were Brenda, Starling, Foss, and Hurly Burly, the latter owned by Miss Grey.

Then in 1921, Walesby Select became the first post-war Shetland Sheepdog champion. He won a third challenge certificate at Cruft's, under judge H. Ainscough. His breeder was E. H. Phillips, and he was owned jointly by Phillips and Miss Beryl Thynne. He was by Kilravock Laddie, out

Nutkin of Houghton Hill.
*Ralph Robinson, Redhill*

Ch. Downfield Olaf of Walnut Hall.

Ch. Helensdale Myrtle, owned by
Mrs. H. W. Nichols, Jr.     *Brown*

Ch. Nicholas of Exford.

Ch. Eltham Park Ena, owned by Miss Fredericka Fry.

Ch. Wee Laird O'Downfield.

of Shadforth Bretta, a 1915 challenge certificate winner that had once beaten Ch. Clifford Pat for best of breed. Ch. Walesby Select was sold to America. He has left little impression on the breed in either country.

Because their kennels made lasting contributions to the breed on both sides of the Atlantic, we are listing some of them.

| | | | |
|---|---|---|---|
| Cameliard | Mrs. Allen and Miss P. M. Allen (later Mrs. Nicholson) | Helensdale | James G. Saunders |
| Clerwood | Dr. Margaret C. Tod | Houghton Hill | Mrs. Baker |
| Dryfesdale | E. Watt | Larkbeare | Clara Bowring |
| | | Netherkeir | A. Watt |
| Eltham Park | E. C. Pierce | Riverhill | The Misses Rogers |
| Exford | Mrs. Sangster (daughter of Mrs. Baker) | from Shiel | Margaret Osborne |

Mrs. Baker's Houghton Hill Kennels made major contributions to the breed for 30 years. Riverhills bred for nearly as long. The influence of Eltham Park on Shetland Sheepdogs in America is beyond computation. Mrs. Sangster, previously Mrs. Geddes, backed up her mother's kennels most successfully. Miss Osborne's "from Shiel" was registered in 1936. Her kennels are world famous. Moreover, she is the author of the excellent English breed book, *The Popular Shetland Sheepdog.* Miss D. Macdougal Currie was for some years secretary of the English Shetland Sheepdog Club.

Ch. Tiny Honey of Walnut Hall.

Tiny Nola of Walnut Hall, owned by Mrs. H. W. Nichols, Jr.

*Brown*

Ch. Farburn Captain, owned by Catherine Coleman Moore.

# 8

# The Shetland Sheepdog
# Comes to America

N O ONE knows when the first Shetland Sheepdogs reached America. Visitors to the Shetland Islands might have brought home "Shetland Collies" as pets long before the breed became fully established in either the Shetland Islands or in Northern Scotland. Such dogs would have left no impression in North America. Since so many Shetlanders immigrated to Canada rather than to the United States, it is likely that the first such dogs came to Canada.

John G. Sherman Jr. of New Rochelle, New York, and who had an office on W. 24th St. in New York City, was the first to import registered dogs. His father had been the chief steward on a passenger ship sailing between Lerwick, Shetland and Aberdeen, Scotland. Later, he managed the Queens Hotel in Lerwick.

Lerwick records show that the younger Sherman imported two dogs. One was Lord Scott, bred by A. Stephen of Aston Villa, Scalloway, Shetland. Lord Scott, erroneously listed as a bitch, was No. 61 in the stud book. He was whelped Feb. 11, 1905, by Carlo, out of Daisy by Hero, and he was a pure golden sable.

The second was Lerwick Bess, bred by J. H. Hunter but owned by James A. Loggie. Bess was whelped Sept. 8, 1908, a sable and white by Trim, out of Cary II by Winkie, No. 35 in the stud book. Lord Scott was sold to E. H. McChesney, who registered him in the AKC stud book.

Ch. Beech Tree Corporal. *Jones*

Ch. Sheltieland Laird O'Page's Hill. *Brown*

58

Sherman bred Lerwick Bess to Lord Scott, and from this litter Mrs. K. D. McMurrich of Knaelcrest Kennels, Manotto, N. Y., registered Shetland Rose. The imports came over in 1910, and all three were registered in 1911. Sherman requested, and was given, permission to offer "The Shetland Sheepdog Club's American Challenge Cup" to be won three times by a dog or bitch for permanent possession. Lerwick Rex apparently won this trophy.

In 1912, eight dogs were registered, and four of these were direct imports. Since the breed was still young, the record of these is remarkable.

Alderbourne Kennels in England have been world famous for nearly three quarters of a century. The author's father imported "two Pekingese Spaniels" from Alderbourne in 1906. And while Alderbourne is still noted primarily as a Pekingese kennel, it has had other breeds. Thus, Mrs. Ashton Cross of this kennel sent two Shetland Sheepdogs to the United States in 1911 or 1912. They were registered in 1912.

They were Jack McEwen, a black and tan, whelped April 9, 1910, and Sandy McPherson, a fawn and white, born Feb. 28, 1910. Both dogs were pure Alderbourne breeding, which indicates that this kennel had been interested in Shelties for several canine generations at least.

By far the most famous of the dogs of 1912 was Lerwick Rex. J. G. Sherman imported him. He was by Berry out of Bee, and was bred by a Mr. Henderson of Lerwick, Shetland. He was whelped Mar. 26. 1910, and was black and white. Sherman also imported Scalloway Belle. Belle was whelped May 22, 1910. She was bred by William A. Low of Shetland, and was by Trim out of Asta Flo.

These dogs were used extensively for breeding. Kenneth McMurrich had bought Shetland Rose for his wife. Rose was bred to Lerwick Rex, and she produced Lerwick Spot, Chucky, and Sheltie. Mrs. T. D. McChesney bred Scalloway Belle to Lerwick Rex and got Lerwick Belle. Meanwhile, Mrs. W. F. Parker of Meriden, Conn. had brought over Sable. She was bred by W. H. Wilkinson of Shetland, and was a sable and white whelped Oct. 23, 1909.

That year, 1912, Shetland Sheepdogs were shown at the Westminster Kennel Club show. Sexes were combined. Lerwick Bess was first, Shetland Rose second, and Lord Scott third. Sexes were split at Nassau. Lerwick Rex was winners dog and Jack McEwen, reserve. Lerwick Bess was winners bitch, and Shetland Rose, reserve. At Long Island, Jack McEwen was winners, and Lerwick Rex, reserve. Sable was winners bitch and Scalloway Belle, reserve.

With the sexes combined at Ladies Kennel Association, Lerwick Rex took the points with Jack McEwen reserve. The results were the same at the Toy Spaniel Club, but Lerwick Bess took the bitch points, as she did at Plainfield where Lord Scott was winners dog.

In 1913, 12 dogs were exhibited, but only three were registered. All

Ch. Arthea Blue Sparkler, owned-bred by Dr. and Mrs. Arthur W. Combs, Best of Breed 41 times and group winner.

Ch. Geronimo Little Gremlin, owned by Billy Kennedy.

*Athos Nilsen*

Ch. Wayfarer's Girl of Pocono, owned by Elaine Samuels, Best of Breed at Tri-State SSC Specialty.

*Brown*

Ch. Joyful O'Page's Hill, owned by William W. Gallagher.     *Brown*

Ch. Piccolo O'Page's Hill, owned by William W. Gallagher.

61

three were of American breeding. In 1914, only three were registered. Mrs. Wilbur F. Parker of Meriden, Conn., registered Highland Laddie and Highland Lassie. And Mrs. Lillian Rague registered Lerwick Laddie. He was bred by Mrs. T. D. McChesney.

Lerwick Rex became the first champion of the breed in the United States, winning his title in 1915. It is odd that he should have won his championship in the same year that Clifford Pat became the first champion of record for the breed in England.

Mrs. McChesney had sold Lerwick Belle to Miss J. Fritz. The dog was shown in 1917, as was Lerwick Rex. But World War I was now in its third year. Breeding in the British Isles had been cut to a minimum, and dog shows were cancelled. The effect upon the Shetland Sheepdog was disastrous in the United States.

Only a dog called Daisy was shown in the United States in 1916. And Ch. Lerwick Rex and Lerwick Belle were the top winners among those shown in 1917. But breeding and importing had ceased. And it would be six years before interest in the breed revived in the United States.

Ch. Mowgli.

Ch. Peabody Pan.

# 9

# Renewal of American Interest in Shetland Sheepdogs

IN July 1923, Mrs. Byron Rogers of Manhasset, Long Island, N.Y., registered two English imports. They were Kilravock Shrew of Misty Isles, a bitch bred by Miss Beryl Thynne, and Lady Park of Misty Isles, a bitch bred in England by J. G. Saunders. The former was by English Champion Walesby Select, out of Kilravock Naomi, a sable and white whelped July 31, 1921. The latter was also a sable and white by Rip of Mountfort out of Farburn Bo Bo, whelped June 16, 1921.

These two bitches made a tremendous impression upon those who saw them. One who liked the dogs was Edward R. Stettinius. In September, he registered two imports which had been sent to him in care of Mrs. Rogers. These were Kilravock Lassie and the sire of Kilravock Shrew of Misty Isles, Eng. Ch. Walesby Select. Lassie was bred in Scotland by a Mr. Cusin. She was a sable and white, whelped Oct. 11, 1922, by Irvine Ronnie out of Chestnut Lassie. Thus, on her dam's side, she came from one of the most famous bloodlines in the British Isles.

Walesby Select was bred by E. H. Phillips of Scotland, and was whelped June 1, 1919. He was by Kilravock Laddie out of Shadforth Bretta. He

Best Team in Show, Westminster 1940, with Dr. Samuel Milbank presenting trophy to owner-handler, Elizabeth D. Whelen. Left to right: Ch. Bil-Bo-Dot Blue Flag of Pocono, Timberidge Truth of Pocono, Ch. Pentstemon of Beech Tree, and Ch. Sea Isle Merle Legacy. Miss Whelen's Pocono Kennels won Best Team at Westminster in 1940, 1941, 1942, 1943 and 1953.

Left to right, Ch. Victory of Pocono, C.D.X., and Ch. Larkspur of Pocono, C.D.X., both owned by Miss Whelen.

Ch. Frigate of Faunbrook, owned by Miss Margaret Thomforde.

was inbred both to his sire and to Ch. Woodvold, one of the first pre-World War I champions. He won challenge certificates at the Kensington and Crystal Palace shows in 1920 and at Crufts in 1921.

In 1924, five Shelties were registered. One of these was Eng. Ch. Nettle of Mountfort, imported by R. E. Gregg. The breeder was Miss E. P. Humphries. The dog was a sable and white, whelped April 10, 1921, by the famous War Baby of Mountfort out of Christmasbox of Mountfort.

By this time, Kilravock Lassie had come into the possession of Catherine E. Coleman of Williamsburg, Mass. She was bred to Eng. Ch. Nettle of Mountfort. From the resulting litter, Gregg registered Saucy Boy, Wee Man, and Dusk. And Miss Coleman registered Prince of Whales.

Kilravock Lassie should probably be given credit for establishing the breed in America. This would not be so much because of what she produced, but because she started Miss Coleman in the breed. Her Sheltieland Kennels became one of the most famous in America, and it has existed longer than any other kennel in either the United States or Canada. Miss Coleman was the author of *The Shetland Sheepdog* and later, as Catherine Coleman Moore, of the revised edition, *The Complete Shetland Sheepdog*.

In 1926, Miss Coleman was given an imported male, Misty of Greyhill, born July 7, 1924, by Tarn out of Siria. Miss Fry brought over Eng. Ch. Eltham Park Esme. The following year, Miss Coleman imported Farburn Captain. He became the breed's first champion since Ch. Lerwick Rex in 1915. He was bred by W. M. Saunders, and was a sable and white, born Oct. 28, 1924, by Forward out of Farburn Bo Bo.

Miss Fredericka Fry had founded her Far Sea Kennels at Cos Cob, Conn. Her Eng. Ch. Eltham Park Esme became an American champion in August, 1928. Miss Fry understood that a successful kennel builds a foundation upon high quality brood matrons. Esme had become a champion and now Miss Fry brought over a succession of excellent bitches from Eltham Park, the kennels of E. C. Pierce. Among her imports, not all bitches, were Eng. Ch. Eltham Park Ellaline, Eltham Park Bluette, and in 1928 Eltham Park Ensor of Far sea.

The same year, Mrs. William F. Dreer imported Eltham Park Anahassitt. Mrs. Dreer had founded the Anahassitt Kennels, and these became nationally famous. Her new bitch was bred by E. C. Pierce. In addition, she brought over Merlyn of Cameliard, a dog bred by Mrs. J. A. and Miss P. M. Allen. He was by Eng. Ch. Eltham Park Eureka out of Aberlady Dot. It is interesting to note that Eltham Park Ensor of Far Sea was sired by Eltham Park Eurekason.

Homebreds were now beginning to appear. So in 1928, Kilravock Lassie was represented in registrations by puppies from two different litters. Wiggles, a son of Farburn Captain, was registered by Ellen B. Slater. And Miss Coleman, now of South Ashfield, Mass., registered Black Eyed Susan and Sheltieland Sue. These puppies were by Misty of Greyhill.

Blue Treasure of Pocono, Winners Bitch, with owner-handler Elizabeth D. Whelen; judge H. W. Nichols, Jr., and Beech Tree Corporal, Winners Dog, with handler Nate Levine, owned by Mrs. Ruth Taynton; at Framingham Kennel Club show 1946. *Jones*

Best Brace in Show, Westminster 1950. John Cross, show chairman; Sandra Ferry, showing her Feracres Bluejeans and Feracres Bluestocking; judge George Hartman. *Shafer*

In 1929 Miss Coleman imported Farburn Ellaline and Helensdale Lassie. Miss Fry brought over Eltham Park Eros of Far Sea, and registered a puppy, Rosette of Far Sea, sired by Ensor out of Esme. The following year Miss Fry imported Eltham Park Emmie of Far Sea, and Mrs. G. H. Edgell brought over Bushwave Baby Bunting. She was by Eltham Park Eurekason out of Brendagard by Eng. Ch. Walesby Select.

The famed Walnut Hall Kennels of Mrs. Katherine H. Edwards now appears. She registered Jock of Walnut Hall, a dog bred by Mrs. Dreer, and imported Downfield Olaf of Walnut Hall. Bred by J. C. Ramsay, Olaf was by Eng. Ch. Blaeberry of Clerwood—a dog figuring prominently in American Shetland Sheepdog history—out of Downfield Ethne.

Mrs. Dreer imported Ashbank Fairy, a sable and white also sired by Eng. Ch. Blaeberry of Clerwood, out of Ashbank Sheila. Downfield Olaf of Walnut Hall and Ashbank Fairy became American champions. In the meantime, William W. Gallagher, who founded the O'Pages Hill Kennels had imported Helensdale Laddie, a full brother to Miss Coleman's Helensdale Lassie. He was an English champion, and became an American champion. He was sired by the famed Chestnut Bud out of Aberland Wendy.

Here are the early champions in the order they won their titles:


1915   Ch. Lerwick Rex

1927   Ch. Farburn Captain

1928   Ch. Eltham Park Esme

1929   Ch. Wee Laird O'Downfield

       Ch. Eltham Park Ena
       (not registered)

1930   Ch. Downfield Grethe


1931   Ch. Downfield Olaf of Walnut Hall
       Ch. Ashbank Fairy

1932   Ch. Miss Blackie
       Ch. Mowgli
       Ch. Adorable of Anahassitt
       Ch. Bodachan of Clerwood
       Eng. Ch. Helensdale Laddie
       Ch. Sprig of Houghton Hill

68

1933    Ch. Piccolo O'Page's Hill
        Ch. Helensdale Sapphire
        Ch. Ariadne of Anahassitt
        Ch. Downfield Jarl
        Ch. Golden Girl of Walnut Hall (unregistered)
        Ch. Tilford Tulla
        Ch. Pegasus O'Page's Hill
        Ch. Tiny Betty of Walnut Hall

1934    Ch. Gigolo of Anahassitt
        Ch. Lady Tamworth O'Pages Hill
        Ch. Eltham Park Elyned of Far Sea
        Ch. Kim O'Pages Hill
        Ch. Alice of Anahassitt


1935    Ch. Coltness Commander
        Ch. Neilsland Nuffsaid
        Ch. Dancing Master of Anahassitt
        Ch. Tiny Chloe of Walnut Hall
        Ch. Peter Pan O'Pages Hill
        Ch. Anahassitt Aphrodite
        Ch. Promise O'Pages Hill
        Ch. Wee Cubby of Far Sea
        Ch. Sheltieland Thistle


If we ignore Ch. Lerwick Rex, as indeed we must, then the others can be considered to be the true foundation stock upon which the subsequent history of the Shetland Sheepdog in America rests. Some additional information should be given about them.

Miss Catherine Coleman claims the honor of breeding the first America-bred champion. She bred Ch. Miss Blackie. She sent Ch. Sheltieland Thistle, the first blue merle champion, to English and American Ch. Helensdale Laddie, owned by W. W. Gallagher. Miss Blackie, one of the puppies from this mating went to the ownership of Mr. Gallagher. As her name suggests, she was black, white and tan, whelped May 30, 1931. In May 1932, the American Kennel Club recorded her championship at about 10 months of age.

During that same May, the championship of Mowgli was recorded. So Miss Blackie beat him out by only a couple of dog shows. And in July of 1932, the American Kennel Club published the championship of Adorable of Anahassitt. She, too, was American-bred. Adorable was bred by Mrs. William F. Dreer of Rosemont, Pa., and she was a tri-color sired by Ch. Wee Laird O'Downfield out of Natalie of Clerwood.

Ch. Sheltieland Thistle was owned by Catherine Coleman. She was

La Belle Dame of Scotleigh, winner of working group at International Kennel Club show 1951. Owned by Ruth E. Wilcox.     *Frasie Studio*

Ch. Ray-Eden's Ricardo, owned by Dr. and Mrs. George H. Ray, winning Best in Show at Louisville Kennel Club show 1950. Left to right: Dr. Ray; T. H. Carruthers III, judge; Karl Straub, handler; and Dr. W. S. Carter, Club president.     *Frasie Studio*

Best Team in Show, Westminster 1953. Elizabeth D. Whelen, owner-handler with Katie-J's Blue Dawn of Pocono, Katie J's Little Boy Blue, Blue Legacy of Pocono, and Ch. Larkspur's Finalist of Pocono; judge James A. Farrell, Jr.                                    *Evelyn Shafer*

Interstate SSC of Pa., Southern N.J. and Del. Specialty, 1953. Left to right: Ch. Frigate's Emblem of Astolat, Best of Breed, with owner-handler Mrs. E. F. Hubbard; judge Alex Gibbs; Golden Sequin of Lillegard, BOS, with handler Elizabeth Whelen, owned by Vernon and Kay Johnson.                                    *Shafer*

Tri-State Specialty 1953. Best of Breed Ch. Pixie Dell Theme Song with owner-handler Mrs. A. R. Miller; judge Mrs. Henry Gray; BOS Ch. Nashcrest Golden Note, owned by Sea Isle Kennels. *Shafer*

Interstate SSC Specialty 1954. Best of Breed Ch. Nashcrest Golden Note; judge Robert G. Wills; BOS Ch. Va-Gore's Bright Promise owned by A. R. Miller. *Shafer*

Ch. Tri-Acres Mr. Sandman, owned by Mrs. Julia T. Alexander, shown by Mr. Alexander to Best in Show at Marion, Ohio, KC 1955. *Frasie Studio*

Ch. Noralee Forecaster, owned by Dr. and Mrs. Earle J. Hansch, Best of Breed SSC of So. California Specialty 1955; judge Mrs. Florence B. Cleveland. *Ludwig*

73

Ch. Classic's Kingly Khan, owned by Classic Kennels; judge, the late Alva Rosenberg; handler Dick Cooper.                                                                      *H. Tepe*

Thistlerose Robbie, owned by C. P. Ellerd, Best Working Dog Wheaton KC 1957. Judge, at left, is Mr. Riddle.                                                            *Frasie*

Ch. Pixie Dell Royal Jester, owned by Mr. and Mrs. A. R. Miller, Best of Breed at Tri-State SSC Specialty 1958.            *Brown*

Ch. Badgerton Alert Alec, owned by Tobruk Kennels, Best in Show Panhandle KC 1959.            *H. Tepe*

Ch. Pixie Dell Royal Blue, owned by Mrs. A. R. Miller; Best of Breed at Tri-State SSC Specialty 1959; judge Haworth Hoch.            *Shafer*

the first blue merle champion; her official AKC registration lists her breeder as Mrs. James G. Saunders of Scotland. Thistle was by Montlethen Blue Prince out of Helensdale Lassie, and the latter was imported by Miss Coleman. Thistle was imported "in utero" and was whelped at Sheltieland Kennels, hence her name, Sheltieland Thistle.

Ch. Wee Laird O'Downfield and Ch. Downfield Grethe were full brother and sister, though Grethe was some 15 months older than her brother. Mrs. Dreer imported Grethe in 1929, and Wee Laird a year later. Mrs. J. C. Ramsay was their breeder. It would be impossible to overestimate the influence they made on the breed through Ch. Mowgli.

His pedigree tells a great deal about how a breed is made. In those days, the modern Shetland Sheepdog type had not been fixed. Inbreeding was used when dogs of the correct type, or when dogs with especially desirable characteristics, appeared. The simplest way to express the meaning of inbreeding is to say that it is a contraction of the words, incestuous breeding. A brother and sister mating is the closest incestuous breeding which is possible.

Mowgli's dam was Jean of Anahassitt, and she was the result of a brother-sister mating of Ch. Wee Laird O'Downfield and Downfield Grethe. His sire was Ch. Wee Laird O'Downfield. Mowgli was whelped July 2, 1931. He was owned by William W. Gallagher of O'Pages Hill. Mowgli appears to have had quality hitherto undreamed of. Most breeders know that the British Isles have a six months quarantine period for dogs coming from North America. This effectively prevents the shipment of most dogs from the United States to England. Yet Mowgli's son, Ch. Sheltieland Laird O'Pages Hill, was sent to England just before World War II. There, despite the war, the dog became a well known sire. In England, he represented three of America's greatest early kennels— Sheltieland, Anahassitt, and O'Pages Hill.

# 10

# American Shetland
# Sheepdog Association

INTEREST in the Shetland Sheepdog grew so rapidly in the United States that, by 1928, fanciers began to talk about organizing a parent club. In those days, the first club to be organized to sponsor and promote a breed would be considered to be the parent club of the breed by the American Kennel Club. This was true whether the founding group had purely local ideas and local membership or was national in scope.

Many clubs then—and now—hold annual meetings at the time of the Westminster Kennel Club show at Madison Square Garden. Some of these clubs hold their meetings in club rooms at Madison Square Garden itself. Others meet at nearby hotels. At the "old Garden" which has been torn down, dressing rooms for the various athletic teams often served as meeting rooms. One room was used by the press corps; the other housed the meetings of various clubs during the two day show.

Thus it was that the organization meeting of the American Shetland Sheepdog Association was held in a dressing room at Madison Square Garden. The date was Feb. 12, 1929. Less than 30 people attended. Of these, 23 became founding members. Only two are still active. They are Mrs. Catherine Coleman Moore (then just Catherine Coleman) and J. Nate Levine, the professional handler. Both are now life members.

Miss Fredericka Fry of New York City and Cos Cob, Conn., was

77

The American Shetland Sheepdog Association meeting at Westminster. At head of table, William Gallagher, President. At his right, Mrs. Erma S. Huhn; at his left, Mr. and Mrs. Nate Levine. Along table on left of picture: Mrs. Ray Miller, Tobi Ain, Mrs. Ben Cooley, Eleanor Mann, Mrs. Ruth Taynton, Peggy Thomforde, Mrs. Neva Wray. Along table on right of picture: Mrs. Vance O'Bryan, Elizabeth Whelen, Miss Dorothea Murray, Mary Van Wagenen, Dona Hausman (second row) and Raymond Miller behind her.

elected president. Mrs. W. F. Dreer of Rosemont, Pa. was made first vice president and A. A. Parker of Worcester, Mass., second vice president. Miss Catherine Coleman of South Ashfield, Mass. was elected secretary, and George C. Carr of Reading, Pa., treasurer.

The executive committee was made up of Mrs. Gladys Funke of New York City (she had served as temporary chairman of the meeting), Miss Gertrude Sampson of New York City, C. J. Spill of Garden City, N.Y., Oscar Day of Fulton, N.Y., and J. Edward Shanaberger of Ravenna, Ohio.

It is worth noting that J. Nate Levine became one of America's top professional handlers. J. Edward Shanaberger became an all-breed judge, then turned to professional handling, and finally left the sport of dogs to train trotting horses. Benjamin Richardson, also a founding member, was a professional handler from Cos Cob, Conn. So far as the writer remembers, he handled the dogs for Miss Fry, and at least for a time, managed her kennel. Such early importers as Mrs. Byron Rogers, Edward R. Stettinius, and Robert E. Gregg seem never to have been members of the association.

Several months after the association was founded, and after a meeting at the Boston show in early March, the club applied for membership in the American Kennel Club. The association had studied the constitutions of other clubs, and had adopted its own at the New York meeting. At the Boston meeting, it had formalized procedures for elections and other matters. Miss Fredericka Fry then presented the association's application to the American Kennel Club. Membership in the American Kennel Club costs $250. Miss Fry personally paid the fee. Miss Fry later became Mrs. Enrico del Guercio.

Miss Katherine H. Edwards (later Mrs. H. Willis Nichols, Jr.) became a member of the executive committee in 1930, and Miss Katherine Lindsay in 1933. Miss Elizabeth D. Whelen became an executive committee member in 1936, and A. Raymond Miller in 1941. Mr. Miller died just after completing his 1973 Westminister K. C. judging assignment. The other three, with Mr. Levine and Mrs. Moore, are the oldest—in point of service—living life members. Mr. Miller represented the American Shetland Sheepdog Association to the American Kennel Club for many years until his death.

Mr. Stanley Saltzman of 130 Easton Rd., Westport, Conn. is the president, and Mrs. Thelma Mauldin of 1042 Lindsey, Rosenberg, Texas, is secretary, at the time of writing.

Of course, national officers change from time to time. But the national association remains. Readers wishing to reach the officers can always do so through the American Kennel Club, 51 Madison Ave., New York, N.Y., or by checking the list of member clubs as published monthly in *Pure-Bred Dogs, American Kennel Gazette.*

Ch. Nicholas of Exford, owned by Mrs. H. W. Nichols, Jr., winner of the 1936 ASSA Specialty.

*Brown*

# 11

# The National
# Specialty Show

A SPECIALTY SHOW is one for a specific breed, given by a breed club. The breed club can be the national parent club of the breed, or it can be a regional club. The club can give its own show, separate from any other. Or, it might join a group of other breed clubs and form a specialty club's association. The association would then give a show for its member clubs. Finally, either a national or a regional club can designate the classes at an all breed show as its specialty show. A regional club must, however, obtain permission for any kind of show from its parent club.

After its formation, the American Shetland Sheepdog Association grew strong enough to hold a specialty show. It decided to designate the classes at the Morris & Essex Kennel Club show as its specialty. This was a natural choice. Morris & Essex was the greatest outdoor show of its day. It was held in May when Shelties are usually in good coat. Thus, the association's first specialty show was held in May, 1933, in conjunction with Morris & Essex.

Edward D. McQuown, who for many years was one of America's finest all-breed judges, officiated. There were 15 dogs and 18 bitches which actually competed. Tilford Tulla, owned by Mrs. W. F. Dreer, was winners dog. Ariadne of Anahassitt, also owned by Mrs. Dreer, was winners bitch and best of winners. Ch. Piccolo O'Pages Hill, owned by W. W. Gallagher, was best of breed. It is noteworthy that the winner of both the puppy and novice dog classes was Gigolo of Anahassitt.

The next year, William H. Schwinger, an officer of the famed Collie Clan of the Midwest, was the judge. This show, as were those of 1935 and 1936, was also held in conjunction with Morris & Essex. That year, Morris & Essex had 2,431 competing dogs. Gigolo of Anahassitt, now a champion, was best of breed and went on to place second in a strong working group to the Great Dane, Nero Hexengold. The group judge was Dr. T. D. Buck.

Today it is not usual for a champion to enter the open class. But they are not barred from doing so. Gigolo was entered in the open class, and so, he went on to a group second from it. The winners bitch was Eltham Park Elyned of Far Sea, owned by Mrs. Fredericka Fry del Guercio. She had won both the limit and the open classes. There were 18 dogs and 24 bitches in competition.

The 1935 show had 2,784 competing dogs—an amazing entry for that time—and there were 19 Sheltie dogs and an equal number of bitches competing. Joseph Burrell was the judge. Ch. Piccolo O'Pages Hill was best of breed, as he had been in 1933. Winners dog was Peter Pan O'Pages Hill. The great producing bitch of a later time, M. J. Kennedy's Keep Goin', was winners bitch and best of winners from the novice class.

The famed Dancing Master of Anahassitt was reserve winners dog, and Captivator Jenny Wren, owned by E. S. Huhn, was reserve winners bitch. Oddly, she, too, had come from the novice class.

Nicholas of Exford, who later became a champion, was best of breed at the 1936 show. The next year, the specialty was moved to Cleveland. Again the judge was William H. Schwinger. His best of breed was Lady Precious O'Pages Hill, and she came up from the puppy class. She was owned by W. W. Gallagher. Kalandar Prince O'Pages Hill, also owned by Gallagher, was winners dog.

The 1937 show was notable for the great producing dogs and bitches which were entered in the classes—26 dogs, 25 bitches, and three for specials only. These were Tiny Margaret of Walnut Hall, owned by Mr. and Mrs. H. W. Nichols Jr. (whose her daughter Tiny Margurite of Walnut Hall was best of breed in 1940); Ch. Lady Tamworth O'Page's Hill, owned by Gallagher; and Ch. Dancing Master of Anahassitt. Ch. Mowgli, and the previous year's winner, Ch. Nicholas of Exford, an imported dog, were entered for exhibition only.

In the classes at that great show of March 13–14, 1937 were such all-time great dogs as Merrymaker of Pocono, China Clipper O'Pages Hill, Melchior of Anahassitt, Black Sachem O'Pages Hill, Ch. Gigolo of Anahassitt, Kelpie, Beach Cliff's Lizette (first Sheltie ever to win a Utility Dog obedience degree), Ronalee Norseman, Gregor MacGregor of Bagaduce, and Ch. Ariadne of Anahassitt.

Ch. Pixie Dell Little Gamin, owned by Mr. and Mrs. A. R. Miller, winner of the 1945 ASSA Specialty.

1948 ASSA Specialty. Best of Breed Creole Babe O'Page's Hill, shown by owner Nate Levine; judge Edward McQuown; Best Opposite Sex Wil-O-Mel's Scotch Piper shown by owner Mrs. W. G. Pietz. *Shafer*

83

Ch. Sea Isle Peter Pan, owned by Mr. and Mrs. George F. Bozenhard, Jr., winner of 1950 ASSA Specialty.                          *Brown*

Ch. Va-Gore's Bright Promise, owned by Mrs. George M. Howard; Best of Breed 1955 ASSA Specialty.
                          *Brown*

Ch. Brandell's Break-A-Way II, owned and shown by Nate Levine, winner of 1958 ASSA Specialty.

Ch. Gigolo of Anahassitt had won the second specialty show. He and Ch. Ariadne of Anahassitt were entered in the open classes at this show. It is hindsight, perhaps, but few shows in the history of the breed, or of any breed, could boast so great a group.

Thus far, there have been 40 national specialty shows. Three judges have officiated three times each. They are the all-breed judges Edward D. McQuown (now deceased), Alva Rosenberg (also deceased), and Miss Mary Van Wagenen. Four dogs have won it twice each—Ch. Piccolo O'Pages Hill, Ch. Timberidge Temptation, Ch. Va-Gore's Bright Promise, and Ch. Malpsh Great Scott.

Dogs owning the O'Pages Hill affix (the kennels of William W. Gallagher, and later, J. Nate Levine) have been best of breed eight times. Dogs with the Pixie Dell prefix of Mr. and Mrs. A. R. Miller, have been best of breed four times. Seven dogs came up from the lower classes and were not yet champions when sent to the top of the show. All later became champions. They are: Nicholas of Exford, Lady Precious O'Pages Hill, Victory of Pocono, Tiny Marguerite of Walnut Hall, Confection O' The Picts, Creole Babe O'Pages Hill, and Golden Sequin of Lillegard.

Twenty-three of the shows have been held in the East; 12 in the Midwest four on the Pacific Coast; and two in the Deep South (if one can call Midland, Texas, the Deep South). At one time, professional handlers were permitted to judge at specialty shows. J. Nate Levine judged twice, in 1940 and in 1947.

## Complete List of ASSA Specialty Winners

| | | | |
|---|---|---|---|
| 1933 | Ch. Piccolo O'Pages Hill | 1944 | Ch. Timberidge Temptation |
| 1934 | Ch. Gigolo of Anahassitt | | |
| 1935 | Ch. Piccolo O'Pages Hill | 1945 | Ch. Pixie Dell Little Gamin |
| 1936 | Ch. Nicholas of Exford | | |
| 1937 | Ch. Lady Precious O'Pages Hill | 1946 | Ch. Timberidge Temptation. |
| 1938 | Ch. Sheltieland Laird | 1947 | Ch. Confection O'The Picts |
| 1939 | Ch. Kalandar Prince O'Pages Hill | 1948 | Ch. Creole Babe O'Pages Hill |
| 1940 | Ch. Tiny Margurite of Walnut Hall | 1949 | Ch. Noralee Autumn Gold |
| 1941 | Ch. Will O'The Mill O'Pages Hill | 1950 | Ch. Sea Isle Peter Pan |
| 1942 | Ch. Victory of Pocono | 1951 | Ch. Ald-A-Beth Flintlock |
| 1943 | Ch. Windrush O'Pages Hill | 1952 | Ch. Pixie Dell Theme Song |

Ch. Mori-Brook's Country Squire, owned by
Mori-Brook Kennels, winner of 1959 ASSA
Specialty. *Brown*

Am. & Can. Ch. Banchory High
Born, owned by Kismet Kennels.

Ch. Flair Peg o'My Heart, owned by
Shirley Valo, winner of 1972 ASSA
Specialty.

| | | | |
|---|---|---|---|
| 1953 | Ch. Golden Sequin of Lillegard | 1963 | Ch. Tess's Trump Card of Wadmalaw |
| 1954 | Ch. Nashcrest Golden Note | 1964 | Ch. Laurolyn Patti O'M. B. |
| 1955 | Ch. Va-Gore's Bright Promise | 1965 | Ch. Elf Dale Viking |
| 1956 | Ch. Va-Gore's Bright Promise | 1966 | Ch. Malpsh Great Scott |
| 1957 | Ch. Brandell's Break-A-Way II | 1967 | Ch. Malpsh Great Scott |
| 1958 | Ch. Dark Stream O'Pages Hill | 1968 | Ch. Halstor's Peter Pumpkin |
| 1959 | Ch. Mori-Brook's Country Squire | 1969 | Ch. Lencrest Rebel Rouser |
| 1960 | Ch. Tiny Toby of Walnut Hall | 1970 | Ch. Banchory High Born |
| 1961 | Ch. Pixie Dell Royal Blue | 1971 | Ch. Tiree Hall Jedelan Scot |
| 1962 | Ch. Pixie Dell Bright Vision | 1972 | Ch. Flair Peg O' My Heart |
| | | 1973 | Ch. Reveille's Reflection of Sheldon |

Amer. and Can. Ch. Tiree Hall Jedelan Scot, owned by Mrs. Helen Hendrickson, Best of Breed 1971 ASSA Specialty.                                    *Lloyd W. Olson*

# 12

# The Shetland Sheepdog
# Futurity Stakes

---

A FUTURITY is a special event which has been copied after those given at horse races. It is essentially an event for breeders. In the case of horses, the race is for two year olds. In dog events it is usually for puppies. However, national breed governing bodies make up their own rules. And some futurities, particularly for field dogs, cover dogs up to 18 months of age.

About 1957, the American Shetland Sheepdog Association altered its futurity rules. These have remained essentially the same ever since. So in this chapter, we report on the victors beginning with 1958. Since that time Mrs. June Korenko of Badgerton Kennels, 7266 Hopkins Rd., Mentor, Ohio, has been in charge.

Before giving the rules, let us try to report in as simple a fashion as possible what a futurity really is. A bitch is bred and high hopes are expected for the litter. So, before the pups are born, she is nominated and a small fee is paid.

At some period after the litter is whelped, a second fee is paid. This fee is for each individual puppy. For example, let us say that four puppies still look promising. Then the additional fee would be paid on all four. But if only one turns out well, then only it would be nominated.

Still a third fee would be paid at a future date, usually when the puppy is six months old. Then it would have to be nominated under its registered name. In addition, there is the entry fee for the show; usually, this is paid to the specialty show, less the superintendent's handling charges. All the money which has come in through the futurity nominations themselves is paid out to the winners. There are usually special cash awards which go to breeder and to the owner of the sire.

The rules which govern the American Shetland Sheepdog Association futurity follows: The futurity is open to all members of the association. Futurity classes are judged in advance of the regular classes at the specialty show. Dogs entered in the futurity must also be entered in the regular breed classes at the show.

There are two classes, 6 to 9 months, and 9 to 12 months of age. The two puppy winners then compete for best in the futurity. Nominations of bitches must be made before the puppies are whelped. And puppies eligible for competition must be born within a year to six months before the futurity show date. Nomination fee for the bitch is $2.

Ten weeks after the date of birth, a second payment of $1 must be made, and the puppy's sire, dam, and sex must be given. Then at six months of age, a final $2 payment must be made, and the puppy's name, sex, and color must be given.

Nomination fees for 6 to 9 months competition are used for that class, and fees for 9 to 12 months competition are used for that class. Prize money is divided as follows: First, 40%; second, 30% third, 20% and fourth, 10%. Special prizes of $15 each are given by the American Shetland Sheepdog Association to the breeder of the best in the futurity, and to the owner of the sire.

These are the basic rules for the futurity. A full set of rules and entry blanks can be obtained from Mrs. Korenko, or from the American Shetland Sheepdog Association itself. Officers of the club change from time to time. But since, the association is a member of the American Kennel Club, the address of the secretary can be obtained from it. However, those wanting to enter the futurity must join the ASSA itself to become eligible.

Perhaps here it should be pointed out that since a futurity is a non-regular part of a dog show, the judge does not have to be licensed by the American Kennel Club. Often, a noted breeder will be asked to officiate. Sometimes, breed specialists will be asked to judge the regular classes, and multiple- or all-breed judges will preside over the futurity.

Here are the winners, judges, and owners starting with the inception of the new rules:

| Year | Judge | Dog | Owner |
|------|-------|-----|-------|
| 1958 | A. R. Miller | Fascination O' Page's Hill | Page's Hill Kennels |
| 1959 | Louis Murr | Grayson's Bright Minx | W. & E. Brady |
| 1960 | Mrs. W. H. Gray | Kiloren Toby of Pocono | Mrs. Walter Ford |
| 1961 | Alex Gibbs | Fast Brook O' Pages Hill | Page's Hill Kennels |
| 1962 | Mrs. H. W. Nichols Jr. | Ch. Gra-John's Little G-Man | Gra-John Kennels |
| 1963 | Mrs. James Hausman | Goodhill Blue Mist | Mrs. J. Gooding |
| 1964 | Alva Rosenberg | King Hector O' Page's Hill | Page's Hill Kennels |
| 1965 | M. T. L. Downing | Gra-John's Mollie Bea | Gra-John Kennels |
| 1966 | Robert Reedy | Storm Signal O' Page's Hill | Page's Hill Kennels |
| 1967 | Constance Hubbard | Tiree Hall Merry Marquis | S. & H. Hendrickson |
| 1968 | Mary Van Wagenen | Merri Lon Night Shadows | D. & Vernon Peterson |
| 1969 | Mrs. Lloyd Johnson | Scotchguard The Admiral | J. & D. Towne |
| 1970 | Mrs. Helen Hendrickson | Beltane The Buccaneer | P. & B. Curry |
| 1971 | Laura Sawin | Tentagel The Folk-Singer | D. Reeves & R. Fletcher |
| 1972 | Mrs. Kitty Reconnu | Betit's Mr. Louisiana | Betty Impastato & Sharlene DeFee |

Amer., Can. Ch.
Browne Acres
Bette.

Can. Ch. Wee Bonnie Blue Lass,
also Amer. and Can. C.D., owned
by Bonnie Lafferty.

# 13

# Canadian Shetland
# Sheepdog Pioneers

THE CULT of the Shetland Sheepdog began later in Canada than it did in the United States. It is not known when the first Shelties arrived. The first to be registered, in 1930, were owned by Miss Sybil Fincham of Montreal. Miss Fincham was an importer who bought and imported dogs of a dozen breeds, and in astonishing numbers. The Canadian Kennel Club took punitive action against her, but not before she had made a lasting impression on several breeds, and particularly on the Shetland Sheepdog.

Her first import was Queen of Mountfort, a daughter of Specks of Mountfort, which arrived in Canada in April, 1930. Several weeks later, Wizbang Godiva and Wizbang Magnus came. On May 27, 1930, a large consignment of dogs arrived for Miss Fincham. There were Nan of Mountfort with her progeny, littermates Sable Jock and Sable Naneen; Wizbang Luxury; and Eng. Ch. Specks of Mountfort. The same consignment included a Wire-haired Fox Terrier and an English Setter.

The next year seven dogs were registered, all by Miss Fincham. These were Callah Mohr, Can. Ch. Marbles of Greyhill, a blue merle Ros Mairl, Roseberry and three littermates sired by Eng. Ch. Gawaine of Cameliard. They were Wizbang Fairy Queen, Wizbang Gold Gawaine, and Wizbang Joy. Their dam was Wizbang Godiva and, as the saying goes, they were imported "in utero." If Wizbang Joy can be said to have

93

been bred in Canada, since she was born there, then she can be called the first Canadian-bred champion.

Actually, the first Canadian Shetland Sheepdog champion of record was Eltham Park Anahassitt. Mrs. William F. Dreer had shown the dog in Canada in 1929. In 1930, Mrs. Harkness Edwards took the dog back to Canada to complete its championship. Mrs. Dreer also exhibited Wee Laird O'Downfield in Canada, but he did not complete his championship.

The rules then for registration and for the granting of championships were less stringent in Canada than they are now. This was also true to some extent with the American Kennel Club. Thus, a dog with a slightly defective pedigree, or none, might have won a championship. It could not be registered, but if bred to a registered dog, the offspring would be eligible for registration. In those days, a dog registered by the American Kennel Club could win a championship without going through the formality of being registered by the Canadian Kennel Club. Today, the Canadian Kennel Club will not issue a championship certificate until the dog has been registered with it.

Wizbang and Marbles of Greyhill won championships in 1931. The following year, two unregistered dogs, Dixie and Patch, won championships. Owned by Mrs. W. G. Clark, they won at shows in the Vancouver, B.C. area. They were bred by G. B. Caird of the English registered Chestnut affix after he moved to Vancouver but not CKC registered.

James D. Strachan is one of the immortals of Canadian dogdom. He served as an officer of the Canadian Kennel Club for at least 22 years. Strachan was already well known as a Collie breeder when he became attracted to the Shetland Sheepdog. His first Sheltie was Nattie Gallagher O'Pages Hill, whom he bought from William W. Gallagher.

In 1933, Nattie Gallagher won her championship. Gallagher himself campaigned Piccolo O'Pages Hill to a Canadian title that year. Also winning championships in 1933 were Ch. Sable Naneen, owned by Miss E. E. Sparrow, and Ch. Tiny Betty of Walnut Hall, owned by Miss Katherine H. Edwards. These two American dogs won at Oakville, National Kennel Club, Toronto Ladies Kennel Association, and Guelph.

Eltham Park Anahassitt, Piccolo O'Pages Hill, and Tiny Betty of Walnut Hall were never registered with the Canadian Kennel Club. They returned to the United States. Their only direct influence upon the breed comes from the attraction they drew from Canadian breeders. However, since Canadian and American breeders have cross-bred their stock, all three can be found far back in Canadian as well as in American pedigrees.

One of the greatest of the early Canadian breeders was William Henderson of Toronto. He established the Alford Kennels. Henderson had bought Ch. Wizbang Joy and Wizbang Godiva from Miss Fincham. Ch. Wizbang Joy, a great producer, was the dam of champions Alford Achievement, Alford Clansman, Alford Heatherbelle, and Alford Guinea Gold. Wizbang

Godiva produced Ch. Alford Champagne Bubble. Henderson also imported Lord Lovell O'Pages Hill from Gallagher, and he bred Kingsvale Lad. Both became champions.

James Strachan's Coltness Kennels appear in the champions' lists in both the United States and Canada. Among his better known champions was Coltness Little Lizbeth. He also owned Ch. Pocono Pimpernel, whom he bought from Dorothy A. Foster of Austel, Ga. This dog combined the bloodlines of two great American foundation kennels. These were Elizabeth D. Whelen's Pocono Kennels, and Mrs. Foster's Timberidge Kennels. Strachan also owned Ch. Alford Champagne Bubble.

However great his dogs, and however broad his breeding program, Strachan's greatest contribution to the breed came through his prestige. He was the secretary-treasurer of the Canadian Kennel Club, and he was among the leaders of the Collie fraternity on both sides of the border. When the great Collie breeder turned to the Sheltie, people everywhere became interested in it.

The breed spread quickly across Canada. MacKenzie Matheson of Caulfield, British Columbia, founded his Caulfield Kennels, and the Caulfield name quickly became famous on both sides of the border. Matheson bought Black Sachem O'Pages Hill from Gallagher, and the dog easily became a champion. Two of Mathesons other foundation dogs were Ch. Caulfield Little Joker and Can. Ch. Caulfield Silver Lady.

These, then, were the pioneers of Sheltie-dom in Canada. They imported top dogs from England, and they freely used the best of the early American dogs. And in doing so, they laid a solid foundation for the healthy growth of the breed in Canada.

Ch. Hi-Hope's Merry Imp, U.D., Am. C.D.X. Dam of two champions; holds honor of both U.D. title and Best in Show win.

*E. M. Allen Ltd.*

Can. and Amer. Ch. Hi-Hope's Echo o'Imp, leading Canadian winner.

*G. Wynne Powell*

# 14

# Modern Shelties in Canada

C<small>ANADIAN</small> Shetland Sheepdog breeders and owners have unfortunately—and unfairly—been forced to live under the shadow of their American counterparts. There has been a general lack of familiarity on the part of the Americans with Canadian dogs. And there has been a tendency to down-grade the Canadian dogs.

Yet the border between the two countries has not been an iron curtain. Dogs have crossed the border both ways, both for show and for breeding purposes. There are many dogs which are Canadian and American champions, and more Canadian dogs which have won American championships than the reverse. Yet the general unfamiliarity of Americans with Canadian successes is great. And because of it, we are departing from the general format of this book to give the records of some of the older Canadian kennels. They indicate how the Canadian lines have been established, and they also prove the points made above.

Basically, the Canadians have achieved greatest success by line-breeding to the lines which produced Ch. Timberidge Temptation and Ch. Prince George O'Pages Hill. One of the fine kennels, Ronas Hill, based its program on Alford dogs (see the previous chapter), also Pocono, and then Helensdale. Pocono and Badgerton often appear in Canadian pedigrees.

Ch. Coltness Commander was the first Canadian-bred dog to win an American championship. He was a son of Ch. Nattie Gallagher O'Pages Hill who was sent back to the United States to be bred to Ch. Mowgli. He is proof of the points made above.

In the following analysis of kennels, we are presenting five not so much in the order of their successes as in the order of their founding. It has been observed that the average life of people in the dog game is five years. But with Shetland Sheepdogs, this has not been true, either in Canada or the United States. Many of the great kennels, which were founded 25 years ago, are still both active and successful.

Ronas Hill Kennels of Mrs. E. F. Lovett of Stittsville, Ontario, was founded in December, 25 years ago. The foundation dogs were Ch. Alford Laddie of Glenleigh, Ch. Alford Ballerina (a half sister), and Aylmer Chorine. Chorine produced five champions, including two American champions. It is worthy of note that these latter two dogs—American and Canadian Ch. Dixie Belle of Ronas Hill and American Ch. Orange Flare of Ronas Hill—produced American champions for Hampshire Kennels in the United States.

Another Ronas Hill foundation bitch was American and Canadian Ch. Pocono Trinket of Windy Oaks. Trinket was a remarkable dog. She was shown at an American Shetland Sheepdog Association national specialty show in the veterans class. She was 16½ years old at the time, and she won an ovation.

In 1953, Ronas Hill imported English Ch. Helensdale Wendy from James Saunders of Scotland. She was a great producer. And so it can be seen that Helensdale has played an important part in Canada just as it has in the United States.

E. H. and Frances Clark established their Hi-Hope Kennels at Richmond, British Columbia, in 1954. Their first champion was Hi-Hope's Merry Imp. She won a Utility Dog title in Canada and a Companion Dog Excellent title in the United States. To the best of the writer's knowledge, she is the only Shetland Sheepdog in North American history to win an all-breed best in show and a U.D. degree.

This kennel purchased and imported Timberidge Typesetter. He became a Canadian champion and won his major points in the United States. A son of this dog, out of Merry Imp, was Ch. Hi-Hope's Echo O'Imp. He, too, was a best in show winner. When bred to Badgerton Vain Vanessa, he sired a litter of five champions, two of which won American championships as well. Again, the high quality of the Canadian dogs is proven.

Badgerton Vain Vanessa also produced four champions when bred to Ch. Timberidge Typesetter. One of these, Ch. Hi-Hope's Badgerton Canadienne has been a producer for Badgerton Kennels in the United States. Kinswood bloodlines also appear in Hi-Hope pedigrees.

The Terian Kennels of Joan Wiik of Saskatoon, Saskatchewan, were founded in late 1958. Saskatoon is not well located for making either great production or show records. Yet Terian has one of the best records in Canada.

Mrs. Wiik won her first championship with Terian's April Lass, C.D.,

Ch. Sunnycrest Black Topper, owned by
Mr. and Mrs. R. C. Kress.

Ch. Kel-Lani's Claire de Lune.

Left to right: Ch. Terians Aire Fare, owned by Mrs. Deanna Roche; Ch. Pattoo's Song
of Holly and Ch. Allmac's Le Centenaire, C.D., owned by Mrs. Joan Wiik.

a daughter of Ch. Timberidge Typesetter, C.D. She added to her kennels Ch. Saravan's Elegant Lad, of Thistlerose breeding, and later, Ch. Kawartha's Fair Game. The Terian record also includes a best in show winner—Ch. Terian's Tuesday Wendy.

Another kennel founded in 1959 is Kel-Lani, developed by Mrs. D. O'Dare, Miss C. O'Dare, and J. Horton. They started basically with Hi-Hope stock. But they bred to a famous American dog, Ch. Geronimo Son Rey, C.D., who was an American, Mexican, and Canadian champion. From him they got Ch. Kel-Lani's Moonglow, C.D., dam of five champions. Moonglow was bred to the great American winner, Ch. Elf Dale Viking, and produced Ch. Kel-Lani Moonshine, which had a great show record, and is now one of Canada's leading sires.

It is not possible to analyze all the great Canadian kennels here, though their records will appear later. However, as a measure of Canadian and American cooperation, we do give here the Meridian Kennels of Mrs. Hazel Slaughter, Bois des Filion, Quebec. To mention it, however, we must also mention Summit Kennels, formerly of Quebec, but now in the United States. The two kennels have continued their cooperation, even though now so widely separated.

Meridian Kennels was founded basically on Ronas Hill stock. Hazel Slaughter, under the Meridian name, has bred 19 champions. Her American and Canadian Ch. Meridian's Miss Behave was the top winning Sheltie in Canada in 1968, and the dam of Ch. Summit's Gay Nineties, the second top winner in 1970. Miss Behave is the dam of six champions, and her daughter, Ch. Summit's Gay Abandon, of eight.

Ch. Summit's Gold Dust, C.D. is by Ch. Nashcrest Golden Note out of Ch. Cinderella's Gypsy of Ronas Hill. He has sired 12 champions, and some of his progeny have been excellent sires and producers on both sides of the border.

Most of these Canadian breeders have paid particular attention to temperament and character. In all that has gone before in this chapter, there is evidence of this by the number of dogs mentioned which have won obedience titles.

Here we give some of the great records of Canadian kennels, sires and dams with number of champions produced by each. To the best of our knowledge, these records are accurate. However, it has been some years since the Canadian Kennel Club published a stud book. This has made it quite difficult to get late records. Readers should bear this in mind in studying the following lists:

## Leading Breeders

| | | |
|---|---|---|
| E. H. & Frances Clark | Hi-Hope Kennels | 28 |
| Mrs. E. F. Lovett | Ronas Hill | 26 |
| Mrs. Hazel Slaughter | Meridian | 19 |
| Mrs. Ariel Sleeth | Sovereign Kennels | 18 |
| William Henderson | Alford Kennels | 15 |
| Mrs. Joan Wiik | Terian Kennels | 14 |
| Mr. & Mrs. R. D. Smuck | Willow Acres Kennels | 13 |
| O'Dares & Horton | Kel-Lani Kennels | 12 |
| Mrs. G. Taylor | Glen-El-Tee Kennels | 12 |
| Laura & George Getty | Quarrybrae Kennels | 10 |

## Leading Sires

| | | | |
|---|---|---|---|
| Ch. Timberidge Typesetter | 17 | Ch. Brigdale Renown | 5 |
| (Can. & Am. C.D.) | | Can. & Am. Ch. Camian's | 5 |
| Ch. Willow Acre's Golden | 16 | Clansman of Hi-Hope | |
| Rocket | | Ch. Doron Brusi Of Note | 5 |
| Ch. Summit's Gold Dust, C.D. | 12 | Am. & Can. Ch. Hi-Hope's | 5 |
| Eng. & Can. Ch. Honey Boy | 9 | Echo O'Imp | |
| of Callart | | Ch. Piper Glen's Christopher | 5 |
| Ch. Minonamee Prince | 9 | Robin | |
| Ch. Saravan's Elegant Lad | 8 | Ch. Ronas Hill Frolic | 5 |
| Ch. Kel-Lani's Moonshine | 7 | Ch. Summit's Night And Day | 5 |
| Ch. Sunnycrest Black Topper | 7 | Sunnycrest Target | 5 |
| Ch. Alford Wee McGregor | 6 | Willow Acres Golden Note | 5 |
| Ch. Hi-Hope's Highrigger | 6 | | |

## Leading Dams

| | | | |
|---|---|---|---|
| Badgerton Vain Vanessa | 9 | Eng. & Can. Ch. Helensdale | 5 |
| Ch. Summit's Gay Abandon | 8 | Wendy | |
| Aylmer Chorine | 7 | Ch. Kel-Lani's Moonglow | 5 |
| Alford Jay Jay's Lassie | 6 | Ch. Minonamee Eugenie | 5 |
| Ch. Willow Acres Golden | 6 | Sunnycrest Merry Imp | 5 |
| Charm, C.D. | | Can. & Am. Ch. Hi-Hope's | 4 |
| Ch. Cinderella Gypsy of | 5 | Bonnie Naiad | |
| Ronas Hill, U.D.T. | | Kel-Lani's Autumn Blaze | 4 |
| Ch. Dilhorme Fortune | 5 | Little Miss Muffet | 4 |
| (imp. from England) | | Mantoga Christmas Carol | 4 |
| Doron's Taffy Ann | 5 | (Eng. import) | |

| | | | |
|---|---|---|---|
| Sandy of Evergreen Acres | 4 | Ch. Hjalti Melrose | 3 |
| Ch. Sovereign Victorious | 4 | Samantha of Sanroc | 3 |
| Astolat Glengowan Symphony | 3 | Ch. Summit's Forever Amber | 3 |
| Ch. Hi-Hope's Badgerton Canadienne | 3 | Ch. Terian's April Lass, C.D. | 3 |
| | | Ch. Terian's Gay Solitaire C.D. | 3 |
| Ch. Kinsman Penny At Quarrybrae | 3 | The Wyke's Doll Baby | 3 |
| | | Ch. Wizbang Joy | 3 |

Ch. Sovereign Trailblazer, owned by Mrs. Jane Farmer.

Ch. Sovereign By Jingo, owned by Sovereign Kennels.

Ch. Pattoo's Song of Holly, owned by Mrs. Joan Wiik.

# 15

# The Modern
# Shetland Sheepdog
# in Great Britain

---

This chapter has been contributed by Miss Felicity Rogers, who with her sister, has operated the Riverhill Kennels for more than 40 years. The author of this book has taken the liberty to rearrange the chapter slightly, and to try to clarify certain parts for the benefit of American readers. Otherwise, the text, and Miss Rogers' accuracy remain as she wrote it.

SINCE World War II, the Shetland Sheepdog has gone from strength to strength. In 1951, there were 788 registrations at the Kennel Club. In 1972, registrations had jumped to 5,800. For the last four years, the breed has stood seventh in the all-breed list of registrations. Indications are that it will hold, or improve, this position in 1973.

I think the reason for the breed's increasing popularity is the fact that Shelties do make wonderful companions. They are a handy size. They neither fight, hunt, nor wander off. They can take as little or as much exercise as their owners want to give them. They are extremely clean in the house. And, they are easily house trained.

Originally, there were three breed clubs. These were: the original Shetland Islands club, now barely alive; the Scottish Shetland Sheepdog Club; and the English Shetland Sheepdog Club. The latter is by far the largest, and has some 780 members. After World War II, the Northern Counties Shetland Sheepdog Club was organized, and this was followed by the Midwestern Shetland Sheepdog Club. All these clubs, except the original Shetland Islands club, hold championship shows. The latest club to be formed is the Welsh Shetland Sheepdog Club. It has not yet attained championship status. But from the way it is growing, it should achieve this very shortly.

Entries are high, especially at the club shows. Thus, the English Shetland Sheepdog Club show in 1972 had 309 dogs entered, of which 61 were in obedience classes. The Northern club show had 205 dogs, and the Scottish Club had 94. As a comparison, the Richmond one day all breed show at Olympia in mid-December, had 167 Shelties, making up an entry of 280 dogs, and an average of 23.3 per class.

Progressive retinal atrophy has appeared in the breed in Britain, as it has in other parts of the world. It is perhaps less common than in some other breeds and in some other countries. In more than 40 years of breeding, I have not seen a blind Sheltie, except for a white dog which came from the mating of two blue merles. And this dog was immediately put to sleep. Reputable breeders, however, have all their dogs checked. The English Shetland Sheepdog Association keeps a registry of certified clear dogs for the benefit of its members.

Aside from a certainly minimal amount of this defect, Shetland Sheep-dogs in Great Britain are free from hereditary defects. And this, despite the phenomenal growth of the breed in recent years. Our clubs, and the Kennel Club itself, are on the alert to keep it so.

The top producing sire line (called in Britain "BB") is that descending from Hector of Aberlour and Ch. Nicky of Aberlour. The latter is the dog to whom I gave best of breed in 1939 at the last Crufts show before World War II. His record is especially remarkable, both because of the war, and because he lived in North Scotland where he had fewer chances than most dogs to establish a line.

He sired Ch. Riverhill Red Coat, from whom was descended Ch. Brigdale Renown. The latter was sent to Canada, but not before he had sired Ch. Midas of Shelert. The line of descent goes on through Ch. Sea Urchin of Shelert down to Ch. Riverhill Richman. The latter was twice best in show at the English Shetland Sheepdog Club specialty shows. He was also the top home-bred stud of 1971.

Ch. Nicky of Aberlour was also the sire of Helensdale Gentle Lady, the dam of Ch. Helensdale Ace. Ace was the result of an unplanned mother-son mating. He was a glamorous dog who brought great honor to the breed by going best in show on the first day of the Birmingham City show.

104

Ch. Riverhill Rufus. *Fall*

Ch. Riverhill Rogue. *Fall*

Ch. Riverhill Rare Gold with her three sable daughters: Chs. R. Real Gold, R. Ready Cash, (R. Rare Gold herself), and R. Rather Rich. *Sally Anne Thompson*

First three generations of champion bitches in Shelties: Chs. R. Rare Gold, R. Rarity of Glenmist, and Sypay Star of Glenmist. *Thompson*

Four champion grandchildren of R. Rare Gold sired by Ch. R. Rather Rich: Chs. R. Richman, R. Rather Dark, R. Raider, and R. Rather Nice.       *Diane Pearce*

Ch. Dilhorne Blue Mirth, winner of many bitch CC's.       *C. M. Cooke & Son*

His son, Ch. Alasdair of Tintobank, was also a great sire, and he was responsible for Ch. Riverhill Rare Gold. Rare Gold was best of opposite sex to best in show at the Ladies Kennel Association championship show. Her victory came before the days of group judging. She is perhaps the greatest brood bitch in the history of the breed in Britain. Some 15 champions and eight other challenge certificate winners descend in tail female from her. These include three lots of three generation champion bitches.

The line of Hector of Aberlour descends in this way—Ch. Orpheus of Callart, Ch. Riverhill Rescuer, Hartfield Herald, Ch. Ebony Pride of Glenhill, Carousel of Melvaig, Riverhill Rolling Stone, and Strikin Midnight of Shelert. It is notable that Carousel of Melvaig sired Ch. Charval The Delinquent, winner of 15 challenge certificates or more than any other Sheltie.

Riverhill Rolling Stone sired three working group winners in Ch. Antoc Sealodge Spotlight, Ch. Tumblebays Topaz of Monkswood, and Ch. Deloraine Ditys of Monkswood. The latter won the working group at Crufts in 1968. Strikin Midnight of Shelert has already sired eight champions, and he is still reasonably young. It should be noted that in earlier days, there were no such awards as first in the working group. Also, it is so difficult to win championships in Britain that the siring of eight champions is a great record.

Before World War II, the top winning producing line—called "C.H.E."—was the one which produced such great sires as Ch. Gawaine of Cameliard, Chestnut Rainbow, Nutkin of Houghton Hill, and Ch. Uam Var of Houghton Hill. All these dogs appear in early American pedigrees, and Nutkin came to America. The line produced Ch. Riverhill Rufus, first champion in that kennel.

Rufus is responsible for several strong lines. One comes down through Ch. Exford Piskeigye Taw and Ch. Lothario of Exford. It includes such famed dogs as Ch. Delwood Terence, Ch. Viking of Melvaig, Ch. Dilhorne Norseman, and others. Ch. Riverhill Rufus also sired Ellington Encore, a leading post war sire, whose champion sons, Ellington Easter Parade and Ellington Esquire, came to the United States.

The top female line in Britain today—called No. 9—started out as a blue merle family. It traces back to a lovely blue merle, Ch. Blue Blossom of Houghton Hill, one of Britain's great brood bitches before 1939. Riverhill Rouge was a great-granddaughter of Ch. Blue Blossom, and she was sired by Riverhill Rufus. Riverhill Rare Gold stems from Rouge. And she seems mainly responsible for the change in a blue merle family to an almost entirely sable one. To return to Ch. Blue Blossom of Houghton Hill, she was the dam of three champions.

Her record was not surpassed until Ch. Tilford Tontine. Ch. Riverhill Rare Gold had the first three generations of champion bitches descended from Ch. Tilford Tontine. And then there followed three generations of blue merles—Ch. Francehill Glamorous, Ch. Francehill Glamour Girl, and Ch. Francehill Painted Lady. And these were followed by two blue merles and a tricolor—Ch. Joyful of Exford, Ch. Bluebird of Exford, and Ch. Blackhare of Exford.

Those female lines designated 1, 2, 3, 5, 13, and 24 are all going strong, and are producing winners. Line 24 holds greatest interest for us at Riverhill since it mainly stems from our first bitch, Riverhill Rosette. Her dam came from the Shetland Islands, and thus is a direct link with the breed's origins. Probably the most important bitch in the family was Ch. Riverhill Rugasd who served as a model for the English Shetland Sheepdog Association standard of the breed. She is also behind Ch. River- hill Rogue, the only dual winner at Crufts. Major kennels whose female lines belong to this family include Toonytown and Loughrigg.

Ch. Sharval the Delinquent winning his 15th Challenge Certificate and Best of Breed at Cruft's 1972. *C. M. Cooke & Son*

109

Ch. Sea Isle Serenade.                    *Shafer*

Ch. Rorralore Robert the Bruce.

Ch. Pixie Dell Royal Blue, owned by Mr. and Mrs. A. R. Miller.

*Norton of Kent*

# 16

# Shetland Sheepdog Litters

THE READER will recall that in 1910 James A. Loggie wrote an article for Sydney Turner's *Kennel Encyclopaedia.* In it, he wrote: "They are not prolific, having generally litters of about three or four; strange to say, females invariably predominate, being generally two to one." One cannot help wondering if this is true today. The Shetland Sheepdog has been bred world wide for more than 50 years. Also, Shetland Islanders told the author that their sheep, cattle, ponies, and dogs tended to lose their native characteristics when bred away from the islands.

The American Kennel Club records litters. Periodically, since 1953, the author has made litter studies at the American Kennel Club. Among other things, a record is made at the AKC of the largest litters ever whelped in each breed. The records are based upon the number of puppies living at the time application is made to register the litter. A bitch might, for instance, whelp 20 puppies. However, 15 might die within the first few days after birth. The litter would then be registered as one of five.

Let us suppose that the breed record is a litter of 16. If an application comes in listing a litter of 17, the American Kennel Club will investigate to be certain that the litter actually is one of 17 as claimed. If found to be true, then a new breed mark is made. The largest litter ever whelped is said to have been 23 puppies, born to a Foxhound. However, no effort was ever made to register the litter. American Kennel Club officials believe the puppies came from three litters whelped on the same day.

At the time of the author's first study in 1953, the largest recorded litter of Shetland Sheepdog puppies was one of eight. A few years later,

Mrs. Alane L. Lubker (now Gomez) reported a litter of 10 with nine survivors litter-registered by the AKC. But litters of nine or 10 are very rare. Only two of 731 litters had as many as nine or ten puppies.

This data was taken from computer records which listed litters in brackets of 1–2, 3–4, and on to 21–22 and 22 plus. If memory serves correctly, the 22 figure belongs to a St. Bernard. All 22 puppies were living at the time the AKC received the application, but more than half had died by the time an AKC field officer investigated. We cannot say for certain, because of the above bracketing, whether the two Sheltie litters were of nine or 10 puppies, or one of nine and one of 10. The data do show that 292 of the 731 litters had either three or four puppies. That is a percentage of 39.9. The 5–6 bracket had 33.5% or 245 litters. And the 1–2 bracket had 141 litters or 19.2%. Of the balance, 51 litters or 6.9% had seven or eight puppies, and the two litters in the 9–10 bracket represented only 0.2%.

A. Hamilton Rowan Jr., secretary of the American Kennel Club, then personally helped the writer in a random study of 105 litters. Two were litters of eight; 22 contained four puppies each; 16 had six; 19 had five; 15 had three, 16 had two, and seven had one. In this case, we were more interested in the ratio of males to females than in actual litter size. There were 206 bitch puppies and only 135 males. Thus, Loggie's ratio of two to one no longer holds. But females do enjoy a strong lead over males. In seventeen of the litters there were no males among the 40 puppies. There were seven all male litters totalling 15 puppies. It will be seen from this that when only one sex is present in the litter, that litter is usually small. When there are large one sex litters, they are usually female. There were three litters of five bitches each.

It can be said that, in general, the largest dogs have the largest litters, and the smallest dogs have the smallest litters. We mentioned the St. Bernard litter of 22. A Great Dane had a litter of 19. At least 48 breeds have had litters of 12 or more. Collies have recorded many large litters, including one of 16. In an early study, 1957, the the author made a random breed check of 506 litters totalling 2,490 puppies. There were 1,301 males and 1,189 females.

# 17

# Color and Coat
# in the Shetland Sheepdog

MAMMALS as a group are among the most colorless of nature's creations. They cannot match the colors of the fish and reptiles. And they are hopelessly common when compared to the fantastic plumage and colors of the birds. Men and dogs are mammals. Men, perhaps envying the reptiles and birds, have tattooed their bodies and painted their faces. They have stretched ear lobes and lips, and have even altered the shapes of the breasts. Probably they first wore clothes more as ornamentation than as a protection from the weather.

Charles Darwin gave an example of this in his book *The Cruise of the Beagle*. The Beagle lay off shore of Tierra Del Fuego. Curious natives came out in their canoes to see the ship and the strange white men. All were naked. Among them were women who were nursing new-born babies. Crewmen gave them blankets. But the blankets were immediately torn into strips and distributed among the people to be used as decorations.

Perhaps you wonder how this preamble affects dogs. Dogs are said to be color blind. Yet, if so, of what use is the remarkable range of coat color shown by purebred dogs? This question is asked because it is a general rule that animals use color as a means of identification. With the dog, a possible answer is that man, unable to develop color and plumage in himself, has done so in his dogs. He could, and did, develop exotic skin colors in the hairless dogs. And he developed dogs with wire coats, short coats, off-standing guard hairs, and coats of astonishing length. He also developed dogs which, like the Shetland Sheepdog, have an outer, harsher coat, and a softer, dense undercoat. And finally, he produced some dogs which, like the Maltese, have no undercoat at all.

Now if the dog is color blind, it is not necessarily form blind. There is excellent evidence to indicate that dogs of a given breed can easily identify others of their breed. And evidence also exists to suggest that dogs have a sense of beauty as well as of form. Bitches, when in season, will seek a mate of their own breed. If they cannot reach such a male, then they tend to seek out certain males. Thus, a given mongrel may be the sire of half the dogs in a village. This evidence suggests that they recognize what is to them beauty of form. And the dogs which seem to them to be the most beautiful are those which have thick, heavy coats—specifically Shetland Sheepdogs, Collies and Chow Chows.

The climate of the Shetland Islands is about as inhospitable for a sheep dog as any in the world. We must believe that the islands' sheepdogs were, in 1900, well able to stand the climate. But the dogs of that day would be considered severely lacking in coat if brought into the modern show ring. Modern breeders have developed coats which probably would be more of a handicap than an aid to a working sheepdog in any climate. But the modern Sheltie coat satisfies the esthetic senses of both the breeders and their dogs.

Most mammalian color, whether of skin or of hair, in man or dog, is dependent upon a pigment named melanin. Melanin may be said to be controlled by a gene. A given gene may express itself in various ways, and these expressions are called allelic genes or alleles. For example when two genes are not identical, with one representing black hair and the other yellow, they are called alleles.

A dog's color is dependent upon the deposit of melanin in the pigment cells of the skin or hair. One set of allelic genes will control the deposit of melanin. But another set determines the actual color the melanin will be. The melanin will vary from black to mahogany red to pink. And the so-called yellow series of melanin will vary from tan and yellow to a whitish cream. Often the cream is so nearly absent as to make the dog appear to be almost wholly white, as in the Samoyed or West Highland White Terrier.

Lack of any melanin produces albinism. The albino is considered to be the result of a genetic error. It should be pointed out here that albinism is not limited to the hair and skin, but affects all the tissues of the body. True albinos are rare among dogs. The only ones ever observed by the author were three Pekingese puppies. As will be seen later, white or whitish Shetland Sheepdogs sometimes do appear. But they are not albinos.

There are dogs whose color we call blue. But pigment blue is very rare in mammals and it is entirely absent in the hair of dogs. The author

114

Ch. Richmore Gamblin Man, Best
of Winners SSC of So. California
1964. Owner-breeder Betty L.
Hansen. *Ludwig*

Am., Can., Bda. Colombian and
Mexican Ch. Astolat Gold Award,
also international CD, owned by
Constance B. Hubbard. *Shafer*

Am., Can., and Bda. Ch. Astolat Enchantor,
owned by Constance B. Hubbard, group winner
1969. *Shafer*

115

has researched world literature, and has studied the results of analyses of more than 200 furs, but can find no mention of blue pigmented hair. He has also queried research professors and geneticists. Blue pigment simply does not exist in dogs; but more about this later.

Shetland Sheepdogs have a wider range of color patterns than almost any other breed, Collies and the Arctic breeds excepted. These colors are black and white; black and tan; black, white and tan; sable (ranging from golden through mahogany) and white; and blue merle and white. There are, of course, prohibitions and penalties. Rustiness in a black or blue coat, washed out or degenerate colors (such as pale sable and faded blue), conspicuous white body spots, and with more than 50 per cent white, are among the prohibitions. Sable merles bring severe penalties in some countries, and all bar brindles. The white, or whitish dogs, mentioned earlier are usually destroyed at birth, as explained later.

It is not our purpose to go into a detailed explanation of color inheritance in Shetland Sheepdogs. Indeed, such an explanation is beyond all but those who have spent a lifetime studying the color genetics of dogs. Often these people do not agree. And few have made a thorough study of the Shetland Sheepdog. Those interested in this immensely complicated field are referred to three excellent texts:

*The Inheritance of Coat Color in Dogs,* by C. C. Little,
   Howell Book House, N.Y., 1957
*Inheritance in Dogs*, by O. Winge,
   Comstock Press, Ithaca, N.Y., 1950
*Dog Breeding and Reproduction and Genetics,* by S. A. Asdell,
   Little Brown, 1966

We will, however, report that information which Shetland Sheepdog breeders themselves have found. And we will include some additional information on the somewhat puzzling problems of the blue merle. Two tri-colors can produce golden sable. Two sables can produce black and white. Two blue merles can produce tri-colors. "It is that mixed up," as one Sheltie breeder put it. One reason is that the color alleles can be affected by others known as color intensity factors. For example, one of these can reduce ruddy colored melanin to tan. And the same factor, or another, can reduce orange to golden or cream. One intensity factor can change a dark color to a gray, or even to a whitish shade. Still another can produce patches of black on a lighter ground color, with interruptions of white. This factor produces the harlequin in Great Danes, and possibly the blue merle of Collies and Shetland Sheepdogs.

In discussing color, one Collie breeder remarked to the author "Blue merles are not blue, they are gray." But they are not the gray known to geneticists as agouti, nor are they a true gray of any kind. And neither are they a pigment blue. The blue color is an illusion. The reader will

Ch. Lencrest Mona Lisa, breeder-owner
Dee Dee Lenney.

Ch. Royal K Bandaleer, owner Shari
Kooyman.

Ch. Lencrest Roustabout, owners Helen
and Don Ostlund.

get a partial explanation of this in the chapter on eye color. But we might cite here a similar illusion which we sometimes see in the human face. A man has a very black head of hair and a very heavy beard. When he is clean shaven, his beard appears blue, and we sometimes speak of the blue beard.

An independent gene series determines that certain hairs will be black. An intense black melanin will be spread evenly through the hair. But a modifier, an allele known as the blue dilute will affect other hairs. In these, the black pigments will be clumped and scattered, with larger or smaller spaces between them. Then we will have the blue effect known as Tyndall blue. Submicroscopic particles refract and reflect the blue and violet rays, thus creating the blue effect. The blue will be deeper or grayer according to the spacing of the clumps of pigment. The black melanin tends to absorb the light, while the submicroscopic particles in between diffuse, reflect, and refract the blues and violets.

Recently, a Shetland Sheepdog breeder remarked that one of her blue merles sometimes appeared to be a lavender color. This could mean simply that more violet rays are being diffused than are pure blue rays. But we speak of blue and lavender sheens. The author has no authority for what follows. But it seems to him that some blue merles show iridescence. This is the quality of being able to change colors when reflecting light from various angles. Iridescence is caused by another factor known as interference. Whether or not it is actually a factor in creating the sheen in some blue merles remains to be studied. But in the light of our present knowledge, it should not be ignored.

Since possible Shetland Sheepdog colors can be so varied, and yet so pleasing, we can dismiss all of them here except the blue merle. The reason is that breeding for blue merles can be dangerous, and even disastrous, unless the breeder understands the problems involved. For that reason, we go into the problem to some depth.

The color is said to have come into the Shetland Sheepdog through Collie crosses. Many such crosses were known in the early history of the breed. Yet J. A. Loggie's 1910 article, which we have quoted in full, and actually written in 1909, indicates that the blue merle was already an established breed color before any serious crosses to Collies were introduced.

Bennett, writing about Collies in 1917, said that blue merles and black and whites without tan, were extremely common in the working sheepdogs of 1867. Ten years later, sable became so popular that both blue merles and black and whites began to disappear. He added: "Not withstanding the fact that Collies of the black and white and blue merle colors combined in forming the foundation of the pedigrees of every modern show Collie, black and white has become extinct."

However, blue merle still existed. But, says Bennett, "the material of the color available for resuscitation was not of much account." In 1907, the Rough Blue Merle Collie Club was formed in England, at Railway Tavern, Kyrwicks Lane, Birmingham. The next year the Birmingham Club gave classes for blue merles. William Arkwright, perhaps the greatest dog man of all time, is credited with saving the color. He bred scientifically for it, and his Blue Rain became the first blue merle champion in any breed.

Bennett seems to have known nothing of Shetland Sheepdogs. At any rate, he assumed that blue merle was a color limited to Collies alone—this, even though he know of the blue merle background in all working sheep-dogs. It seems likely to the author that Shetland Sheepdogs inherited blue merle color from the early working sheepdogs of Scotland just as the Collie did. One must add that, Bennett and others to the contrary, the blue merle factor is not limited to Collies and Shelties, but appears in the harlequin Great Dane, and probably in the Australian Cattle Dog, or blue heeler.

Dr. Leon Whitney, the brilliant American geneticist, worked on the problem, as far as the Australian Cattle Dog is concerned. Dr. Whitney pointed out that the blue of the American Blue Tick Coonhound is controlled by a different set of genes than those involved in the others. But the genetics of the blue merle in Collies and Shetland Sheepdogs are the same. And so we discuss the problem briefly here.

Different researchers have used different symbols for the blue merle gene or factor. Here we use Dr. Little's symbol, M. Most blue merles would be heterozygous, that is, they would carry a gene for another color also. We can use the symbol m for this. Thus, the heterozygous blue merles would carry the genetic combination Mm. If two Mm dogs are mated, and if four puppies are born, we could expect to have two heterozygous blue merles (Mm and mM); one homozygous (MM); and one homozygous (mm). The latter would be a dog of another color, perhaps a tri-color. The MM dog would be white, or whitish. It would have abnormally small eyes and it would be blind, or it might have no eyes at all. It probably would be deaf and, if allowed to live, probably sterile.

The ratio we have given above might not work out exactly to the figures given, except over many litters. One might, for example, come up with three whites in a single litter. But, even if only one white dog were born in the litter, the economic loss to the breeder would be greater than most breeders could stand. It is therefore a working rule not to breed blue merles to blue merles unless, with a specific purpose in mind, you are willing to put the defective puppies to death. Tri-colors are often used to darken sable colors, or to bring back black shading. But this may not work if the tri-colors come from blue merle backgrounds.

119

Ch. Sea Isle to a Wild Rose, owned by Sea Isle Kennels.

Ch. Skyways Sa-Wen, owned by Randy and Kathy Spencer.

Am. and Can. Ch. Someday's Stainless Steel, owned by Dr. and Mrs. J. R. Frazier.

Ch. Shanteroo Shady Colleen, owned by Shanteroo Shelties.

Ch. Merri's Daring Matador o'Capri, owned by Mary T. Boyle.

121

Ch. Flair Phoenix Blue, owned by Shirley Valo, Best in Show Des Moines KC 1971.

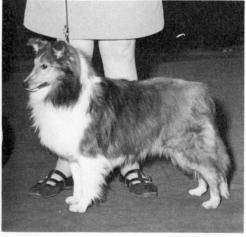

Ch. Pixie Dell Thistledown, owned by Mr. and Mrs. A. R. Miller, BOS Westminster 1972. *Gilbert*

Alkan's Dusty Rose, bred by Kandy Crocco, owned by Mr. and Mrs. A. R. Miller, BOW Westminster 1972. *Gilbert*

# 18

# Eye Color
# in the Shetland Sheepdog

$A$ MAJORITY of Shetland Sheepdogs have brown eyes. A few have lighter, yellowish eyes. Others have blue eyes, and these are variously known as wall, China, watch or pearl. In this chapter we will use the term blue. Some dogs have one brown eye and one blue. An occasional dog will show an iris which is half brown and half blue.

It is the blue eye which puzzles owners and breeders. Much has been written about the inheritance of blue eyes, but almost nothing as to what a blue eye actually is. In this chapter, we will try to explain the nature of color as it occurs in Shetland Sheepdogs.

In nature, basic colors are formed in one of three ways. The first is by pigments; the second by light scattering; and the third by interference We are hardly concerned with the interference in this chapter. Interference colors are those of iridescence. In the dog iridescent colors occur only in the whites of the eyes, some internal structures, and perhaps in the luster of the hair.

Pigments, called melanins, are responsible for all the blacks, browns, and grays of the animal world, whether in skin, hair, fur, or eyes. Here we are considering only the eye. It is the iris which is "colored" and which therefore gives an eye its color.

The colored portion of the iris is made up of a thin membrane. At the back of this membrane is the uvea. It normally contains deposits

123

of black or brown melanin. These melanins act as light absorbing curtains, and in this way protect the eye from harmful rays.

In the eyes of all brown eyed individuals, whether people or dogs, there is an additional layer or coating of melanin in the outer surface of the iris. It is this outer layer which gives the eye its color. The melanins absorb the other rays of the spectrum, but reflect back those which we see as brown or black.

Now we have said that the melanins in the uvea are "normally" present. When they are not, then the eye is an albino. Albinism is a genetic error which, fortunately, is rare in Shetland Sheepdogs. Since the melanins are missing, light strikes the thin walled capillaries and reflects back the pinks and reds of the haemoglobin. Albinos, therefore, have pink eyes.

Now, if the melanins which form the light curtain are present, but are absent in the outer portion of the iris, then the eye is blue. Remember, true blue pigments are extremely rare in mammals. And in mammalian eyes, they are totally absent.

The blue of the eye is called structural blue, or Tyndall blue. When we look at the sky on a sunny day, it appears to be blue. The reason is that white light is broken up and scattered. Some of the rays of the spectrum are lost in one way or another. But the blue rays are polarized and beamed to us. Thus, our blue sky is really only the result of having white light broken and scattered by colliding with particles in the upper air.

In considering Tyndall or structural blue, we are dealing with colloidal systems. A colloid is a subdivision of matter in which the particles, often protein molecules, are of sub-microscopic size. These particles, which usually range in size from one to 100 millicrons, are evenly dispersed in a medium. Scientists speak of a solid-in-medium, liquid-in-liquid, or gas-in-solid medium. All three are responsible for Tyndall blue.

White light consists of all the colors of the spectrum, ranging from the short violet and blue rays to the progressively longer ones ending in red. In the blue eye, there are no black or brown melanins in the outer layer of the iris. So the browns or blacks are not reflected back. The colloidal system then operates. Submicroscopic particles scatter the blue rays, but polarize them in a plane which is in the line of the light beam. The light beam returns to the viewer as blue—structural or Tyndall blue. The quality, that is the depth or the paleness of the blue, depends upon the size of the particles which scattered the blue rays. In some cases, the eye may appear almost white. The larger the particles, the paler will be the blue.

It is possible to extract melanin, or color, from any pigmented tissue. But you cannot do this with any structural blue. You can destroy the color by grinding or crushing the tissue because you have destroyed the light scattering mechanism, the colloidal system. You might inject a liquid into a gas-in-solid colloidal system and thus cause the blue to disappear. But if the liquid is allowed to disappear, as by drying, then the blue color is restored.

There is a widespread belief that the blue eye in a Shetland Sheepdog is a faulty eye, and that the dog may be subject to early blindness as a result. There appears to be no basis to this, despite the claims of some authorities. One has argued that blue eyed Nordics—those from northern countries—must squint a lot in order to protect their eyes from the hot sun of temperate or tropical countries.

This claim seems hardly tenable, especially when made in the case of dogs. No light can be stronger than that of the sun upon snow. Many Arctic dogs have blue eyes. Had these been faulty eyes, it is certain that Eskimo breeders would long ago have eliminated the blue eyes from their dogs.

Other authorities have tried to understand the purpose in nature of structural blue, whether in the eyes, skin or hair. They have found no answer. But they have decided that the light absorbing curtain of the uvea is sufficient protection for the eye. In the Shetland Sheepdog, the eye has additional protection from bright light. It is not set out prominently and it is adequately protected by eye lashes and brows.

The inheritance of eye color is a complex problem. There are many books on genetics which go into great detail upon the subject. Since they are easily available to the student, we will give only a brief generalization here.

True albinism involves the total dog—hair, eyes, skin, and internal tissues. Albinos bred to albinos would produce only albinos—in this case, pink eyes. Since no reputable person would make such a mating, it is unnecessary to consider the subject further.

There are only three colors which are common to the eyes of Shetland Sheepdogs. These are dark brown, light brown (sometimes called yellow) and blue. Dark brown eyes are dominant over light brown. Two pure brown eyed dominants can produce only brown eyed puppies. But one or both brown eyed dogs may carry a recessive gene for light brown. In that case, about 75 per cent of the puppies will be brown eyed, and 25 per cent will have light brown eyes. If only one of the parents carries the recessive gene for light brown, all the puppies will have dark brown eyes, but about 25 per cent would carry the recessive light brown factor.

The problem with blue eyes is more complex and is less well understood. As we have pointed out earlier, a dog might have two blue eyes, or one brown and one blue. Occasionally, a dog will be seen which has one blue eye and one which is about half blue and half brown. In such cases, the brown is usually dark brown.

Some researchers have felt that blue eyes are linked with coat color, and usually to blue merle. Perhaps a majority of Shetland Sheepdog

125

fanciers have believed this. For the breed standard calls the blue eye a "merle eye" and permits them only in blue merle dogs. Others have postulated the belief that blue eyes are in some way linked to tri-color coats. In such cases, they have claimed to see a lighter tan in the hair about the eyes.

Most researchers have noted that blue eyes can occur independently of merle coat color. When blue eyes occur in blue merles many researchers have felt that they are then dominant. But when one or both eyes are blue, and are not joined by a blue merle coat, then the gene for blue eyes must reverse its dominance.

To put it another way, a different set of "determiners" must be present to cause a reversal of the dominance. If one eye is brown and one blue, then some other modifier must be present. And, when the eye is half blue and part brown, either a different set of determiners, or a sub-determiner apply.

Whatever the facts may be, the breeding of blue merle to blue merle, and especially when the eyes are blue, is extremely dangerous. Some excellent puppies may result. But many of the pups will be a defective white. Many will suffer from an hereditary disease known as micropthalmia, that is, they may be born with no eyes, or with abnormally small eyes with oblique pupils. Many will be blind, or will shortly become blind. And some may be deaf as well.

Ch. Philidove Heir Presumptive, sire of 10 champions, owned by Philidove Kennels.

# 19

# Character

# of the Shetland Sheepdog

I N CREATING the standard for the Shetland Sheepdog, breeders placed a great deal of emphasis upon temperament. Leaving out the preamble, it is the fourth heading in the standard, and comes after General Description, Size, and Coat. This would indicate the importance which early breeders placed upon character, even though only 10 points were allowed for it in the Scale of Points at the end of the standard.

The temperament section says: "The Shetland Sheepdog is intensely loyal, affectionate, and responsive to its owner. However, he may be reserved toward strangers, but not to the point of showing fear or cringing in the ring. Faults—Shyness, timidity, or nervousness. Stubbornness, snappiness, or ill temper."

Now the phrase, 'intensely loyal" is a cliche, a hackneyed and virtually meaningless phrase. At least this is so when it is used to define character in a dog. Every breed fancier in the world claims this quality for his, or her, breed. Yet how do you define loyalty in a dog? And how "intense loyalty?"

Is a loyal dog one who follows the children to school? Is it one which shadows its master? Will it attack the charging bull which threatens its owner? If the owner engages in a fight with another, will the dog attack the owner's opponent? Will the loyal dog rush into the street and drag a child out of the path of a car?

Dogs do these things. But they rarely have the chance to prove themselves. The dog which shadows its master may do so out of an innate fear of being alone, rather than out of loyalty. Similarly, the dog which barks when strangers approach may be doing so out of fear, and may feel no real sense of loyalty.

Similarly, it is the rare dog in any breed which does not show affection for its master and family. This is a quality of being a dog. So, as in the case of loyalty, this really tells us nothing about Shetland Sheepdog character. It is the third word in that sentence—responsive—which has real meaning.

The major quality in the character of a sheepdog is responsiveness. It must respond quickly to training. It must respond quickly, quietly, and without question to commands. And, when herding, it must respond with lightning speed to every move of a wild sheep.

To do this, it must have great powers of concentration. A truism in training dogs, or children, is that you can't teach them unless you can capture their attention. So a sheepdog must give absolute attention to its master during training, and while working in the field. If its attention strays, the lesson is lost, or the sheep bolts from the flock and may cause a stampede.

A sheepdog must have a high degree of intelligence. It gains understanding of sheep through experience. But, unless it has great intelligence, it will be discarded by the herdsman long before it has a chance to gain much experience.

Courage can be measured in a variety of ways. A dog which may show fear under certain conditions, will show courage under others. The sheepdog must demonstrate its courage in certain very important ways.

It must not be afraid to go far afield in search of a lost lamb. It must show courage when an enraged ram or the angry mother of a lamb charges it. It must not fear to plunge into the flood swollen waters of a stream. It must not fear to attack wandering dogs which menace the flock.

The good sheepdog has an innate aptitude or instinct for herding. This has been bred into herding dogs since men first began to change from hunters to agriculturists and herders. Their ancestors for possibly 10,000 years have been herders. Of course, bidability or responsiveness, attention giving, and intelligence are all a part of the innate herding aptitudes. Still others are nipping at the heels, rather than biting or slashing, and silent fighting. The noisy fighter might cause the herd to stampede.

Shetland Sheepdogs have been impressive in obedience trials. Many of them win highest scoring dog in trial honors. They show the result of those thousands of years of breeding for such qualities as response.

Obedience training and trial do not, in the author's judgment, demonstrate intelligence, or even require it. But they do demonstrate other character qualities—attention-giving, trainability, response, steadiness, and obedience to command.

"However," says the section on temperament, "he may be reserved toward strangers." This is again a quality which belongs innately to a sheepdog. Such dogs live on lonely farms. They have work to do, and they know it. They may have to work in gales of rain or snow, and they must work to a large extent alone. So it is natural that they should be reserved, or suspicious, of strangers. Moveover, the demand for good herding dogs has always been great. One not suspicious of strangers would be easily stolen, and it could as easily be sold on a "no questions asked" basis for a high price.

These are some of the positive qualities in the character of the Shetland Sheepdog. It is true that few, if any, ever get a chance to demonstrate them in sheepherding trials or in actual farm work. But the author cannot believe that a thousand generations of breeding for innate aptitudes can be eliminated in a few show generations. But they can be nullified by serious character faults.

The sentence in the standard quoted above ends "but not to the point of showing fear or cringing in the ring." It is a tragic fact that thousands of Shelties are being shown which show fear, and which cringe pathetically in the ring. Moreover, many of them are winning. So you have remarkable working Shelties in one ring, and shy ones in another.

No one can question the fact that shyness, snappiness, and fear biting, have crept into the breed. There is no point in trying to blame anyone or any dog for this. Shyness is an hereditary curse in all of dogdom, in mongrels and in purebreds alike. It is a curse, and as a curse, it should be avoided as a plague. It is assumed that every breeder and every exhibitor has, at some time read the standard. Yet many breed and show shy dogs.

Judges are often amused by the imagination used by exhibitors to excuse shyness. But after a time, they get simply bored. They've heard all the phony reasons. Here are some of them.

"He is not used to men." "He won't show in a building." He's not used to showing on grass." "The last judge squeezed his testicles." "Another dog lunged at him just before we entered the ring." "He doesn't like to have you open his mouth." "He fell on the ice and skinned his testicles, so he won't let you check his rear end." "This is his first show." "He's only a puppy." "He's got a phobia on women's skirts." "Ever since the vet gave him a shot, he's been afraid of people in white." And so on, ad infinitum.

As a judge, it has not been the writer's experience that Shelties are fear biters. They may cringe away in fear, but they do not try to bite. This is quite different than the situation in some other breeds in which there are dogs which will try to bite the judge.

Am. Can., Mex. Ch. Grador's Robin of Windy Hill, owned by Frank and Irene Brown.

Ch. Thistlerose Sir Reginald, owned by Pinefrost Kennels. *Neetzel*

Shiloh's Mountain Echo, C.D., owned by Deana B. Rogers.

Ch. King of the Blues O'Page's Hill, owned by Karol A. O'Connell.

Ch. Starhaven's Mini Brat, owned by Marabelle Miller.

Ch. Lobo Dell's Charm Bracelet.
*Ludwig*

Ch. Rorralore Mickey Dazzler, owned by Charlotte C. Clem.

Am. and Can. Ch. Roydon's Queen Kandi, owned by Roydon Shelties.

Snappiness is, perhaps, a different type of character fault. Thus, the Sheltie on our farm will try to bite you if you try to clean its ears or trim its toe nails. And many veterinarians report that Shelties try to bite them when they are being treated.

This is not necessarily a fault in Sheltie character. It can be poor training on the owner's part. It is natural for dogs to use their teeth. Millions of dogs have to be taught that they are not allowed to bite human beings. And they can be taught this. But hundreds of thousands of doting owners fail to discipline their dogs.

It is a part of sheepdog character to be possessive. The dogs had to be possessive to the sheep they herded. They had to know the limits of the farm or grazing lands. They had to keep the sheep from straying onto another's property, and to keep strange animals and people off their land.

Such dogs may be possessive of the food dish, of their beds, of toys. But they can be taught that they must not be; that the baby can take away the toy or food dish, or crawl into the dog's bed.

We did not know the Sheltie on our farm when it was young. Nor does it live in our house now. So we had no chance to train it. But we did have the Belgian Sheepdog from its puppyhood. Belgians are somewhat sharper by nature than are Shelties. Or, perhaps we should say that Sheltie character is of a gentler sort.

We had to teach the Belgian that she had to permit us to cut her nails, and that she could not bite if hurt while combing out hair mats. When she would be hurt, she would yelp and turn her head to bite. Turning the head is the first step toward biting. So we disciplined her sharply. Then we tried to show her that we did not mean to hurt her, and that we would be as gentle as possible. Now few dogs are so gentle.

This is the sort of training which any dog can receive. Were it given to all Shetland Sheepdogs, the vast majority of them could not be faulted for snappiness or ill temper.

There are two others under Temperament which should be discussed. One is nervousness, and the other is stubbornness. The first is almost always an hereditary fault. Highly nervous dogs, and those which are actually hysterical, should not be used for breeding. The standard requires that they be faulted in the show ring. But breeders should make no excuse for them, and should guarantee that they do not spread their faults further in the breed.

Many breeders make the excuse that "She'll be all right after she has a litter." She won't be. And neither will her puppies be. As a rule, the puppies will be more shy than is their dam.

Whether stubbornness is a fault is a debatable point. Stubborn dogs are often hard to train. But once trained, the stubborn dog may be a gem. It will not quit when herding during gales. It will work until exhausted. And while it may be lacking in some degree in intelligence, it will make up for it by following orders perfectly.

However, if the stubborn dog dislikes dog shows, its stubbornness may prevent it from winning. It will refuse to cooperate with its owner and handler. In that sense, stubbornness is certainly a fault.

If one enters a home which has Shetland Sheepdogs, the dogs will normally dance just out of reach of the newcomer. This is not generally a form of shyness. It is a form of caution which has been bred into sheepdogs for thousands of years. They dance just out of reach of strangers who might steal them. They also dance just out of reach of the rams and wild sheep which might butt or charge them.

Recently, a Sheltie breeder put it this way: "People have got to learn that Shetland Sheepdogs are not Cocker Spaniels. It is not in their nature to fawn upon strangers. Nor should it be." In determining the character of their breeding stock, Sheltie owners should make this distinction between true shyness, true fear, and the prudence which Shetland Sheepdogs should possess.

Ch. Catamount Charade, owned and bred by Mrs. Stanley Saltzman.

133

Ch. Tentagel Mr. President, shown above at age 10 months, and here at age 2½ years.

# 20

# About Measuring
# Shetland Sheepdogs

---

SIZE is a problem in Shetland Sheepdogs today as it always has been in the past. The standard calls for the disqualification of all dogs which are under or over the desired heights, that is, under 13 or over 16 inches at the highest point of the shoulders. This disqualification applies only to dogs in the show ring.

When registering dogs the American Kennel Club ignores height, as it does also brindle color (brindle is also a disqualification). If a Sheltie is a brindle, 10 inches tall, or a brindle 20 inches tall, the American Kennel Club will register it so long as its papers are in order.

The American Kennel Club does, however, set up rigid rules for dogs which enter the show ring. At the present writing, any exhibitor competing in the ring at the time can demand that a competing dog be measured. Or, the judge can demand that a given dog be measured.

The present AKC rule calls for a committee designated by the show giving club as the measuring committee to be summoned to the ring. This committee must measure the dog in the presence of the superintendent, and often in the presence of an American Kennel Club field representative.

The owner or handler of the dog is not allowed to participate. Thus, three strangers take over the dog. A measuring standard which might best be described as a Guillotine type, is placed over the dog. A rod with a blade at the end is dropped to the dog's shoulders. Hair is lifted so that the blade rests on the shoulders, and then a screw on the cross bar is tightened. The standard is then lifted off the dog. The distance from the floor to the edge of the blade is the height of the dog. (The AKC has under consideration a rule change that would eliminate the measuring committee and leave the measuring to the judge and exhibitor.)

Another measuring procedure is possible. An exhibitor can ask that his dog be pre-measured. This must be done before judging starts for that breed. The measurement made at that time then stands for that show, that is, neither an exhibitor nor the judge can then demand that the dog be measured.

It is a common saying—and a common observance—that if the dog is measured three times, three different measurements will come up. Perhaps for that reason, the AKC permits the measuring committee to make only one measurement. But it often happens that a dog is measured "in" at one show, and "out" the next day.

As noted above, a pre-measurement stands for only that show. But, if a dog is measured out in the ring, then it is disqualified from all competition at succeeding shows until the dog is granted a reinstatement.

The procedure is to make a formal request, in writing, to the American Kennel Club. It will then designate a special committee in the owner's area to remeasure the dog. If it is found to be within the standard limits, the American Kennel Club will reinstate it.

Now there are some moral considerations involved. First, the exhibitors make the standard. In this case, the height disqualifications were made by the American Shetland Sheepdog Association after a long, and often bitter, battle with the American Kennel Club. It is therefore the duty of Sheltie breeders and exhibitors to see that the height specifications are enforced.

The trouble is that most exhibitors think that it is poor sportsmanship to demand that a competing dog be measured. Except under one circumstance, which will be discussed later, this isn't true, and it is a misconception which should be banished from the minds of all Sheltie exhibitors.

The judge also has a moral responsibility. He is, in a very real sense, the custodian of the standard. The trouble is that most judges are afraid to call for measurements. They fear the ill will of exhibitors. They also know that the measurement is likely to be as much as an inch off, and so they feel that it is futile to call for a measurement. Moreover the procedure takes time, and may keep the judge from staying on schedule.

Some exhibitors and some judges will demand that a class dog be measured. But they are afraid to ask for a height determination of a champion. They feel that, if other judges have passed the dog, it is safe to assume that it is within the standard. Yet if an oversized dog runs

Ch. Lingard Catamount Cameo, owned by Mr. and Mrs. Stanley Saltzman.

Ch. Shanteroo Black Jack.

*Mik-Ron*

Ch. Hallmark's the Black Watch, owned by Sheila T. Slick and Dr. Howard Cadwell.

*Shafer*

into a string of weak kneed exhibitors and judges, it can easily become a champion.

There are two conditions under which it is unfair for an exhibitor to call for a measurement. Shelties are not notably enthusiastic about being taken over by strangers, horsed about, and having a Guillotine standard put over them.

It may then become difficult for the committee to make any kind of a measurement. In such cases, the judge and committee certify that the dog could not be measured, and it is disqualified for that show. This is, then, a method by which a dishonest exhibitor can get rid of a likely winner.

Shetland Sheepdogs, Miniature Schnauzers, and Great Danes are breeds which also have minimum height standards. If a dog which is close to the minimum height, and is a bit shy, it will cringe when the measuring committee takes over. The best measurement the committee can then make may be so much less than the actual height of the dog that it will be disqualified.

Recently, the American Kennel Club has been investigating the system used in other countries—that which it barred the author from using. So it should happen that, within the next couple of years, the wicket will be the formal measuring device used at dog shows. But, whether it is or not, all responsible Sheltie breeders can make their own wickets. And there can then be no excuse for exhibiting a dog which is not within the limits set by the standard.

Now we have said that breeders and exhibitors have a moral responsibility not to exhibit over or undersized dogs. Yet few of them have measuring standards, and accurate measuring takes two or more people. Yet it is reasonably simple to determine whether or not the dog is within size. And this is all the breeder really wants to know.

Soft iron dowel rods are available at all hardware stores. One can bend and hammer a slender dowel rod into the shape of a croquet wicket. Two of these should be made. The ends of one should be cut off so that the wicket stands exactly 16 inches tall; the other, 13 inches.

The dog is placed in show pose. The first wicket is then set on the shoulders under the hair. If it does not touch the floor, then the dog is over 16 inches tall. The second wicket is used in the same way. However, if it does not touch the floor, then the dog is taller than the required 13 inches.

# 21

# How to Groom
# Your Shetland Sheepdog

In discussing grooming with a number of Shetland Sheepdog breeders who show their own dogs, and with two professional handlers, all said that Mrs. Barbara Curry of Beltane Kennels had written the finest article ever produced on the subject. We therefore asked Mrs. Curry to write this chapter.

Mrs. Curry says modestly that she has learned much from Collie fanciers as well as from Sheltie exhibitors. While her article deals mainly with preparation of the Sheltie for the show ring, it is equally valuable for those who do not exhibit, but who want always to be proud of their dogs.

Mrs. Curry's article is substantially the same as one she wrote some years ago for the *Sheltie Special*.

**Grooming the Sheltie for the Show Ring**

Just as many paths may lead to the same road, so may different methods of grooming result in the same finished product. The grooming methods described herein have been developed after much trial and error by the author, who feels that you do your dog an injustice when you take him in the ring poorly groomed.

ALL trimming should be done at home a day or two before the show, leaving only coat preparation—which takes no more than 30–45 minutes, depending upon the amount of coat carried by the dog—to be done at the show. It is not necessary to do the trimming one to two weeks before the show to allow for growth of hair to cover the mistakes. Trimming techniques should be practiced and perfected by the novice on a dog other than one being currently exhibited. All trimming should be done in such a subtle manner as to appear to be the normal growth of hair. When one trims the skull, for example, to the point where it becomes obvious, one might just as well hang a sign on the dog pointing out to the judge the fault one is supposedly trying to minimize.

The tools needed for trimming are a thinning shears (with double thinning blades), barber's scissors, stripping knife, and a fine tooth comb, along with the normal steel comb set with medium and coarse teeth.

Trim the feet first, removing the hair with the barber's scissors from the area between the large heel pad and the toes. Grind down the toenails with either a grinding appliance or steel file. With the scissors trim the hair around the foot even with the nails. If there is a large amount of hair growing between the toes, hand-pluck this out with your fingers. Older dogs have a tendency to grow "snow-shoes" between the toes. If this is allowed to occur it will spread the feet, and when removed leave a gap between the toes. It is best to keep this removed all the time to prevent the spreading of the toes.

To trim the back pastern, comb the hair with the fine tooth comb straight out and use the thinning shears to trim it, rounding it out evenly with the heel pad. The use of barber's scissors leaves a "scissored" look, where the thinning shears, which take longer, gives a more natural appearance. Use the thinning shears on the back of the front pastern also, cutting the hair close at the heel pad and tapering it into the longer feathering on the front leg.

Head trimming is difficult and the area where many over-do it. Clean out the long hairs on the inside of the ear with the thinning shears, and drastically reduce the large tuft of hair in front of the ear, taking several cuts with the thinning shears and combing out to see the result before proceeding further. Do not remove the hair that frames the front of the ear, but just clean away the long straggly hairs and the thick tuft mentioned above. The back of the ear should be handplucked, again to remove the straggly hairs. If the ear carries a very heavy coat and tips too far, excess hair may be removed with the stripping knife or the thinning shears. Avoid "Doctoring" the back of the ear too much, as it is readily visible. Where the inner corner of the ear joins the skull one usually finds a long growth of hair. Grasp the ear in the one hand and extend the ear away from the head, creating a straight edge, which may then be trimmed with the thinning shears. Low-set ears may be made to appear higher set by trimming some hair away from the outer ear edge. If ear is properly set, leave this area alone, as the longer hair here help to frame the face.

Carefully remove the whiskers and mole hairs (over the eyes, on the side of the head and under the jaw.)

If the dog is wider in skull than desired, or carries a thick growth of hair on the sides of the skull, trim the skull as follows. Picture a triangle, from the corner of the eye to the lowest point where the ear joins the skull, and from the corner of the eye to the highest point where the ear joins the skull, the base of the triangle being the ear itself. This is the area to be thinned out. If one examines the dog, one will see that (except in the tricolor) the hair is light at the base and darker at the end. The darker color forms the mask in the sables. If the hair is cut at the base, it will not be missed. If just the black portion is removed, the light part will show, leaving a gap in the mask. This is where the trimming becomes obvious. Therefore, the hair must be cut at the base, and this can be done only with the thinning shears. With your hand, make a part in the hair and lay the thinning shears against the skin, taking only one or two cuts. Comb out before going further. Repeat this procedure, making new parts, and staying within the triangle. This will trim out the side of the skull above the level of the eye, without it becoming noticeable.

The side of the head below the level of the eye can also be trimmed out by inserting the trimming shears into the mass of thick heavy hair and laying it as closely to the skin as possible, combing out and surveying the results frequently. Proper skull trimming on the short, wide headed dog will give the illusion of a longer, leaner skull.

After all trimming is done, brush the dog thoroughly, *to the skin,* using a bristle brush. Pin brushes are fine to remove dead coat on the shedding dog, but are not recommended for the healthy coat, as it does do some damage. Brushing out to the skin separating each and every hair, takes longer with a bristle brush, but does not damage healthy coat. Train the dog to lie quietly on his side while you meticulously part the coat and brush it out. Then turn him over to do the other side. This procedure is essential on heavy coated dogs if the dog is to appear in the ring "without a hair out of place." If the undercoat is clumped, the dog will look "lumpy."

After the dog has been thoroughly brushed out, put him in the tub and wash the white areas only, with tepid water and shampoo. Occasionally one sees the dog whose coat still appears lumpy in spite of thorough brushing. This is usually caused by an accumulation of oils from the skin and the only solution is a complete bath. There are risks with bathing however, for if the dog is due to shed, the bath will hasten shedding. It is perfectly safe to bathe a dog just coming into a new coat.

At the show, first prepare the white areas with Foo-Foo Powder (available at the concessions) and Precipitated Calcium Carbonate (available at the drug store), mixed half and half. After spraying the legs lightly with water and rubbing to distribute the moisture evenly, apply large amounts of this mixture with a woman's teasing brush, working it in with the brush, against the lay of the hair (place an old towel on the grooming table to collect the excess, removing it after the whites are done). If the dog does not have white legs, apply plain Foo-Foo sparingly, working it in with the fingers or brush. Leave all the excess powder temporarily on the legs and proceed to the collar and skirting. Spray the collar lightly and distribute the moisture evenly with your hands. Sprinkle heavily with baby powder, working it into the coat with your free hand as you sprinkle. (Foo-Foo can cut coat, and should therefore not be used liberally on the collar. Although baby powder may soften coat, it does not damage the coat when used as frequently as is necessary when campaigning a dog.) Then rub it in thoroughly with both hands. Spray the skirting in the back and the underside of the tail and repeat the same process with the baby powder. Now remove all the excess powder. Use the teasing brush and brush the legs against the lay of the hair until all the excess powder is removed and the legs are dry. Comb out the back pastern with the fine tooth comb. To remove the excess powder on the collar, face the dog and start at the lowest point of the bib, holding the hair above it out of the way with your left hand. Brush down vigorously toward the table, and in this manner work your way up to the chin and around the collar. *Be certain to remove all the excess powder!* This method whitens and brightens the white areas, setting them off from the body color, adds "bone" to the legs and separates and fluffs out the collar.

If the dog has a blaze, chalk it heavily with a piece of white chalk, including the underjaw, and then use a hand towel to wipe off the excess. Put a small amount of vaseline on your finger and apply to the nose, making a straight line across the nose so that the blaze is well defined from the nose. Put a small amount of vaseline on the fingers and rub your hands together and then smooth down the sides and top of the skull. (If you apply too much it can easily be removed with the towel.)

Spray the body coat with water. If the coat has been thoroughly brushed the night before the show, it is not necessary to dampen the coat heavily which requires longer drying time and more brushing. A moderate amount of water, distributed throughout the coat with the hands, will provide enough moisture to "stand" the coat up. Brush the dog vigorously with the bristle brush toward the head, including the belly coat and thighs, also brushing up the collar, until he is fairly well dry and all the hair well separated. Use the rat tail end of the teasing brush to work the show lead in out of sight directly behind the ears. Take the dog off the grooming table and encourage him to shake and settle the coat in place, and then place the coat over the hips in proper place with the wide tooth section of the steel comb.

# 22

# How to Show
# Your Shetland Sheepdog

THERE IS a rather special art to showing a Shetland
Sheepdog. Since the writer of this book is an all-breed judge, what is
said below is based partly on how the good professionals and amateurs
show their Shelties, and partly on how judges want them to be shown.
Since, as a rule, the judge first sees the dogs in action—in gaiting—let
us discuss this first.

Judges customarily send the dogs in each class around the ring once
or twice before having them posed ("set up" or "stacked" are terms
often used). Judges may then have the dogs gaited before having them
posed, or they may have them posed, examine each dog individually,
and then may gait them. Some judges may take each dog separately from
the group, examine it, and then gait it.

Gaiting usually consists of having the dog trot away from the judge,
and then back. The judge will stand in such a position that the dog is
moving back and forth directly in the judge's line of vision. Some judges,
particularly in classes of one or two dogs only, may require a triangle
pattern. That is, the dog moves away along one side of the ring. It then
crosses the far end of the ring, then comes back to judge diagonally.

Still others want a T pattern. In indoor shows this is most often used
when the center mat forms rectangles on each side of it. The dog is
then sent out on this center mat. It is than taken across the far end

143

Ch. Flair on Parade, owned by Shirley Valo, group winner.

*Lloyd W. Olson*

Ch. Valdawn's Talk of the Towne, owned by Kathleen A. and Herbert S. Searle, Best of Breed Westminster KC 1973. Judge A. Raymond Miller; handler Barbara Kenealy. Mr. Miller died of a heart attack two hours after this picture was taken.    *Gilbert*

144

mat, back across again, and then is returned along the center mat. This method will give the judge evidence of the dog's ability to cover a lot of distance with the fewest number of steps.

It is the exhibitor's job to study the judge's ring methods, note the procedure used, and then follow it. You can do this by watching part of the judging of a previous breed, or the earlier judging in your own breed. A judge must make hundreds of decisions during a day's judging, and must shrug off many annoyances and irritations. One such annoyance comes when an exhibitor, say the fifth in the class to be gaited, asks: "How do you want me to move?" If the judge wishes to see your dog gait in any pattern other than those used by the preceding dogs, he will tell you.

In gaiting, the judge is attempting to determine several things. The front legs should move forward in parallel lines with the elbows close to the body. There should be no crossing over, that is, with one front foot crossing over the other and into the line of that foot's progress. Crossing over is a serious fault.

Some dogs "single track," and especially if pulling on the leash. In such cases, the front legs appear to move in to a single forward line which would represent the center balance line of the dog's body. There would be no true crossing over. Usually a dog on a tight lead—"strung up" as the saying goes—both single tracks and crosses over. And, moreover, the dog cannot be kept along a true course. At a fast trot a Sheltie will single track naturally.

The hind feet, too, may tend to single track at a fast trot. There should be no crossing over. The hock joints should not be so close together that the feet drive outward instead of straight forward. When the feet drive outward, the dog is using energy to move its feet away from the line of forward motion. It is also losing ground with each step.

Crabbing, or side-winding, is also a serious fault of gait. The dog does not move forward in a straight line. The rear end is swung slightly to the right or left, so that the body is actually diagonal to the true line of forward motion.

Crabbing may be the fault of the handler. It may be due to a fault of conformation. Or it may result from lack of experience. When not due to conformation, crabbing can be corrected. The dog needs plenty of experience at gaiting so that it doesn't unconsciously pull itself out of line. Since most indoor shows use mats, the dogs are required to move along on them. This suggests a way of training your dog.

Try gaiting your dog along the edge of a sidewalk so that, if it doesn't move in a straight line, its rear end will fall off the edge of the walk. Or work with it along the street, and very close to the curb. If along the curb, then close enough so that it is almost crowded against it. If on the tree lawn, then close enough so that its rear end will fall over

Ch. Lencrest Renegade o'Tara Hill, owned by Dorothy Aldrich, group winner.                  *Earl Graham*

Ch. Raetta's Mark of Jobe, owned by Mrs. Henrietta Huston.
*Don Petrulis*

Ch. Catamount Black Phantom, owned and bred by Mr. and Mrs. Stanley Saltzman.          *Tauskey*

if it does not go straight. Your goal is double: to get the dog to move in a straight line beside you, and to do so on a loose leash.

Judges and breeders often complain that many Shetland Sheepdogs have a stilted gait, that is, they move forward with mincing, prancing, almost dancing steps. The Sheltie is a working dog. It should reach out with its forelegs and then drive hard with the hind legs. Part of the trouble can be yours. You move too slowly, and the dog keeps pace with you. Speed up a bit. Teach your dog to move forward as fast as it can without breaking into a gallop.

Most Shelties are posed in such a way that they stand truly, look upward at the exhibitors, and carry their ears at alert. Since Sheltie ear placement, size, and correct tilt of the tips is so important, you can't expect to win unless you can "alert" your dog. This is done by "baiting." Usually the exhibitor keeps the dog's attention by teasing it with a bit of fried or boiled liver, or even a bit of dog biscuit.

The exhibitor teaches the dog to stand while on a loose leash. The handler stands in front of the dog and holds the bait in one hand. If the dog tries to move forward, the handler moves a knee forward so that the dog must stop. The dog is thus kept in relatively good position, as far as head, ears, neck, and front legs are concerned.

But, if the dog is continuously moving forward, the exhibitor is in danger of backing into the dog ahead of it. In such cases, many inexperienced exhibitors tend to turn toward the edge of the ring, thus presenting the rear of the dog to the judge. But, whether the handler turns toward the outside of the ring or toward its center, the judge is given a three-quarters view of the dog when a full profile view is wanted.

If your dog does get out of line, tighten your leash, take the dog out of line, make a reasonably large circle, and then replace the dog as it should be. The judge may wish to see all the dogs posed for a front view. If so, be alert for this, and turn your dog so that it faces the judge.

If the class is large, the dog may become impatient. In such cases, give it a nibble on the liver or biscuit. Give it just enough to get it interested again. Be sure that the hand holding the liver is directly in front of the dog, so that its head is not turned to either side.

Many Sheltie exhibitors concentrate too intensely upon getting the front legs set truly and the ears alert that they forget the rear end entirely. Consequently, they may not be aware that the dog has moved one or both rear legs forward and under the body. The hocks are too far under, the rump is too high, and the dog appears to have a sway back.

In training, glance back occasionally at the hind end. Train yourself to be aware of the instant the dog moves a leg out of position. When this happens, tighten the leash, hold it in such a way that the dog will keep its head up, and then reset the hind leg. This is done by grasping the leg at the stifle joint, lifting it slightly and placing it in position. This

147

Ch. Kismet's Centurion, owned by Guy and Thelma Mauldin, Best in Show at Clearwater, Fla., June 1973. Judge is the author.

requires considerable training since the first few times you try it, the dog will move—and probably because you pulled it out of position.

Many an exhibitor complains that the dog stands and moves perfectly at home. But then they add such excuses as: "He doesn't like the leash." "He doesn't like to show inside." "He can't stand to have strangers go over him." "He won't let anyone look at his mouth." "He can't bear to have anyone touch his testicles."

In most cases, these are really excuses for lack of training. When you are training your dog, make sure that it is hungry—at first, very hungry. Then when the training lesson is over, it is fed. If you do this regularly, the dog will begin to look forward to training because it knows that it will get fed, or at least get delicious snacks, as soon as the training period is over.

Always take the dog to the show hungry. Give it snacks when it leaves the ring, plus plenty of petting and praise. It is not unusual to see people hug and pet their dogs even when the dog has done no better than to get fourth in the class. Tomorrow, the dog might win. And alertness in the ring may be a major factor.

Thus far, we have said nothing about the examination the dog must undergo. The dog must not pull away from the judge. Neither should it cringe. The judge will want to see the teeth. It is a courtesy to him if you pull up the lips, or open the mouth for the judge. Apart from the courtesy, you may be preventing the spread of disease.

The judge must check for soundness of front, eye size and color, ear size and placement, shoulder placement, back roached or swayed, angulation at the stifle, the testicles, hocks, coat texture, etc. If the dog cringes, he will have difficulty and you may lose. Yet you can condition your dog to stand this examination and even to enjoy it.

As in other training, the dog should be hungry, and should be rewarded afterward. Each member of the family should go over the dog as you have seen dog show judges do it. And this should be done repeatedly. Always afterward, the bit of fried or boiled liver, or the biscuit snack should be given. Finally, strangers should be asked to use your procedure. At first, have them do it in your own home, then on the street.

Your dog must also become accustomed to strange noises, strange buildings, and strange dogs. So take your dog to shopping centers. Praise it when people pet it. Remember to do this when it is hungry, and to feed it upon return home. Take it for long walks. Accustom it to car riding. And take it to sanction match shows where it can meet and get used to being around many dogs.

When you take your dog to its first show, take it when the show opens, even if you are not judged until afternoon. This will give it a chance to settle down, to get used to the building, the loud speakers, and the strange dogs. After you've been judged, stay until the end of the show.

149

Amer. and Can. Ch. Markrisdo's B.A.'s Patt'chez, owned by Charles and Patti Bruce, herding champion of American Sheep Trial Club 1966, 1967, 1968 and 1969.

# 23

# Shetland Sheepdog
# Working Trials on Sheep

*"There is no good flock without a good shepherd
And no good shepherd without a good dog."*

The quotation above is taken from the French Shepherds Club, and it is also the motto of the Shetland Sheepdog Trials Association of the Shetland Islands, Scotland. So far as the writer has been able to determine, this is the only club in the world which gives sheepdog trials exclusively for Shetland Sheepdogs. And one would be less than truthful if he did not admit, that, today, Border Collies do more sheepherding in Shetland than do Shetland Sheepdogs. Even in the islands, one constantly hears such things as: "Shetland Sheepdogs are only toy dogs," or "They are only show dogs."

J. A. Reid, a successful breeder and competitor in sheepdog trials for working, or Border Collies, wrote the article on working Collies for Brian Vesey-Fitzgerald's *The Book of the Dog*. He dismissed the Shetland Sheepdog in these words: "Nor need anything be said about the so-called 'Shetland Sheepdog'; for it is not a worker but merely, in the main, a miniature show Collie, and as such, is a production of yesterday." Thus does he dismiss both the Collie and the Sheltie.

And yet, just after World War I, Shetland sheepmen determined to save the great little workers which had for so long herded their sheep. Thus, in 1923, the Shetland Sheepdog Trials Association was formed.

151

It has held trials every year since. These trials do not differ in any respect from those given for Border Collies. And the dogs which compete are the equal of the Border Collies.

Perhaps here, we need to give some qualifications to the above remark. No dog is better than its trainer, just as no trainer can be a winner without a dog which lives up to its trainer. The ability of any dog to win is based on the perfection of its unison with its trainer. More trainers work with Border Collies, and so it may be possible that more of them are better trainers than are their opposite numbers among the Sheltie owners. It is also true that the Shetland Islanders are not professional trainers. They are herdsmen who compete with their private working dogs, as much to determine future breeding stock as to win prizes.

The original Shetland working dogs were much larger than those of today. They were called Haad Dogs. They were used to chase, trip and throw and hold wild Shetland sheep until their masters could tie them. But such dogs and such methods disappeared with the advent of Scottish shepherds, (It is to be remembered that the Shetland Islands were once Norse). The Scottish shepherds brought their own dogs, and they had already developed modern means of controlling sheep with dogs.

Again, to be truthful, we must admit that the Shetlanders speak of two breeds of Shetland Sheepdogs, even though both might be registered under the one breed name. There are the working Shelties and the show Shelties. The former are selected for self reliance, intelligence, trainability and stamina. Herdsmen boast that the dogs can run 60 miles in a day and do the work of 20 men. Show Shelties, they say, are selected chiefly for show points, and only afterward for temperament. One can draw a parallel between the modern field dogs, such as field-bred and bench-bred English Springer Spaniels. They are so different in appearance and in working abilities as to appear to be different breeds. There is, however, less difference between the working and the show Shelties.

Competition is keen. The 1972 trials were held at Swinster, Tingwall. There was a junior class for "boys and girls under 18." The Limit Class was for dogs which had not won a prize in the open class. The Open Class was open to "all dogs not entered in the Limit Class or eligible for the Championship Class; also the first three prize winners of the Limit Class. The Championship Class is confined to the prize winners in last year's class, and the first three prize winners of the Open Class on the day of the trials. There is also a Doubles Class.

In all, 50 dogs competed. They performed before a highly knowing, or expert, audience and before an outside judge. The winner of the Champions Class was C. R. Nicholson of Weisdale with a dog listed only as Glen. Glen had had to take second in the Open Class to Roy, a dog brought over from Aberdeen on the Scottish Mainland by his owner, Andrew Sutherland.

152

Before indicating the tests given to working sheepdogs in trials, the author would like to insert a personal comment. He judges as many as 10,000 dogs a year of all breeds. He attends, and sometimes judges, a variety of sporting dog field trials. And he has attended sheepdog trials on three continents. He does not think the Shetland Sheepdog can be sold so short. Shelties are trainable and biddable, and most of them have a high degree of intelligence. So it cannot be taken for granted that they would fail if given a chance, from weaning, at sheep work. Their background as workers is still too intense for that.

Still, Sheltie breeders and exhibitors, and especially those interested in obedience, should attend sheepdog trials. They would find the performances simply breathtaking. And they would gain a new concept of obedience work. Dogs may be sent off by an imperceptible (to people) movement of the foot, or by an almost inaudible hiss. They may drop instantly on a hand signal, or to a whistle. They anticipate the moves of wild sheep, and when they think the sheep are alarmed, they may drop and remain absolutely still until the sheep have calmed.

Sometimes at winter shows, such as Westminster, Border Collies demonstrate the penning of wild sheep. But the writer has seen Kelpies herd three day old chicks into tin cans; has watched Border Collies send sheep down a chute at a speed which just allows a man to force the sheep's mouth open and shove a worm capsule down its throat before the next sheep comes along. The dogs will herd geese. And they will not hesitate to run over the backs of closely milling sheep when it becomes necessary to get them moving in the right direction.

The trials given on Shetland do not differ greatly from those given for Border Collies in the British Isles, in the United States, Canada, Australia and New Zealand. A dog will have to go out on the "outrun," that is, take a circular run until it gets in back of some wild sheep some 200 yards straight away from the shepherd. It must then drive the sheep—three at Shetland trials—directly toward the shepherd, between two gates, around a pen behind the shepherd, then through another gate. It must then drive the sheep at right angles, across to the other side of the course, through a gate, and then into the "shedding ring" behind the shepherd.

In brace stakes, two dogs go out on the "outrun" on opposite sides of the course. They must get behind the sheep, which are at a greater distance from the shepherd than in singles trials. All six sheep must then be herded over a course similar to the one described above, and must then be penned.

At international championship trials, dogs might have to go out as far as 800 yards, and each dog of a brace might have to pen 10 of 20 sheep. Other tests are correspondingly difficult.

Have Shetland Sheepdogs ever been used for herding sheep in the United States? Have they ever competed in sheepdog trials in this country?

153

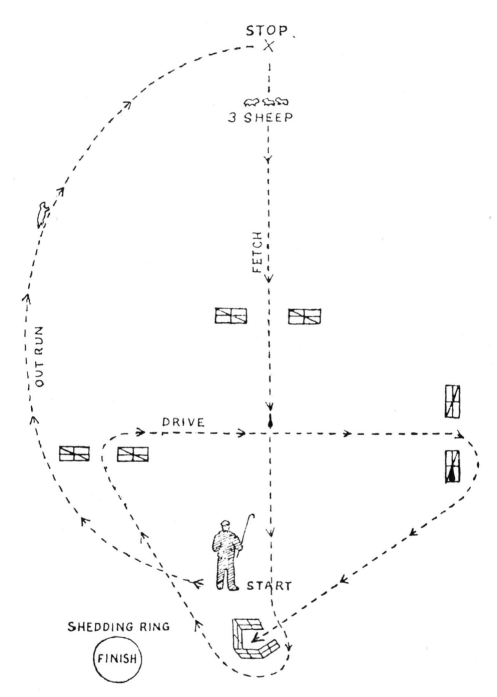

**All dogs must be kept on lead when not working.**

154

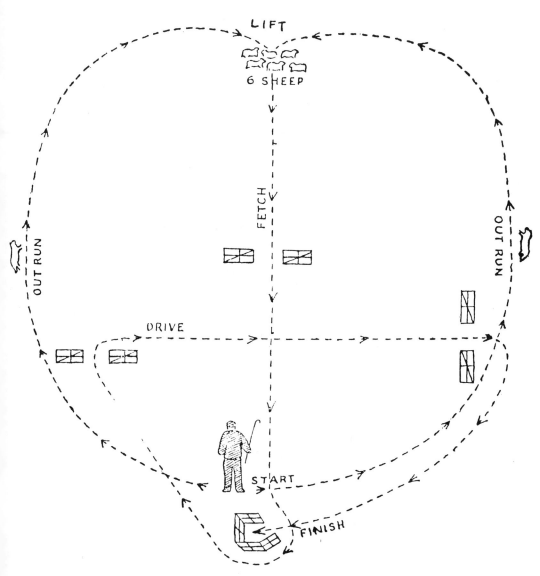

**Each dog is expected to keep its own side and do its fair share of the work.**

The answer to both questions is "yes." However, they have been used sparingly. They had to compete against already established breeds—the Border Collie and the Australian Shepherd (a breed now unknown in Australia). Their records in sheep herding are mostly unknown for such records were never kept.

Louise Knowles of Brookridge Kennels, Gunnison, Colorado, was an early Sheltie breeder and her family owned a ranch. In 1943 Miss Knowles bought Pixie Pan of Laurelridge from Mr. and Mrs. Ben Cooley of Laurelridge Kennels, Hillsboro, Oregon. The dog lacked one point for its championship. The Cooleys had just imported Ch. Laird of Exford. Miss Knowles had Pixie Pan bred to Laird before she was shipped to Colorado. She whelped seven puppies, four bitches and three males.

Three of the pups were kept for use on the Knowles Ranch. "They didn't need any training to be good stock dogs," she writes. But let her tell of two of the litter.

"One was sold to a sheepman here in Gunnison. He always took his sheep to high range for the summer, and this was the first time he had had a dog to help with the sheep. He had a herder who stayed with the sheep. About every two weeks, the sheepman would take food and supplies to the herder. And he also took food for the dog.

"One of the times the sheepman took food to his herder, he became very ill. The herder had to stay with the sheepman until he could get word to someone to get an ambulance up there to bring the man to the hospital. It took six days before anyone passed by so that the herder could get word to the doctor. The little dog, Wee Cadet of Brookridge, took the sheep from the bed ground every morning and brought them back at night without losing a single one from the flock.

"After he had got his sheep down from the range, the sheepman sold both his sheep and the ranch. Since he didn't want to keep the dog in town with nothing to do, I bought him back. Many of the ranch men wanted him, but they wouldn't pay my price. They all said that no dog was worth that price.

"Another pup went to a family here in Gunnison to be a pet for a two year old youngster. She made a wonderful pet for the child. She wouldn't let the child catch her and wool her. She just kept far enough away from the little boy to keep him from reaching her. There were several little children in the neighborhood and they all played together. They would run around the block, and the puppy herded them as she would have sheep or cattle when they are being driven to a certain location.

"She was named Pixie after her mother, and people called her Little Pixie. Little Pixie wouldn't let any of the children get off the sidewalk. The mothers knew that when Pixie was with the children, they were well taken care of.

"I sold Wee Foxy to a farm family in Kansas. She always went with the man when he went out to the barn to do the chores. One

156

morning, one of the cows ran after the man and knocked him down and began trampling him. If Foxy hadn't been with him, the cow would have killed or seriously injured him. But Foxy diverted the cow's attention and got her away so that the farmer could escape.

"I sold a pup from another litter (Pixie had been bred again to Ch. Laird of Exford) to a dog trainer in La Junta, Colorado. He trained all breeds of dogs. This dog was named Trinket. And when this trainer got Trinket, he wrote me that she was the easiest dog to train he had ever trained.

"He trained Trinket for sheep trials and entered her in one in Utah. She had to compete against all breeds of sheepdogs. The dogs had to work rams. And as more dogs worked them, the rams became meaner and more difficult to handle. Trinket worked late in the trials. She was the only dog which was able to corral all the rams. But to do this, she had to get a bit rough with them, and the judge refused to give her the winner's points. She was never entered again."

The trainer to whom Miss Knowles refers is Don Evett. He operated a dog training school for some years. He confirms what Miss Knowles has said about Trinket.

"I never had a dog easier to train," he says. "In fact, she really trained me. I used her for years to train the other dogs. She was one of the few that was not timid, and she was wonderful to handle."

Sheepdog trials were first held in Great Britain just one hundred years ago. They began in the United States some two years later. One of the clugs organized at that time was the American Sheep Trial Club. It was organized in Oregon, and it has held trials ever since.

Though it is not as well known as other clubs, trials have been held on member club ranches from time to time. Dogs competing have been Border Collies, Australian Shepherds, and a breed known locally as the Black and Tan Shepherd.

Shetland Sheepdogs were considered to be only "Toy Collies" and as one man expressed it "more toy than anything else." It was not until 1966 that a Shetland Sheepdog proved the contrary. The dog who did this was Markrisdo's B. A.'s Patt'Chez, generally called simply "Patches."

He was sired by Am. & Can. Ch. Malpsh The Duke of Erle out of Am. Ch. Markrisdo's Highlands Wendy, and he was bred by Mr. and Mrs. C. A. Buckmiller of Markrisdo Kennels, Beaverton, Ore. Charles and Patty Bruce of Kelso, Washington bought him, and Mr. Bruce trained and handled him.

During the next four years, Patches won the herding championship of the club, defeating Border Collies, Australian Shepherds, the Black and Tan Shepherds, and other Shetland Sheepdogs which were attracted to the trials. In all, he won all the 33 trials in which he competed. A perfect score is 200, and Patches, or Patt'Chez, never scored lower than 195.

He won three trials in 1970 before being injured while successfully shoving a child out of the path of a car. The dog was something more than just a herding dog, however. The Bruces owner-handled him to both his American and Canadian bench championships. He was ten times best of breed, and got one second and one fourth in group.

It is worthy of note that 20 Shelties were competing in the American Sheep Trial Club's events during 1968, and four of the six division winners were Shelties. For this proof of the working abilities which Shetland Sheepdogs still retain, American and Canadian Ch. Markrisdo's B. A.'s Patt'Chez is responsible.

# 24

# Shetland Sheepdog
# in Obedience

OBEDIENCE trials were designed to counteract the wide-spread belief that "show dogs are beautiful but dumb" (meaning stupid). Almost immediately, the trials turned out to be a fascinating and fun filled additional activity for the owners of purebred dogs. And they have done much to convince the general public that the owners of purebred dogs are responsible citizens who do not let their dogs become public nuisances.

We have already remarked that Shetland Sheepdogs have three great qualities—a high degree of intelligence, an aptitude for training, and what we can call "bidability"—the willingness to obey. No dog can be trained in obedience unless it will give absolute attention to its owner or trainer. Nor can it win unless it will obey instantly and correctly. Most Shelties fit these qualifications.

Obedience work should be taught to every Shetland Sheepdog whether or not it is to be entered in a show, or in obedience competition. The well trained dog is always a great joy to its owners, and a cause for neighborhood pride. Most cities and towns have primary obedience training classes. In these, the dogs learn to obey such simple commands as to come when called, to walk at heel on or off the leash, and to sit and lie down upon command.

Some of these dogs go on to advanced training. Many enter competition

Hi-Hope's Merry MacDuff, Can. U.D., and Can. Ch. Hi-Hope's Merry Imp, C.D.X.          *E. M. Allen Ltd.*

Ch. Wee Lassie of Eve-Bart, U.D., owned by Daniel Kerns. Leading Sheltie obedience winner.

at the shows. But those which do not are still a source of pleasure and pride to their owners. They help to improve the image of both dogs and dog owners in their home neighborhoods. And, of course, they advance the Shetland Sheepdog as a breed.

It is not our intention here to give an exhaustive report on obedience procedures. There are excellent books available on this, including the training of the dogs. But a short outline is in order. Obedience work is divided into four divisions: Novice, Open, Utility and Tracking. Dogs getting three qualifying scores in the novice classes win a Companion Dog (C.D.) title. They may then compete in the open classes. When the dog gets three qualifying scores in these classes, it earns a Companion Dog Excellent (C.D.X.) title. It can then compete in the utility class. Three qualifying scores are required to win the Utility Dog (U.D.) title. Tracking tests are given in open country. If the dog passes, it can add Tracking Dog (T) to its titles. A dog winning a U.D.T. title has won the highest award that can be given in U.S. and Canadian obedience competition.

Before obedience trials were formally adopted by the American Kennel Club, the American Amateur Training Club was organized at Chicago. It then permitted the organization of a Cleveland chapter. These clubs were basically for Doberman Pinschers and German Shepherds. When the American Kennel Club formally established obedience trials, the Cleveland chapter became the amateur training division of the Western Reserve Kennel Club. Thereafter dogs of all breeds were permitted to enter for training. The sole qualification was that the dog should be purebred. However, puppies had to be six months old, or older.

It is not surprising then that the first Shetland Sheepdog to win a U.D. title was a Cleveland area dog. Her name was Beach Cliff's Lizette. She was bred at the Merrilynn Kennels of Basil and Agnes Benson. The Bensons had been Collie breeders before adding Shelties. Basil Benson had been a long distance (20 miles) Lake Erie swimming champion, and as was Ella B. Moffit of Rowcliffe Kennels, he was also interested in spaniel field trials.

Lizette was whelped April 25, 1936. She was by Ch. Pegasus O'Pages Hill out of Longleigh Merrilynn. The Bensons sold her to Mrs. Irma Werner of Beach Cliff Kennels at six weeks of age. At eight weeks old, Lizette would, upon command, dive into a fish pool.

Mrs. Werner had been a German Shepherd fancier since her childhood in Denmark. She became an early member of the Cleveland training group. When World War II came, she became a member of the Dogs For Defense Cleveland chapter. And she was one of those who gave basic training to the dogs which were then to be sent to Army war dog training centers. Counting German Shepherds and Shelties, there was a time when more than a dozen of her champions had one or more of the obedience titles.

161

Amer., Can. and Berm. Ch. Sea Isle Rhapsody of Halstor, owned by Edith Overly.

Ch. Starhaven's Rockin' Robin, C.D., owned by Carl and Amy Langhorst, and shown by Amy Langhorst. Highest scoring dog in Cleveland Shetland Sheepdog Specialty, 1968.

*William E. Kelly*

Ripple Laddie became the second Shetland Sheepdog to win a Utility Dog title. He was bred by Margaret Perry of Hancock, N.H. He was whelped April 7, 1938 by Sheltieland Little Tartan out of Flagstone Tess. Eleanor S. Lundberg trained him and campaigned him to the U.D. title. Both Lizette and Laddie competed in the days before the tracking test was added by the American Kennel Club. In the lists given below, they are considered to have won this also, since they had won all they could.

It is hard to realize now the sensation these two dogs created. They were competing in a branch of the sport which, except for a few Poodles, was considered to be the domain of the German Shepherds and Doberman Pinschers. These two dogs did much, therefore, to open the classes to all breeds. And, of course, they did much to promote the Shetland Sheepdog.

Many Shetland Sheepdogs have won highest scoring dog in show honors. So it is hard to single out one dog as having been the greatest of all. We do, however, single out one dog as a perfect example of what the Sheltie can do. She is Ch. Wee Lassie of Eve Bart, U.D., owned by Mr. and Mrs. Dan Kerns of Center Valley, Pa. Note that she is a champion and a U.D. title holder. She was the nation's top obedience dog of all breeds in 1970. Moreover, she is the first champion in any breed to earn the title of top obedience dog, all breeds, in the United States. She is by Lonnie Du of Eve-Bart out of Wendy of Eve-Bart.

Through 1972, 387 Shetland Sheepdogs have won Utility Dog titles. Many others have won one or more of the lower titles, and some have passed their tracking tests as well. Obviously, the number of dogs winning the U.D. title is much less than the number winning the C.D.X. which, in turn, are fewer than those winning only the C.D. title. At least 1,000 have won the C.D. title.

## Sheltie Champions and Utility Dog Titlists

1. Ch. Geronimo Little Gremlin
2. Ch. Sea Isle Wee Bairn
3. Ch. Badgerton Flirt
4. Ch. Prince Patches of Feracres
5. Ch. Pameron's Copper Penny
6. Ch. Astolat Emblem of Merit
7. Ch. Merrywood's Candy of Pintura
8. Ch. Geronimo Little June
9. Ch. Sheldor Honor Guard
10. Ch. Blue Beau of Pocono II
11. Ch. Kawartha's New Gal in Town
12. Ch. Mr. Sunshine of Teradane
13. Ch. Playmate's Beau of Teradane
14. Ch. Sea Crag's Golden Bonnie
15. Ch. Lingard Danwyn's Gay Miss
16. Ch. Shalimar's Donnybrook Fair
17. Ch. Wee Lassie of Eve-Bart
18. Ch. Dreamalot Max
19. Ch. Marjan's Teddy of Scarlet Oak
20. Ch. Nodsoc Taro Blue Thunder

## American Shetland Sheepdogs with U.D.T. Titles

*1. Beach Cliff's Lizette
*2. Ripple Laddie
3. Sea Isle Little Tinker
4. Christopher Boy
5. Sandy of Brunhal
6. Ch. Sea Isle Wee Bairn
7. Pameron's Little Rascal
8. Sheltie Glen Shagbark
9. Minden
10. Golden Cove Shadow
11. Torlea's Brinda
12. Gail Patricia O'Pages Hill
13. Dusty Chiquita
14. Chiquita's Suzanne
15. Astolat Mr. Wonderful
16. Phillida of Hillswick
17. Hooligan of Orchid Lake
18. Tenorap's Lady Luck
19. Gillian O'Hillswick
20. Ch. Sea Crag's Golden Bonnie
21. Grayfield Peach Brandy
22. Carla's Little Peek-A-Boo

*Dogs 1 and 2 are included because they won the highest training awards possible in their day, before Tracking degrees were officially awarded. However, passing a Tracking Test was required then for the U.D. degree.*

One of these dogs rates with the greatest dogs of all time in all breeds. She is Ch. Wee Lassie of Eve-Bart, U.D., owned by Mr. and Mrs. Daniel Kerns of Talisman Kennels, Walnutport, Pa. She was called "Missy" for short, and she was purchased just to be a pet. But the Kerns recognized her quality in conformation and as an obedience prospect. By then, she was 15 months old.

People say that obedience training spoils a dog for the show ring. Missy was a perfect proof that this isn't so. She competed in both obedience and conformation at the same time. In fact, she won her championship one show prior to completing her Utility Dog title.

The now defunct magazine, *Chips,* rated Missy the top dog of all breeds in obedience for 1970. That year, she competed in 53 shows and won 80 first places in Open B and Utility. Moreover, she was highest scoring dog in trial in 29 of those shows. A study of highest scoring honors indicates that they go chiefly to winners of the Novice classes with the relatively simpler work required. But Missy was competing in the extremely difficult Open B and Utility classes. Also, since she often competed in both classes at the same show, she had two chances to make severe faults as against one in the Novice classes.

Missy's 1970 point average was 198.5 out of a possible 200 for the 53 shows. This is a remarkable average. Also, during a five year career in licensed and match trials, she was highest scoring dog more than one hundred times. And her five year licensed trial average was 198 out of a possible 200. We believe that no champion in any breed in history has made such a record. Finally, Ch. Wee Lassie of Eve-Bart, U.D. was owner trained and handled both in conformation and in obedience.

# 25

# Great Shetland Sheepdog Sires

I T has been said that records live; opinions die. The records of the great sires will stand forever. Arguments as to which was the greatest will always occur. Though inevitably the records must speak for themselves, a comment must be made on them.

The records of some sires would be greater if we included champions they sired in other countries. And there has long been an argument as to whether a certain dog was the actual sire of one particular champion. The truth may never be known. But the record stands.

We believe our list is complete up to the time of writing. But a number of the dogs in the list are still siring; so their records may still grow with the years.

In the lists of champion progeny for each sire the abbreviation "Ch." is omitted to conserve space.

Ch. Timberidge Temptation, Best of Breed Framingham KC 1946. Left to right: William W. Gallagher, judge H. W. Nichols, Jr., owner Dorothy Allen Foster.

*Percy T. Jones*

Ch. Merrymaker of Pocono, C.D. Leading foundation sire of both sable and white and blue lines.

## 23 Top Champion-Producing Sires

| | | | |
|---|---|---|---|
| Ch. Lingard Sealect Bruce | 42 | Ch. Pixie Dell Bright Vision | 18 |
| Ch. Halstor's Peter Pumpkin | 40 | Ch. Elf Dale Viking | 18 |
| Ch. Timberidge Temptation | 32 | Ch. Bil-Bo-Dot Blue Flag of Pocono | 14 |
| Ch. Sea Isle Serenade | 29 | Ch. Shelt-E-Ain Reflection O'Knight | 14 |
| Ch. Nashcrest Golden Note | 26 | Ch. Chisterling Florian | 14 |
| Ch. Merrymaker of Pocono | 25 | Ch. Prince George O'Page's Hill | 13 |
| Ch. Kawartha's Match Maker | 24 | Ch. Frigate's Emblem of Astolat | 13 |
| Ch. Mountaineer O'Page's Hill | 22 | Ch. Geronimo Crown Prince | 13 |
| Ch. Merry Meddler of Pocono | 21 | Ch. Astolat Future Emblem | 13 |
| Ch. Musket O'Page's Hill | 20 | Ch. Brandell's Break-A-Way II | 12 |
| Ch. Malpsh Great Scott | 20 | Ch. Diamond's Robert Bruce | 12 |
| Ch. Mowgli | 19 | | |

## Ch. Lingard Sealect Bruce

(By Ch. Nashcrest Golden Note ex Timberidge Sandstorm. Whelped 10/26/60. Sable. 1966 champion.)

| | |
|---|---|
| Malpsh Great Scott (D) | Lingard Fair Lady O'Four Winds (B) |
| Malpsh Woodwind of Sea Isle (D) | Badgerton Scheherazade (B) |
| Malpsh Autumn Gold (B) | Win-Dee-Hil Bronze Satellite (D) |
| Naripa Enchantment of Note (B) | Lingard Sunset's Delight (B) |
| Lingard First Lady (B) | Ken-Robs That's Life (D) |
| Wickiup Topsy Turvy (B) | Lingard Golden Glow (B) |
| Diamond's Robert Bruce (D) | Lingard's Butch Cassidy (D) |
| Malpsh Stormy Weather (B) | Tiny Tuck of Walnut Hall (D) |
| Lingard Donna of Northwood (B) | Richmore Wheeler Dealer (D) |
| Lingard Western Heir (D) | Schoodic Helzablazen (D) |
| Lingard Wee Geordie (D) | Lingard Catamount Cameo (B) |
| Meadow Ridge of Birch Hollow (B) | Karelane Banshee O'Faunbrook (B) |
| Candlewood's Charlie My Boy (D) | Sun Goddess of Sealect (B) |
| Astolat Enchantor (D) | Lingard Bruce Junior (D) |
| Lingard Congenial Timmy (D) | Edanjo Classic Cassandra (B) |
| Malpsh Hanky Pank O'Briarwood (B) | Northwood The Sundance Kid (D) |
| Malpsh Windhover Sorcery (B) | Benayr Bonfire, C.D. (D) |
| Lingard Mighty MacDuff (D) | Lingard Rosmoor Upsy Daisy (B) |
| Lingard Dawn of Bruce (B) | Lingard Gold A Glow (B) |
| Briarwood Playboy's Playmate (B) | O'Bare's Double Take of Astolat (D) |
| Lingard Highland Piper (D) | Shurdale Charlie Brown (D) |

Ch. Kawartha's Matchmaker.

Ch. Merry Meddler of Pocono, C.D.X.

## Ch. Halstor's Peter Pumpkin

(By Fair Play of Sea Isle ex Can. & Berm. Ch. Sea Isle Rhapsody of
Halstor. Wh. 7/13/65. Sable. 1967 ch.)

Philidove Macdega Miracle (B)
Habilu Inspiration (B)
Marjan's Vagabond (D)
Marjan's Flower Power (B)
Sandmere Peter Piper (D)
Betsubar Masterpiece (D)
Ilemist Impossible Dream (D)
Sheldor Cinderella (B)
Beltane The Buccaneer (D)
Four Winds Filibuster (D)
Kiloren September Song (B)
Mountainlair Sandmere Margo (B)
Shu-La-Le's Gerth Rapunzel (B)
Beltane The Standardbearer (D)
Willow Wand Touch O'Gold (B)
Elite's Select Pumpkin (D)
Sandmere Tommie Tucker (D)
Shu-La-Le's Pocketful of Rye (B)
Four Winds Jasmyn O'The Glenn (B)
Macdega The Prophet (D)

Four Winds Baron O'The Glenn (D)
Philidove Pumpkin Seed (D)
Spook Holler's Peter Pan (D)
Talisman's Peebles v. Linzmeyer (B)
Betsubar Ringmaster (D)
Shu-La-Le Twinkle Star (B)
Beltane Checkmate (D)
Carmylie Elusive Dream (D)
Astolat Galaxy (D)
Beltane Bannerette (B)
Marjan's Nifty (B)
Sandmere Starina (B)
Carmylie Call To Promise (B)
Bob's Mt. Piper O'Tentagel (D)
Rosmoor Repete (D)
Kidwelly Two For The Show (D)
Beltane Scotch Gambit (B)
Shu-La-Le Summer Sunshine (B)
Willow Wand Gold Rush II (D)
Barwoods Rhapsody (B)

## Ch. Timberidge Temptation

(By Ch. Kalandar Prince O'Page's Hill ex Ch. Timberidge Temptress.
Wh. 6/9/42. Sable. 1944 ch.)

Geronimo Crown Prince (D)
Lady Libby (B)
Timberidge Taffy of Pocono (B)
Geronimo Guardsman O'Noralee (D)
Timberidge Topaz (B)
Gleeful of Mar-Nor-Wil (B)
Gay Pilot of Mar-Nor-Wil (D)
Geronimo Russet (B)
Timberidge Black-Eyed Susan (B)
Brandell's Butterfly (B)
Wayfarer of Pocono (D)
Tiny Badger of Walnut Hall (D)
Heather For Luck (B)
Timberidge Amber (B)

Meadow Ridge Rascal (D)
Meadow Ridge Another Ridge (D)
Precision of Pocono (D)
Genairn Devil May Care (D)
Golconda of Timberidge (D)
Arthea Jaunty Jon (D)
Golden Crown of Faunbrook (D)
Gold Sixpence O'Faunbrook (B)
Bogota Sunbeam (B)
Timberidge Penelope (B)
Gingerbread Lady of Pocono (B)
Timberidge Talisman (D)
Geronimo Lend Lease (B)
Arthea Dot and Dash (B)

Brandell's Beacon (D)
La Belle Dame of Scotleigh (B)

Falkirk's Whimsical Susie (B)
Genairn Joy O'Shelt-E-Ain (B)

## Ch. Sea Isle Serenade

(By Ch. Nashcrest Golden Note ex Ch. Sea Isle Serenata.
Wh. 3/22/56. Sable. 1957 ch.)

Sea Isle Bard of Bagaduce (D)
Sea Isle Tay of Eltham (D)
Badgerton Pantomime Patsy (B)
Badgerton Proud Prince (D)
Sea Isle Calypso's MacDuff (D)
Markrisdo's Highlands Wendy (B)
Ken-Robs Gay Blade (D)
Malpsh The Duke of Erle (D)
Rickwood Acres Miss Serenade (B)
Malpsh Winter Wind (B)
Hatfield's Sultan of Lorel (D)
Kerry Poole of Rabbit Run (D)
B.A.'s Lucky Fella of Highlands (D)
Bright Angel's Highlands Buz (D)
Highland's High Sea (D)

Browne Acres Prince Consort (D)
Sea Isle Rhapsody of Halstor (B)
Carmylie Bravo O'Banchory (D)
Rebmel Barnstormer (B)
Barwoods Bonanza O'Merri Lon (D)
Barwoods Bold Venture (D)
Ken-Robs Partners Choice (D)
Scotchguard Sea Chantery (D)
Alnphyll Aristocrat (D)
Camian's Clansman of Hi-Hope (D)
Keynote of Sealect (D)
Bilgowan Grenadier (D)
Vanity Fair of Carmylie (B)
Diamond's Redbud (D)

## Ch. Nashcrest Golden Note

(By Ch. Prince George O'Page's Hill ex Nashcrest Rhythm. Wh. 1/21/51.
Sable. 1952 ch. Note Prince George and Timberidge Temptation,
above, are full brothers.)

Sea Isle Serenata (B)
Sea Isle Sheila (B)
Sea Isle Serenade (D)
Sea Isle Cadenza (D)
Sea Isle Stanza of Astolat (D)
Stylish Miss of Hatfield (B)
Hatfield's Stardust (B)
Notable Lad of Sea Isle (D)
Sealect Christmas Holly (B)
Lingard Sealect Bruce (D)
Timberidge Target (D)
Timberidge Honey Gold (B)
Kildoona Tori of Sea Isle (B)

Katie-J's Ronny (D)
Badgerton Alert Alec (D)
E-Danha Babalu (D)
Sea Isle Merchant Prince (D)
Sea Isle Autumn Glory (B)
Sea Isle Rebecca (B)
Rosslyn's Magic Touch (B)
Thistlerose Milord (D)
Sheltilore Queen of Hearts (B)
Browne Acres Bandleader (D)
Ray Eden's Golden Dove (B)
Ray Eden's Golden Chord (D)
Golden Pines Wee Angus (D)

Ch. Chisterling Florian.

Ch. Bil-Bo-Dot Blue Flag of Pocono, leading blue merle sire.

## Ch. Merrymaker of Pocono

(By Ch. Peabody Pan (import) ex Ch. Syncopating Sue of Anahassitt. Wh. 10/10/35. Sable. 1938 ch.)

Adoration (B)
Merry Maid of Anahassitt (B)
Beach Cliff's Mischief (D)
Rockwood Candlelight (B)
Mischief Maker of Pocono (B)
Noralee Black Dougal (D)
Timberidge Temptress (B)
Bogota Silhouette (B)
Merry Meddler of Pocono (D)
Kiloh Son of Merrymaker (D)
Pocono Merry Lass (B)
Pocono Ginger of Bagaduce (B)
Tiny Ebony of Walnut Hall (D)

Victory of Pocono (D)
Altair Ann of Pocono (B)
Smokecloud of Pocono (D)
Token of Pocono (D)
Yankee of Keprell (D)
Meadow Ridge Golden Dawn (B)
Genairn Gay Teddybear (D)
Blaeberry Jean (B)
Faunbrook Fairy of Pocono (B)
Genairn Gay Laird (D)
Black Witch of Pocono (B)
Pocono Pirouette (B)

## Ch. Kawartha's Match Maker

(By Ch. Sheltieland Kiltie O'Sea Isle ex Ch. Kawartha's Sabrina Fair. Wh. 12/7/56. Sable. 1958 ch.)

Crawford Matchless (D)
Kawartha's Auntie Mame (B)
Kawartha's New Star's Born (B)
Gigi of Holly Hill (B)
Kawartha's Sheena O'Hushco (B)
Sea Isle Sound O'Victory (D)
Marjan's Commander of Sea Isle (D)
Marjan's Destiny Maker (D)
Marjan's Pattern Maker (B)
Marjan's Rorralore Riddle (B)
Marjan's Bonny of Scarlet Oak (B)
Tamworth Tempo Primo (D)

Malpsh Texas Loner (D)
Allmac's Starlit Rhapsody (B)
Marjan's Music Maker O'Waljon (D)
Marjan's Major of Sea Isle (D)
Marjan's Daisey Belle (B)
Marjan's Teddy of Scarlet Oak (D)
Westwood's Mischief Maker (B)
Crawford Myth-Maker (D)
Marjan's Legend Maker (D)
Westwood Pace Maker (D)
Brujean Magic Maker O'Waljon (D)
Westwood Merry Maker (B)

## Ch. Mountaineer O'Page's Hill

(By Ch. Kim O'Page's Hill ex Coquette O'Page's Hill. Wh. 5/18/41. Sable. 1942 ch.)

Olympic Flower O'The Picts (B)
Gipsy's Audacious (D)

Geronimo Little Garland (B)
Country Gossip O'The Picts (B)

Remembrance O'The Picts (D)     Laird O'The Picts (D)
Geronimo Little Starlight (B)     Gipsy's Adorable (B)
Mountain Missy O'The Picts (B)     Mountain Ann of Windy Oaks (B)
Sheltieland Peg O'The Picts (B)     E-Danha Fanciful Wishing (B)
Redledge Cherry Blossom (B)     Bil-Bo-Dot Adorable Miss (B)
Sheltieland Shasta Geronimo (B)     Ayr's Prince Consort (D)
Gay Dirndl O'The Picts (B)     Zetland Glufft (D)
The Chief Geronimo (D)     Confection O'The Picts (B)
Bit O'Honey O'The Picts (B)     Zetland Sturla (B)

## Ch. Merry Meddler of Pocono

(By Ch. Merrymaker of Pocono ex Ch. Merry Memory of Pocono.
Wh. 1/2/37. Tricolor. 1941 ch.)

Bil-Bo-Dot Blue Flag of Pocono (D)     Bluet of Pocono (B)
Pollyana of Pocono (B)     Blue Talisman of Pocono (D)
Michael of Beech Tree (D)     Pocono Carefree of Sea Isle (B)
Blue Iris of Pocono (B)     Blue Treasure of Pocono (B)
Arthea Blue Sparkler (D)     Alice Blue of Pocono (B)
Forget-Me-Not of Pocono (B)     Miss Meddlesome of Pocono (B)
Pocono Portia of Arthea (B)     Tailor Made of Pocono (D)
Blue Petal of Pocono (B)     Night Rider of Pocono (D)
Pocono Pennyroyal of Sea Isle (B)     Pocono Trinket of Windy Oaks (B)
Blue Elegance of Pocono (B)     Shelmar Songbird O'Pocono (B)
Valiant of Pocono (D)

## Ch. Musket O'Page's Hill

(By Musketeer O'Page's Hill ex Peablossom O'Page's Hill.
Wh. 2/7/45. Sable. 1948 ch.)

Va-Gore's Classy Miss (B)     Pixie Dell Encore (B)
Va-Gore's Bright Promise (B)     Kacing Summer Sprite (B)
Va-Gore's Brigadier (D)     Eltham's High Gun (D)
Lillegard Golden Talisman (D)     Bandmaster O'Page's Hill (D)
Va-Gore's Cheer Leader (B)     Cheery Carol of Hobby Ho (D)
Meadow Ridge Stitch In Time (F)     Victory Song of Hobby Ho (D)
Pixie Dell Firebrand (D)     Ald-Abeth Flintlock (D)
Meadow Ridge Hot Sunday (B)     Sir Charles of Kenloch (D)
Pixie Dell Little Minstrel (D)     Magnet O'Page's Hill (D)
Pixie Dell Theme Song (B)     Pixie Dell Echo (B)

# Ch. Malpsh Great Scott

**(By Ch. Lingard Sealect Bruce ex Malpsh Her Royal Madjesty
Wh. 11/23/63. Sable. 1964 ch.)**

Malpsh Kathy's Clown (B)
Malpsh Windhover Whichery (B)
Lanbur's Great Fortune (D)
Nightfall's Star Bright (B)
Ronann's Tawny Miss (B)
Ken-Robs Kenny (D)
Ken-Robs Bobbie (D)
Timewell's Something Special (B)
Malpsh Golden Dancer (B)
Sparkling Sherry of Aron-Kae (B)

Marjan's Mystery of Sea Isle (B)
Marjan's Mystic Scot O'Sea Isle (D)
Lanbur's Mostly Mischief (F)
Malpsh Spookey (B)
Malpsh Sandman of Robinaire (D)
Briarwood Carey's Clown (D)
Debonaire's Prince Scot (D)
Beltane Solitaire (B)
Sugar Hill's Aron-Kae Glory Be (B)
Honeywynd's Rob Roy (D)


# Ch. Mowgli

**(By Ch. Wee Laird of Downfield (import) ex Jean of Anahassitt.
Wh. 7/2/31. Sable. 1932 ch.)**

Pegasus O'Page's Hill (D)
Lady Tamworth O'Page's Hill (F)
Kim O'Page's Hill (D)
Coltness Commander (D)
Tiny Chloe of Walnut Hall (B)
Peter Pan O'Page's Hill (D)
Promise O'Page's Hill (B)
Pied Piper O'Page's Hill (D)
Sheltieland Little Boy (D)
Kalandar Prince O'Page's Hill (D)

Lady Precious O'Page's Hill (B)
Sheltieland Laird (D)
Ronalee Norseman (D)
Petticoat O'The Picts (B)
Cock O'The North O'Page's Hill (D)
Otseningo Dinah Mite (B)
Will O'The Mill O'Page's Hill (D)
Sheltieland Atlantis (D)
Leif The Lucky O'Page's Hill (D)


# Ch. Pixie Dell Bright Vision

**(By Ch. Brandell's Break-A-Way II ex Ch. Va-Gore's Bright Promise.
Wh. 6/17/57. Sable. 1958 ch.)**

Dan-Dee Petite Regards (B)
Sutter's Golden Masquerade (D)
Dan-Dee Sun Struck (D)
Albershel Sundrops (F)
Meadow Ridge On Time (B)
Ray-Eden's Sundown (D)
Goodhill Black Mist (B)

Smokeywood New Vision (D)
Meadow Ridge Baby Jane (B)
Meadow Ridge Bright Holiday (B)
Meadow Ridge Norgay Red Raven
(D)
Sharlin's Oh-Suzanna (B)
Forecaster Wee Bairn of Heidi (D)

174

Sharlin Ringo (D)
Sharlins Penny Brite (B)
Ric-Lyn's Bright Magic (B)

Meadow Ridge It's Me (D)
Meadow Ridge So What's New (B)

## Ch. Elf Dale Viking

(By Ch. Noralee Forecaster ex Ch. Elf Dale Heidi.
Wh. 6/29/58. Sable. 1960 ch.)

Elf Dale Golden Legacy (D)
Elf Dale Pride of Dale (B)
Starcastle Vanity Fair Angel (B)
Elf Dale Spartacus (D)
Elf Dale Mr. Wonderful (D)
Starcastle My Valiant Laddie (D)
Clelland's First Impression (D)
Starcastle Angelic Vixen (B)
Elf Dale Captain's Choice (D)

Tiger Adonis (D)
Richmore Fascinating Lady (B)
Elf Dale My Fair Lady (B)
Elf Dale Golden Glow (B)
Elf Dale Wee Warrior (D)
Viking's Tamerlark O'Sherwood (B)
Blucreek's If I Had My Way (B)
Zelbrae Sugar N'Spice (B)
Richmore Stylish Miss (B)

## Ch. Bil-Bo-Dot Blue Flag of Pocono

(By Ch. Merry Meddler of Pocono ex Ch. Pentstemon of Beech Tree.
Wh. 7/21/38. Blue Merle. 1940 ch.)

Pixie Dell Blue Splendor (B)
Silhouette Sue of Pocono (B)
Valse Bleu of Faunbrook (B)
Little Blue Of Gnilwoc (D)
Happy-Go-Lucky of Pocono (B)
Blue Flageolet of Faunbrook (D)
Laurelridge Fuzzy Wuzzy (D)

Shelcort Anne (B)
Royal Blue of Montrose (D)
Scottish Grey of Faunbrook (D)
Black Royalty of Montrose (D)
Bogota Blue Thistle (D)
Larkspur's Finalist of Pocono (D)
Blue Storm of Pocono (D)

## Ch. Shelt-E-Ain Reflection O'Knight

(By Ch. Shelt-E-Ain Black Knight ex Shelt-E-Ain Lucky Penny.
Wh. 6/4/50. Tricolor. 1951 ch.)

Blue Echo of Pocono (D)
Blue Heritage of Pocono (D)
Kiloren Nightstorm O'Alandie (D)
Kiloren Silver Mist of Pocono (B)
Lingard Blue Boy (D)
Prince Patches of Feracres (D)
Blue Beau of Pocono II (D)

Ro-Jay's Blue Angel (B)
Kiloren's Silver Legend (D)
Kiloren's Sprite of Pocono (B)
Cherrilon Blue Moon (B)
Feracres Hercules (D)
Blue Blend of Pocono (D)
Blue Destiny of Pocono (B)

Ch. Halstor's Peter Pumpkin.

Ch. Astolat Future Emblem.

Ch. Nashcrest Golden Note.

176

## Ch. Chisterling Florian

(By Ch. Astolat Future Emblem ex Lillegard Golden Charm.
Wh. 5/8/60. Sable. 1961 ch.)

Chisterling Golden Boy (D)
Gra-John's Muffit O'Philamour (B)
Gra-John's Twinkle O'Al-Jo (B)
Chisterling Cadet O'Taralane (D)
Chisterling Scarlett O'Hara (B)
Tara of Jo-Bet Valley (B)
Chisterling Bronze Prince (D)

Timtone's Amber Lady (B)
Chisterling Black Fortune (D)
Chisterling The Phanton (D)
Timtone's Golden Image
Chisterling King of Diamonds (D)
Diamond's Golden Girl (B)
Sass-Shan O'Triciel (B)

## Ch. Prince George O'Page's Hill

(By Ch. Kalandar Prince O'Page's Hill ex Ch. Timberidge Temptress.
Wh. 6/9/42. Sable. 1944 ch.)

Nashcrest Golden Note (D)
Of All Delight of Perkasie (B)
Pixie Dell Royal Jester (D)
Parson of Kenloch (D)
Lee Brae's Little Miss Muffet (B)
Nightfall of Perkasie (D)
Count Rinaldo O'Page's Hill (D)

Katie-J's Royal Ace (D)
Lee Brae's Gay Cockade (D)
Lovely Chorale of Hobby Ho (B)
Somber Chorale of Hobby Ho (B)
Lee Brae's Georgie Porgie (D)
Bradford King O'Page's Hill (D)

## Ch. Frigate's Emblem of Astolat

(By Ch. Frigate of Faunbrook ex Astolat Snow Flurry.
Wh. 7/6/47. Sable. 1948 ch.)

Astolat Golden Symbol (D)
Lingard Dark Elegance (B)
Wansor's Dusky Lassie (B)
Astolat Emblem's Onyx (B)
Gold Farthing O'Faunbrook (B)
Astolat Good Luck (D)
Astolat Emblem's Libby (B)

Astolat Emblem of Merit (D)
Astolat Future Emblem (D)
Sally Girl (B)
Roc-Sycamore's Little Honey (B)
Feracres Daisy Mae (B)
Astolat Emblem's Rhoda (B)

## Ch. Geronimo Crown Prince

(By Ch. Timberidge Temptation ex Ch. Sheltieland Shasta Geronimo.
Wh. 8/25/50. Sable. 1951 ch.)

Geronimo Highland Bruce (D)
Elmwood's Tom Thumb (D)

Geronimo Diamond Jubilee (B)
Geronimo Rex (D)

Geronimo Son Rey (D)
Sea Crags Urchin of Geronimo (D)
Golden Prince of Timberidge (D)
Badgerton Impersonator (B)
Pemaquid's Merran (B)

Geronimo Little Hi-Lite (D)
Fairy Prince of Candy Lane (D)
Elf Dale Little Doll (B)
Shady Lodge Crown Princess (B)

## Ch. Astolat Future Emblem

(By Ch. Frigate's Emblem of Astolat ex Astolat Emblem of Hope.
Wh. 10/26/52. Sable. 1955 ch.)

Chisterling Dawn O'Maryknoll (B)
Chisterling Trade Winds (D)
Donajoan Golden Leaf (D)
Donajoan Rambunctious (B)
Fawley's Bonnie Blue Flag (B)
Fawley's Emblem of Dixie (B)
Bykenhall's St. Andrew (D)

Taralanes Love N'Kisses (B)
Chisterling Florian (D)
Donajoan Golden Corker (D)
Whitwood's Dark Secret (B)
Chatawae's Witch Doctor (D)
Chisterling Bold Venture (D)

## Ch. Brandell's Break-A-Way II

(By Brandell's Bric-A-Brac II ex Brandell's Bettina of Tobruk.
Wh. 12/6/52. Sable. 1955 ch.)

Apple Valley's Gleaming Star (B)
Brandell's Bronze Beulah (B)
Isolde O'Page's Hill (B)
Pixie Dell April Lady (B)
Pixie Dell Black Tulip (B)
Pixie Dell Bright Vision (D)

Pixie Dell Penrod (D)
Dark Lagoon O'Page's Hill (D)
Magic Dream O'Page's Hill (B)
Stronghold O'Page's Hill (D)
Dream Girl O'Page's Hill (B)
Lamp Lighter O'Page's Hill (D)

## Ch. Diamond's Robert Bruce

(By Ch. Lingard Sealect Bruce ex Ch. Diamond's Black Velvet.
Wh. 7/11/64. Sable. 1965 ch.)

Rosmoor Braecarel Bonnie (B)
Tentagel It's A Man's World (D)
Diamond's Robin of Hymettus (D)
Bob's Mt. Fire O'The Picts (B)
Almost Angel of Hymettus (B)
Diamond's Red Rover O'Tentagel (D)

Cherden Sock It To 'Em (D)
Markrisdo's Patti Kate O'Roydon (B)
Joelle's Hello Holly (B)
Tambrae Aquarius (B)
Cherden Light My Fire (D)
Tentagel Donka Belle Starr (B)

## China Clipper O'Page's Hill

(By Ch. Mowgli ex Pandora O'Page's Hill.
Wh. 6/13/36. Sable.)

Lord Lovell O'Page's Hill (D)
Frigate of Faunbrook (D)
Dunrobin Bijou O'Page's Hill (B)
Black Crusader O'Page's Hill (D)
Royal Scot O'Page's Hill (D)

Primrose O'Page's Hill (B)
Yankee Clipper O'Page's Hill (D)
Falcon of Faunbrook (D)
Alrho's Beau Brummell (D)
Chosen Damsel O'Page's Hill (B)

Ch. Diamond's Robert Bruce, owned by Tentagel Shelties, as painted at home by noted artist, Jean Simmonds.

179

Ch. Larkspur of Pocono, C.D.X., owned by Elizabeth D. Whelen, dam of 16 champions.

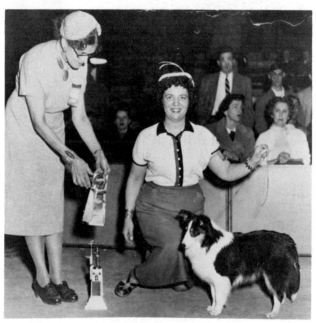

Ch. Thistlerose Class Moderne, owned by Thistlerose Kennels, judge Mrs. Irma Werner, handler Mrs. Al Jolly. *Norton of Kent*

# 26

# Great Shetland Sheepdog
# Dams

BITCHES have less chance to produce champions than do males. At most, a bitch can be bred twice a year. A noted male could be bred to several dozen bitches during the same year. The production record made by Ch. Larkspur of Pocono is therefore astonishing. She outranks all but 12 sires. It will be noted that every male which sired 12 or more champions was itself a champion. But ten of 25 dams of five or more champions were not themselves champions.

In researching these producers, we asked help from the American Kennel Club. It could not locate three of the non-champions on the list. Eventually, of course, we found them. An oddity is that Lady Diana of Rowcliffe belonged to Ella B. Moffit. Mrs. Moffit's lasting fame lies in her pioneering of Cocker and Springer field trials, and in the book which she wrote— *Elias Vail Trains Gun Dogs.*

# 25 Top Champion-Producing Dams

| | | | |
|---|---|---|---|
| Ch. Larkspur of Pocono | 16 | Tiny Penny of Walnut Hall | 5 |
| Ch. Larkspur's Replica of Pocono | 8 | Malpsh Her Royal Madjesty | 5 |
| Ch. Thistlerose Classic Moderne | 7 | Ch. Songstress O'Page's Hill | 5 |
| Ch. Gra-John's Little Tim Tam | 7 | Pris | 5 |
| Ch. Stylish Miss of Hatfield | 7 | Ch. Kawartha's Sabrina Fair | 5 |
| Ch. Sheltieland Shasta Geronimo | 6 | Ch. Dan-Dee's Portrait in Gold | 5 |
| Ch. Lady Diana of Rowcliffe | 6 | Ch. Richmore Repeat Performance | 5 |
| Annie Laurie of Cross Acres | 6 | Faharaby Blue Babe of Pocono | 5 |
| Ch. Kerianne Sweetquean | 6 | Ch. Christerling Falkirk's Flame | 5 |
| Ch. Westwood's Suzy Q | 6 | Ch. Olympic Fairy Flower | 5 |
| Anahassitt April Lady | 5 | Timberidge Crown Jewel | 5 |
| Anahassitt Atalanta | 5 | Ch. Va-Gore's Bright Promise | 5 |
| Keep Goin' | 5 | | |

## Ch. Larkspur of Pocono

(By Ch. Sea Isle Merle Legacy ex Merry Meddley of Pocono.
Wh. 6/22/39. Blue Merle. 1940 ch.)

| | |
|---|---|
| Pollyanna of Pocono (B) | Pocono Carefree of Sea Isle (B) |
| Forget-Me-Not of Pocono (B) | Blue Treasure of Pocono (B) |
| Blue Petal of Pocono (B) | Alice Blue of Pocono (B) |
| Pocono Pennyroyal of Sea Isle (B) | Tailor Made of Pocono (D) |
| Blue Elegance of Pocono (B) | Night Rider of Pocono (D) |
| Valiant of Pocono (D) | Pocono Trinket of Windy Oaks (B) |
| Bluet of Pocono (B) | Shelmar Songbird O'Pocono (B) |
| Blue Talisman of Pocono (D) | Larkspur's Finalist of Pocono (D) |

All but the last one on the list were sired by Ch. Merry Meddler of
Pocono. Larkspur was bred to Merry Meddler 7 times and champions
were produced in every litter: in order—one, three, two, three, two, two,
two.

## Ch. Larkspur's Replica of Pocono

(By Ch. Larkspur's Finalist of Pocono ex Abendruhe Carolynann's Pixie.
Wh. 3/21/55. Blue Merle. 1956 ch.)

| | |
|---|---|
| Blue Heritage of Pocono (D) | Blue Blend of Pocono (D) |
| Blue Heirloom of Pocono (D) | Blue Echo of Pocono (D) |
| Blue Destiny of Pocono (B) | Kiloren Sprite of Pocono (B) |
| The Lone Ranger of Pocono (D) | Kiloren Silver Mist of Pocono (B) |

## Ch. Thistlerose Classic Moderne

(By Ch. Timberidge Black Crusader ex Hobert's Tawny Lady.
Wh. 6/16/53. Tricolor. 1958 ch.)

Thistlerose Silver Belle (B)
Thistlerose Miss Park Avenue (B)
Thistlerose Mister Broadway (D)
Thistlerose Arcwood Aladdin (D)

Thistlerose V.I.P. (D)
Thistlerose Sun Dance (B)
Thistlerose Blue Heather (B)

## Ch. Gra-John's Little Tim Tam

(By Ch. Gilmanor Sugar Daddy ex Tiny Herdsman's Lady Cricket.
Wh. 5/27/58. Sable. 1959 ch.)

Gra-John's Diamond Lill (B)
Gra-John's Little Lu-Lu (B)
Aron-Kae Golden Tamara (B)
Gra-John's Muffit O'Philamour (B)

Gra-John's Lady n'Red (B)
Gra-John's Julie Ann (B)
Gra-John's Twinkle O'Al-Jo (B)

## Ch. Stylish Miss of Hatfield

(By Ch. Nashcrest Golden Note ex Ch. Bonnie Lass of Hatfield.
Wh. 6/10/57. Sable. 1959 ch.)

Kerry Poole of Rabbit Run (D)
Ken-Robs Partners Choice (D)
Hatfield Sultan of Lorel (D)
Highland Laird of Hatfield (D)

Ken-Robs Kenny (D)
Ken-Robs Bobbie (D)
Ken-Robs That's Life (D)

## Lady Diana of Rowcliffe

(By Ch. Piccolo O'Page's Hill ex Lady Patricia of Add-A-Bit.
Wh. 8/7/33. Tricolor.)

Ronalee Norseman (D)
Otseningo Dinah Mite (B)
Pocono Blue Thistle O'Noralee (B)

Valse Bleu of Faunbrook (B)
Blue Flageolet of Faunbrook (D)
Scottish Grey of Faunbrook (D)

## Ch. Sheltieland Shasta Geronimo

(By Ch. Mountaineer O'Page's Hill ex Sea Isle Nancy.
Wh. 2/22/44. Sable. 1946 ch.)

Geronimo Guardsman O'Noralee (D)
Timberidge Topaz (B)
Geronimo Little June (B)

Geronimo Crown Prince (D)
Timberidge Amber (B)
Geronimo Lend Lease (B)

183

Ch. Chisterling Falkirk's Flame, owned by Don. K. Combee.

Ch. Richmore Repeat Performance. *January*

# Annie Laurie of Cross Acres

(By Ch. Valiant of Pocono ex Cross Acres Memory of Pocono.
Wh. 1/1/46. Sable.)

Ray-Eden's Ricardo (D)
Ray-Eden's Queen O'Sheba (B)
Ray-Eden's Scheherazade (B)

Ray-Eden's Don Juan (D)
Ray-Eden's Rhapsody (B)
Ray-Eden's Mr. Fell (D)

# Ch. Kerianne Sweetquean

(By Ch. Highland Laird of Hatfield ex Ch. Badgerton Bashful Baby.
Wh. 3/26/60. Sable. 1962 ch.)

Bee-Jay's Brannigan (D)
Bee-Jay's Miss Behaving (B)
Bee-Jay's Typical of Skyways (D)

Kismet's Coquette (B)
Bee-Jay's Cayenne of Aron-Kae (D)
Bee-Jay's Lady Starlight (B)

# Ch. Westwood's Suzy Q

(By Westwood's Dapper Dan ex Starlight's Baby Doll.
Wh. 5/29/62. Sable. 1965 ch.)

Westwood Merry Maker (B)
Westwood Pace Maker (D)
Westwood Copper Penny (B)

Westwood Fella O'Alpha (D)
Westwood's King of Hearts (D)
Westwood's Mischief Maker (B)

# Anahassitt April Lady

(Ch. Wee Laird O'Downfield ex Ch. Ashbank Fairy.
Wh. 4/27/31. Sable.)

Dunrobin Bijou O'Page's Hill (B)
Mazeppa O'Page's Hill (D)
Que Vive O'Page's Hill (D)

Light Brigade O'Page's Hill (D)
Meadowsweet O'Page's Hill (B)

# Anahassitt Atalanta

(By Ch. Wee Laird O'Downfield ex Ch. Ashbank Fairy.
Wh. 4/27/31. Sable.)

Gigolo of Anahassitt (D)
Anahassitt Aphrodite (B)
Sheltieland Atlantis (D)

Anahassitt Animation (B)
Syncopating Sue of Anahassitt (B)

# Keep Goin'

(By Ch. Bodachan of Clerwood ex Glenisla Elegance.
Wh. 7/16/33. Tricolor.)

Ardland Ann (B)
Ardland Admiral (D)
Ardland Adorable (B)

Ardland Atom (D)
Ardland Artist (D)

## Tiny Penny of Walnut Hall

(Jock of Walnut Hall ex Tiny Barbara of Walnut Hall.
Wh. 7/15/39. Sable.)

Falcon of Faunbrook (D)
Frigate of Faunbrook (D)
Parliment Penny of Faunbrook (B)

Gold Sixpence O'Faunbrook (B)
Golden Crown of Faunbrook (D)

## Ch. Songstress O'Page's Hill

(By Musicmaster O'Page's Hill ex Madame Pompadour O'Page's Hill.
Wh. 5/21/46. Sable. 1947 ch.)

Bandmaster O'Page's Hill (D)
Pixie Dell Encore (B)
Pixie Dell Firebrand (D)

Pixie Dell Little Minstrel (D)
Pixie Dell Theme Song (B)

## Malpsh Her Royal Madjesty

(By Ch. Sea Isle Serenade ex Sea Isle Dusky Belle.
Wh. 12/24/61. Sable.)

Malpsh Great Scott (D)
Malpsh Autumn Gold (B)
Malpsh Shower of Gold (D)

Malpsh Hanky Pank O'Briarwood
(B)
Briarwood Playboy's Playmate (B)

## Pris

(By Ch. Sea Isle Serenade ex Sea Isle Dusky Belle.
Wh. 12/21/62. Sable.)

Malpsh Windhover Wichery (B)
Malpsh Kathy's Clown (B)
Malpsh Golden Dancer (B)

Malpsh Windhover Sorcery (B)
Malpsh Spookey (B)

186

## Ch. Kawartha's Sabrina Fair

(By Ch. Teaberry Lane's Little Pecos ex Miss Ruffles of Oak-Lawn.
Wh. 5/9/55. Sable. 1956 ch.)

Kawartha's Match Maker (D)
Kawartha's Fair Game (B)
Kawartha's Mr. Alpha (D)

Kawartha's Mist O'Gold (B)
Kawartha's Me Candido (B)

## Ch. Dan-Dee's Portrait in Gold

(By Ch. Elf Dale Golden Legacy ex Dan-D's Merry Maggie.
Wh. 3/9/62. Sable. 1965 ch.)

Dan-Dee Prima Dona (B)
Dan-Dee's Samantha (B)
Dan-Dee's Miss Fashion (B)

Premaur's Lyric O'Dan-Dee (B)
Dan-Dee Cabaret (D)

## Ch. Richmore Repeat Performance

(By Ch. Geronimo Son Rey ex Can. Ch. Willow-Acres Patty.
Wh. 2/3/60. Sable. 1961 ch.)

Richmore Top Brass (D)
Richmore Fascinating Lady (B)
Richmore Stylish Miss (B)

Wyndcliff-Richmore Striking (D)
Richmore Royal Flush (D)

## Faharaby Blue Babe of Pocono

(By Ch. Blue Heritage of Pocono ex Tiny Leatha of Walnut Hall.
Wh. 3/16/59. Blue Merle.)

Van's Blueberry Cookie (C)
Faharaby Blue Cloud (D)
Faharaby Blue Larkspur (B)

Faharaby Blue Heidi (B)
Faharaby Blue Chips (B)

## Ch. Chisterling Falkirk's Flame

(By Ch. Pixie Dell Firebrand ex Ch. Falkirk's Whimsical Susie.
Wh. 4/22/54. Sable. 1955 ch.)

Chisterling Trade Winds (D)
Chisterling Pipe Dreams (B)
Chisterling Bold Venture (D)

Chisterling Scarlett O'Hara (B)
Chisterling Bronze Prince (D)

### Ch. Olympic Fairy Flower

(By Ch. Mountaineer O'Page's Hill ex Ch. Olympic Flower O'The Picts.
Wh. 9/13/46. Sable. 1947 ch.)

Zetland Peerie Jenta (B)
Zetland Storting (D)
Zetland Glufft (D)

Zetland Sturla (B)
Zetland Lille-Venn (B)

### Timberidge Crown Jewel

(By Ch. Geronimo Crown Prince ex Ch. Timberidge Gold Standard.
Wh. 8/8/52. Sable)

Browne Acres Bette (B)
Browne Acres Blaze (D)
Browne Acres Blossom (B)

Browne Acres Butterscotch (B)
Banchory Sis O'Browne Acres (B)

### Ch. Va-Gore's Bright Promise

(By Ch. Musket O'Page's Hill ex Ch. Creole Babe O'Page's Hill.
Wh. 5/4/51. Sable. 1952 ch.)

Pixie Dell Bright Vision (D)
Pixie Dell April Lady (B)
Pixie Dell Bright Beacon (D)

Pixie Dell Little Hobo (D)
Pixie Dell Mr. MacDuff (D)

# 27

# The Great Shetland
# Sheepdog Winners

THERE is a saying that records are made to be broken. There is another which says that the greatest dog in the world may be in someone's back yard—unknown to the show dog world. What the former means is that there will always be someone—man, dog, or horse—ready to shoot at, and go over, the current record. The second saying needs some adaptation to the present subject.

A great dog may appear, shine brilliantly, then to disappear. Any number of things can happen. The dog may become ill and be retired, or it may suffer an injury. The owner may be unable to show the dog in an appreciable number of shows. The dog disappears and is quickly forgotten. Anyone who has remained in dogs for a period of years will remember several such cases.

But these cases cannot in any way lessen the brilliance of the dogs which do make the records. They appear in show after show. They are always in tip top condition. They stand travel perfectly. Their temperaments catch the eyes of the judges. They face the best dogs of their time, and they win. In short, they are remarkable.

Given below are the records of the great winners, past and present. The records are necessarily those at the time of writing. At least three of them are still campaigning: Ch. Meadows Fire of Bryce-Star-Lit, Ch. Wyndcliff Richmore Striking, and Ch. Tiree Hall Jedelan Scot. Any of the three might conceivably beat Ch. Elf Dale Viking's record of 173

Ch. Elf Dale Viking, owned by Elf Dale Kennels, pictured here winning Best of Breed at No. California Specialty 1965. Judge Elizabeth D. Whelen, handler Wayne Baxter. *Bennet Associates*

best of breed victories. But it appears unlikely at this date that they could catch up to his 16 best in show victories.

Aside from these three, there are others in the wings, waiting to take over. Many of them are group winners, and Ch. Flair Phoenix Blue has already won a best in show award. We honor our great winners. But all responsible breeders dream of the youngsters who will come on to join the record holders.

Perhaps another word of explanation should be given. In former years, best of breed winners at specialty shows were often given credit for best in show awards. And, in a sense, they were best in show winners. However, the American Kennel Club ordered the practice stopped. This was to avoid the inevitable confusion. Today, only those dogs winning best in show in all-breed competition may claim the honor.

In the following tables, dogs listed as winning best of breed may have won in both categories. Thus, for example, Ch. Wyndcliff Richmore Striking has been best of breed at 14 specialty shows. Similarly, Can. and Am. Ch. Tiree Hall Jedelan Scot defeated an entry of 114 at the 1971 national specialty show. And these are but two examples. Their great specialty show victories are simply listed among their best of breed victories. Those dogs which have won one hundred or more best of breed victories are said to belong to the "Century Club." To be eligible, a dog must have won 100 or more bests of breed. So far, 14 dogs have done this. All are given in the following list of great winners. Others may shortly join.

| Dog | Best of Breed | Group First | Best in Show |
|---|---|---|---|
| Ch. Elf Dale Viking | 173 | 46 | 16 |
| Ch. Mori-Brook's Icecapade | 150 | 15 | 5 |
| Ch. Meadows Fire of Bryce-Star-Lit | 152 | 17 | 2 |
| Ch. Sutter's Golden Masquerade | 123 | 4 | 3 |
| Ch. Cee Dee's Squire | 118 | 11 | |
| Ch. Badgerton Alert Alec | 117 | 10 | 3 |
| Ch. Malpsh Great Scott | 110 | 3 | 1 |
| Ch. Wyndcliff Richmore Striking | 109 | 14 | 1 |
| Ch. Nashcrest Golden Note | 105 | 7 | 0 |
| Ch. Mori-Brook's Country Squire | 104 | 8 | 1 |
| Ch. Just-A-Mere Brandy | 104 | 4 | 0 |
| Ch. Etwin's Lil Timmie O'Cor-Mik | 103 | 3 | 0 |

| | | | |
|---|---|---|---|
| Ch. Frigate's Emblem of Astolat | 101 | 4 | 0 |
| Ch. Dark Lagoon O'Pages Hill | 100 | 1 | 0 |
| Can. & Am. Ch. Tiree Hall<br>Jedelan Scot | 94 | 13 | 0 |
| Ch. Tess's Trump of Wadmalaw | 90 | 9 | 0 |
| Ch. Pixie Dell Bright Vision | 85 | 1 | 0 |
| Ch. Pixie Dell Epicure | 85 | 7 | 3 |
| Ch. Crawford Matchless | 69 | 1 | 0 |
| Ch. Laurolyn's Patti O'M-B | 67 | 16 | 1 |
| Ch. Elf Dale Golden Legacy | 63 | 4 | 0 |

Recent spectacular victories include five group firsts for Ch. Halstor's Peter Pumpkin and three for Ch. Skyway's Sa-Wen. And in winning his Canadian title, Ch. Tiree Hall Jedelan Scot won three straight bests of breed and one first in group.

Ch. Meadows' Fire of Bryce-Star-Lit, owned by Pat Meadows.     *Bergman*

Amer. and Can. Champion Mori-Brook's Icecapade, C.D., bred by Mori-Brook's Kennels, owned by Mrs. Lee O. Martin.

Ch. Sutter's Golden Masquerade, owned by Mrs. James Hausman.

Amer. and Can. Ch. Cee Dee's Squire, C.D., owned by Mr. and Mrs. Don Henderson.

Ch. Wyndcliff Richmore Striking, owned by Joan Surber.

Amer. and Can. Ch. Mori-Brook's Country Squire, owned by Mori-Brook's Kennels. Picture taken when dog was 14½ years old.

*Martin Booth*

Ch. Frigate's Emblem of Astolat, owned by Mr. and Mrs. E. F. Hubbard. *Shafer*

Ch. Pixie Dell Epicure. *Shafer*

Amer. and Can. Ch. Laurolyn Patti O'M-B, owned by Mori-Brook Kennels, top-winning bitch.

# 28

# Birkie, The Shetland Sheepdog Film Star

---

ON March 11, 1973, Walt Disney Productions released a motion picture on television called *The Little Shepherd Dog of Catalina Island*. The film was one of the Wonderful World of Disney releases, and it was a one part film produced by Harry Tytle, based on an original script by Rod Peterson. The film was sponsored on TV by Ralston Purina, and millions saw it on a national hookup, either that night or later.

The story features a Shetland Sheepdog, a champion, who becomes lost on Catalina Island. He finds his way to a farm where his natural herding abilities are quickly discovered. Bud Parker, the farm's assistant manager, gives him what training he needs.

Eventually, the dog's Mainland California owner, discovers his whereabouts. But the dog and Parker are inseparable. And at the moment of coming upon his lost dog, Birkie is engaged in the dangerous job of rescuing an Arabian stallion who seems likely to fall to his death off a cliff.

Mason decides to leave the Sheltie, Birkie, at Middle Ranch. There, among his normal duties, he stands at stud to bitches sent over to Catalina by his real owner, Mason.

Birkie is a registered Sheltie whose real name is Gaywyn Sandstorm (Shane for short). He is owned by Carol Snip of 5560 Limerick Dr., St. Louis, Mo., 63128. He is a grandson of two Sheltie greats, Ch. Malpsh

197

Gaywyn Sandstorm who, as Birkie, starred in Disney's "The Little Shepherd of Catalina." Owned by Carol Snip.

"Birkie" and Bud Parker in the story of the Sheltie that is stranded on Santa Catalina Island, telecast on The Wonderful World of Disney in March 1973. © *MCMLXXIII Walt Disney Production world rights reserved.*

Great Scot on his sire's side, and Ch. Kawartha's Matchmaker on his dam's side.

The Disney people say they searched for a year before selecting Gaywyn Sandstorm and Gaywyn Pipedream. Sandstorm had already been given basic obedience training. But let Rod Peterson tell it.

"We brought in the most lovable and understanding Sheltie we had. He walked into Tytle's office confident and self-assured, like any well-trained professional. Tytle stared at the Sheltie for a long moment, and Shane stared right back in eager anticipation. After a few minutes you could see that Harry had taken a liking to him. He issued a couple of simple commands which Shane obeyed perfectly. Then the dog moved up beside Harry's desk and shook hands with him. That sealed the deal. Tytle threw up his hands and said: 'Okay, he gets the part!' "

Of course, it wasn't quite that simple. Tytle and Peterson wanted two identical Shelties in markings. They had to be of show dog quality. And they had to be sable color with plain face markings so that they couldn't be confused with the Collie Lassie. The two dogs, Gaywyn Sandstorm and Gaywyn Pipedream fitted those requirements. It was the former who won out, and who became Birkie in the picture. His training took seven months.

Now the Collie movie star, Lassie, is not really a lassie but a male dog. Moreover, there are three or four Lassies. They may be used for specialized scenes according their special abilities. And if one should become ill or otherwise incapacitated, one of the others could take its place. And "Lassie" can be making personal appearances at three or four different places at once.

In *The Little Shepherd Dog of Catalina* there were actually four Shelties. But Gaywyn Sandstorm (the Birkie of the picture) was used in all close-ups, all stills, climbing and running in field scenes, and in some of the tricks which were done. The other three were Piper, Cookie, and Banner.

Banner and Cookie were used in some of the herding and chasing scenes. Banner had been trained to attack any animal which the trainers ordered it to do. The trainers, incidentally, were Clint Rowe and Hubert Wells. The former played the part of Bud Parker in the picture.

These four dogs, but in particular, Gaywyn Sandstorm (Shane in his kennel, and Birkie in the film) have done a great deal to tell the American public about Shetland Sheepdogs. To them all, honor!

Ch. Timberidge Typesetter, Can. and Amer. C.D., sire of 17 champions. Owned by Hi-Hope Kennels.

Can. and Amer. Ch. Camian's Clansman of Hi-Hope. Sire of 5 champions. *Wainwright Photos*

# 29

# Great Canadian Kennels, Sires, and Dams

---

$M$AINLY through the meticulous record keeping and great research of Miss Francis Clark of Hi-Hope Kennels, Richmond, British Columbia, we are able to give you a comprehensive record of Shetland Sheepdogs in Canada.

Canada is a vast country, larger than the United States. There are fewer shows, and they are far apart. Canadian records are therefore seemingly less impressive than are American. But, on a comparative basis, they are equally great.

In the list of leading breeders appears the name of William Henderson, who established his Alford Kennels at Toronto. The kennel no longer exists, yet it lived long enough to establish an immortal record. For it was one of the pioneer kennels of Canada.

## Leading Kennels

| | | Champions bred |
|---|---|---|
| Hi-Hope Kennels | E. H. and Frances Clark | 28 |
| Ronas Hill | Mrs. G. F. Lovett | 26 |
| Meridian | Mrs. Hazel Slaughter | 19 |
| Sovereign | Mrs. Ariel Sleeth | 18 |
| Alford | William Henderson | 15 |
| Terian | Mrs. Joan Wiik | 14 |
| Willow Acres | Mr. and Mrs. R. D. Smuck | 13 |
| Kel-lani | Mrs. D. and Miss C. O'Dare, and Mr. J. Horton | 12 |
| Glen-El-Tee | Mrs. G. Taylor | 12 |
| Quarrybare | Laura and George Getty | 10 |

## Leading Sires

| | |
|---|---|
| Can. & Am. Ch. Timberidge Typesetter | 17 |
| Ch. Willow Acre's Golden Rocket | 16 |
| Ch. Summit's Gold Dust, C.D. | 12 |
| Ch. (Eng. & Can. Ch.) Honey Boy of Callart | 9 |
| Ch. Minonamee Prince | 9 |
| Ch. Saravan's Elegant Lad | 8 |
| Ch. Kel-Lani's Moonshine | 7 |
| Ch. Sunnycrest Black Topper | 7 |
| Ch. Alford Wee McGregor | 6 |
| Ch. Hi-Hope's Highrigger | 6 |
| Ch. Brigdale Renown | 5 |
| Ch. Piper Glen's Christopher Robin | 5 |
| Ch. Ronas Hill Frolic | 5 |
| Ch. Doron Brusi of Note | 5 |
| Ch. (Am. & C.) Hi-Hope's Echo O'Imp | 5 |
| Can. & Am. Ch. Camian's Clansman of Hi-Hope | 5 |
| Willow Acres Golden Note | 5 |
| Can. & Am. Ch. Camian's Clansman of Hi-Hope | 5 |
| Ch. Doron Brusi of Note | 5 |
| Can. & Am. Ch. Hi-Hope's Echo O'Imp | 5 |
| Ch. Ronas Hill Frolic | 5 |
| Ch. Summit's Night and Day | 5 |
| Sunnycrest Target | 5 |
| Willow Acres Golden Note | 5 |

# RECORDS OF THE GREAT CANADIAN SIRES

In the following compilation champion progeny are shown in the left column under each sire and their dams. appear in the right column. Since all progeny listed are champions, the abbreviation "Ch." is omitted to conserve space.

## Can. & Am. Ch. Timberidge Typesetter
### (By Ch. Timberidge Target ex Timberidge Lettie)

| | |
|---|---|
| Camelot's Major of Hi-Hope | Ch. Hi-Hope's Golden Schilling C.D. |
| Camelot's Appalachian Spring C.D. | Ch. Hi-Hope's Golden Schilling, C.D. |
| Hi-Hope's Merry Caroline C.D. | Pixieland Joy |
| Hi-Hope's Viscount of Sunset | Ch. Hi-Hope's Merry Imp, U.D. |
| Hi-Hope's Echo O'Imp | Ch. Hi-Hope's Merry Imp, U.D. |
| Hi-Hope's Gay Shiralee, U.D. | Timberidge Copper Penny |
| Hi-Hope's Merry McMorland C.D. | Noralee Naiad, C.D. |
| Hi-Hope's Flag of Thornmor | Sunset's Black Lady |
| Hi-Hope's Airdive Sandpiper C.D. | Badgerton Vain Vanessa |
| Hi-Hope's Regal Canuck | Badgerton Vain Vanessa |
| Hi-Hope's Princess Patricia | Badgerton Vain Vanessa |
| Hi-Hope's Badgerton Canadienne | Badgerton Vain Vanessa |
| Sunset's Silhouette of Hi-Hope | Ch. Hi-Hope's Merry Caroline C.D. |
| Samarcan's Golden Moment | Merry Meg of Keltie |
| Sunset's Miss Viela of Hi-Hope C.D. | Ch. Hi-Hope's Golden Echo O'Sunset |
| Terian's April Lass, C.D. | Terian's Sugar Candy |
| Terian's Gay Solitaire, C.D. | Terian's Dark Moment, C.D. |

## Ch. Willow Acres Golden Rocket
### (By Willow Acres Golden Note ex Ch. Willow Acres Fanfare)

| | |
|---|---|
| Alford Tam-O-Shanter | Helensdale Lady Luck |
| Alford Lizette | Helensdale Lady Luck |
| Doron Cameo | Doron's Taffy Ann |
| Doron Charles | Doron's Taffy Ann |
| Dorlee's Sweet Colleen | Yankee Doodle Tar Baby |
| Gfelic Glen's Lad O'Mine | Ch. Willow Acres Golden Fancy |
| Helreg's Rock-A-Babe | Ch. Willow Acres Golden Charm C.D. |
| Helreg's Rock's Parader | Ch. Willow Acres Golden Charm C.D. |
| Helreg's Starlett | Ch. Willow Acres Golden Charm C.D. |
| Helreg's Bit-O-Brass | Ch. Willow Acres Golden Charm C.D. |
| Helreg's Autumn Gold | Ch. Willow Acres Golden Charm C.D. |
| Sir Chester of Sanroc | Sandy of Evergreen Acres |
| Shasta of Evergreen Acres | Sandy of Evergreen Acres |
| Vi-Liz-Bai Cheryl's Glory | The Wyke's Doll Baby |
| Hewmac's Billie-G | The Wyke's Doll Baby |

## Ch. Summit's Gold Dust C.D.

### (Can. & Am. Ch. Nashcrest Golden Note ex Ch. Cinderella's Gypsy of Ronas Hill, U.D.T.)

| | |
|---|---|
| Braedon's Fancy That | Little Miss Muffet |
| Meridian's Gypsy Baron | Ch. Gypsy Rose of Ronas Hill C.D. |
| Meridians Gypsy Serenade | Ch. Gypsy Rose of Ronal Hill C.D. |
| Meridian's Truly Truly Fair | Ch. Gypsy Rose of Ronas Hill C.D. |
| Rosslynn's Dainty Dividend | Sutherland Little Luana |
| Rosslynn's Ban Jo of Summit | Sutherland Little Luana |
| Summit's Forever Amber | Ch. Wee Honey of Ronas Hill |
| Summit's Kissin Cousin | Ch. Meridian's Miss Behave |
| Summit's Night And Day | Ch. Meridian's Miss Behave |
| Summit's Holiday | Ch. Meridian's Miss Behave |
| Summit's Venus | Flying Saucer o'Jubilee |
| Uam-Var All Aglitter | Uam-Var All Aglow |

## Eng. & Can. Ch. Honey Boy of Callart (import)

### (By Ch. Miel of Callart ex Tanera of Callart)

| | |
|---|---|
| Meridian's Summer Conquest | Ch. Meridian's Gypsy Serenade |
| Manor Pride's Harvest Gold | Ch. Hjalti Melrose |
| Manor Pride's Rag-A-Muffin | Ch. Hjalti Melrose |
| Manor Pride's Carmen | Ch. Hjalti Melrose |
| Soleste Fiesta | Soleste Ski Jumps |
| Sno-Lane Bean Geste | Ch. Tobermory Tinker Belle |
| Sno-Lane Playboy of Uam-Var | Ch. Tobermory Tinker Belle |
| Sno-Lane Bright Brandy | Sno-Lane's Mistinguette |
| Uam-Var Bright Enchantress | Riverhill Roll Away |

## Ch. Minonamee Prince

### (By Am. Ch. Noralee Bronze Nugget ex Alford Jay Jay's Lassie)

| | |
|---|---|
| Belpequa's Lucky Gold Piece | Gaelic Glenn's Tisa |
| Glen-El-Tee's Little Black Joe | Quarrybrae Lindy Lou at Glen-El-Tee |
| Nelius Blue Peter | Quarrybrae Little Blue Met |
| Quarrybrae Little Princess II | Ch. Quarrybrae Little Topsy |
| Quarrybrae Little Valentine | Ch. Kinsman Penny at Quarrybrae |
| Quarrybrae Little Valentino | Astolat's Emblem's Taffy |
| Quarrybrae Little Bobo-Link | Ch. Lingard Laurie at Quarrybrae |
| Quarrybrae Little Miss Muffett | Quarry Brae Honey Locust |
| Wee Brucie of Glen-El-Tee | Quarry Brae Honey Locust |

### Ch. Saravan's Elegant Lad

(By Ch. Thistlerose Milord ex Saravan's Autumn Dream)

| | |
|---|---|
| Elegant Lad's Cari of Mini Col, C.D. | Camelot's Perky of Hi-Hope C.D. |
| Terian's Echo Lass | Ch. Terian's April Lass C.D. |
| Terian's Hi-land Fling | Terian's Fireball |
| Terian's Tricolor | Terian's Fireball |
| Terian's Peg o'My Heart | Ch. Terian's Gay Solitaire C.D. |
| Terian's Prairie Promise | Terian's Tempest Tyke |
| Terian's Burnished Copper | Ch. Terian's Gay Solitaire C.D. |
| Terian's Fair Match | Ch. Kawartha's Fair Game |

### Ch. Kel-Lani's Moonshine

(By Ch. Elf Dale Viking ex Ch. Kel-Lani Moonglow)

| | |
|---|---|
| Kel-Lani's Autumn Leaves | Kel-Lani's Autumn Blaze |
| Kel-Lani's Chieftain | Kel-Lani's Marquita |
| Kel-Lani's Clair De Lune | Ch. Kel-Lani's Moonglow C.D. |
| Kel-Lani's Melody C.D. | Ch. Kel-Lani's Autumn Blaze |
| Kel-Lani's Musketeer | Ch. Kel-Lani's Autumn Blaze |
| Kel-Lani's Corky McKinnon | Ch. Kel-Lani's Autumn Blaze |
| Paddy of Scalloway | Kel-Lani's Minuet |

### Ch. Sunncrest Black Topper

(By Ch. Mori-Brook's Icecapade ex Sunnycrest Black Bonnet II)

| | |
|---|---|
| Hjalti Tip Top | Ch. Dilhorne Fortune |
| Hjalti Tawny Top | Ch. Dilhorne Fortune |
| Jo Ro's Topper's Trademark | Ch. Jo-Ro's Jancee |
| Jo Ro's Starboy of Marshelt | Ch. Jo-Ro's Jancee |
| Marshelt's Golden Topper | Okopaw Golden Mischief |
| Marshelt's Miss Topper | Okopaw Golden Mischief |
| Silence of Hjalti | Hjalti Festivity |

### Ch. Alford Wee McGregor

(By Ch. Lord Lovell O'Pages Hill ex Ch. Alford Heatherbelle)

| | |
|---|---|
| Alford Winsum o'Wil-O-Mel | Alford Miss Black Watch |
| Alford Ballerina | Alford Black Jewel |
| Alford Laddie of Glenleigh | Coltness Caramita |
| Alford Petite Marie | Coltness Caramita |
| Quarrybrae Little Topsy | Ch. Kinsman Penny At Quarrybrae |
| Wil-O-Mel's Wee Robbie | Alford Golden Ray o'Wil-O-Mel |

# Ch. Hi-Hope's Highrigger

### (By Ch. Diamond's Robert Bruce ex Ch. Hi-Hope's Bonnie Naiad)

| | |
|---|---|
| Quilcheena's Blue Hylite | Quilcheena's Surprise Package |
| Quilcheena's Blue Legend of Hi-Hope | Quilcheena's Surprise Package |
| Maverick The Mark of Miskela | Miskela's Scamperina |
| Miskela's Mis Behave | Ch. Sunset's Miss Kela of Hi-Hope |
| Rodwin's Charmer of Hi-Hope C.D.X. | Rodwin's Charming Lady |
| Aljoran's Flair of Hi-Hope | Bonnie's Gay Cinderella |

Ch. Summit's Gold Dust, C.D., owned by Ruth E. Lane, sire of 12 champions. Best Veteran under judge Virginia Hampton.

## The Great Canadian Brood Matrons

As we have said earlier, Canada is a vast land, and distances between dog shows—and kennels—are very great. Therefore, Canada has not produced the number of champions that has the United States. The great brood matrons, because of the distances between kennels, have had less opportunity to produce. Yet their records are quite remarkable. In recognition of this, we have carried the production records further than we could do for the American matrons. First, we list the entire group, and then we give details individually in so far as space permits.

It will be noted that two of these matrons have (Imp) after their names. This indicates that they were brought to Canada from England. Canadian and American dogs have been so inter-changed that we have not listed those American matrons as being imported. On the whole, their names indicate this. Moreover, several Canadian kennels have functioned on both sides of the border.

### The Leading Canadian Dams

| | |
|---|---|
| Badgerton Vain Vanessa | 9 |
| Ch. Summit's Gay Abandon | 8 |
| Aylmer Chorine | 7 |
| Ch. Willow Acres Golden Charm, C.D. | 6 |
| Alford Jay Jay's Lassie | 6 |
| Ch. Cinderella Gypsy of Ronas Hill | 5 |
| Ch. Dilhorne Fortune (imp.) | 5 |
| Doron's Taffy Ann | 5 |
| Ch. Helensdale Wendy (imp.) | 5 |
| Ch. Kel-Lani's Moonglow C.D. | 5 |
| Ch. Minonamee Eugenie | 5 |
| Sunnycrest Merry Imp | 5 |
| Can. & Am. Ch. Hi-Hope's Bonnie Naiad | 4 |
| Kel-Lani's Autumn Blaze | 4 |
| Little Miss Muffett | 4 |
| Mantoga Christmas Carol (imp.) | 4 |
| Sandy of Evergreen Acres | 4 |
| Ch. Sovereign Victorious | 4 |

## RECORDS OF THE GREAT CANADIAN DAMS

In the following compilation champion progeny are shown in the left column under each dam and their sires appear in the right column. Since all progeny listed are champions, the abbreviation "Ch." is omitted to conserve space.

207

Badgerton Vain Vanessa. Dam of 9 champions. Owned by Hi-Hope Kennels.

Can. Ch. Summit's Gay Abandon. Dam of 8 champions. Bred by Ruth E. Lane Owned by Hazel Slaughter.

### Badgerton Vain Vanessa

(By Ch. Sea Isle Serenade ex Ch. Badgerton Impersonator, C.D.)

| | |
|---|---|
| Hi-Hope's Bonnie Naiad | Ch. Hi-Hope's Echo o'Imp |
| Hi-Hope's Golden Echo o'Sunset | Ch. Hi-Hope's Echo o'Imp |
| Hi-Hope's Golden Schilling, C.D. | Ch. Hi-Hope's Echo o'Imp |
| Hi-Hope's Pilot of Coppertone | Ch. Hi-Hope's Echo o'Imp |
| Ch. Hi-Hope's Happy Prince C.D. | Ch. Hi-Hope's Echo o'Imp |
| Hi-Hope's Badgerton Canadienne | Ch. Timberidge Typesetter C.D. |
| Hi-Hope's Princess Patricia | Ch. Timberidge Typesetter C.D. |
| Hi-Hope's Regal Canuck | Ch. Timberidge Typesetter C.D. |
| H-Hope's Airdive Sandpiper C.D. | Ch. Timberidge Typesetter C.D. |

### Ch. Summit's Gay Abandon

(By Ch. Ken-Rob's Gay Blade ex Ch. Meridian's Miss Behave)

| | |
|---|---|
| Meridian's County Fair | Ch. Ken-Rob's Kenny |
| Meridian's Vanity Fair | Ch. Ken-Rob's Kenny |
| Meridian's Savoire Fair | Ch. Ken-Rob's Kenny |
| Meridian's Fair Warning | Ch. Ken-Rob's Kenny |
| Meridian's Rain Storm | Capewind's Storm Warning |
| Meridian's Rain Check | Capewind's Storm Warning |
| Meridian's Rain Dance | Capewind's Storm Warning |
| Meridian's Lone Shot | Ch. Ken-Rob's Benchmark |

### Aylmer Chorine

(By Ch. Alford Wee MacGregor ex Bonny Lou)

| | |
|---|---|
| Cinderella's Gypsy of Ronas Hill U.D.T. | Ch. Magic Talisman of Ronas Hill |
| Dixie Belle of Ronas Hill | Ch. Alford Laddie of Glenleigh |
| Dixie Charmer of Ronas Hill | Ch. Blue Flag of Ronas Hill |
| Wee Tammas of Ronas Hill | Ch. Magic Talisman of Ronas Hill |
| Wee Honey of Ronas Hill, C.D. | Ballerina's Lance of Ronas Hill |
| Orange Flare of Ronas Hill, C.D. | Ch. Wee Tammas of Ronas Hill |
| Moon Mist of Ronas Hill | Ch. Blue Flag of Ronas Hill |

### Ch. Willow Acres Golden Charm C.D.

(By Ch. Nashcrest Golden Note ex Ch. Minonamee Eugenie)

| | |
|---|---|
| Helreg's Golden Nomie | Willow Acres Golden Note |
| Helreg's Rock A Babe | Ch. Willow Acres Golden Rocket |

| | |
|---|---|
| Helreg's Rock's Parader | Ch. Willow Acres Golden Rocket |
| Helreg's Starlet | Ch. Willow Acres Golden Rocket |
| Helreg's Bit-O-Brass | Ch. Willow Acres Golden Rocket |
| Helreg's Autumn Gold | Ch. Willow Acres Golden Rocket |

### Alford Jay Jay's Lassie

(By Ch. Alford Wee McGregor ex Alford Miss Black March)

| | |
|---|---|
| Minonamee's Prince | Ch. Noralee Bronze Nugget |
| Minonamee Eugenie | Ch. Geronimo Crown Prince |
| Minonamee Majestic | Ch. Geronimo Crown Prince |
| Piper Glen's Christopher Robin | Sunnycrest Target |
| Piper Glen's Red Roberta | Sunnycrest Target |
| Piper Glen's Ebony Prince | Sunnycrest Target |

### Ch. Cinderella Gypsy of Ronas Hill

(By Ch. Magic Talisman of Ronas Hill ex Aylmer Chorine)

| | |
|---|---|
| Summit's Gold Dust C.D. | Ch. Nashcrest Golden Note |
| Summit's Golden Shelley, C.D.X. | Ch. Nashcrest Golden Note |
| Summit's Golden Promise, U.D. | Ch. Nashcrest Golden Note |
| Summit's Golden Rod, C.D. | Ch. Nashcrest Golden Note |
| Summit's Fiesta, C.D. | Ch. Blue Flag of Ronas Hill |

### Ch. Dilhorne Fortune (import)

(By Eng. Ch. Antoc Sealodge Spotlight ex Ch. Dilhorne Festivity)

| | |
|---|---|
| Hjalti's Melrose | Ch. Alford Tam O'Shanter |
| Hjalti's Felicity | Ch. Sno Lane's Beau Geste |
| Hjalti's Tip Top | Ch. Sunnycrest Topper |
| Hjalti's Tawny Top | Ch. Sunnycrest Topper |
| Hjalti's Kevin | Ch. Sno Lane's Beau Geste |

### Doron's Taffy Ann

(By Can. & Am. Ch. Keystone's Timmie of Tarsus ex Astolat
Emblem's Taffy)

| | |
|---|---|
| Doron Cameo | Ch. Willow Acres Golden Rocket |
| Doron Charles | Ch. Willow Acres Golden Rocket |

| Doron Dell | Ch. Doron Brusi of Note |
| Doron Dee Dee | Ch. Doron Brusi of Note |
| Doron Fern | Ch. Doron Brusi of Note |

## Ch. Helensdale Wendy (import)

(By Ch. Helensdale Ace ex Helensdale Fantasia)

| Foxfire of Ronas Hill | Ch. Chatawae's Foxfire |
| Jewel of Ronas Hill | Texas Blue of Ronas Hill |
| Kerry Music of Ronas Hill | Ch. Chatwae's Foxfire |
| Piper of Ronas Hill | Ch. Brass Tacks of Ronas Hill |
| Pipe Dream of Ronas Hill | Texas Blue of Ronas Hill |

## Ch. Kel-Lani's Moonglow C.D.

(By Ch. Geronimo Son Rey, C.D. ex Kel-Lani's Little Replica)

| Kel-Lani's Tycoon | Ch. Starcross Wonder Boy of Hi-Hope, C.D.X. |
| Kel-Lani's Moonshine | Ch. Elf Dale Viking |
| Kel-Lani's Martini | Ch. Elf Dale Viking |
| Kel-Lani's Clair De Lune | Ch. Elf Dale Viking |
| Kel-Lani's Mountain Dew | Ch. Elf Dale Viking |

## Ch. Minonamee Eugenie

(By Ch. Geronimo Crown Prince ex Alford Jay Jay's Lassie)

| Willow Acres Fanfare | Ch. Noralee Forecaster |
| Willow Acres Patty | Hallinwood Skylon |
| Willow Acres Golden Charm, C.D. | Ch. Nashcrest Golden Note |
| Willow Acres Golden Fancy | Ch. Nashcrest Golden Note |
| Willow Acres Gai Cheri | Hallinwood Skylon |

## Sunnycrest Merry Imp

(By Sunnycrest Golden Rippet ex Sunnycrest Golden Duchess)

| Sunnycrest Dark Bell II | Ch. Diamond's Robert Bruce |
| Sunnycrest Golden Samuel | Ch. Diamond's Robert Bruce |
| Sunnycrest Golden Elf II | Ch. Diamond's Robert Bruce |
| Sunnycrest Golden Splendour | Ch. Scotchguard Sea Chantey |
| Sunnycrest Amber Prince | Ch. Manor Pride's Harvest Gold |

Can. and Amer. Ch. Hi-Hope's Echo o'Imp, left, with 5 champions he sired in litter ex Badgerton Vain Vanessa: Can. & Amer, Chs. Hi-Hope's Bonnie Naiad, Hi-Hope's Golden Echo o'Sunset; Can. Chs. Hi-Hope's Golden Schilling, C.D., Hi-Hope's Pilot of Coppertowne; and Can. & Am. Ch. Hi-Hope's Happy Prince, C.D.

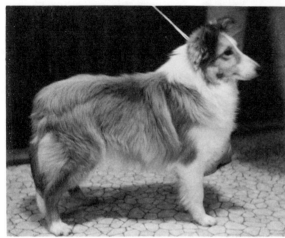

Ch. Kel-Lani's Moonglow. C.D., dam of 5 champions.

Ch. Kel-Lani's Moonshine, sire of 7 champions.

212

## Can. & Am. Ch. Hi-Hope's Bonnie Naiad

(By Can. & Am. Ch. Hi-Hope's Echo o'Imp ex Badgerton Vain Vanessa)

Hi-Hope's Contessa of Miskela     Ch. Camian's Clansman of Hi-Hope
Hi-Hope's Jolly Jack     Ch. Camian's Clansman of Hi-Hope
Hi-Hope's Highrigger     Ch. Diamond's Robert Bruce
Hi-Hope's Highwayman     Ch. Diamond's Robert Bruce

## Kel-Lani's Autumn Blaze

(By Ch. Olympic Nettle ex Kel-Lani's Penny Serenade)

Kel-Lani's Autumn Leaves     Ch. Kel-Lani's Moonshine
Kel-Lani's Melody C.D.     Ch. Kel-Lani's Moonshine
Kel-Lani's Muskateer     Ch. Kel-Lani's Moonshine
Kel-Lani's Corky McKinnon     Ch. Kel-Lani's Moonshine

## Little Miss Muffet

(By Ch. Summit's Gold Dust ex Wee Bonnie's Janie Mite O'Scot)

Braedean's Fancy That     Ch. Summit's Gold Dust C.D.
Braedean's Dusty Miller     Glenroyal Lariot
Braedean's Special Dividend     Ch. Rorralore Robert The Bruce
Braedean's Bra Bricht Nicht     Ch. Summit's Golden Rod C.D.

## Mantoga Christmas Carol (import)

(By Mantoga Clanna Consort ex Ch. Alasdair of Tintobank)

Amethyst of Mantoga U.D.     Ch. Okopaw Sonny Boy
Astra of Mantoga     Ch. Okopaw Sunny Boy
Bronze of Mantoga U.D.     Ch. Doron Brusi of Note
Brilliant of Mantoga     Ch. Doron Brusi of Note

## Sandy of Evergreen Acres

(By Waljon's Red Rocket of Lorel ex Lady Star Bonnie C.D.)

Sir Chester of Sanroc     Ch. Willow Acre's Golden Rocket
Shasta of Evergreen Acres     Ch. Willow Acre's Golden Rocket
Sherry of Evergreen Acres     Ch. Foxfire of Ronas Hill
Temptor's Belle of Scottsvale     Scottsvale Tawny Temptor

## Ch. Sovereign Victorious

### (By Ch. Dunderraw's Koko ex Helreg's Golden Victory)

| | |
|---|---|
| Sovereign Golden Conquest | Ch. Sovereign Flash Fire |
| Sovereign Bonfire | Ch. Sovereign Fire Chief |
| Sovereign Victory Maid | Ch. Sovereign Fire Chief |
| Sovereign By Jingo | Ch. Sovereign Fire Chief |

# 30

# Shetland Sheepdog
# Eye Disease

M ODERN dogs are afflicted with a variety of hereditary problems. Among these are eye problems causing blindness. Some breeds, such as Cocker Spaniels, have had a greater than average incidence of glaucoma. Miniature Schnauzers often suffer from hereditary cataracts. Irish Setters, Poodles, Collies, Norwegian Elkhounds and some other breeds have had a terrible scourge known as progressive retinal atrophy or PRA.

PRA ultimately causes blindness. It is difficult to determine in young puppies. So dogs may be used for breeding before the disease is discovered. The disease may appear in any breed at any time. That is to say, it cannot be stated that it will not suddenly develop in some breed which has hitherto had no cases of it.

Although Shetland Sheepdogs seem to be free of this disease, it is necessary to describe it in order to separate it from a somewhat similar problem which does occur in Shelties. PRA affects the entire retina. As the dog ages, the retina begins to lose cells, and to become thinner. There will also be a lack of adequate blood supply, itself caused by the loss of cells. Eventually, the dog becomes blind. The disease is called progressive, because it develops slowly and cannot be stopped. It is called atrophy since the retina is actually wasting away.

PRA is caused by a recessive gene. That is, the gene for a normal retina is dominant. A puppy gets a gene from each of its parents. The pair of genes is called an allele. If the puppy has two dominant genes, DD, then it will have a normal retina. And if two DD dogs are mated, all the puppies will have normal retinas.

If, however, one parent has DD and the other Dd, with the "d" representing the gene for PRA, all the puppies will be normal. But half the puppies will carry the recessive gene for PRA. If two such dogs, both with normal vision, but carrying the recessive gene (Dd × Dd), then one puppy will be DD normal, two will be normal but carriers (Dd, Dd) and one will have PRA (dd).

If two dogs carrying the dd genes are mated before it is recognized that they have PRA, then all the puppies will have PRA and will ultimately become blind, as will have their parents before them.

There is a similar disease in Shetland Sheepdogs which is a serious problem. It is called Central Progressive Retinal Atrophy, or CPRA. In this disease, the central, or best seeing, part of the retina is gradually destroyed.

A Sheltie with advanced CPRA will be neither night nor day blind. It will be able to distinguish stable objects very poorly, or not at all. However, it will be able to see moving objects. This is because the rods and cones in the periphery of the retina have not been affected. Thus, the moving object crosses the retina from peripheral sight, to central retina blindness, to peripheral sight.

Some researchers believe that CPRA is transmitted by recessive genes, as is the case with PRA. But others feel that the reverse may be the case, at least in some breeds. More research is being conducted on this at the present time.

A comparatively recent veterinary discipline is that of the ophthalmologist, or veterinary eye specialist. Such specialists are still comparatively rare, and may not always be within the reach of breeders. Usually, your local veterinarian can tell you where they are located. Or the veterinarian can give you the address of the American or Canadian Veterinary Medical Association, organizations which can supply the information.

Ophthalmologists use an instrument known as the ophthalmoscope. It has a high degree of accuracy in diagnosing both progressive retinal atrophy and central progressive retinal atrophy. The difficulty is that, with the exception of Irish Setters, PRA may be impossible to diagnose until the dog is two to seven years old, depending upon the breed. And CPRA in Shetland Sheepdogs may not be detectable until the dog is two years old. Thus unsuspecting owners may breed carriers before they are aware of the trouble.

Any Sheltie owner who has any reason to suspect its dog has the disease, or is a carrier, should delay using the animal for breeding until a competent specialist can check the eyes, and until the parents of possible carriers have been certified clear.

Recently, a method of diagnosing PRA has been developed, called electroretinography, or ERG. The electroretinogram, which is produced, will give an absolutely correct diagnosis of PRA in puppies four to 10 weeks of age, depending upon the breed. Unfortunately, at the time of writing, this method had not been worked out for the diagnosis of CPRA.

There are two excellent sources for information on this. One is the Seeing Eye Foundation Laboratory of the Cornell Research Laboratory for Diseases of Dogs, Cornell University, Ithaca, N.Y. The other is the School of Veterinary Medicine, University of Pennsylvania, Philadelphia, Pa. Research at Cornell was done by Dr. Stephen Bistner and Dr. Gustavo Aguirre. Dr. Aguirre is now at Pennsylvania.

In a personal letter to the writer, Dr. Aguirre makes these points:

> "The most successful means of decreasing the incidence of C.P.R.A. in Shetland Sheepdogs would be by ophthalmoscopic examination of large numbers of dogs in order to eliminate from a breeding program affected animals.
>
> "One of the existing problems in the control of C.P.R.A. in Shetland Sheepdogs is in determining the exact mode of inheritance of this disorder. Some individuals believe it to be a dominant trait, but enough dogs have not been examined to determine if there is complete or partial penetrance of the genetic trait. This would be necessary before any measures are attempted to eradicate the disease.
>
> "Utilization of a modified ERG would not be difficult provided sufficient dogs were bred to develop the disease so that diagnostic tools could be developed."

Although Dr. Aguirre did not suggest it, this might be accomplished by donating C.P.R.A. dogs to his laboratory, together with sufficient funds to support a breeding colony.

Artful Dodger of Anahassitt
Grey Mist of Pocono
    Peabody Silver Phantasy
Ch. Sea Isle Merle Legacy
    Nutkin of Houghton Hill
Parkswood Little Symphony
    Parkswood Patience

## CH. LARKSPUR OF POCONO

    Ch. Peabody Pan
Merrymaker of Pocono
    Ch. Syncopating Sue of Anahassitt
Merry Medley of Pocono
    Ch. Bodachan of Clerwood
Sunny Girl of Anahassitt
    Ch. Anahassitt Animation

Ch. Sprig of Houghton Hill
Anahassitt Atalanta
Peabody Silver Prince
Peabody Pegamy
Nut of Houghton Hill
Toddles of Houghton Hill
Ch. Piccolo O' Pages Hill
Ch. Sheltieland Thistle

Peabody Paulet
Peabody Plume
Ch. Dancing Master of Anahassitt
Anahassitt Atalanta
Eng. Ch. Euan of Clerwood
Bracken of Clerwood
Ch. Dancing Master of Anahassitt
Anahassitt Atalanta

218

# 31

# Shetland Sheepdog
# Pedigrees

---

One of the most boring things in any breed book is what Elsworth Howell and the Bible call "the begats." The "begats" are long sentences, paragraphs, and pages, detailing the pedigrees of dogs, and including such things as "grandson of this dog," half sister to that one, litter mate to so-and-so. The result is often complete confusion for the reader.

In this book, we have tried to avoid this. And we have tried to get around it in the only way this is possible. Here we are including the pedigrees of the great dogs of the breed. But more than that, we have selected them on the basis of their bloodlines. We hope, therefore that most people will be able to trace the background of their dogs through these pedigrees.

Moreover, these pedigrees show, better than any other method, the systems used in developing the breed. For they indicate the ways in which inbreeding, line breeding, and the adding of importations have been used to develop the breed.

```
                Ch. Sea Isle Serenade           Ch. Nashcrest Golden Note
         Ch. Malpsh the Duke of Erle            Ch. Sea Isle Serenata
                Sea Isle Dusky Belle            Ch. Pixie Dell Bright Vision
    Fair Play of Sea Isle                       Bagaduce  Hannah of Sea Isle
                Ch. Sheltieland Kiltie O' Sea Isle   Ch. Bogota Blaze
         Ch. Kawartha's Fair Game               Ch. Sheltieland Peg O' The Picts
                Ch. Kawartha's Sabrina Fair     Ch. Teaberry Lane's Little Pecos
                                                Miss Ruffles of Oak Lawn
CH. HALSTOR'S PETER PUMPKIN

                Ch. Nashcrest Golden Note       Ch. Prince George O' Pages Hill
         Ch. Sea Isle Serenade                  Nashcrest Rhythm
                Ch. Sea Isle Serenata           Ch. Nashcrest Golden Note
    Ch. Sea Isle Rhapsody of Halstor            Ch. Sea Isle Sandra
                Ch. Sheltieland Kiltie O' Sea Isle   Ch. Bogota Blaze
         Ch. Colvidale Soliloquy                Ch. Sheltieland Peg O' The Picts
                Ch. Lochelven's Reverie         Ch. Grayson's Range Rider
                                                Ch. Lochelven's Caprice
```

220

Timberidge Tricolor
Ch. Noralee Bronze Nugget
Timberidge Tessa
Ch. Noralee Forecaster
Ch. Timberidge Temptation
Noralee Indian Summer
Ch. Noralee Autumn Gold

Bagaduce Bronze O' Timberidge
Timberidge Sparkle
Ch. Timberidge Temptation
Ch. Helensdale Myrtle
Ch. Kalandar Prince O' Pages Hill
Ch. Timberidge Temptress
Timberidge Tricolor
Noralee Cherry

## CH. ELF DALE VIKING

Ch. Merrywood's Charter Member
Merrywood's Junior Member
Merrywood's Will O' The Wisp
Ch. Elf Dale Heidi
Ch. Sea Isle Dappled Grey
Ch. Geronimo Little June, C.D.X.
Ch. Sheltieland Shasta Geronimo

Ch. Remembrance O' The Picts, C.D.
Ch. Gleeful of Mar-Nor-Will
Ch. Little John of Alandie, C.D.
Alandie Blue N' Black
Ch. Bil-B-Dot Blue Flag of Pocono
Parkswood Little Symphony
Ch. Mountaineer O' Pages Hill
Sea Isle Nancy

221

```
                                      Ch. Frigate's Emblem of Astolat
            Ch. Astolat Golden Symbol  Astolat Marigold
        Park Crest Aladdin             Ch. Astolat Golden Symbol
            Park Crest Princess Hiedi  Ch. Lady Libby
    Lonnie Du of Eve-Bart              Marion's Donacha Dhu
            Ch. Puck of Perkasie       Marion's Perkasie Goldilocks
        Peggy of Fairview              Knight Errant of Perkasie
            Victoria of Perkasie       Silver Mist of Perkasie

CH. WEE LASSIE OF EVE-BART, U.D.
                                      Ch. Frigate's Emblem of Astolat
            Ch. Astolat Golden Symbol  Astolat Marigold
        Park Crest Aladdin             Ch. Astolat Golden Symbol
            Park Crest Princess Hiedi  Ch. Lady Libby
    Wendy of Eve-Bart                  Jills Crusader of Pocono
            Honey Boy of Perkasie      Jills Honey Bun of Pocono
        Honey Girl of Eve-Bart         Ch. Puck of Perkasie
            Peggy of Fairview          Victoria of Perkasie
```

Within the American trade, however, one small group not only shared in these unquestionable benefits from the removal of Spencer Perceval, but were engaged in the three-way Russian trade that would have brought them into contact with John Bellingham. Several of their names appear repeatedly in the minutes of the chamber of commerce – Tom Hazard, brother of Sam, whose partner Henry Cabot took care of the agency in Boston; Abraham Barker, whose brother Jacob handled the New York end of the business; and Elisha Peck, whose partner Anson Phelps had also remained in New York. The nature of their trade not only gave them an interest in removing the multiplicity of blockades that choked their business, but a passionate concern to preserve the peace between their native country and their adopted home.

At the hub of Liverpool affairs was the enigmatic figure of Richard Statham. While mayors came and went every year, the town clerk was permanent. An attorney-at-law with many wealthy clients, Statham had served a long apprenticeship on the town council before his appointment as clerk in 1807. He was efficient and generally well-regarded by the ruling Tory and West India group, except in one regard. Large sums of money passed through his hands, both as a private solicitor and as a public official, and much of it stuck to Statham's fingers. His business files were thick with letters of complaint from clients about his slowness in paying out funds that he controlled. Twice he had to be sued in order to force him to disgorge money belonging to other people. But the habit had helped him grow wealthy, and presumably he knew too many secrets to be forced out of office.

Statham's overriding concern at the time of the assassination had been to protect the town's reputation. He had raced south with testimony to suggest that an obsessed Bellingham had acted alone, and he had raised money for Mary Bellingham with the clear understanding that she supported this view. He was unlikely to have preserved any papers that suggested the contrary.

Nonetheless, had John Vickery been given access to Statham's private papers, the detective might have found overlooked among the thousands of documents in the town clerk's files a scruffy affidavit on rag paper dated 18 March 1810 attesting that William Gee 'was a fit person' to be considered for the post of keeper of the King's Dock timber yard. Three people had signed it – T. Browne, J. Parton and E. Peck. Browne was a Liverpool merchant who traded with Scandinavia, later to be Swedish consul in Liverpool, but of no immediate interest to an investigator. J. Parton, however, was John Bellingham's business partner, and E. Peck's cramped handwriting had inscribed the name of Peck & Phelps in the minutes book of the American Chamber of Commerce as one of its founding members in 1801.

It was a tenuous link at best, but it took on more significance when seen in the context of the extraordinary letter that Bellingham wrote to Parton just before the murder. Although dated 11 May, the very day he killed Perceval, it was clearly the letter given to Mary Stevens on Sunday, the previous day, when Bellingham brought her the account books. On 25 May the *Mercury* printed a copy of it provided by 'a friend' who, unmistakably, was Parton himself. The critical passage, according to the *Mercury*, was the last, chilling paragraph, which demonstrated Bellingham's indifference to the shedding of life. To avoid embarrassment, Parton blanked out all names connected to Liverpool, but it is still possible to fill in the spaces, at least in general terms:

London May 11 1812. Dear ——— [*Parton*], I have to acknowledge your favour of the 4th. Ten days ago I wrote to ——— [*presumably a merchant*] to forward the ——— [*some form of goods*] which suppose he will do without loss of time. As you have not mentioned any thing about the Russian ship, suppose nothing has been done by you; or that —— [*someone interested in the Russian trade*] has procured one through another channel. Herewith a letter to —— [*probably his solicitor, Thomas Avison*] and get the —— [*terms*] explained. —— [*a merchant, possibly Russian given the context*] had returned home some days before your letter came to hand, as you must most likely be apprised. £17 is the price here, six months credit out of the yard for duty paid; that is to say for such as has paid duty, and the seller retaining the drawback; so that it ought to be £2 less at least. If —— [*the Russian merchant*] is inclined for it, the strong (quality) would be objectionable to him but that can be given off to advantage at home. A Russian friend has offered me the loading of four vessels to —— [*presumably Archangel or St Petersburg*], and to receive the return cargo on consignment.

I wish my affairs were come to a conclusion; everything in point of law is in my favour; but Mr Perceval and the ministry have shewn themselves more inclined to favour Lord Gower than do justice to me; however as I am resolved on having justice, in case of need, I will very shortly play a court card to compel them to finish the game. I am yours sincerely John Bellingham.

To the *Mercury*, the final paragraph's throwaway allusion to murder as the last play in a card game was truly shocking. On the face of it, this was the outlook of a psychopath. But, as Mary Stevens had witnessed, Bellingham was undoubtedly repelled by the thought of murder. Thus what is most striking about the casual tone is how completely Bellingham had grown accustomed to thinking of Perceval's assassination as part of a legal process. Once it had come to a conclusion, he could concentrate all his attention on business. And, despite all the woes he had suffered in Archangel, that business was almost exclusively concerned with Russia. For Bellingham, trading there was not history, but the future.

Clearly he did not have the money to get back into the business on his own account but, as his instructions to Parton showed, he hoped to do so by finding a suitable ship for another Liverpool merchant interested in the country's products. Nor could he take up his Russian friend's offer of four cargoes of goods, or finance the complex deal concerning a commodity – possibly Burton's beer, much in demand at the time in Russia – whose price was £17 duty paid, but £15 with the 'drawback', or repayment of duty. Nevertheless, his tone indicated that they were live projects and that his partner needed to be told what was going on.

For any investigator, the letter radically changed the context of Bellingham's visit to London. Throughout his time in the capital, he was pursuing two objects at once, the quest for justice and a return to the Baltic trade. As Vickery had already discovered, his original commercial intention was simply to purchase some iron. This must have been a commission from a client since he could not afford it on his own behalf. In London Bellingham would have been expected to deal with a specialist Baltic broker, negotiate a price, and arrange the means of shipment to the customer. It was certainly within his competence, but, given his uncontrollable urge to rant about the injustices done to him whenever the subject of Russian trade was raised, the client who commissioned him could not have escaped hearing about his past and his plan for getting compensation. A Liverpool businessman only interested in acquiring iron would hardly have commissioned as his agent a man with such an unreliable history and so obsessive a frame of mind. Yet someone did. At which point, the question becomes inescapable – why deliberately choose Bellingham?

From Bellingham's blinkered perspective, the answer would have been because he was a merchant with unique experience of Russia, eager to get back into his old business. In the longer term, as he frequently indicated when writing to those closest to him, including his wife and Mary Stevens, achieving justice was only a step towards the larger goal of escaping poverty. His reference to finishing the game with 'a court card', a pun meant in the legal as well as high-ranking sense, made this explicit. The assassination was the last move in a play that would inevitably bring his legally watertight case into court, where he was bound to be paid compensation of £8,000. All he needed was some time in London.

No businessman interested purely in its money-making potential would have been attracted to such a scheme, but at the end of 1811 with trade in ruins other priorities came to the surface. Like the Birmingham businessman who regarded the murder of Perceval as providential, a Liverpool merchant could well have learned of Bellingham's plan for forcing the government into court by means of killing the Prime Minister, and wondered whether this was Providence at work.

Bellingham's client evidently did think like this. There would be no direct involvement. The commission to buy iron would merely set matters in motion. But anyone who knew about the mad obstinacy with which Bellingham fought to obtain compensation from the tsar's despotic rule could be sure that he had the crazy determination needed to carry out the plan. At which point, a second question must be asked – what sort of person would make it possible for John Bellingham to assassinate the Prime Minister?

The pre-eminent London bank dealing with American affairs was Baring Brothers. It was used by both British and American citizens. Barings had financed the Louisiana Purchase by the United States from France in 1803 with a loan of $15 million, and was deeply involved in lending to the booming market in American land speculation. For many United States merchants, trading in anything from salt fish to slaves, Barings was the banker of choice to provide the necessary finance. But in Liverpool, one particular section of those in the Atlantic trade preferred another London banker when they needed long terms of credit.

Thomas Wilson of 98 Leadenhall Street in the City of London, once a partner of William Roscoe, certainly understood the risks of the agents who ran the Atlantic trade. In normal times, Wilson & Co. advanced the money to pay Liverpool exporters for their goods when they left the port, and passed on to their American customers the price plus interest at 6 per cent for the six weeks or so it took for the shipment to arrive. On the other side of the Atlantic, the bank did the same for American cotton exporters, but billed the Liverpool importers who settled up more quickly something nearer 5 per cent. As Wilson's reputation grew, a network of New York merchants and financiers including Jacob Barker and Gabriel Shaw sent business his way. Wilson's Russian connection, however, was what chiefly attracted the agents of United States merchants in Liverpool.

Russian producers insisted on being paid in advance for ore and timber, and so not only was local knowledge essential but also a line of credit that might have to stretch from the import of goods in one season through the winter freeze-up of the Baltic and Archangel until the waters opened up six or seven months later. It was useful, therefore, that Wilson's cousin, John, a longtime resident of St Petersburg, happened to be a partner in the brokerage agency of Porter, Brown & Wilson. As a result, Thomas Wilson & Co. could guarantee both to find a market for rice or tobacco or calico sent on from Liverpool, and to arrange the finance for a cargo back to the United States where the American merchant fleet was as desperate for Russian produce as the Royal Navy. 'The hemp, iron and duck [sailcloth] brought from Russia have been to our navigation and fisheries like seed to a crop,' exclaimed George Cabot, brother of Sam Hazard's former partner.

To underfunded American shipowners, the backing of such a well-connected banker was essential. Thus when Henry Ladd, a New Hampshire merchant, discovered that the value of the barrels of sugar in the hold of his vessel, *Hannah*, was not enough to pay for a full load of hemp in St Petersburg, he turned to Wilson who advanced the credit to cover the shortfall. The advantages of Wilson's deep pockets and good contacts made it doubly attractive for American shippers to ship goods first to Liverpool rather than directly to Russia. They were paid immediately for the first leg of the voyage, and they were then safeguarded against emergencies in a distant country.

John Bellingham could have used such backing in Archangel instead of relying on his own credit and his own contacts. When he went to London in 1812, the banker providing the finance for the purchase of iron would most probably have been Thomas Wilson & Co. Not only was the commodity Russian, but among Liverpool's merchants the only sector with a strong interest in buying iron was the American trade. On both counts Wilson was the financier most likely to be used. And of all his clients, the one most in need of iron was Elisha Peck.

In the United States, Phelps & Peck specialised in importing metal. Other companies might ship linen or flax or hemp, but theirs concentrated on pigs of iron, lead ingots, copper, brass and tinplate, the hard materials that the rural economy of the United States needed for its growth. Eventually they would establish a near monopoly in the United States as metal merchants, paying fees of around £12,000 a year to Thomas Wilson & Co., and earning fortunes for the two principals, Elisha Peck and Anson Green Phelps. Although they rarely saw each other, Peck and Phelps acted like brothers, tied to one another by religion and upbringing.

Peck was a Baptist, born in 1781, who came originally from New London, Connecticut, whereas Phelps was a Presbyterian, but they shared the same stern understanding that their faith was a covenant demanding conditions of behaviour as strict as those of a business contract. The ruthlessness with which each of them drove bargains and enforced contracts was equalled by the ferocity of their interior battles against temptation and idleness. Phelps's account books showed him by day suing his debtors for every penny they owed, while at night he berated himself in his diary for allowing 'the variety of business and cares for the present life' to distract him from the renewal of his 'covenant of faithfulness with God'. He and Elisha Peck had grown up together in Connecticut, and been friends since boyhood.

As adults, each felt a compelling desire to obey God's will and to make money. The solution was to go into business together, and to trust no one except themselves. At first the pair specialised in leather goods – saddles in particular that they made and sold in the south – but they did not take long to realise that there was more profit in metal. This had to be imported from England, and so at the age of twenty-one, Elisha Peck moved to Liverpool. There he set up the company of Peck & Phelps, the reversal of names reflecting the fact that it was simply the other side of the American coin.

Initially he engaged in the classic two-way trade, American raw materials, mostly cotton shipped out of Savannah and Baltimore, in exchange for tinplate, nails, lead and brassware shipped back to New York. But at some date before 1811 he had added the third leg that took Peck & Phelps into the Russian trade, and led him to employ Thomas Wilson as his banker.

By December of that year, in common with other American merchants in Liverpool, Phelps had certainly come to realise that one man was single-handedly driving the United States and Britain into war. That conclusion was obvious to every American on the eastern side of the Atlantic. Even in distant St Petersburg, the ambassador, John Quincy Adams, expressed conviction that 'the

British Orders in Council unless abandoned would inevitably produce a war between us and England', and that 'the most powerful patron and supporter of the Orders in Council [is] Mr. Perceval, First Lord of the Treasury and Chancellor of the Exchequer'. In December 1811, American expatriates learned from the newspapers that Congress had told President James Madison that Britain's economic blockade would justify a declaration of war. That recommendation was hammered home by hawkish supporters.

'We must now oppose the farther encroachments of Great Britain by war,' insisted Congressman Richard Johnston of Kentucky. Only by a drastic change of policy could bloodshed be avoided. 'I wish to see Great Britain renounce the piratical system of paper blockade,' he demanded, 'liberate our captured seamen on board her ships of war; relinquish the practice of impressment on board our merchant vessels; repeal her Orders in Council.'

So long as Perceval remained alive none of those measures would be taken. Thus hostilities would break out, thousands would be killed and many more horribly mutilated. Homes would be destroyed, towns burned, trade brought to a standstill, and the affairs of Peck & Phelps ruined. It was apparent to anyone whose prosperity depended on keeping the peace that the time had come to intervene.

# Where the Money Came From

I consider his Majesty's Government to have completely endeavoured to close the door of justice, in declining to have, or even to permit, my grievances to be brought before Parliament for redress, which privilege is the birthright of every individual.

John Bellingham to the Bow Street magistrates, April 1812

When he left Liverpool, three days after Christmas 1811, Bellingham apparently allowed only a few weeks for the operation of his plan to wring £8,000 from the government. From the delivery of his petition to the head of state, the Prince Regent, in January, he evidently expected to have reached the endgame by late February. Either his petition would have been presented to Parliament, or he would be ready to play 'the court card'.

Through no fault of his, however, the original timetable immediately fell apart. The inefficiency of the prince's office in losing his letter, and the delay in discovering the mishap, meant that by the middle of February the first card in the game had not even been played. It would take at least another month to carry out his plan, and already he owed six weeks' rent. Without new funds, he would shortly be forced to return home.

In the United States the military clock was ticking faster. In January news arrived in Liverpool that Congress had voted $11 million for armaments and authorised the establishment of a militia army of fifty thousand men. No one yet believed the United States to be prepared for hostilities, and its armaments budget was dwarfed by Britain's annual expenditure on the army and navy of almost £40 million, equivalent to about $200 million. Nevertheless, the War Hawks were gaining support, and not only from those infuriated by the Royal Navy's repeated press-ganging of American citizens. In the western states, settlers moving into the prairies joined the call for war when they discovered that the Native Americans resisting their advance had been armed by the British.

For Americans who did not share the interests of slave owners, these were powerful arguments, but not yet decisive. Thus in February 1812, the outcome still hung in the balance.

That same month, Spencer Perceval won his power struggle with the Prince Regent, guaranteeing that his policies would not be changed for the foreseeable future. And in February John Bellingham also ran out of money.

What Bellingham needed was a maintenance until his case could be heard in court. Whoever put up the money would be an investor to be paid back out of the compensation Bellingham would receive from the government. The possibility that this person might be considered an accomplice never entered Bellingham's precise mind. What Elisha Peck needed was someone to save the world from war. Whether Peck was indeed the person who commissioned Bellingham to buy iron in London and subsequently paid his maintenance is impossible to know. All that can be said is that he fits the profile better than anyone else. What little is known of his character shows him to have been a typically stubborn, flinty-souled Yankee trader. His handwriting is small, spare and tucked-up, his religion was strict, his education minimal, his domestic situation solitary – he was thirty-seven when he married – and his accounts meticulous. He regarded making money as next to godliness, and nothing would shake him from a bargain once made.

Either Peck, or someone remarkably like him, already had a commercial arrangement with Bellingham. Now he promised to pay a maintenance of £20 a month drawn on his bank, Thomas Wilson & Co. But the schedule was to be unshakable. The case must be brought to court without delay.

Bellingham's acceptance of the contract was rewarded with a first payment at the end of February 1812. He celebrated with a spending spree, and at the beginning of March began the process of winning justice again, with another petition to the royal household.

The need for haste had become urgent. On 3 March, Henry Brougham presented a motion in the House of Commons calling for an inquiry into the effects of the Orders in Council. James Stephen led the government side, blandly declaring in the face of the nation's appalling economic distress that the Orders had actually led to an increase in trade. In reply, an outraged Alexander Baring came close to calling him a liar, exclaiming 'Nothing could more surprise him than to hear an honourable and learned gentleman . . . asserting that they had produced great commercial prosperity'. Even General Gascoyne, a lifelong supporter of Pitt's Tories, broke ranks and voted with Brougham and the Whigs. His defection showed that the West India lobby, once supporters of the economic blockade, had been engulfed like the rest of Liverpool by the trade recession.

At the end of the debate, however, Perceval made it plain that no criticism, either British or American, would shake him. 'As England is contending for the defence of her maritime rights, and for the preservation of her national existence which essentially depends on the maintenance of these rights,' he explained in his dull, persistent voice, 'she could not be expected, in the prosecution of this great and primary interest, to arrest or vary her course to listen to the pretensions of neutral nations.'

Sitting in the gallery listening to the debate was Jonathan Russell, the United States chargé d'affaires. The following day he wrote to James Monroe, the Secretary of State: 'If any thing was wanting to prove the inflexible determination of the present ministry to persevere in the orders in Council, without modification or relaxation, the declarations of leading members of the administration on these measures must place it beyond the possibility of a doubt. I no longer entertain a hope that we can honorably avoid war.'

The eleventh hour had come, and all hopes of peace and prosperity now lay in Bellingham's hands. On the surface, his justice programme was going according to the worst-case expectations. The Prince Regent rejected his petition, followed by the Privy Council, and the Foreign Office, and the Treasury. But during those fraught days, as one department after another refused to allow him to petition Parliament, the conflict in John Bellingham's nature between the beautiful and the sublime became extreme. By early April every avenue had been explored. The Bow Street magistrates had not responded to his clear threat to execute justice himself. A perfunctory note from them told him his letter would be forwarded to the Home Secretary, but nothing more. That marked the end of what was small and beautiful. He had now reached the endgame that consisted of one terrifying, sublime act.

His first instinct was to find some way out.

In mid-April, he sent a second, written appeal to the Treasury, fielded again by John Beckett. He followed it up by going in person once more to Downing Street to plead his cause. There he met yet another civil servant, a Mr Hill, who, failing to realise that he was dealing with a man at the end of his tether, replied that he was at liberty to take 'such measures as he thought proper'. It was intended as a brush-off, but to Bellingham, who believed he had given clear warning of his intentions, it sounded as though he had been given '*carte blanche* to act in whatever manner I thought proper'.

In that agonised state of mind, he went to see General Isaac
Gascoyne again, this time in his Mayfair house. It was a strange
encounter that lasted, according to the general, for about an hour.
By Gascoyne's account, he recommended that Bellingham again
ask the ministers to present his petition to Parliament. Each of
them knew this to be a pointless exercise that had already been
tried, and that Perceval's mind was unchangeable. But the general's
advice was not entirely neutral. He was about to present a massive
petition from Liverpool against the Orders signed by more than six
thousand people, and knew that Perceval already regarded him as a
turncoat. True to his instinct for personal abuse, Perceval publicly
labelled Gascoyne a subversive troublemaker, lumping him in with
factory-burners, machine-breakers and those responsible for 'exciting outrageous spirits through the country including the Luddites'.

At their lengthy meeting, it is possible that, like Mr Hill, the
peppery general told Bellingham to do what he felt he had to do.
Unlike Hill, however, the general was familiar with Bellingham's
implacable obstinacy and with the anger in his Liverpool background. Exasperated as he was with both Perceval and Bellingham,
Gascoyne might have suspected the consequences, and wished the
worst on both of them.

Shortly after this meeting Bellingham went to purchase a brace
of pistols from William Beckwith. But even then, he could not
force himself to take the last step.

The strain in his face immediately struck Mary Stevens when she
saw Bellingham on 8 May 1812. For more than three weeks he had
put off playing the final fatal card. He had bought the weapons, a
concealed pocket had been added to his coat, and he had familiarised himself with the Prime Minister's appearance. Then nothing.

Bellingham understood acutely the obligations of a contract.
His entire campaign for compensation sprang from his resentment
at the government's failure to perform the reciprocal duties it owed

to its citizens. Now, having promised to bring the business to court, he had failed to carry out his side of the bargain. On the weekend of Mary Stevens's arrival he suddenly broke down, and admitted that he was close to suicide. He had been so forthright about the infallibility of his plan, and so direct in telling his wife of its impending success. Mary Stevens herself must have added to the nightmare by her unmistakable scepticism. But, as his behaviour was to demonstrate, it is also evident that the source of his maintenance had lost all patience with the delay. A contract had been made, Bellingham had been paid, and the case needed to be taken to court at once.

Information from New York made it clear that the absolutely final second was approaching before war was declared. On 2 April, Congress took the long-discussed measure of forbidding all shipping to enter or leave United States ports for ninety days. This was seen as the last step before a declaration of war. By 1 July, therefore, either the embargo would have been lifted or war would have been declared.

Information took four to six weeks to cross the Atlantic from east to west. A United States sloop, *Hornet*, carrying diplomatic despatches from London had sailed early in April, and was generally thought to be the last official carrier of news about the British government's intentions. Its message was simply that no change had taken place. But conceivably an unofficial courier could have left with good news as late as the first week of May, and still have been in time to prevent war breaking out.

During these last moments, Perceval and Stephen were becoming more isolated. In the Commons, Henry Brougham was finally granted the House of Commons inquiry he had pressed for into the economic effects of the Orders. Even former hardliners like the new Foreign Secretary, Lord Castlereagh, now argued for concessions. On 21 April the Prime Minister gave way sufficiently to allow the Prince Regent to announce that the Orders in Council might be withdrawn on condition that Napoleon publicly revoked the 1806 Berlin decree without secret caveats. Beyond that Perceval would not yield a step, and no one had the power to make him.

The stakes could not have been higher. In the United States, there was growing opposition to the war from New York merchants like Anson G. Phelps and Jacob Barker, and from New England shippers like Henry Cabot. A writer to the *New York Evening Post* appealed to the hawks to draw back from a declaration of war: 'The measure is perfect madness. You will lose millions when you will gain a cent. The expense will be enormous. It will ruin our country.' In Congress a substantial minority of congressmen and senators were adamantly against hostilities.

A handbill circulating in New England condemned the war as a device by rich, southern slave owners to gain control over the yeomen farmers and shopkeepers of the north. 'Ye who live by farming, by the mechanic arts, and by commerce,' it demanded, 'where and what would you be, at the end of a five years war with England, directed by Southern planters? If you escape a war, you are doomed to be deprived of your commerce; and with your commerce goes your freedom.' So deeply did this suspicion run that Governor Caleb Strong of Massachusetts refused to participate or even let the state's militia be called up for service. Nationwide, less than one-fifth of the expected volunteers had come forward to enlist. It only required the removal of the Orders in Council and the fragile momentum for war would collapse.

By Sunday, 10 May, John Bellingham was at breaking point. Psychologically, he still recoiled from murder. But there was nowhere else to go. He had broken his contract. As a result April's maintenance had not been paid. And now his money had run out.

Mary Stevens's arrival exposed his desperate position. The whole point of her coming to London was to be given the business free of debt, and an essential part of the process was for Bellingham to introduce her to creditors and suppliers so that they knew the arrangement. Have confidence in me 'to do what is right and proper', he had told her in his letter. 'You will not be deceived . . .' But he had deceived her.

Instead of meeting Miss Stevens off the coach as he promised, Bellingham avoided her for two days, and only made contact at the weekend when businesses were closed. Although he examined the accounts she had brought, there were no introductions to trades people, and no handover of half the business. Evidently he could no longer afford to do so and, since a husband was responsible for his wife's debts, presumably he himself could not face Mary Bellingham's creditors. On top of that, he owed his landlady for a further five weeks' rent and firing. Rebecca Robarts was prepared to extend him credit, but Bellingham's display of anger at the shilling charged by the washerwoman on the Monday morning showed how thin his well-disciplined nerves were stretched.

Dire though Bellingham's financial situation was, his sponsor evidently refused to pay him another penny until the contract was fulfilled. Yet with so great a prize so close at hand, he clearly hoped that even at the very last second Bellingham could still be persuaded to play 'the court card'. As much as any other detail, this adamant insistence on the terms of the deal points to Elisha Peck as the paymaster. That weekend he must have been in London because only his presence would explain Bellingham's extraordinary behaviour on the day of the assassination. Everything Bellingham did was dictated by the need to ensure that on Monday evening, as John Vickery could testify, Rebecca Robarts would be in possession of Wilson's note promising to pay £20 to John Bellingham.

Manifestly Bellingham could only have acquired the note just before the killing, otherwise he would immediately have turned it into cash. In court, Mrs Robarts's chambermaid Catherine Figgins testified that he left the lodging-house at noon on the day of the assassination for about an hour. Presumably that is when he met his investor, and secured an agreement that he would be paid April's maintenance, on the strict condition that he carried out his side of the contract that very day. While the American, if that's who he was, went off to 98 Leadenhall Street to make arrangements with his banker, Bellingham returned to New Millman Street and suggested to his landlady an expedition to the European Museum. Of all the strange events of that day, their last outing together was in many ways the most curious.

At about one o'clock on Monday afternoon, John Bellingham took Rebecca Robarts and her young son to an exhibition at the museum in King Street, next to St James's Square. They walked there from New Millman Street, a journey of about forty minutes. Tucked into the secret pocket of his coat was a primed and loaded pistol, while another bulged in his yellow ochre, nankeen pantaloons. The inconvenience, danger and sheer eccentricity of going so far for such a trivial reason, armed with two loaded weapons that were to be used to commit murder immediately afterwards, would have struck a mind far less fastidious than Bellingham's as bizarre.

It is impossible to suppose that he undertook the expedition simply to entertain a landlady who had been remarkably forbearing about his rent. At that moment, worlds kept apart in his viscous mind were in gross danger of colliding. The self-possessed, gentlemanly Bellingham, appreciative of beauty, of well-fitting, well-laundered clothes, and of the discreet affection of a young mother, was threatened by the terrifying reality of Peck's contract – the 'abhorrent but compulsive alternative' of killing the Prime Minister.

The trio spent more than two hours enjoying the exhibits at the European Museum. When they came out, it was some time after four o'clock. Hearings into the Orders in Council organised by Henry Brougham were publicly scheduled to begin at 4.30 p.m.

Bellingham should have chosen the direct route from St James's Square to Parliament Square, cutting through St James's Park. It takes about fifteen minutes. He would have arrived shortly before the start of the hearings, in good time for the appearance of the Prime Minister. Instead, he, Mrs Robarts and her son walked away in almost the opposite direction towards Leicester Square.

They went to Sidney's Alley, a short street leading into the square, where a row of smart shops sold jewellery, lace and silk. Bellingham would have needed some privacy for his last transaction with his sponsor. At 7 Sidney's Alley, Thomas Challenier offered fine linen for sale, material that came from both Russia and Ireland, and he might once have been one of Bellingham's customers. On this occasion, his flinty-souled sponsor had with him a note promising to pay £20, issued by Thomas Wilson. No doubt Bellingham had to prove that he did finally intend to carry out his plan. In the back of Challenier's shop, out of his landlady's sight, a glimpse of the two pistols would have carried conviction. The note was handed over. Bellingham rejoined Mrs Robarts, gave her the promise of £20, then politely excused himself, saying, as his landlady recalled, that he had to go to Westminster to buy a prayer book. Rebecca Robarts and her son would have arrived back at the lodging-house at about quarter past five, just as Spencer Perceval was being murdered.

He could not have avoided the detour. Indebtedness made it necessary. But it could have ruined everything. Had Spencer Perceval left 10 Downing Street at half past four for the start of the hearings on the Orders in Council, or at ten minutes to five to see his friend James Stephen open the defence, John Bellingham's plan would have collapsed. The promissory note would have been revoked, Rebecca Robarts would reluctantly have been forced to admit that her finely dressed lodger could not pay his rent, and a homeless

Bellingham would have had to return to Liverpool. Mary Stevens would not have been surprised.

As it was, anxiety must have squeezed the air from his lungs all the way down crowded Whitehall and up the steps into the lobby of the Houses of Parliament. The deep gasping for breath that struck William Jerdan when he caught Bellingham testified to the tension he had been under. At no time in all his tense life had John Bellingham been so completely alone with his fear of the sublime.

It is possible that one other person was also suffering from a similar degree of anxiety.

At the moment John Bellingham fired his shot, General Isaac Gascoyne sat in an upstairs committee room with yet another Liverpool petition against the Orders. He had made a private appointment to go through its terms with Perceval, and having been savaged for his irresponsibility in presenting the previous petition, he was presumably prepared for a bruising exchange. Like Brougham, he had expected Perceval to arrive earlier, and, when he did not turn up, Gascoyne had walked upstairs to the committee room which opened onto a balcony overlooking the lobby.

Despite his distance from the scene, the general claimed under oath that sounds travelled so clearly, 'it was nearly the same thing as to hearing, as to being in the lobby of the House'. Accordingly when he heard the pistol shot followed by cries to close the door, he 'rushed down stairs, through the House into the lobby'. There someone said to him, 'that is the man who fired the pistol', and he saw a crowd gathered around Bellingham, whom he either did or did not recognise according to the particular version of the story he told. But there was one obvious flaw in every version.

While those in the lobby had seen Perceval fall dead, Gascoyne had only heard a shot. He could not have known that anyone was killed, still less that it was the Prime Minister.

The natural reaction to the sound of a pistol shot would be to step out onto the balcony and look down to the lobby to see what was happening. The general never explained why he decided to rush directly to the scene without looking, nor did he ever reveal at what point he discovered the identity of the victim. His testimony always implied that he knew immediately that it was Perceval who had been shot.

The most innocent explanation is that his knowledge of Bellingham, and especially the tone of their last encounter, had given the general some inkling of what he intended to do. Thus, when he saw Bellingham pointed out in the lobby as the man who had fired the shot, he instantly realised what must have happened.

A less innocent explanation is that Gascoyne had more than an inkling of Bellingham's intentions, but did nothing about it. Unlike the London magistrates and civil servants, he was aware of Liverpool's hatred of the Prime Minister, and the risk of it taking violent form. The fury with which Gascoyne attacked Bellingham, like his pretence at suddenly recognising him in the Commons, could be taken to be the result of bad conscience.

The least innocent explanation is that he had prior knowledge. Bellingham's story was sufficiently remarkable, and his persistence sufficiently irritating, to ensure that Isaac Gascoyne would have talked about him to friends in Liverpool, and especially to the Atlantic traders whose petition he had just presented in Parliament. Conceivably, they discussed the steps that Bellingham was prepared to take, and both the traders and the general had concluded, like Elisha Peck, that it might be providential if one life were sacrificed *pro bono publico*. In that case, there would have been no need to step out onto the balcony to find out who had fallen victim to a pistol shot. Only the pressing urgency to show that he was in no way complicit.

\* \* \*

The relief that everyone noted in the assassin after his deed was not one that came from killing the Prime Minister, but from being able to return to the world of beauty. Convinced that the justice of his action would be recognised and that the government would have to pay the compensation he demanded, Bellingham was at last free from anxiety. His triumph would soon be known to his wife and to Mary Stevens, and beyond that there extended a limitless future as a successful Russian merchant, growing in wealth and basking in the affection of his three sons.

The first indication of this brighter future arrived in his cell on Thursday afternoon, just before the trial. While Mary Stevens was visiting him, *The Times* reported, the prisoner 'received a small box, containing one fifty, one twenty, and several Bank-notes for smaller sums, amounting altogether to about an hundred guineas [£105]. It was not ascertained whether this sum was an anonymous gift, or came from a known friend to meet the expenses of the trial.'

The report was not published until Monday, 18 May, and the paragraph was crammed into the foot of the right-hand column well away from the main story, clearly provided by Newgate's Keeper, John Newman, that on his last full day alive Bellingham had complained that he would not be shaved before his execution and 'he thus will not be able to appear as a Gentleman!' The item about the money came from a different source, and appeared at the last moment as the paper was being made up late on Sunday night. By any journalistic standards, however, it should have been the headline news. The thirty or so pounds in coin and small notes might well have been contributions from anonymous sympathisers, but the two large-denomination notes, for £50 and £20, represented something quite different. Such sums could only have come from one or more wealthy individuals.

The smaller note was presumably from his sponsor and represented May's instalment of the maintenance. In strict justice, it was not due until the end of the month, but even the moralistic, materialistic Peck could have guessed that Bellingham was not going to live that long.

The origin of the larger note can only be conjectured. But the one other person who knew of Bellingham's contract was Thomas Wilson himself. The banker shared to the full Alexander Baring's hatred of the Orders in Council, and his bitterness at James Stephen's dishonest attempt to justify their continued existence. Wilson understood better than most the catastrophic economic effects of a war with the United States. He had already warned his American clients of the difficulties they would face, and his prescience would be confirmed in 1813 when the war forced him to suspend all financial business with them. But Wilson had another reason for wanting to express his appreciation of what Bellingham had done.

In common with other British financiers, he had expanded his operations into South America, and Brazil's slave economy in particular. It was impossible for Thomas Wilson & Co. not to be involved with the ramifications of the illegal slave trade because every aspect of Brazil's cotton plantations, copper mines and coffee farms depended on slave labour. Brazil had no banks of its own. Its development could not take place without British finance. Wilson, Baring and their banking colleagues paid for everything, from government bonds to ships and the gaudy produce used in barter to buy the slaves in Africa. The more Spencer Perceval choked the slave trade, the tighter the bankers' profits were squeezed. Among those who gained most from his assassination were the mandarins of the City of London.

Late on Sunday, 17 May, John Bellingham finished his last letter to his wife. 'My blessing to the boys,' he wrote, 'with kind remembrance to Miss Stevens, for whom I have the greatest regard in consequence of her uniform affection for them.'

All that remained was to tell their mother his last thoughts. 'As we shall not meet any more in this world, I sincerely hope we shall do so in the world to come.' John Newman, the keeper, made copies of his letter for sale to the newspapers, and so this most intimate communication was quickly made public. There was just one backward look at his failures – 'With the purest of intentions it has always been my misfortune to be thwarted, misrepresented and ill-used in life . . .' – but in general the tone of Bellingham's final words was that of a soul at rest. Although he had never quite arrived at security, he was consoled by 'a happy prospect of compensation in a speedy translation to life eternal'.

Compensation was all he had ever wanted. It would have balanced the books between his suffering in Russia and the failure of the government to protect him. It was the lack of it that had forced him to execute justice. But his reward was now to be eternal freedom from penury and misrepresentation. The hangman's rope carried no terrors. A divine accountancy would ensure that the deficits of mortality were cancelled out: 'It's not possible to be more calm or placid than I feel, and nine hours more will waft me to those happy shores where bliss is without alloy. Yours ever affectionate, John Bellingham.'

Then, after laying the letter aside, he recalled some practical details and added what amounted to a will disposing of his worldly goods:

Sunday Night 11 o'Clock
Dr Ford [the prison chaplain] will forward you my watch, my prayer book with a guinea and note. Once more, God be with you, my sweet Mary. The public sympathise much for me, but I have been called upon to play an anxious card in life.

Of the hundred guineas delivered to his cell before his trial, no trace remained. With luck the money travelled north with Mary

Stevens, otherwise it would probably have been confiscated by the City of London sheriffs responsible for his custody. For an hour or so he dozed. The money no longer bothered him, but he was kept awake by a sense of the unfairness that had cheated him of the reward his meticulous plan deserved. Eventually he sat up and added a final postscript:

> Twelve O'Clock I lost my suit solely through the improper conduct of my Attorney and Counsel, Mr Alley, in not bringing witnesses forward (of which there were more than 20); in consequence, the Judge took advantage of the circumstance, and I went of [*sic*] the defence without having brought forward a single friend – otherwise I must inevitably have been acquitted. – J Bellingham

## 18

## An Execution Ends all Cares

The police officers and the Secretary of State might have known what would happen a fortnight past. I have obeyed them. I have done my worst, and I rejoice in the deed.

John Bellingham before the bar of the House of Commons,
11 May 1812

Conscious that he was in a way blameless, both for what he had done and for what was about to happen to him, John Bellingham behaved in his last hours with an inner dignity that impressed all those who observed him. Even the solidly Tory *Morning Post* remarked that 'his deportment was calm, manly, and even at times dignified; and had he perished for almost any other crime than that of assassination, he would justly have excited the pity and respect, if not the admiration, of everyone who beheld this extraordinary close of his wretched career'.

He was woken early, and William Cobbett, sharing the same prison, recorded that Bellingham had been 'sleeping sound in his cell, and upon being called between six and seven, said he was called too soon'. It was a justifiable complaint. Having washed and dressed, he read his prayer book for half an hour, then took holy communion, and still there was time to wait. Meanwhile in the dark grey light of a rainy dawn, large crowds had been gathering outside Newgate prison. They surrounded the scaffold that had been constructed opposite the debtors' door in the prison wall, and were soon filling Newgate street for a hundred yards in either direction. More spectators packed the windows and rooftops of nearby houses, among them Lord Byron, who had sat up all night in order to see 'Bellingham launched into eternity'.

There had been a riot the previous month at a double hanging, and posters warned spectators in large black letters of the danger they faced. 'Beware of entering the crowd! Remember! thirty poor creatures were pressed to death by the crowd when Haggerty and Holloway were executed!' Some latecomers were deterred and walked away, but unlike most execution crowds, this one's mood was subdued rather than excitable. It might have been the result of the steady downpour – 'the Old Bailey,' said the *Public Ledger*, 'seemed to be paved with umbrellas' – but it was also because, as Bellingham had said, 'the public sympathise much with me'.

Exactly a week had passed since the mob had taken to the streets celebrating Perceval's assassination as an act of liberation, and applauding the murderer as a hero. The authorities were taking no chances. There were constables and bludgeon men posted around the scaffold, and along the walls of the prison, while soldiers were posted in backstreets out of sight. The fear of revolution had not disappeared.

At about half past seven the two sheriffs, William Heygate and Samuel Birch, followed by the lord mayor, and about twenty official guests all dressed in black, assembled in the prison yard. Bellingham was told that they were waiting, and replied clearly, 'I am perfectly ready also.' He was still wearing the double set of fetters at wrist and ankle, and these had to be struck off before his execution. As he was led towards a small anvil in the middle of the yard, the watchers noted that he walked 'with a firm and intrepid pace, and looking up, he observed, with great coolness – "Ah! it rains heavily." '

He placed first his hands then his feet on the anvil so that the rivets could be driven out of his fetters, and it was only as the inexperienced jailer began to hammer at the chains close to his feet that he showed any sign of nerves, crying out 'Mind, mind – take care, take care.' With the chains struck off, he was taken to the condemned prisoners' room by the two sheriffs. Although he had not been allowed to shave, he had dressed with the care of a gentleman – the chocolate-brown greatcoat he had worn on the day of the assassination, a buff and blue-striped waistcoat in kerseymere, clay-coloured pantaloons, white stockings and, unfortunately, a pair of down-at-heel prison shoes made necessary by the iron rings around his ankles. But once the shackles had been removed, he and the sheriffs went into the executioner's room accompanied by a few of the dignitaries. There, he kicked off the shoes and pulled on his smart hessian boots. So far as he could, Bellingham remained stylish to the end.

With the hanging rope coiled on a table next to them, the law officers returned to the one question that still nagged at the authorities. Sheriff Samuel Birch voiced again the government's haunting anxiety that he might have had an accomplice in the murder. For the last time, as every newspaper reported, Bellingham 'solemnly assured the Sheriff that the act of killing Mr. Perceval was entirely his own'.

According to one of the black-clad witnesses in the room, someone called out, ' "Then it was your own affair; it was from personal resentment." Bellingham appeared hurt at the latter expression, and after repeating the words "personal resentment" with an indignant or rather dignified tone, said, "I bore no resentment to Mr Perceval as a man; and as a man, I am sorry for his fate . . . It was my own sufferings that caused the melancholy event, and I hope it will be a warning to future Ministers, to attend to the applications and prayers of those who suffer by oppression." '

It was a remark that suggested he had come to see the assassination as more than a balancing of the books, and something closer to a political act. At one point during the trial, he had demanded 'What is my crime to the crime of government itself?', language that would not have been inappropriate to Thomas Paine, or even to a late nineteenth-century anarchist like Prince Peter Kropotkin. Sensing that even on the verge of his execution, Bellingham's inner convictions represented some sort of challenge to the society they lived in, those in the executioner's room began to throw jibes at him. 'I hope you feel deep contrition for the deed,' Sheriff William Heygate exclaimed. Gracefully, Bellingham deflected the remark. 'I hope, sir,' he replied, 'I feel as a man ought to do.' And when someone from the surrounding group called out that he hoped he had repented so that 'you will meet the Almighty with a pure soul', Bellingham responded, 'No one can presume to do that, sir. Only our Saviour went from this world with a pure spirit.'

As the hour hand neared eight, the executioner, William Brunskill, entered the room. Bellingham turned to the table where the thick hanging rope lay. Beside it were two thinner cords to tie his wrists and arms. 'Gentlemen,' he said, 'I am quite ready.' Then he rolled back his sleeves and held out his clasped hands to the executioner. 'So?' he asked. He waited like that while his wrists were pinioned, then asked for the sleeves of his coat to be turned down neatly to cover the ties.

The second rope went around his elbows, and was passed behind his back to prevent him scrabbling upwards to loosen the noose as he swung. When it was tied, he tested to see how high he could reach, and asked for the cord to be tightened. 'I wish not to have the power of offering any resistance,' he explained. As the executioner left the room with the hanging rope, Bellingham asked whether it would be strong enough to bear his weight. Brunskill, by then in his late sixties, promised him with all the authority of almost thirty years' experience in the business that it would not break. Bellingham thanked him for that assurance. His composure and unfaltering voice astonished those present. He seemed to have no fear of what lay ahead. If so, it was not from a lack of feeling. As the procession walked out of the room into the prison yard, it was observed that the condemned man ducked his head down to his shoulder as though to wipe away a tear.

Cobbett, who was standing by the window of his cell, watched Bellingham emerge into the street and step lightly up the stair to the scaffold. But his attention was immediately diverted by the reaction of the crowd. 'I saw the anxious looks,' he wrote, 'I saw the half-horrified countenances; I saw the mournful tears run down; and I heard the unanimous blessings. What then, were these tears shed, and these blessings bestowed by Englishmen upon a murderer!' Searching for an explanation for this surprising, even shocking, display of sympathy, Cobbett decided that people felt grateful to Bellingham for having 'ridded them of the leader amongst those whom they thought totally bent on the destruction of their liberties'. Cobbett was not unbiased, but it was clear to him that in the public mind Perceval's murder had indeed been a political assassination.

On the scaffold, Bellingham looked about him with a lively interest, much as he had at the Old Bailey. William Brunskill, who had knotted one end of the rope around the beam above him, now removed Bellingham's cravat, and placed the noose over his head. Standing near to him, Dr Samuel Forde, the Newgate Ordinary, or chaplain, asked him whether he had any last words. Almost as a reflex, Bellingham once more began to tell the story of his Russian experience, but stopped when Forde reminded him that he had no more time left. Then he joined Forde in a short prayer. When it was over, Brunskill placed a white cap over his head. Bellingham asked to have it removed, but was told that it was obligatory.

This, the last stage, provoked more cries of 'God bless you!' and 'God save you!' from the crowd. Forde asked Bellingham whether he could hear them. Bellingham said he heard the shouting but could not make out the words. Then he was asked how he felt, and replied that he thanked God for enabling him to meet his fate with fortitude and resignation. Brunskill had done his job with swift efficiency, and for a long minute John Bellingham stood there on the trapdoor, blindfolded, noosed and pinioned, before a crowd that had fallen utterly silent.

Then the Newgate clock began to strike eight o'clock and, according to the *Edinburgh Annual Register*:

> while it was striking the seventh time, the Clergyman and Bellingham both fervently praying, the supporters of the internal square of the scaffold were struck away, and Bellingham dropped out of sight down as far as the knees, his body being in full view, the clergyman being left standing on the outer frame of the scaffold. When Bellingham sunk, the most perfect and awful silence prevailed, not even the slightest attempt at a huzza or noise of any kind was made. He did not struggle at first, and but little afterwards, the executioner below pulling his heels that he might die quickly.

Except for the clues left by his spending, that might have been the final act in a murder that seemed to make no sense. Bellingham's body swung on the rope till nine o'clock and was then taken down to be dissected by Sir William Blizzard at St Bartholomew's hospital. According to the *Annual Register*, when the chest was opened, Bellingham's heart was observed to be still beating. 'The expanding and contracting powers continued perceptible till one o'clock in the day,' it reported, 'a proof of the steady, undismayed character which he preserved to the last gasp.'

It was the sort of mythical detail that should have entered folklore. But with astonishing speed, the existence of John Bellingham was erased from public memory, until only a faint shadow labelled 'a deranged merchant' remained to show where he had been. 'You'd be astonished to find how shy people are of speaking on the subject,' an anonymous letter-writer reported from Liverpool just weeks after the execution. Obliterated with him were the mysteries of the crime, the bizarre motivation, the intricate planning, and the finances needed to carry it out.

Yet in his fumbling, anguished, obstinate way, Bellingham truly was someone who changed the course of history. Had he missed his encounter with the Prime Minister, the campaign to choke off the illegal slave trade would have continued, Judge Thorpe would have remained dispensing rough justice on slavers of every nationality, compulsory slave registers would have been extended to every West Indian colony, and as many as forty thousand Africans a year would have been saved from slavery.

Had Bellingham brought himself to carry out his plan as he intended and shot the Prime Minister in April, the news would have reached the United States in time to prevent the outbreak of war. Instead, Perceval's successor, Lord Liverpool, was not appointed until 8 June, and although the Orders in Council were withdrawn at the first opportunity, on 16 June, war had already been formally declared two days earlier. Only in August did James Madison's government learn that the Orders had been withdrawn. By then, the first American troops had invaded Canada and Fort Detroit was under siege by Canadian forces. On 19 August the humiliating surrender of the United States garrison in Detroit under General William Hull left such a wound that there could be no pulling back until honour had been regained.

Elisha Peck sailed back to the United States before the end of 1812. Reunited, he and Phelps moved the company headquarters to a prominent location in Manhattan, and set about creating a company that eventually held a virtual monopoly on the import of sheet metal into the United States. Once peace returned, Elisha Peck went back to Liverpool where he continued to make money until his retirement in 1834. By that year, the annual turnover of Peck & Phelps had reached £270,000 a year, and in the village of West Haverstraw beside the Hudson river Bellingham's paymaster had built a rolling steel mill imported from England, which he named Samsondale. Not far away, he constructed a massive mansion looking over the Hudson with a Palladian entrance modelled apparently on Liverpool's Athenaeum. He spent his remaining years there until his death in 1851.

After his retirement, Phelps & Peck changed its name to Phelps, Dodge and Co., eventually metamorphosing into today's Arizona-based mining conglomerate of the same name whose annual sales amount to more than $7 billion. Anson Phelps died a year after his partner, and was buried in the odour of sanctity despite having participated with Thomas Wilson's sons, Melvin and Fletcher, in an elaborate scam to milk more than three million dollars from investors following the bankruptcy of Thomas Wilson & Co. in 1837.

Although no one in Liverpool wanted to remember John Bellingham, the newspapers made it clear that Mary Bellingham was an innocent bystander to her husband's crime. In Liverpool, the West India group ensured that she was looked after, and authorised Richard Statham to set up a fund to support her and the boys. In response to an anonymous letter revealing that she was suffering from shock and was 'left totally unprovided for, with three helpless children dependent upon her', a surprisingly generous donation of £50 came from the good-looking Lord Leveson-Gower. The money was delivered in person by Peter Bourne, son of the mayor, together with an explanatory letter from the former ambassador.

Aware that Bellingham's accusations implied 'gross neglect of my duties', Leveson-Gower had written to the Foreign Secretary even before the trial, to defend himself and the consul, Stephen Shairpe. His need to send this document to Mary Bellingham, with a sum of money large enough to keep her family for a year, suggested at least the hint of an uneasy conscience. Publicly, however, he insisted there was nothing he could have done to help Bellingham. Once more he went through the sequence of events – Shairpe's discovery that Bellingham was undeniably Dorbecker's partner, Bellingham's refusal to accept the arbitration award made by Archangel's commercial court, the *duma's* requirement that he pay the 2,000 roubles, and Bellingham's subsequent committal to prison. Gower ended the letter by claiming to have given Bellingham 'small sums of money' while in prison, and to have secured his release after a private talk with the minister for foreign affairs.

Peter Bourne reported back that Mary Bellingham did not feel inclined to blame Lord Leveson-Gower. She said that while she was in St Petersburg, Stephen Shairpe had explained the background of the case and convinced her that the ambassador was unable to help. As Bourne and Mrs Bellingham talked, the protective Mary Stevens appeared and, with her friend beside her, Mary Bellingham went on to explain that 'she did all in her power to persuade her husband of the folly and impropriety of his claims for remuneration'.

But money alone could not alleviate Mary Bellingham's distress. 'Her delicate frame has received a blow,' the anonymous writer to Gower revealed, 'which totally incapacitated her to attend to her affairs for the present in order to procure immediate Subsistence of Herself and her Family.' And when Mary Stevens announced the display of her summer collection, 'a new and elegant assortment of Millinery, dresses &c' in early June, she also had to declare that her partner would not be participating. She hoped that their clients would sympathise with them 'under their very peculiar situation'.

Six months after the assassination, Mary Bellingham still had not recovered. In November a sad little advertisement appeared in the *Liverpool Mercury*: 'M. Bellingham presents her best respects and sincere thanks to the Ladies of Liverpool and its Environs who have favoured her and her Partner, Miss Stevens, with their Orders; she is sorry to inform them that she has been reduced by unprecedented misfortunes and distress to the necessity of compounding with her Creditors for ten shillings in the pound . . .' In other words, she was bankrupt.

The two Marys may simply have decided to put Leveson-Gower's money aside, including perhaps the hundred guineas sent to Newgate prison, and start afresh somewhere else. Mary Bellingham's disreputable father, John Neville, had caused her deep embarrassment by advertising a fund-raising concert to celebrate Spencer Perceval's assassination, and to raise money for 'the widow of the assassin'. She wanted no publicity of that kind. The concert was condemned, and in search of anonymity she reverted to her maiden name but spelling it 'Nevill', the form used by her uncle, James, in Wigan. It is probable that she and Mary Stevens returned to live in the town together.

Although their subsequent history disappeared into obscurity, one intriguing glimpse remained. In 1875 the death was recorded in London of Henry Stevens Neville, who was married to James Nevill's granddaughter. Almost certainly, this was former baby Henry whose welfare had so concerned John Bellingham. That Henry should have taken the name of Miss Stevens as his own would seem to point to a continuing and happy partnership between the two Marys. And, given the anxieties of his ever insecure father, it is worth noting that Henry died prosperous.

# Understanding Why it Happened

With every private virtue however which could adorn an human being, he was unquestionably the most mischievous of all the bad ministers who for these thirty years past have been placed at the head of affairs in this country; – and with totally opposite intent the political years of his life were employed in bringing this empire to the brink of ruin.

*Edinburgh Review*, June 1812

The body of Spencer Perceval had been carried to 10 Downing Street early in the morning of Tuesday, 12 May, after the last rioters had left the area. It was laid out in what had been his dressing room, surrounded by tall candles and attended by members of his family. The jibes that Sydney Smith once made about his pallor – 'the sepulchral Perceval', 'the sallow surveyor of the meltings' – were now literal description. His wide eyes were closed and his expression had taken on the peaceful indifference of death. 'Nothing could be more calm and undisturbed than his countenance,' wrote his sister Frances.

At the time of his murder, Jane Perceval had been visiting her closest friend, Frederica Ryder, wife of the ineffectual Home Secretary. The Ryders lived in Great George Street, opposite Parliament Square, and their house must have resounded to the cheers and jubilant cries of the mob as they too learned of her husband's death. The news, and perhaps the glee outside, left her too shocked for tears. Jane's dazed, dry-eyed calm lasted until the next morning when she was taken in to see the body. She had spent all her adult life with him. He was not yet fifty, and in less than a week the youngest of their twelve children would celebrate his fifth birthday. It was then, confronted by his familiar appearance and strange stillness, that she burst into uncontrollable weeping.

The backbenchers who had followed him so loyally wanted a public funeral, and a monument in Westminster Abbey, but Spencer Perceval's grieving widow was adamant about her husband's resting place. Parliament was informed that the family would have a private funeral, and early on Saturday morning – to avoid hostile crowds according to Cobbett – a hearse drawn by six, black-plumed horses and bearing the 'very superb' lead-lined coffin moved out of Downing Street followed by five mourning coaches carrying the Prime Minister's children, and most of the cabinet. The procession crossed Westminster Bridge, and followed the course of the Thames down towards its mouth until they came to Charlton where Jane Wilson had fallen in love with an impoverished young lawyer twenty-two years before. In the little church of St Luke's, Spencer Perceval was buried in the Egmont family vault beside the father who had taught him too well to resist all change.

The plain ceremony was in keeping with the way they had lived their lives. Already in the days following the murder, details had emerged that pointed up the simplicity of the Percevals' family life compared with the self-indulgent dedication to expense and pleasure that characterised fashion in the Regency era. The last meal shared by the Prime Minister and his wife had been a family lunch eaten at 2.30 with the daughters and youngest sons present. At this sort of occasion, said Robert Plumer Ward, 'Perceval was never more easy or more cheerful.' The previous day he had been present when two of his daughters were confirmed by the bishop of London, and the following day he was due to take part in his eldest son's speech-day celebration at Harrow school. Nothing could have been more domestic.

Returning home on Sunday, he had asked his valet whether he had any further engagements that day, and when told there were none, he had replied, 'What none to dinner? Then I am happy for I shall have a pleasure I very seldom enjoy, of dining alone with my family.' And, Ward said, after family prayers that evening, the Prime Minister had begged Jane to let the children linger a little longer before going to bed. At last they had gathered round and kissed him in a family ritual they would never know again.

As Perceval's family and companions looked back at the quiet flow of his private life, they felt sure that he had some premonition that it would be cut short. During the spring, he had scribbled a makeshift will on half a sheet of paper leaving all his possessions to his wife. A friend, Matthew Montagu, testified that he had 'strong apprehensions of his impending fate for several days before it took place'. Much earlier, soon after he became Prime Minister, he had written to his eldest son about his conviction that his life must serve some purpose, and his 'sense of the improbability of its long continuance'. Almost inevitably reports of similar clairvoyance came from around the country, as though so great an event must throw out a warning bow-wave before its actual occurrence. The best attested of them was that of John Williams, a famous Cornish mining engineer, who dreamed of a small man that he subsequently felt to be Spencer Perceval being shot dead in the House of Commons, and told friends of it, ten days before John Bellingham pulled the trigger.

The 'murder money', as frivolous-minded descendants of the Percevals referred to the £50,000 grant from Parliament, ensured that well into the twentieth century most of the Prime Minister's vast dynasty were preserved from poverty. But the immediate family had to find ways of coping not only with grief but the shock to their belief in the workings of Providence.

The option chosen by his widow, Jane, aroused profound, and almost universal disapproval. In the words of Henry 'Orator' Hunt, self-appointed voice of the people and enthusiastic scandalmonger, 'in a very few months after the decease of that best of all possible husbands, that nonpareil of married males; yes, in a few short months after her irreparable loss, his disconsolate widow concealed herself in the arms of another and a younger husband!' This was not entirely accurate – she did not remarry until January 1815, more than two and a half years after the assassination – but it was certainly true that at thirty-seven years old, her new husband, Lieutenant-Colonel Sir Henry Carr KCB, was eleven years younger. As would happen after President Kennedy's widow remarried, Jane Perceval's choice of partner was widely condemned as a betrayal of the memory of her murdered husband.

Yet becoming Lady Carr did provide a means of escape from the burden of being the widow of a political martyr. Her second husband was the younger son of the vicar at Ealing, and a wounded hero of Wellington's Peninsular War. In caring for him, Jane Carr no doubt found distraction from her own wounds, and relief from the demands of public life. Henry Carr died in 1821 and, during their short life together, he and Jane lived in Elm Grove, the plain, stuccoed, three-storey building surrounded by parkland that Perceval had bought when he was still a high-earning lawyer. It was the family home, and for some of her children the presence of the lieutenant colonel in their father's place was hard to bear. But they too were burdened with the problem of making sense of the tragedy of their father's murder.

Some of the younger children followed their mother's example by stepping away from the problem altogether. Isabella, the ninth child, married Spencer Walpole, a middle-of-the-road politician who became a progressive-minded governor of the Isle of Man, and betrayed no tendency to mysticism. Ernest, the youngest, took to being a country gentleman, strolling his estate with a terrier named Slut bouncing at his side. But at least four of the daughters, including the sharp-tongued Fanny, never married, and most, like the elder sons, were gripped by religious fervour.

Unable to find comfort in an Evangelical reliance on the Bible, they followed the lead of their eldest brother, Spencer Perceval junior, who left the Church of England altogether. Influenced by his wife, Anna MacLeod of MacLeod from Skye, he joined one of the earliest Pentecostal churches in Britain, the Catholic Apostolic Church. This was led by Edward Irving, who opened a chapel in a former art gallery near Portland Square in London, where speaking in tongues was encouraged.

The fashion-seeking MP, Charles Greville, went there in 1833 to hear Spencer Perceval junior speak, significantly about the fragility of human government. To Greville's annoyance, Perceval's sermon was almost immediately interrupted by several women moaning and crying out aloud. Perceval covered his head in his hands and fell silent, except for occasional exclamations of 'Hear the voice of the Lord', until Irving took over and began preaching in 'a mystical, incomprehensible rhapsody with extraordinary vehemence of manner and power of lungs'.

To his credit, Perceval did not restrict his preaching to the converted. He also made William IV and the Privy Council listen to a charismatic sermon on the degeneracy of the times, which began unpromisingly, 'You are aware that God has been pleased to make especial communications of His will to certain chosen instruments in a language not intelligible to those who hear, nor always to those by whom it is uttered. I am one of those instruments.' Appointed an 'angel' of the Catholic Apostolic Church with a particular duty to convert Italy, Perceval went to Rome where, helped by Henry Drummond, a fabulously wealthy banker who had married a Perceval sister, he delivered a similar sermon to the Pope. When he visited Lord Holland for the same purpose, Lady Holland placed two pageboys outside the study door with orders to scream for help in case the unpredictable preacher attacked his lordship.

What the charismatic movement offered was an escape from rational to revealed truth. It accepted that the human mind could not comprehend the working of Providence. To understand how the murder of a Prime Minister fitted into the improvement of the world was not necessary. A believer had only to receive the Holy Spirit whose message was true but incomprehensible. Taken to extremes, such an assumption might propel a fragile mind towards insanity. This was the fate of John Perceval, the Prime Minister's tenth child.

He was eight when his father was murdered, and approaching puberty when his adored mother married again. Weighed down by this Hamlet-like legacy, he was determined to wring from heaven some understanding of what it all meant. Bypassing the Catholic Apostolic Church, he went north to Scotland in search of the origin of Irving's charismatic beliefs. In the reformed Presbyterian kirk at Rhu in Dumbartonshire, he found the remarkable source of the modern tradition of speaking in tongues. In 1825 Isabella and Mary Campbell, the two sisters of the minister John McLeod Campbell, had both begun speaking when possessed by the spirit, and the practice quickly attracted an enthusiastic following, including Irving.

For John Perceval, it seemed to offer the way to ultimate truth, and he followed it with deadly passion. When Mary Campbell tried to moderate his zeal, he left the congregation to take his own extreme route. After a ferocious regime of fasting, praying and speaking in tongues, he went mad in 1830. Like John Bellingham senior, he became so violent he had to be restrained in a strait-jacket, and was occasionally chained up. For four years, he was incarcerated in two of the most advanced lunatic asylums in the land, Brislington near Bristol and Ticehurst in Sussex, before recovering almost spontaneously.

Although he remained as obsessive about the truth as Bellingham was about justice, John Perceval was helped to recovery by the gradual realisation that he had been too serious. God was the god not just 'of the sincere, the grave, the sober and chaste . . . but also of fun, of humour, of frolic'. Neither reason nor revelation was sufficient for understanding. At times John Perceval seemed to reach an almost Buddhist sense of detachment from material events, and a corresponding appreciation for the cosmic joke of existence. But in the agonising memoir he wrote about his lunacy, he confessed, 'I fear the death of my poor father was at the root of all my misfortune. I was then a little boy. But . . . I do not YET understand his loss.'

In 1832 the Reform Bill became law. Industrial towns such as Birmingham were allowed to return their own Member of Parliament, many of the urban middle-class were given the vote for the first time, and the sort of parliamentary seats that were controlled by a single noble family were abolished. It represented the first small expansion of democracy in a system that Spencer Perceval would have kept unchanged until the Book of Revelation came true. With the Bill's passage, the political ice age that he had inaugurated started to come to an end. In this new climate, it became possible to discern another, more political explanation of what had happened twenty years earlier.

What emerged was the uncomfortable realisation that the Evangelical Prime Minister had broken the constitutional rules.

Convinced of the truths revealed to him, he ceased to take account of other opinions. Nor could any power in the unreformed parliamentary system force him to do so. His predecessors, from Lord North to Pitt and Portland, had all been subject to the moods of the country gentlemen and the prejudices of George III. By coincidence, both these restraints were removed while Spencer Perceval was Prime Minister. The country gentlemen increasingly identified their interests with his, and the king went mad. Supreme authority allowed Perceval to exercise powers that were close to autocratic.

'If the laws had been made by persons chosen by the whole people, Mr. Perceval would not have been shot,' argued Henry Hunt. 'It was the want of an honest House of Commons that made Mr. Perceval a tyrant.'

Yet that cannot be quite the last word. Spencer Perceval's life and death would have been very different had they been shaped simply by politics. Without his obstinacy, guile and faith there would have been no heroic efforts to keep an army in Spain and to kill the slave trade. Nor would there have been his contemptible desire to silence Catholics, factory workers and political reformers. An older model offers a better way of explaining why the arc of his life should have ended as it did.

No Prime Minister should claim a monopoly on rightness. Perceval's hubristic conviction that he acted as a providential agent ensured that he would be met by nemesis, because sooner or later he was bound to encounter someone else whose conviction of his own rightness was equally fixed. In John Bellingham, with his single-minded conviction that he was owed justice and could achieve it with a pistol shot, the Prime Minister met that person.

# Notes

Every modern account of the assassination of Spencer Perceval has rested on the indefatigable researches of Mollie Gillen, an Australian-born Canadian and self-taught historian, whose *Assassination of the Prime Minister* will always remain essential reading for anyone interested in the subject. She uncovered in the Public Records Office the cache of documents, now labelled BM Add Mss 48216, containing the vital information of Mary Stevens's affidavit and Bellingham's financial accounts and personal receipts that make it possible to link his plan for justice to the pattern of his expenditure and the political events of the day. The other substantial source of information is Denis Gray's assiduous and now somewhat outdated biography, *Spencer Perceval: The Evangelical Prime Minister*. The time is long overdue for a new look at Spencer Perceval's political leadership.

## Chapter One: A Horrible Event

p. 1    'The assassin was late.' John Bellingham's movements were minutely recorded in contemporary pamphlets and newspapers. Bellingham himself, his landlady Mrs Robarts in evidence to John Vickery, the Bow Street officer, and her maid, Catherine Figgins, in court, were the prime sources. From 1760 to 1833 the House of Commons usually sat at 4 p.m., according to the 2009 House of Commons Factsheet 'Sittings of the House'. To accommodate the hearings when outsiders presented petitions against the Order in Council, the Commons designated itself a Committee of the whole house whose proceedings began at 4.30 p.m. after the attention to routine business. Most people had expected Spencer Perceval to be present from the start. A week earlier, on 5 May, he had actually arrived before hearings into petitions took place. In *Evangelical Prime Minister*, p. 457, Gray explains that Perceval 'was so absorbed [by work] that he was late starting for the Commons'. His lateness provoked the anger of Henry Brougham at his absence.

p. 1    'Prime Minister'. Throughout the book, Perceval is designated as the Prime Minister, but it should be noted that this title had only recently come into use. In parliamentary reports, he was commonly referred to as the Chancellor of the Exchequer, and elsewhere as the First Lord of the Treasury. Critics of his dominance in cabinet dubbed him 'the Supreme Commander'.

p. 2    'His anxiety would have triggered self-pity.' Bellingham's psychology became the focus of intense speculation following the murder. In his Russian pamphlet and all public utterances after the murder, he invariably portrayed himself as a victim of personal injustice. In private, however, he saw himself as someone who was dogged by misfortune in general and, having been dealt a poor hand, was required, as he put it in his last letter, 'to play an anxious card in life'.

p. 3    'The pavements were obstructed . . .'. In 1809 a complaint that the Privy Council offices at the lower end of Whitehall were 'in a very bad and even dangerous state' (PRO, P.C. 2/184) was symptomatic of a general stress on existing accommodation, as the civil service began to grow beyond its eighteenth-century limits. Parliament had already authorised the redevelopment of buildings around King Street next to Parliament Square in 1806, and, according to the Public Survey of London, buildings were being worked on in Great George Street, Whitehall Gardens, and other streets close to the Houses of Parliament.

p. 3    'his brown coat . . .'. The assassin's clothes were minutely described in newspapers and pamphlets, a tribute to the care he clearly took in choosing them.

p. 4    'The lobby of the Houses of Parliament . . .'. The scene in the lobby of the Houses of Parliament was described in detail by eyewitnesses at committal proceedings, the coroner's inquest and Bellingham's trial. The crowd had gradually dispersed, many to the Strangers' Gallery to listen to the hearings. According to estimates, around twenty or thirty remained when Perceval was murdered.

p. 5    'The anger in the chamber . . .'. The ideological split over the Orders in Council, and their underlying purpose in repressing the illegal slave trade, was apparent in the selection of Thomas Babington, a vehement anti-slaver, as chairman of the committee, and of James Stephen, the policy's architect, as its chief defender. Although no slaver, Henry Brougham, in leading for the opposition to the Order, inevitably was supported by those favourable to continued involvement in slave trading. For the mood of the committee and Babington's exchange see Gillen, *Assassination*, pp. 13–15.

p. 6    'He still sweated . . .'. Bellingham's physical state, the gasping breath and pouring sweat, was noted especially by William Jerdan in personal testimony, and *Autobiography*, vol. 1, pp. 133–41.

p. 6    'He had studied . . .'. Vincent Dowling, parliamentary reporter and government spy, revealed in testimony to the coroner's inquest and in court that Bellingham had appeared in the gallery at least three times.

p. 6    '"I thought he appeared . . ."'. John Norris's testimony in court.

p. 6    'Other people would also remember . . .'. Henry Burgess, William Smith and General Gascoyne all gave testimony at the inquest and in court. Gascoyne also testified at the committal proceedings, changing his account on each occasion.

p. 8    'the most powerful politician . . .'. The power vacuum that occurred after Perceval's death, with the initial paralysis of the cabinet and later the collapse of his policies, testified to the extent of his personal and political influence.

p. 9      'With genuine affection . . .'. A recollection of Wilberforce's friends, cited in J. C. Colquhoun, *William Wilberforce – his Friends and his Times*, London, 1867, p. 27. Wilberforce himself expressed his feelings in his private diary a few hours after the murder: 'Perceval had the sweetest of all possible tempers, and was one of the most conscientious men I ever knew; the most instinctively obedient to the dictates of conscience, the least disposed to give pain to others, the most charitable and truly kind and generous creature I ever knew.' *Life*, vol. 4, p. 95.

p. 9      'Spencer Perceval started up the steps . . .'. Jerdan, *Autobiography*, vol. 1, pp. 133–41.

p. 9      'he had no intention . . .'. Bellingham made this clear when questioned in Newgate prison by City of London magistrates on 12 May 1812.

p. 9      'The Prime Minister said something . . .'. The various witnesses agreed only that he uttered some words, not on what he said.

## Chapter Two: The Identity of an Unfortunate Man is Revealed

p. 13     The scene after the murder was minutely described in newspapers during the following days, and recapitulated by witnesses at the inquest and trial.

p. 13     William Smith's testimony. He later admitted to William Wilberforce that he thought for a moment the victim was Wilberforce himself.

p. 13     '"If he had risen in a minute . . ."', '"Large drops of agonizing sweat . . ."'. Jerdan, *Autobiography*, vol. 1, pp. 133–41; William Jerdan was born in the Scottish Borders, but lived most of his life in London, falling into journalism having failed as a poet, and later becoming editor of the *Literary Gazette*. Despite a tendency to snobbery, he was much loved by authors for his enthusiasm in promoting early Victorian fiction. Even today most writers will sympathise with his assertion that 'the uncertainties and disappointments incident to a life entirely dependent on literature, in 99 out of 100 cases render that life to be at the best precarious and unproductive, and at the worst impoverished and wretched'.

p. 14    General Isaac Gascoyne's behaviour before and after the assassination was riddled with contradictions. Although not physically present, he apparently knew the identity of the victim without being told. He initially affected not to recognise Bellingham despite frequent meetings, the latest having continued for about an hour. Finally his evidence changed repeatedly to present himself arriving on the scene earlier, and taking a more pre-emptive role, than any other witness recalled.

p. 16    The Houses of Parliament lay within Middlesex, hence the lead role taken by the Middlesex magistrates. Once Bellingham was held in Newgate, he fell within the jurisdiction of the City of London.

p. 17    '"he considered the slave trade . . ."'. Lord Howick, later the 2nd Earl Grey, having debated the subject with Gascoyne, 23 February, 1807; 'The Liverpool Abolitionists' by F. E. Sanderson, in *Liverpool, the African Slave Trade, and Abolition*, ed. Roger Anstey and R. E. H. Hair, Historic Society of Lancashire and Cheshire, Occasional Series, vol. 2, 1976.

p. 17    '"he had seen Bellingham often . . ."'. *The Times*, 12 May 1812.

p. 17    'Jerdan found himself doubting . . .'. Jerdan put it politely, 'the consternation that prevailed might well excuse imperfection of memory and the blending of hearsay with what was actually seen and done'. *Autobiography*, vol. 1, pp. 133–41.

p. 18    '"I have been denied the redress . . ."'. *The Times*, and other newspapers, 12 May 1812.

p. 19    New Millman Street. In *The Adventures of Philip*, serialised in *Harpers* in 1862, W. M. Thackeray wrote 'Millman Street is a little cul-de-sac of a street', describing it as 'cheap, unfashionable but cosy'.

p. 20  'a memorandum of twenty pounds . . .'. *The Times*, 13 May 1812. According to the newspaper, Bellingham explained 'it was a bill that he expected would have been paid next day, at half-past nine o'clock'. That is, he expected it to be cashed as soon as the banks opened the following day.

## Chapter Three: Riots Break Out amid Rumours of Revolution

p. 21  The resemblances between Perceval's assassination and that of President Kennedy are striking, but especially in the mysterious, deadly motives of the assassins. Because Bellingham and Lee Harvey Oswald were both killed before they could be properly interrogated, their connection to the illegal activities of, respectively, Liverpool's blockade-busting slavers and traders, and Florida's Cuban exiles, could never be adequately examined.

p. 22  '"They were whipped off . . .'". Bath archives: *Diaries and Letters of Sir George Jackson*, vol. 1, p. 374, ed. Lady Jackson, Bentley, London, 1873.

p. 22  The disturbances in London. *The Times, Morning Chronicle*, and other London newspapers, 13 May 1812.

p. 23  '"Oh I will fire my gun . . .'". Gillen, *Assassination*, p. 15.

p. 23  '"Perceval is down . . .'". *An Irish Beauty of the Regency. Compiled from 'Mes Souvenirs'—The Unpublished Journals of the Hon. Mrs Calvert 1789–1822*, ed. by Mrs Warrenne Blake, London and New York: John Lane, 1911, p. 22.

p. 23  For the measures taken to restore law and order, see Gillen, *Assassination*, pp. 15–16.

p. 23  'Instead of a hired coach . . .'. Gillen, *Assassination*, pp. 15–16.

p. 24  'The keeper loaded . . .'. *The Times* and other newspapers, 13 May 1812.

p. 24  Cabinet meeting. *The Times*, 12 May 1812.

p. 24  For the activities of the Committees of Secrecy, the Aliens Office and the Home Office in gathering intelligence in general, see Porter, *Plots and Paranoia*, and McCalman, *Radical Underworld*. Aliens Office, created 1793, Porter, p. 18; Private Office in Post Office, opening letters, Porter, p. 23; Committees of Secrecy, set up ad hoc, 1794, 1801, 1812 and 1819, Porter, pp. 49–51.

p. 26  "'the speediest and most effectual measures . . .'". *The Times* and others, 12 and 13 May 1812.

p. 27  Journalism and the printing-rooms. *The Cambridge History of English literature*, 18 vols., ed. A. W. Ward, vol. 14, pp. 173–4.

p. 28  John Stoddard's tribute; reports of armed raids. *The Times*, 12 May 1812.

p. 29  "'At all events . . .'". *Irish Beauty*, p. 22.


## Chapter Four: A Free and Easy Conspiracy?

p. 30  Bellingham's self-description as 'dilatory'. Sworn affidavit of Mary Stevens, BM Add Mss 48216, No. 59.

p. 30  'breakfasted with a good appetite off buttered rolls . . .'. *The Globe, Morning Chronicle* and others, 13 May 1812.

p. 31  Bellingham's appearance. Newspapers and shorthand writers in court were quite consistent in their descriptions of Bellingham's height, his long nose, long face and short hair.

p. 31  Bellingham's clothes. *Le Beau Monde or Literary and Fashionable Magazine*, April 1807 – 'A Morning Walking Dress for Gentlemen is composed of a dark brown mixed coat, lappeled, with flat plated buttons and collar of the same cloth; or greenish mixtures lappeled, flat plated buttons and collar of cloth, and the coat must be buttoned close up. Striped toilinet, or plain kerseymere waistcoats, single breasted and bound with silk, and drab coloured kerseymere pantaloons, with Hessian boots.'

p. 31  Thanks to Newman, Bellingham's letter was reprinted in every London newspaper on 13 May 1812.

p. 32   '"a dispute which he had . . .'". *Morning Chronicle*, 13 May 1812.

p. 33   '"At first it was impossible . . ."'. *The Globe*, 13 May 1812; *Liverpool Courier*, 14 May 1812.

p. 33   'His room next to the chapel . . .'. *Old Bailey Sessions Papers*. The odour of Newgate was thought to be the source of the typhus, often known as 'gaol fever', that periodically swept through the prison. Vinegar washes and nosegays of strong-smelling herbs, mint, rue and rosemary, were used to counteract it. In *Tales of Boz*, Charles Dickens described how 'the buildings in the prison, or in other words the different wards – form a square . . . The intermediate space is divided into several paved yards, in which the prisoners take such air and exercise as can be had in such a place.'

p. 34   'Bellingham indignantly rejected the suggestion . . .'. *The Times*, 13 May 1812.

p. 34   The talents of John Vickery are most apparent through his testimony in many different trials between 1800 and 1819 recorded in the *Newgate Calendar*, also known as the *Old Bailey Sessions Papers*. (For details see below.) The two Adkins brothers were solid but less brilliant.

p. 34   Hokkirk is a mystery visitor, recorded only by Newman, who duly shared his information with the newspapers.

p. 35   The 1744 Vagrancy Act allowed two Justices of the Peace to order a violent lunatic to 'be safely locked in some secure place . . . (and if necessary) to be there chained . . . for and during such time only as the lunacy or madness shall continue'. Private funds were raised to build St Luke's, Woodside, London, in 1751. At about the time that Bellingham's father was confined there, 11 staff cared for 260 inmates. Information from Resources for Mental Health Law – www.davesheppard.co.uk.

p. 35   Information about Bellingham's background. Daniel Wilson, *The Substance of a Conversation*, p. 32; Gillen, *Assassination*, pp. 43–5, based on parish registers of St Neots, Huntingdon, Bishop's

Transcripts, St Dunstan-in-the-West, and St George's, Hanover
Square.

p. 35   Bellingham in Russia. BM Add Mss 48216, No. 44. Petition to
House of Commons.

p. 36   Home Office information gathering. Porter, *Social History*;
McCalman, *Radical Underworld*; H.O. 42/108, 115, 118–20;
H.O. 102/22.

p. 37   "'that damned set of Rogues . . .'". Cole, *British Working Class
Movements*, 'A letter to a Huddersfield Master', H.O. 40/41.

p. 38   Gunmakers. Durs Egg, 'Durs Egg, the Gunsmith', *Notes and
Queries*, 15 July 1944; Joseph Manton, http://en.wikipedia.org/
wiki/Joseph_Manton; James Purdey, http://www.purdey.com/
history/history-of-purdey; William Beckwith, 'Muzzle Loaders
Association of Great Britain', http://www.mlagb.com/

p. 38   "'These were the very words . . .'". 'Letter to Robert Southey', 12
May 1812, *Letters of Samuel Taylor Coleridge*, ed. E. H. Coleridge,
Boston & New York: Houghton Mifflin, 1896. In *Biographia liter-
aria* the once-revolutionary Coleridge confessed that 'I am
singular enough to regard [Mr Perceval] as the best and wisest
minister of this reign.'

p. 39   'free and easy' meetings. McCalman, *Radical Underworld*, p. 44.
In 1811 the radical Thomas Spence wrote, 'Even under the modern
tyrannies of China, France, Turkey etc, what can hinder small
companies from meeting in a free and easy convivial manner and
singing their rights and instructing each other in their songs?' The
songs and toasts were faithfully recorded by government spies,
thus preserving them for posterity.

p. 40   "'Perceval's ribs . . .'". Recorded by Frances Calvert in *Irish Beauty*,
ed. Mrs Warrenne Blake, p. 22.

p. 41   'Dowling, however, had a secret . . .'. McCalman, *Radical
Underworld*, p. 98. Dowling had been a Jacobin supporter, but
while working for *The Observer* he was recruited as a government

spy. He was to play a major role in exposing the Cato Street conspiracy in 1822. *The Cambridge History of English Literature*, vol. 14, p. 374.

p. 41 'The inadequacies of the Home Secretary . . .'. Richard Ryder's shortcomings were itemised in Gray, *Spencer Perceval, the Evangelical Prime Minister*, pp. 273–4. Ryder resigned immediately after the assassination.

p. 42 'Richard Ryder could not even speak for crying . . .'. *The Diary and Correspondence of Charles Abbott, Lord Colchester*, vol. 2, London: John Murray, 1862, p. 380.

p. 43 'Lord Eldon, was so convulsed . . .'. *Annual Register*, 1812.

p. 43 The nationwide scenes of joy at Perceval's assassination were reported in most London newspapers of 13 May 1812. The *Nottingham Journal* report, quoted in Gillen, *Assassination*, pp. 33–4.

p. 44 '"The country is no doubt . . .'". *The Love Letters of William and Mary Wordsworth*, ed. Beth Darlington, Ithaca, NY: Cornell University Press, 1981, p. 148.

p. 44 '"all the common people's heads . . .'". 23 May 1812. *Memoirs, Journals and Correspondence of Thomas Moore*, ed. Lord John Russell, London: Longman, Brown, 1853, p. 277.

p. 44 'When the cabinet assembled . . .'. *Courier*, 13 May 1812.

p. 44 Castlereagh's opinion that the murder 'was confined to the individual . . .'. *The European Magazine*, 1812, p. 60.

p. 44 The Eldon-Ellenborough plan to hang Bellingham in front of the House of Commons was still in place on the day of the trial. Lord Ellenborough lost his temper when the plan was criticised, and Lord Grey reported, 'was in so heated a state of mind as is quite frightful in a man in his situation [Lord Chief Justice]'. Gillen, *Assassination*, p. 122.

## Chapter Five: Examining the Enigma of the Assassin's Sanity

p. 46   The choice of James Harmer was probably made by the Whiggish Harvey Combe in the interests of securing as fair a trial as was possible. For Harmer's reputation and Phillips's opinion of him, see May, *The Bar and the Old Bailey, 1750–1850: The Prisoners' Counsel Act Justifying Advocacy*, p. 80.

p. 47   "'The people will now be able . . .'". *The Times*, 13 May 1812.

p. 48   For Earl Ferrers's case, see Richard Davenport-Hines, 'Shirley, Laurence, fourth Earl Ferrers (1720–1760)', *Oxford Dictionary of National Biography*, Oxford University Press, 2004; online edn., January 2008; http://www.oxforddnb.com.ezproxy.londonlibrary.co.uk/view/article/25432, accessed 3 October 2010.

p. 48   Hadfield's case is detailed in 'Counter-Revolutionary Panic and the Treatment of the Insane: 1800' by Valerie Argent, Middlesex University, 1978; http://studymore.org.uk/1800.htm

p. 48   For the evidence of Beckwith and Taylor, see *Old Bailey Sessions Papers*, 'John Bellingham'; Beckwith specialised in very small pistols, thought to have been designed to be carried in ladies' purses and handbags.

p. 49   According to Gillen, *Assassination*, p. 84, he practised on Hampstead Heath, by Primrose Hill.

p. 50   For the story of Bellingham helping to find his landlady's child, see *The Times*, 12 May 1812. Evidently this must have come from John Vickery as a result of his questioning Mrs Robarts.

p. 50   For Bellingham's pamphlet, see BM Add Mss 48216, No. 44; other details from his petition to the Marquess of Wellesley, December 1809, No. 31.

p. 51   For the start of the Baltic Exchange, see http://www.balticexchange.com/default.asp?action=article&ID=19; for British trade see Ryan, 'The Defence of British Trade with the Baltic, 1808–1813', and 'Trade with the Enemy in the Scandinavian and Baltic Ports during the Napoleonic War: For and against'.

p. 52    Bellingham's tangled relationship with the Dutch merchants in Archangel and his fight for justice there are the subject of his pamphlet *op. cit.*, and are covered by Gillen, *Assassination*, 51–4.

p. 54    The intervention of Shairpe, the actions of Lord Leveson-Gower and Bellingham's imprisonment in St Petersburg are described in his pamphlet and in Gillen, *Assassination*, pp. 54–68; and Leveson-Gower gave his own version in a letter to Lord Castlereagh written soon after the trial and reprinted in many pamphlets, including *A Full Report of the Trial of John Bellingham*, Hull, 1812.

## Chapter Six: The Victim is Seen as a Fond Father and Attentive Husband

p. 58    The financial award to Perceval's family was covered by the London newspapers, 14 May 1812; the *Courier* declaring that 'its smallness is utterly unworthy of the national character'.

p. 59    '"the most straightforward man I have ever known . . ."'. George III on his appointment of Perceval as Prime Minister on 4 October 1809.

p. 59    '"No man could be more generous . . ."'. *Memoirs of the life of Sir Samuel Romilly*, vol. III, London: John Murray, 1840, p. 37.

p. 59    For the married life of the Percevals, their irrepressible daughters and disappointing sons, see Gray, *Spencer Perceval*, pp. 10–11, 27 and 428–34.

p. 61    '"with very little reading . . ."'. Romilly quoted in Gray, *Spencer Perceval*, p. 10.

p. 62    For Lord Egmont's political views, see Hassell, *Edward Marsh*, p. 13.

p. 62    '"no information beyond what a classical education gives . . ."'. Brougham quoted in Gray, *Spencer Perceval*, p. 5.

p. 62    Perceval's early career is described in Gray, *Spencer Perceval*, pp. 12–20; '"I am sorry to say"', Gray, p. 16.

p. 63    Perceval's early political career, Gray, *Spencer Perceval*, pp. 19–34.

p. 64   '"The most striking thing I saw . . ."'. Jefferson to John Page, May 1786, *Papers of Thomas Jefferson, General Correspondence*, Library of Congress; http://memory.loc.gov/ammem/collections/jefferson_papers/mtjser1.html

p. 66   'His fourth son, John, carried into old age . . .'. Perceval, *Narrative of the Treatment*. In this tortured account of his descent into madness, John Perceval identified a tune heard on a hurdy-gurdy, or barrel organ, as the emblem of lost happiness. 'I fear the death of my poor father was at the root of all my misfortune for I can trace the notes of this air, to the time we were living happily in Hampstead.' According to *The Globe*, 13 May 1812, one of Perceval's sons, and John is the most likely candidate, was actually in the House of Commons when his father was shot.

p. 66   The political and romantic opinions of the Perceval daughters are from Gray, *Spencer Perceval*, pp. 431–3.

p. 68   Perceval's letters to his son. Gray, *Spencer Perceval*, pp. 429–31.

p. 69   Perceval's comments on Dudley Ryder's losses at faro. Gray, *Spencer Perceval*, p. 17.

p. 70   '"I wish that Wellesley was castrated . . ."'. Wellington to his brother William Wellesley-Pole, October 1809.

p. 70   '"Tricking in love and tricking the public . . ."'. Quoted in *The Gentleman's Magazine*, vol. 82, p. 590.

p. 70   '"You spend a great deal of ink . . ."'. Sydney Smith, *Peter Plymley's Letters*. Letter 1; http://www.gutenberg.org/cache/epub/4063/pg4063.html.

## Chapter Seven: A Prime Minister Put There by Providence

p. 73   'In his novel, *Tremaine* . . .', see Ward, *Tremaine*, vol. 3, p. 236.

p. 73   'It was a physical rather than an intellectual faith . . .'. Ch. 2, 'Knowledge of the Lord' in *Evangelicalism in Modern Britain: A History from the 1730s to the 1980s* by David W. Bebbington,

London: Routledge, 1989, pp. 20–75; Venn, 'Experience is a living proof . . .', ibid., p. 56; Wilberforce, 'God has so assigned . . .', ibid., p. 61; More, 'Action is the life of virtue . . .', ibid., p. 12.

p. 75   For the illness of the Percevals' baby son, and Perceval's response, see Gray, *Spencer Perceval*, p. 12.

p. 75   Perceval's promotion to cabinet office is the subject of Ch. 5, 'Counsel for the Defence', pp. 47–57, in Gray, *Spencer Perceval*.

p. 76   '"Gentlemen, who is Mr. Cobbett? . . ."'. *The Village Labourer, 1760-1832: A Study in the Government of England Before the Reform Bill* by J. L. Hammond; London: Longmans Green, 1920, p. 188.

p. 76   '"a sort of understrapper . . ."'. Gray, *Spencer Perceval*, p. 11.

p. 77   For the slave trade see Anstey, *The Atlantic Slave Trade*; Thomas, *The Slave Trade*; Turley, *The Culture of English Antislavery, 1780–1860*. Liverpool's particular contribution is documented especially in the city's outstanding International Slavery Museum and the Merseyside Maritime Museum.

p. 78   Perceval's contribution to stamping out the slave trade has been ignored by historians, and inexplicably is overlooked even in Gray's biography. Nevertheless it was considered vital by the architects of the campaign, William Wilberforce and James Stephen, and its chief agent, Judge Robert Thorpe in Sierra Leone. Pitt's refusal to move against the slave trade provoked Stephen to complain, 'Mr. Pitt, unhappily for himself, his country and mankind, is not zealous enough in the cause of the negroes, to contend for them as decisively as he ought, in the cabinet any more than in parliament', quoted in Eric Williams, *Slavery and Capitalism*, p. 149. Without Perceval's advocacy of the Guiana Order in Council, Pitt would not have had even that fig leaf to conceal his failure to match actions to words.

p. 79   The collaboration between Perceval and Stephen emerges from Stephen, 'Letters to Spencer Perceval', BL Add. MS 49177; Wilberforce, *Life of William Wilberforce*; Anstey, *The Atlantic Slave*

*Trade*; Wilberforce, "'Guiana slave-trade'", in *Life*, vol. 3, p. 216; "'Busy with [James] Stephen and Attorney-General'", in *Life*, vol. 3, p. 248.

p. 80 Perceval's dealings with Princess Caroline reveal a capacity for combining blackmail and moral righteousness on a par with one of Bertie Wooster's more sociopathic aunts. See, Perceval, *The Book!*, *passim*; and Gray, *Spencer Perceval*, pp. 75–90.

p. 82 "'My principles would govern my vote . . .'". Wilberforce, *Life*, p. 307.

p. 82 "'the best regulated ambition . . .'". Charles Arbuthnot, quoted in Croker, *The Croker Papers*, March 1809, vol. 3, p. 15.

p. 83 "'Mr Perceval's conduct has so fully confirmed . . .'". Windsor Mss, George III to cabinet, 2 Oct. 1809, cited in Gray, *Spencer Perceval*, 254.

p. 83 "'man seems to have been abandoned by Heaven . . .'". Ward, *Tremaine*, vol. 3, p. 236.

## Chapter Eight: The Pervasive Power of Little P

p. 84 "'Mr. Perceval, an insignificant lawyer . . .'". Hunt, *Memoirs of Henry Hunt Esq*, vol. 3, Pt. 1. http://www.fullbooks.com/Memoirs-of-Henry-Hunt-Esq-Volume-31.html

p. 84 'Little P . . .'. Eldon quoted in Gray, *Spencer Perceval*, p. 15.

p. 85 'The king refused to have second thoughts . . .'. Gray, *Spencer Perceval*, pp. 254–74. So fragile was the ministry in its first days that Wellesley, who had to travel back from Spain to take up office, told a friend, 'It is possible I may find the Opposition in before I can reach England.' Gray, *Spencer Perceval*, p. 257.

p. 85 The classic account of the influence of the 'country gentlemen' is Lewis Namier's *The House of Commons*, London: HMSO, 1964.

p. 86 "'in these times of imputed corruption . . .'". *The Day*, January 1810, quoted in Gray, *Spencer Perceval*, p. 272.

p. 86 'In the jaundiced view of Henry Hunt . . .'. Hunt, *Memoirs*, vol. 3, Pt. 1. http://www.fullbooks.com/Memoirs-of-Henry-Hunt-Esq-Volume-31.html

p. 87 'Writing to Wellington in Spain . . .'. Liverpool quoted in Gray, *Spencer Perceval*, p. 426.

p. 88 "'the dear duke of York . . .'". Fanny Perceval, quoted in Gray, *Spencer Perceval*, p. 423. To avoid confusion over military commanders the duke of York was the commander-in-chief, responsible for British forces throughout North America, the West Indies, India, Ireland and the UK, as well as Wellington's army in Portugal.

p. 88 Perceval's effectiveness as a cheese-paring Chancellor is explored in painstaking detail in Gray, *Spencer Perceval*, pp. 305–90; the payment to Wellington's army in silver forced the Treasury to seek dollars where they were most abundant, in Peru and Mexico where four-fifths of the world's silver was mined, and China where dollars ended up having paid for the European demand for tea, silk and china.

p. 90 "'To carry on the war . . .'". Rose, 11 November 1809, quoted in Gray, *Spencer Perceval*, p. 344.

p. 91 'the Bullion committee'. The report of the Bullion committee is taken by economists as the most comprehensive, early analysis of inflationary pressure through an increase in the money supply. However, it is also a classic early demonstration of the capacity of economists to ignore the supreme importance of politics in creating and solving economic crises.

p. 91 "'he was aware that he was not as well informed . . .'". Perceval to Huskisson, 28 October 1810, quoted in Gray, *Spencer Perceval*, p. 375.

p. 92 "'We think this . . .'". *The Day* quoted in Gray, *Spencer Perceval*, p. 377.

p. 92 Perceval's financial efforts compared well with the French who could barely pay their troops, and according to Wellington in late 1811, 'thus a million of men are put into the field . . . for the pay of 4 or 500,000! . . . It is impossible that this fraudulent tyranny can last. If Great Britain continues stout we must see the destruction of it.'

p. 93    '"Of this I am certain, in a democracy . . .'". Burke, *Reflections on the Revolution in France*, 11th edn., London: Dodsley, 1791, p. 186.

p. 93    '"they [the French] have been raised up by Providence . . ."'. Perceval to R. Bosanquet, Perceval Papers, quoted in Gray, *Spencer Perceval*, p. 46.

p. 94    Perceval had applied the prophecy from Daniel initially to the defeat of Napoleon by a British army at Acre in 1800, but evidently it was also applicable to the Peninsular campaign. For his biblical divination with Thomas Walpole see Gray, *Spencer Perceval*, pp. 45–6.

p. 94    Although it is difficult to defend Perceval's readiness to allow policy to be influenced by biblical divination, President Ronald Reagan showed in modern times how effective illogical decision-making could be. At the height of the Cold War, Reagan found it simpler to picture the Soviet Union as 'the evil empire', thereby cutting through the distracting complexities thrown up by Kremlinologists and other experts on Soviet politics. Like Perceval, he too relied on other-worldly guidance when complex choices had to be made, in his case, the readings of San Francisco astrologer, Joan Quigley. According to his chief of staff, Donald Regan, 'every major move and decision the Reagans made was cleared in advance with [her] to make certain the planets were in a favourable alignment'. Obviously Quigley's findings were more effective than any academic analysis in persuading an intellectually lightweight president that he was taking the right executive decision, and doubtless they contributed to the sunny sense of confidence he exuded. Spencer Perceval operated in a similar fashion. Just as

Reagan went to Reykjavik for his second summit meeting with
Mikhail Gorbachev in 1985 strengthened by his astrologer's assurance that the stars were favourable for such an encounter, so
Perceval drew strength for the confrontation with Napoleon from
the insights of biblical prophecy.

## Chapter Nine: The Beauty of Double Bookkeeping

p. 97  Ann Billett's testimony about Bellingham's state of mind was
recorded in *Old Bailey Sessions Papers*, p. 271; her childhood as
Ann Scarbrow was cited in Gillen, *Assassination*, p. 46.

p. 98  Burke's exposition of the sublime/beautiful polarity was exceptional in its emphasis on the sexual nature of the divide, 'its origin
in gratifications and pleasures'; see Burke, *Philosophical Enquiry*,
Section VIII.

p. 100  The insanity of Bellingham's father amid Scarbrow respectability,
and the efforts of uncle William Daw to provide for his future, are
well covered in Gillen, *Assassination*, pp. 43–7.

p. 101  One of the underpinning wonders of modern capitalism is
accountancy based on double-entry bookkeeping in which each
transaction is recorded twice, as an asset and liability, and balanced
over an accounting period, as profit or loss. It began in fourteenth-
century Venice. In *Wilhelm Meister*, Goethe categorised it, half
ironically, as a science that allowed merchants to organise into a
system not only the guesswork of financial trading but the endless
variability of subjective thought: 'It came from the same spirit
which produced the systems of Galileo and Newton and the
subject matter of modern physics and chemistry. By the same
means, it organizes perceptions into a system, and one can charac-
terize it as the first Cosmos constructed purely on the basis of
mechanistic thought.'

p. 103  The picture of Liverpool's recent past was vigorously drawn in

*Recollections of Old Liverpool* by 'a Nonagenarian' in 1836, with indications that his memory went back to the 1780s. More modern accounts are provided by Checkland in 'American Versus West Indian Traders in Liverpool, 1793–1815' and 'Economic Attitudes in Liverpool, 1793–1807'; Hyde and others in 'The Nature and Profitability of the Liverpool Slave Trade'; Hyde in *Liverpool and the Mersey: An Economic History of a Port, 1700–1970*; and Harris, *Liverpool and Merseyside*.

p. 105   Bellingham's early mercantile career is pieced together from the account given by the Reverend Daniel Wilson, *Substance of a Conversation with John Bellingham*, various pamphlets, especially *A Full Report of the Trial of John Bellingham*, and Gillen, *Assassination*, pp. 44–50.

p. 107   'Mary, "a very pleasant, affable woman" . . .'. quoted in Gillen, *Assassination*, p. 147. The strengths of Mary Bellingham's character are obvious both in her ability to maintain herself and her young child in St Petersburg for more than a year, and in her attempts to hold together her family and the unstable Bellingham.

p. 108   Specialist sources for the Russian trade are Ryan, 'The Defence of British Trade with the Baltic, 1808–1813' and 'Trade with the Enemy in the Scandinavian and Baltic Ports during the Napoleonic War: For and against'; Barty-King, *The Baltic Exchange*; and Jackson, *Hull in the Eighteenth Century*.

p. 109   Bellingham's experience in Russia is derived from his pamphlet *op. cit.*, Leveson-Gower's letter to Castlereagh, and Gillen, *Assassination*, pp. 51–4; on his inheritance from William Daw, see Gillen, *Assassination*, pp. 69–70.

p. 110   For Ann Billett's evidence, see above.

p. 112   Mary Bellingham's partnership with Mary Stevens, affidavit of Mary Stevens, see above.

p. 112   For Bellingham's fruitless search for compensation in early 1810, see Billett's evidence above; *European Magazine*, pp. 377–8. His reconciliation with Mary, affidavit of Stevens, Gillen, *Assassination*, p. 73.

p. 114  Despite Gillen's meticulous research, neither in her ground-breaking book nor in subsequent accounts of the assassination is there any attempt to explain the strange gap between Bellingham's two attempts to get compensation in 1810 and 1812, the impact of the economic upheaval that occurred in Liverpool during that period, or the sharp difference in his behaviour in the two episodes.

## Chapter Ten: The Prosecution Presents its Case

p. 115  Bellingham's trial launched a thousand pamphlets, articles and reports. The most complete are in the *Annual Register* and the *Old Bailey Sessions Papers*. The most immediate are in *The Times*, 16 and 18 May 1812, *The Globe* and *Morning Post*, 16 May 1812.

p. 117  For Alley's character see May, *The Bar and the Old Bailey, 1750–1850: The Prisoners' Counsel Act Justifying Advocacy*, p. 83.

p. 124  'as he confessed to Sir William Curtis MP . . .'. Bellingham's evidence during committal proceedings, 11 May 1812.

## Chapter Eleven: Bellingham and the Absence of *malice prepense*

p. 126  The sources for Bellingham's defence are as in the previous chapter. Although more considered accounts, such as the *Annual Register*, imply he must have been mad, newspapers assumed he was sane. The important point was his intention – to make the jury understand his justification for killing the Prime Minister (to secure justice), and thus to see that it was without *malice prepense*, and consequently that it could not constitute murder. 'Had I not possessed these imperious excitements, and had murdered him in cold blood,' he declared, 'I should consider myself a monster.'

p. 130  '"That my arm destroyed him . . ."'. *The Authentic Account*, pp. 24–37.

p. 133 'Amazingly, Sheriff William Heygate returned to announce . . .'. This extraordinary circumstance appears in the *Old Bailey Sessions Papers* for the session beginning 13 May 1812, ref no. 18120513.

## Chapter Twelve: The Compelling Evidence of Miss Stevens

p. 136 'both of Liverpool's papers . . .'. The *Liverpool Courier*, which was solidly Tory and pro-West India interests, and the *Liverpool Mercury*, which was solidly Whig and pro-American trade interests.

p. 136 The few indications of Mary Stevens's character, the common-sense in her affidavit, the loyalty she showed to her friend, Mary Bellingham, the stylishness of her dresses, and the love she inspired in the three Bellingham children, all point to someone who was reliable, good and interesting, a rare combination.

p. 136 For Bellingham's return to Liverpool in 1810 and business there, see Stevens's affidavit, above; Billett's testimony, above, and testimony of James Nevill, PRO 30/29/6/11.

p. 138 The decline in Liverpool's economy can be traced through reports in the *Mercury* from the summer of 1811 showing prices and sales of Irish linens, and Manchester, Birmingham and Sheffield goods all down; 'little demand for cattle', *Mercury*, 19 July 1811.

p. 138 "It is their Traveller's mistake . . .'". Mary Bellingham to John Bellingham, 18 January 1812, BM Add Mss 48216, No. 42.

p. 138 Bellingham's letter to Parton dated 11 May 1812 made it clear that buying iron was part of a larger ambition to get back into the Russian trade.

p. 139 "'I think I need not entreat you . . .'". Mary Bellingham, 18 January 1812, see above.

p. 140 "'I could have wished when you had written . . .'". Bellingham, 16 April 1812, BM Add Mss 48216, No. 49.

p. 141 "'If I could think that the prospects . . .'". Mary Bellingham, April 1812, BM Add Mss 48216, No. 50.

p. 142 Mary Stevens's discussion with Bellingham comes from her affidavit, see above.

p. 147 According to the *Morning Chronicle*, 13 May 1812, Bellingham estimated his losses at '£7000 or £8000'.

## Chapter Thirteen: The Search for the Truth behind the Murder

p. 148 "'I screamed for the gaoler . . .'". Jerdan, *Autobiography* vol. 2, p. 124. Charles Dickens also described the condemned cell in *Sketches of Boz*, 'Visit to Newgate': 'It was a stone dungeon, eight feet long by six wide, with a bench at the upper end, under which were a common rug, a bible, and prayer-book. An iron candlestick was fixed into the wall at the side; and a small high window in the back admitted as much air and light as could struggle in between a double row of heavy, crossed iron bars.'

p. 149 "'Government think to intimidate me . . .'". *Morning Chronicle*, 19 May 1812.

p. 149 "'No person can have heard . . .'". Romilly, *Memoirs*, vol. 2, p. 257.

p. 149 "'he was one of those unhappy men . . .'". Cobbett, *History of the Regency and Reign of George IV*, Ch. III, section 127. Googlebooks.

p. 150 "'And whither can the fainting eye of human misery turn . . .'". Daniel Wilson, *A Defence of the Church Missionary Society Against the Objections of the Reverend Josiah Thomas, M.A. Archdeacon of Bath*, Wilson, London, 1818, p. 37.

p. 151 The character and early life of James Stephen come from *The Memoirs of James Stephen written by himself for the use of his children*, edited by Merle M. Bevington, London: Hogarth Press, 1954. Wilberforce's comments on his character are quoted in Anstey, *The Atlantic Slave Trade*, p. 145.

p. 151 For Stephen's concern for Bellingham's soul, see Wilberforce, *Life*, vol. 4, pp. 26–7: "May 14 . . . Stephen had been this morning,

I found, praying for the wretched murderer, and thinking that his being known to be a friend of Perceval's might affect him [Bellingham], went and devoted himself to trying to bring him to repentance.'

p. 152 "'O! what will be the misery you will endure . . .'". Wilson, *The Substance of a Conversation with John Bellingham.*

p. 153 Butterworth's conversation with Bellingham, *A Full and Authentic Account*, p. 93.

p. 154 Bellingham's 'Washing book', and other receipts and accounts together with Rebecca Robarts's invoices, are all preserved at the British Museum, BM Add Mss 48216.

p. 155 "'If he had known the price would be more than eight pence . . .'". Testimony of Catherine Figgins at Bellingham's trial.

p. 156 'Vickery showed himself to be an exceptional detective . . .'. *Old Bailey Sessions Papers*, 1800–1819: his evidence regarding a theft of timber, 'we moved the timber to the office, and locked it up, (produces one of the pieces;) I put a mark on it that night, with my knife'; concerning a theft of furs, 'I saw Hamlyn the porter with a large load upon his head upon a knot in a basket, and another basket upon that; it was packed in such an awkward loose way it struck me that it was not all right'; concerning stolen bank notes, 'When I came up, I saw the two prisoners very near together, and in the hands of Joel Joseph I saw some paper . . . there was no other person near them within a dozen or twenty yards, they had taken a circular walk round the hall, and where they were there was no company . . . Joseph refused being searched by Preston [another Bow Street officer], and said, Vickery shall search me, he has known me a good while, and whatever he finds he will return me.'

p. 156 For the Bow Street Runners in general, see Cox, 'A Certain Share of Low Cunning – The Provincial Use and Activities of Bow Street "Runners" 1792–1839', School of Historical Studies: Monash University, 2003.

p. 156 Mary Clark's encounter with Bellingham, given in cross-examination at his trial, *Old Bailey Sessions Papers*.

p. 157 It is impossible to trace the source of Bellingham's money, but the quantity of his expenditure makes it clear that someone must have supplied him with funds during his time in London. Had he earned £85 from the purchase of iron, he would surely have remitted some to his distressed family in Liverpool. But his allusion to receiving 'maintenance', and the pattern of his spending, from heavy at the end of February, apparently regular in March and April, but so desperate in May that he grew upset at a charge of eight pence for laundry, indicates that the money came piecemeal, until being withheld at the end.

p. 161 The long-term significance of the Prince Regent's capitulation to Perceval in late February, following the Whigs' refusal to serve, was obvious not merely to the political classes. An intercepted letter from a group of Luddites promising to begin a rebellion explained that 'the immediate cause of us beginning when we did was that Rascally Letter of the Prince Regent to Lords Grey and Grenville which left us no hope of a change for the better'.

## Chapter Fourteen: Choking to Death the Illegal Slave Trade

p. 163 "'It indeed afforded some relief . . .'". *Morning Chronicle*, 13 May 1812.

p. 165 Stephen's character. *Memoirs*, Bevington, pp. 8–20.

p. 166 Hans Sloane, *A Voyage to the Islands of Maderia, Barbados, Nieves, S. Christophers, and Jamaica, with the natural history . . . of the last of those islands; to which is prefixed an introduction wherein is an account of the inhabitants . . . trade, etc.*, 2 vols. (London, 1701–1725), vol. 1, cited in Smandych, 'To soften the extreme rigor of their bondage'.

p. 167 "'I would rather be on friendly terms . . .'". quoted in Leslie

Stephen, *Life of Sir James Fitzjames Stephen, Bart., K.C.S.I.: A Judge of the High Court of Justice*, London: Smith, Elder, and Co., 1895.

p. 168 "'Mr Wilberforce I do not think has behaved . . .'". Fanny Perceval, quoted in Gray, *Spencer Perceval*, p. 205.

p. 169 "'It has been discovered . . .'". *The Fourth Report of the Directors of the African Institution*, London: Hatchard, 1810, p. 2; Googlebooks.

p. 169 'a ship stopped in the Thames in 1810 . . .'. Christopher Lloyd, *The Navy and the Slave Trade*, London: Longmans Green, 1949, p. 31.

p. 170 Measures against the illegal slave trade initiated by Perceval in cabinet. Order in Council 16 May 1808 authorising the payment of a bounty amounting to £40 per man, £30 per woman and £10 per child released, see Tara Helfman, 'The Court of Vice Admiralty at Sierra Leone and the Abolition of the West African Slave Trade', *Yale Law Journal*, vol. 115, 2006; Perceval's instructions to officials in Trinidad and Demerara to put down illegal slaving, 1808, see Gray, *Spencer Perceval*, p. 26; Admiralty order to send two Royal Navy vessels, HMS *Solebay* and HMS *Derwent*, to patrol the west Africa coast, Perceval Papers, Perceval to Stephen, 9 August 1809; creation of West Indian commission to investigate charges of evasions of Slave Trade Act, September 1810, Wilberforce, *Life*, vol. 3, pp. 372 and 382; Order in Council requiring compulsory register of slaves in Trinidad, March 1812, Smandych, "'To Soften the Extreme Rigor of their Bondage'", p. 12.

p. 170 For the activities of Judge Robert Thorpe, see Tara Helfman, 'The Court of Vice Admiralty at Sierra Leone and the Abolition of the West African Slave Trade', *Yale Law Journal*, vol. 115, 2006; *passim.*

p. 172 Although Stephen's plan for a blockade put forward in *War In Disguise, or the Friends of the Neutral* was overtly aimed at France, Wilberforce's sons, Samuel and Robert, who were also his biographers, asserted in a footnote in their *Life of Wilberforce*, vol. 3, p. 234, seemingly based on information from their father, 'Mr Stephen aiming only at its [the slave trade's] suppression published a masterly pamphlet (*War in Disguise*) upon the rights of neutral powers. Fearing, if he mentioned the slave trade that the effect of his arguments might be diminished by a suspicion of his motives, he confined himself entirely to the general question.'

p. 174  '"and in its associated iniquity . . .'". Stephen, *The Dangers of the Country*, p. 114.

p. 175  For the effect of Perceval's measures on Liverpool, see B. H. Tolley, 'The Liverpool Campaign Against the Order in Council and the War of 1812' in Harris, *Liverpool and Merseyside: Essays in the Economic and Social History of the Port and its Hinterland*; Checkland, 'American Versus West Indian Traders in Liverpool, 1793–1815', *The Economic History Review*, New Series, vol. 5, no. 1 (1952), pp. 58–75; Drake, 'Continuity and Flexibility in Liverpool's Trade with Africa and the Caribbean', *Business History* (1976), pp. 85–97; and Hyde, *Liverpool and the Mersey: An Economic History of a Port, 1700–1970*.

p. 177  The extent of illegal slave trading by Liverpool merchants, using foreign flags, masters and documentation, can only be inferred from discrepancies in the Registers of Merchant Ships registers. Those consulted ran from 1805 to 1812. Thus well over half the ships listed in the 1807 register changed ownership within the next two years, a huge increase over previous years. The fifty to sixty ships formerly engaged in the slave trade that left the register in the two years after 1807 represented a significant increase in the rate for former years.

p. 178  '"there was no evidence of smuggling . . .'". Lord Liverpool, quoted in Smandych, '"To Soften The Extreme Rigor of their Bondage"', p. 12.

p. 178  "'to instruct His Majesty's cruizers . . .'". quoted in Helfman, 'The Court of Vice Admiralty at Sierra Leone and the Abolition of the West African Slave Trade'.

p. 179  Growth of the American trade. See Checkland, 'American Versus West Indian Traders in Liverpool, 1793–1815'.

## Chapter Fifteen: How to Kill an Economy

p. 181  "'My Blessed Mary . . .'". quoted in Gillen, *Assassination*, p. 124.

p. 182  "'It is always a matter of dissension between me and Mrs B . . .'". quoted in Stevens, affidavit.

p. 182  "'she had decided never to raise the subject . . .'". quoted in Gillen, *Assassination*, p. 143.

p. 183  "'no person was more inclined to be domestically happy . . .'". quoted in Stevens, affidavit.

p. 183  "'uniformly cruel'". Nevill's testimony, PRO 30/29/6/11.

p. 183  For Liverpool's economic distress, see B. H. Tolley, "The Liverpool Campaign Against the Order in Council and the War of 1812' in Harris, *Liverpool and Merseyside: Essays in the Economic and Social History of the Port and its Hinterland*.

p. 184  The growth of the American trade in Liverpool is treated in Checkland, 'American Versus West Indian Traders in Liverpool, 1793–1815'; it is also apparent from 'The Minutes of the American Chamber of Commerce' Archives, Liverpool Central Library. In 1808 Alexander Baring gave evidence to the House of Commons that 'Liverpool is the principal centre of the American commerce, London houses acting almost solely as bankers for the America trade, receiving the proceeds of consignments', *An Inquiry into the Causes and Consequences of the Orders in Council*, London: Hatchard, 1808.

p. 184  For the development of American trade with Russia, see Kalevi Ahonen, 'From Sugar Triangle to Cotton Triangle: Trade and Shipping between America and Baltic Russia, 1783–1860'.

p. 186 The petition of Birmingham manufacturers is quoted in Holmberg, 'The Acts, Orders in Council, &c. of Great Britain [on Trade], 1793–1812', Napoleon Series; Government and Politics, April 2003. http://www.napoleon-series.org/research/government/british/decrees/c_britdecrees1.html

p. 187  '"Not only are the names forged . . .'". Brougham to the House of Commons, 3 March 1812.

p. 188 The tangled origins of the War of 1812, and the activities of the War Hawks, are examined in Bradford Perkins, *Prologue to War: England and the United States, 1805–1812*, Berkeley and Los Angeles: University of California Press, 1961. Google-books; 'British slavery upon the water', quoted in Perkins, p. 57.

p. 189 Pinkney's negotiations with Wellesley and Perceval, in Gray, *Spencer Perceval*, pp. 450–3; for Perceval's opposition to 'courting of negotiations', Gray, p. 451.

p. 189 Brougham's accusation that Perceval was motivated by 'scorn of the Americans' was cited by Reginald Horsman in *The Causes of the War of 1812*, Philadelphia: University of Pennsylvania Press, 1962, p. 58.

p. 190 '"The Americans swarm on the Coast . . .'". Helfman, 'The Court of Vice Admiralty at Sierra Leone and the Abolition of the West African Slave Trade'.

p. 190 'From a peak of about eighty thousand slaves . . .'. Eltis, 'Slave Departures from Africa, 1811–1867'.

p. 191 The impact of the American embargo on Liverpool trade. Checkland, 'American Versus West Indian Traders in Liverpool, 1793–1815'.

p. 191 '"the distress in this town'". *Liverpool Mercury*, 12 June 1812.

p. 192 '"the temerity in a moment of premature triumph'". *Mercury*, 18 October 1811.

p. 192  '"Rely on one thing . . .'". Grundy to Jackson, 28 November 1812, quoted in Perkins, *Prologue to War*, p. 356.

p. 193 '"Now, after this . . .'". *New York Evening Post*, 26 January 1812.

p. 193 'The *Mercury* columnist who described Perceval . . .'. *Liverpool Mercury*, 19 August 1811.

p. 193 Breed's application for credit. 'A Letter to Messrs Hughes & Duncan' by Richard F. Breed, Liverpool 1812.

p. 194 That Liverpool's most respectable citizens were ready to use violence to attain their ends was attested by William Roscoe. A polymathic poet and banker, and courageous campaigner against the slave trade, he became a Liverpool MP in the election of 1806, but his supporters were beaten up so badly by gangs of dockers that he withdrew from the 1807 contest. The violence, he told the *Mercury*, was organised by the West India merchants who controlled the city.

## Chapter Sixteen: The Russian Connection Returns

p. 196 Lord Holland's meeting with a Birmingham manufacturer. Holland, *Further Memoirs of the Whig Party*, London: John Murray, 1905, pp. 131–2.

p. 197 '"Aye," Castlereagh admitted, "but one does not like to own . . ."'. Wilberforce, *Life*, vol. 4, p. 35.

p. 197 The *Mercury* on rejoicing over the assassination. *Liverpool Mercury*, 25 May 1812.

p. 198 '"about a million in money". . .'. Richardson, evidence to 1812 House of Commons committee on Order in Council, quoted in Checkland, 'American Versus West Indian Traders in Liverpool, 1793–1815', p. 157.

p. 199 For evidence of Richard Statham's business character, see 'Papers of Richard Statham', *passim*, Acc 55, Secure Room, Liverpool Central Library.

p. 200 William Gee affidavit, 'Papers of Richard Statham'.

p. 200 'E. Peck's cramped handwriting . . .'. The evidence that Peck &

Phelps existed in 1801 dates the beginning of their partnership earlier than any of the dates, usually 1818 or 1821, assigned by company histories of their successor company, Phelps Dodge & Co.

p. 200 Letter of Bellingham to Parton. *Liverpool Mercury*, 25 May 1812.

p. 203 British bankers in the American-Russian trade. See Ahonen, 'From Sugar Triangle to Cotton Triangle: Trade and Shipping between America and Baltic Russia, 1783–1860'; Ryan, 'Trade with the Enemy in the Scandinavian and Baltic Ports during the Napoleonic War: For and against'; Dorfman, 'A Note on the Interpenetration of Anglo-American Finance'; Stanley Chapman, 'British Marketing Enterprise: The Changing Roles of Merchants, Manufacturers, and Financiers, 1700–1860', *The Business History Review*, vol. 53, no. 2, Early Commercial Aviation, Summer 1979, pp. 205–34.

p. 205 For the activities of Peck & Phelps, and Phelps & Peck, see Ahonen, 'From Sugar Triangle to Cotton Triangle'; Dorfman, 'Interpenetration of Anglo-American Finance' (especially for the Wilson-Phelps connection); Diary of Anson G. Phelps, Documents Room, New York Public Library. A history of Phelps, Dodge & Co. in 1950 quotes Phelps writing in his diary that while he had not attained 'what my ambitious heart would call worldly prosperity', he had at least been able, 'by the goodness of God', to pay his debts.

## Chapter Seventeen: Where the Money Came From

p. 209 Elisha Peck's character was inevitably subsumed by his American-based partner, Anson Phelps, who morphed the business into the beginning of today's multibillion-dollar metals conglomerate. But the thirty years of their partnership testifies to a harmony of views, and to their common tendency to cut business and financial corners, and adhere to fundamentalist tenets of religious belief.

p. 210 "'Nothing could more surprise him . . .'". Baring, quoted in *Annual Register*, 1813, p. 111.

p. 210 "'As England is contending for the defence . . .'". Perceval to the House of Commons, 3 March 1812.

p. 211 "'If any thing was wanting . . .'". Russell to Secretary of State James Monroe, 4 March 1812.

p. 211 Bellingham's final claims for justice. See Gillen, *Assassination*, pp. 74–80.

p. 214 "'The measure is perfect madness . . .'". *New York Evening Post*, 21 April 1812.

p. 214 "'Ye who live by farming . . .'". Handbill issued in Boston, Massachusetts, April 1812, 'Let every Federalist do his duty and Massachusetts will yet be saved!'

p. 217 Sidney's Alley used to run from Piccadilly Circus to Leicester Square. According to *The Survey of London*, it was redeveloped in the 1840s. But it was evidently a fairly fashionable shopping arcade. Thomas Challenier occupied No. 7, according to *Kent's London Directory*, 1810–11.

p. 218 I have spent more time than I can justify trying to work out how General Isaac Gascoyne could have known that it was Perceval who had been killed.

p. 220 'the prisoner "received a small box . . ."'. *The Times*, 18 May 1812.

p. 223 The poignancy of the final sentence of this last letter, published in almost every London newspaper on 19 May 1812, emphasises how completely Bellingham was caught up in his plan. Nothing existed outside it.

## Chapter Eighteen: An Execution Ends all Cares

p. 224 The scene of Bellingham's execution is a composite of several descriptions, mostly relying on the *Edinburgh Annual Register*, *The Complete Newgate Calendar*, vol. V, and *The Full and Authentic Account*.

p. 224 "'called too soon . . .'". Cobbett, *Political Register*, 23 May 1812, vol. 21, column 669.

p. 228 "'I saw the anxious looks . . .'". Cobbett, *Political Register*, ibid., section 133.

p. 230 "'You'd be astonished to find how shy . . .'". Liverpool letter to J. J. Cossart, of Lombard Street, London, quoted in Gillen, *Assassination*, p. 147.

p. 230 The history of Phelps, Dodge & Co. comes from a company history written in 1950, online 'A history of Phelps, Dodge, 1834–1950'; Phelps's dubious role in the Wilson Bank scam comes from Dorfman, 'A Note on the Interpenetration of Anglo-American Finance, 1837–1841'.

p. 230 Elisha Peck's movements have been deduced from his appearance in New York trade directories from 1812, and his reappearance in *Gore's Liverpool Directory* from 1815. The West Haverstraw Village History, online, records his arrival on the ship *Samson* in 1830 in the United States with a rolling steel mill from England, and his foundation of the company town of Samsondale, named after the ship, on the River Hudson.

p. 231 Leveson-Gower's letter and donation to Mary Bellingham are contained in 'Letters of George Canning to John Drinkwater', 920 CAN, Liverpool Central Library, Archives; quoted in Gillen, *Assassination*, pp. 142–3.

p. 232 Mary Stevens's 'new and elegant assortment of Millinery' was advertised in the *Liverpool Mercury*, 5 June 1812.

p. 233 Advertisement of Mary Bellingham's bankruptcy. *Liverpool Mercury*, 13 November 1812.

## Chapter Nineteen: Understanding Why it Happened

p. 234 "'the sepulchral Perceval . . .'". Smith, *Peter Plymley Letters*, p. 35.

p. 234 "'Nothing could be more calm . . .'". Quoted in Gray, *Spencer*

*Perceval*, pp. 458–9. Jane Perceval's reaction, Gray, p. 458. Perceval's funeral, Gray, p. 461.

p. 235 "'Perceval was never more easy...'". Ward, quoted in Gray, p. 456.

p. 236 Williams's dream. Gillen, *Assassination*, pp. 153–4.

p. 236 The term 'murder money' was used by Edward Marsh, great-grandson of Spencer Perceval and later Winston Churchill's secretary, according to his biographer Christopher Hassell.

p. 237 Henry Hunt's attack on Jane Perceval. Hunt, *Memoirs of Henry Hunt*, vol. 3, online http://www.gutenberg.org/cache/epub/8463/pg8463.txt

p. 237 The lives of Spencer Perceval's children attracted the attention of diarists like Charles Greville, see *The Greville Memoirs*, and John Croker, see *The Croker Papers*. The adherence to Edward Irving's charismatic Church attracted particular attention to Spencer Perceval junior, from both Greville and Hassell, in *Edward Marsh*. John Perceval's descent into and recovery from lunacy were agonisingly described in his *Narrative of the Treatment*, and by its twentieth-century editor, the noted anthropologist Gregory Bateson.

p. 241 Hunt's analysis of Perceval's fate, *Memoirs* vol. 3, online http://www.gutenberg.org/cache/epub/8463/pg8463.txt

# Bibliography

## British Museum Collections

49189. SPENCER PERCEVAL PAPERS. Vol. XVII (ff. 97). 'Memoirs' of Perceval; 1812. Partly (ff. 1–12b) *printed*. An anonymous biography, amplifying the life published in the *National Advertiser*, 20 May 1812, and reprinted in the *Gentleman's Magazine*, May–June 1812. Includes (ff. 95–96) a receipted bill for publication work, 1812. Apparently suppressed (see f. 97) by Lord Arden.

49173–49195. Correspondence and papers of the Hon. Spencer Perceval (b. 1762, d. 1812), Prime Minister, and of his family; 1782–1922, n.d.

Add. MSS. 46920–47213, 48216

Add. Ch. 75439–75450

PRO 30/29/6/11 T 29/116 (747) T 29/117(5215)

HO 42/121, which includes a petition and letter from Bellingham, and HO 42/123

Stephen, James, 'Coup d'oeil on an American War', Perceval Papers, 33/98–105

## Liverpool Central Library Archives

Letters of George Canning to John Drinkwater jun. 1812–14, 1822 transcript 920 CAN

Minutes of the American Chamber of Commerce

Papers of Richard Statham Acc 55; Secure Room

Gore's Directory for Liverpool 1800, 1802, 1807, 1810

Liverpool Register of Merchant Ships 1802–8 Reel 25 Abolition and
    Emancipation Pt. 2 Slavery Collection from the Merseyside Maritime
    Museum; published by Adam Matthews publications, 1998

**New York Public Library**

Documents Room, *Diary of Anson G. Phelps*

**Printed Works by Rt. Hon. Spencer Perceval**

Anon., but really Spencer Perceval, *The Duties and Powers of Public
    Officers with respect to Violations of the Public Peace*, [London, 1792]
—*A Review of the Arguments in favor of the Continuance of Impeachments,
    notwithstanding a dissolution*, p. 123. W. Clarke, London: J. Stockdale,
    1791
—*"The Book!" or, the Proceedings and correspondence upon the subject
    of the inquiry into the conduct of Her Royal Highness the Princess of
    Wales . . . To which is prefixed a Narrative of the recent events that have
    led to the publication of the original documents. With a statement of
    facts relative to the child, now under the protection of Her Royal
    Highness.* [Superintended through the press by the Rt. Hon. Spencer
    Perceval] [With an appendix of documents, depositions, etc.],
    pp. 246, 108, London: M. Jones, 1813
—*The Church Question in Ireland. Speech as prepared by . . . Spencer
    Perceval, for the Debate on the first Roman Catholic Petition to the United
    Parliament,* May 1805. Now first published, . . . with an introduction,
    . . . notes and comments by D[udley]. Perceval, Edinburgh, 1844.

**Pamphlets reporting on John Bellingham's trial, etc.**

*A full and authentic report of the trial of John Bellingham Esq, at the
    sessions; house in the Old Bailey on Friday May 15 1812 for the Murder*

*of the Rt Hon Spencer Perceval, Chancellor of the Exchequer, &c in the Lobby of the House of Commons on Monday May 11 1812* . . . taken in short hand by Thomas Hodgson esq. printed by Charles Squire, Furnival's Inn Ct., Holborn, for Sheerwood, Neely and Jones 20 Paternoster Row, 1812

*The Trial of John Bellingham for the Assassination of the Right Honourable Spencer Perceval* . . . Taken in short hand, by Mr. Fraser. To this is added, an account of Bellingham's execution, etc. p. 103, London: R. Mercer, 1812

*A Full Report of the Trial of John Bellingham for the Murder of the Right Hon. Spencer Perceval . . . in the lobby of the House of Commons . . . Including the arguments of Counsel and his own defence at length. Accompanied with a faithful narrative of every circumstance connected with the atrocious deed, and of Bellingham's conduct from his committal to the time of his execution. Together with a copy of Bellingham's memorial, and of Lord Gower's statement.* To which is added a sketch of the life of Bellingham. [With a portrait.] p. 55, Hull: J. Craggs & J. Simmons, 1812

*An Authentic Account of the Trial and Execution of John Bellingham, for the assassination of the Right Hon. Spencer Perceval; with a vindication of the character of Sir Francis Burdett from the aspersions of some of the London prints.*

*An Account of the Trial of John Bellingham, for the wilful murder of the Right Hon. Spencer Perceval in the lobby of the House of Commons,* Brighton: John Forbes, [1812]

*The Trial of J. Bellingham, a Liverpool merchant, at the Old Bailey, on Friday, May 15, 1812, for the assassination of the Right Hon. Spencer Perceval . . . With every particular attending the sad catastrophe, and other important information.* Taken in short-hand (Second edition), p. 26, London: W. Lewis, [1812]

*An authentic account of the horrid assassination of the Right Honorable Spencer Perceval, (Prime Minister of the United Kingdom,) who was shot in the lobby of the House of Commons, by James [sic] Bellingham, a*

*Liverpool merchant; also, the trial of the murderer, which took place at the Old Bailey, before Lord Chief Justice Mansfield; with a particular account of the execution.* Printed by T. Evans; London, 1812

*Old Bailey Sessions Papers*, John Bellingham, killing: murder, 13th May, 1812

*Annual Register* 1812, 'Assassination of Mr Perceval. Appendix to Chronicle: The Right Hon. Spencer Perceval; Trial of John Bellingham for the murder of the Rt Honourable Spencer Perceval. Assassination of Mr Perceval, and Parliamentary Proceedings thereupon.'


## Newspapers

*The Atlas*
*The Day*
*The Globe*
*The Liverpool Courier*
*The Liverpool Mercury*
*The Morning Chronicle*
*The Nottingham Journal*
*The Times*


## Contemporary Publications

Adams, John Quincy, *The Writings of John Quincy Adams*, vol. 9 (ed. Worthington C. Ford), New York: Macmillan, 1904; www.ebooksread. com/authors-eng/john-quincy-adams

Anon, *Recollections of Old Liverpool by A Nonagenarian*, Liverpool: J. F. Hughes. 1836

Burke, Edmund, *Philosophical Enquiry into the Origin of our Ideas of the Sublime and the Beautiful*, New York: Collier & Son, 1909–14; www. bartleby.com; 2001

Croker, John W., *The Croker Papers* [Correspondence and Writing, ed. Louis Jennings], London: John Murray, 1885

Cruchley, G. F., *Cruchley's London in 1865: a handbook for strangers, showing where to go, how to get there, and what to look at*, London: Cruchley, 1865

Goethe, Wolfgang von, *Wilhelm Meister's Apprenticeship*, New York: Collier & Son, 1917; www.bartleby.com, 2000

Greville, Charles F., *The Greville Memoirs: a journal of the reigns of King George IV and King William IV*, vols. I and II, London: Longmans Green, 1874

Holland, Lord Henry, *Further Memoirs of the Whig Party: 1807–1821 with some miscellaneous reminiscences*, London: John Murray, 1905

Hunt, Henry, *Memoirs of Henry Hunt Esq*, 3 vols., London: Dolby, 1820. www.wattpad.com/12477-memoirs-of-henry-hunt-esq-volume-1

Jerdan, William, *The Autobiography of W. J.*, 4 vols., London: 1852–53.

Paine, Tom, *The Rights of Man being an Answer to Mr Burke's Attack on the French Revolution*, Boston: Thomas & Andrews, 1791

*Parliamentary History*, vol. XXVIII

Perceval, John T., *Narrative of the Treatment experienced by a Gentleman, during a state of mental derangement; designed to explain the causes and the nature of insanity, and to expose the injudicious conduct pursued towards many . . . sufferers under that calamity* [By John Thomas Perceval], p. 278, London: Effingham Wilson, 1838

Smith, Sydney, *Peter Plymley's Letters* [Published from 1804 in *The Edinburgh Review*] http://www.archive.org/details/peterplymleyslet04063gut

Stephen, James, *The Dangers of the Country* [First published 1807, US edition Bradford; Philadelphia, 1897] http://www.archive.org/details/dangerscountry00stepgoog

Stephen, James, *War In Disguise, or the Friends of the Neutral*, London: Hatchard, 1805

Stephen, James, *The Memoirs of James Stephen*, ed. Merle Bevington, Hogarth Press, London, 1954

Walpole, Sir Spencer K.C.B., *The Life of the Rt. Hon. Spencer Perceval*, 2 vols., London: Hurst and Blackett, 1874

Ward, Robert Plumer, *Tremaine: or The Man of Refinement*, London: Henry Colburn, 1825

Wedderburn, Robert, *The Horrors of Slavery; exemplified in the Life and History of the Rev. Robert Wedderburn* [First published 1824], ed. Iain McCalman, New York and Princeton: Wiener Publishing, 1991

Wilberforce R. and I., *The Life of William Wilberforce*, London: John Murray, 1838

Wilson, Daniel, *Sermons and Tracts*, vol. 2, London: George Wilson, 1825

Wilson, Daniel, *The Substance of a Conversation with John Bellingham, the assassin of the late Right Hon. Spencer Perceval, on Sunday, May 17, 1812, the day previous to his execution: together with some general remarks*, London: J. Hatchard, 1812


## Professional Journals

Ahonen, Kalevi, 'From Sugar Triangle to Cotton Triangle: Trade and Shipping between America and Baltic Russia, 1783–1860', *Jyväskyla Studies in Humanities*, no. 38 (2005), University of Jyväskyla, Jyväskyla

Argent, Valerie, 'Counter-Revolutionary Panic and the Treatment of the Insane: 1800', Middlesex University (1978)

Barnhart, William C., 'Evangelicalism, Masculinity and the Making of Imperial Missionaries in Late Georgian Britain, 1795–1820', *The Historian*, vol. 67, issue 4 (2005)

Binfield, Kevin, ed., *Writings of the Luddites*, Baltimore, Maryland: The Johns Hopkins University Press, 2004

Chapman, Stanley D., 'British Marketing Enterprise: The Changing Roles of Merchants, Manufacturers, and Financiers, 1700–1860', *The Business History Review*, vol. 53, no. 2

Checkland, S. G., 'American Versus West Indian Traders in Liverpool, 1793–1815', *The Journal of Economic History*, vol. 18, no. 2 (June 1958), pp. 141–60

Checkland, S. G., 'Economic Attitudes in Liverpool, 1793–1807', *The Economic History Review*, New Series, vol. 5, no. 1 (1952), pp. 58–75

Dorfman, Joseph, 'A Note on the Interpenetration of Anglo-American Finance, 1837–1841', *The Journal of Economic History*, vol. II, no. 2 (Spring 1951), pp. 140–47

Drake, K., 'Continuity and Flexibility in Liverpool's Trade with Africa and the Caribbean', *Business History* (1976), pp. 85–97

Dreschler, Seymour, 'Whose Abolition? Popular Pressure and the Ending of the British Slave Trade', *Past & Present*, May 1994

Eltis, David, 'Slave Departures from Africa, 1811–1867: An Annual Time Series', *African Economic History*, no. 15 (1986), pp. 143–71

Helfman, Tara, 'The Court of Vice Admiralty at Sierra Leone and the Abolition of the West African Slave Trade', *Yale Law Journal*, vol. 115, no. 5 (2006), pp. 11–22

Holmberg, Tom, 'The Acts, Orders in Council, &c. of Great Britain [on Trade], 1793–1812', The Napoleon Series; http://www.napoleon-series.org/research/government

Hyde, F. E., *Liverpool and the Mersey: An Economic History of a Port, 1700–1970*, Newton Abbot: David & Charles, 1971

Hyde, Francis E., Parkinson, Bradbury B. and Marriner, Sheila, 'The Nature and Profitability of the Liverpool Slave Trade', *Economic History Review*, 2nd series, vol. V (1953)

Jackson, Gordon, *Hull in the Eighteenth Century: A Study in Economic and Social History*, London: Oxford University Press, 1972

Kenwood, A. G., 'Fixed Capital Formation on Merseyside, 1800–1913', *Economic History Review*, vol. 31 (1978), pp. 214–37

Moran, Richard, 'The Modern Foundation for the Insanity Defense: The Cases of James Hadfield (1800) and Daniel McNaughtan (1843)', *Annals of the American Academy of Political and Social Science*, vol. 477, The Insanity Defense (January 1985), pp. 31–42

Ryan, A. N., 'The Defence of British Trade with the Baltic, 1808–1813', *English Historical Review*, vol. 74, no. 292 (July 1959), pp. 443–66

Ryan, A. N., 'Trade with the Enemy in the Scandinavian and Baltic Ports during the Napoleonic War: For and against', *Transactions of the Royal Historical Society*, Fifth Series, vol. 12 (1962), pp. 123–40

Smandych, Russell, '"To Soften the Extreme Rigour of Their Bondage": James Stephen's Attempt to Reform the Criminal Slave Laws of the West Indies, 1813–1833', *Law and History Review*, 23.3 (2005), 28 September 2011; www.historycooperative.org/journals/lhr/23.3/smandych.html

Wood, Marcus, 'William Cobbett, John Thelwall, Radicalism, Racism and Slavery: A Study in Burkean Parodics', *Romanticism on the Net*, no. 15 (August 1999), University of Montreal

Worral, David, 'Kinship, Generation and Community: The Transmission of Political Ideology in Radical Plebeian Print Culture', *Studies in Romanticism*, vol. 43 (2004)

## Publications

Anstey, Roger, *The Atlantic Slave Trade and British Abolition*, London: Macmillan, 1975

Barty-King, H., *The Baltic Exchange: The History of a Unique Market*, London: Hutchinson Benham, 1977

Blake, Mrs Warrenne, ed., *An Irish Beauty of the Regency. Compiled from 'Mes Souvenirs' – The Unpublished Journals of the Hon. Mrs Calvert 1789–1822*, London and New York: John Lane, 1911, p. 22

Burton, Elizabeth, *The Georgians at Home*, London: Longmans Green, 1967

Cole, G. D. H., *British Working Movements: Select Documents 1789–1875*, London: Macmillan, 1951

Cox, David J., *'A Certain Share of Low Cunning' – The Provincial Use and Activities of Bow Street 'Runners' 1792–1839*, Cullompton: Willan Publishing, 2010

Crosby, Alfred W. jr, *America, Russia, Hemp and Napoleon: American Trade with Russia and the Baltic, 1783–1812*, Columbus, Ohio: Ohio State University Press, 1965

Gillen, Mollie, *Assassination of the Prime Minister: The Shocking Death of Spencer Perceval*, London: Sidgwick & Jackson, 1972

Gray, D., *Spencer Perceval: The Evangelical Prime Minister, 1762–1812*, Manchester: Manchester University Press, 1963

Greene, Lorenzo Johnston, *The Negro in Colonial New England, 1620–1776*, New York: Columbia University Press, 1942

Harris, J. R., ed., *Liverpool and Merseyside: Essays in the Economic and Social History of the Port and its Hinterland*, London: Frank Cass, 1969

Hassell, C., *Edward Marsh, Patron of the Arts*, London: Longmans, 1959

Hill, Peter P., *Napoleon's Troublesome Americans: Franco-American Relations, 1804–1815*, Washington, DC: Potomac Books, 2005

Longford, Elizabeth, *Wellington: The Years of the Sword*, London: Weidenfeld & Nicolson, 1969

May, Allyson Nancy, *The Bar and the Old Bailey, 1750–1850: The Prisoners' Counsel Act Justifying Advocacy*, Chapel Hill, North Carolina: UNC Press, 2003

McCalman, Iain, *Radical Underworld: Prophets, Revolutionaries and Pornographers in London 1795–1840*, Cambridge: Cambridge University Press, 1988

Parry-Jones, William, *The Trade in Lunacy: A Study of Private Madhouses in England in the 18th and 19th Centuries*, London: Routledge & Kegan Paul, 1972

Pollard, Arthur, ed., *The Penguin History of Literature*, vol. 6, 'Faith and Doubt in the Victorian Age' by A. O. J. Cockshut

Porter, Roy, *A Social History of Madness*, London: Weidenfeld & Nicolson, 1987

Porter, Roy, *Mind-Forg'd Manacles: A History of Madness in England from the Restoration to the Regency*, London: Penguin, 1987

Porter, Roy, *Plots and Paranoia*, London: Unwin Hyman, 1989

Sherwood, Marika, 'Oh, What A Tangled Web We Weave': Britain, the Slave Trade and Slavery, 1808–43; http://www.shunpiking.com/bhs2007/200-BHS-MS-britishStrade.htm

Thomas, Hugh, *The Slave Trade: The History of the Atlantic Slave Trade, 1440–1870*, London: Picador, 1997, p. 589

Turley, David, *The Culture of English Antislavery, 1780–1860*, New York: Routledge, 1991

Ward, William, *The Royal Navy and the Slavers: The Suppression of the Atlantic Slave Trade*, London: Allen and Unwin, 1969

Williams, Eric, *Capitalisation and Slavery*, Richmond, Va; University of North Carolina Press, 1944

# Acknowledgements

Like Blanche Dubois, historians are always beholden to the kindness of strangers. In my case, I am indebted first to the late Mollie Gillen who discovered John Bellingham's laundry book in the Public Records Office. Everything about it was neat: the linen backing, the writing, the lists, the accounts. Nothing could have conveyed more immediately Bellingham's fastidious, organised character. Set against the appalling destruction he was planning, it was impossible not to wonder how the contradiction could have been resolved. My next debt is therefore owed to the staff at the archives of Liverpool City's Central Library and at the International Museum of Slavery who guided, suggested and helped me to sources for the angry decade in the city when it was tipped over like a beehive, its trade in slaves stamped out, more or less, and its American business scattered. The murder was Liverpool's revenge.

For me, the key to the bigoted, but evidently attractive character of the victim, Spencer Perceval, was provided by the extraordinary memoir of madness written by his son, John, and his baffled desire to find a meaning in life. I am grateful to the archivists at the Fitzwilliam Museum, Cambridge, who suggested this source, and at the Wellcome Institute for their expertise on the period's shifting approach to insanity. More generally I owe much to the knowledge of librarians at the London Library, the British Library, and the New York Public Library.

I would also like to record my thanks to my agent, Peter Robinson, to Anna Simpson, senior editor, and to Michael Fishwick, publishing director, at Bloomsbury, for making such a beautiful book out of this idea.

Closer to home, I must express how much it means in the solitude of writing to have the love and support of friends and family, especially of Paul Houlton and Charlotte Desorgher to whom this book is dedicated, of Clico and Gerald Kingsbury, of Lyn Cole, and of my darling wife, Marielou.

Finally, I want to acknowledge with boundless gratitude the unpayable debt I owe to George Gibson, publishing director of Bloomsbury USA, who is the best of editors and the staunchest of friends.

# Index

Abbott, Charles, 26, 42, 64
Abolition Act, 81–2, 165, 168, 176–7
Adams, John Quincy, 172, 206
Addington, Henry (Lord Sidmouth),
    26, 75–6, 162
Adkins, Richard, 34, 48
Adkins, William, 19–20, 34, 48
African Institution, 169, 189
Alexander I, Tsar, 56
Alley, Peter, 48, 56, 117–19, 123, 130–3,
    223
Almack's Assembly Rooms, 59
American Chamber of Commerce, 185,
    198, 200
*Annual Register*, 149, 229
Arbuthnot, Charles, 82
Archangel, 102–3, 176, 185, 204
    and Bellingham's venture, 18, 32,
    50–5, 107–9, 111, 127–8, 137, 182–3,
    201, 205, 232
Arden, Lord, 27, 60
Arden, Lady, 60
Aspinall, John, 176, 178–9
Association for the Preservation of
    Liberty and Property, 25
Austen, Jane, 60–1
Australia, 171
Austria, 87–8, 92–3
Avison, Thomas, 136, 140, 201
Azores, 101

Babington, Thomas, 5, 8, 164
Baltic Coffee House, 51, 157
Baltic trade, 51, 101–3, 159, 176–7, 179,
    185, 192
Bank of England, 26, 39, 89, 91
Barbados, 166

Baring, Alexander, 210, 221
Baring, Sir Francis, 91
Baring Brothers bank, 191, 203
Barker, Abraham, 199
Barker, Jacob, 199, 204, 214
Bathurst, Lord, 174
Beckett, John, 23, 36–7, 40–2, 44, 211
Beckwith, William, 38, 48–9, 122–3, 154,
    212
Bellingham, Elizabeth (née Scarbrow),
    98–9, 109
Bellingham, Henry, 3, 114, 139–41, 183,
    187, 233
Bellingham, James, 52, 55, 110–11, 141
Bellingham, John, senior, 34–5, 98–100,
    130, 141, 240
Bellingham, John
    appearance, 31, 115–16, 226
    arrest and identification, 13–16
    defence case, 46–50, 56–7, 72–3, 97,
        116–18
    early life and career, 97–110
    execution, 224–9
    family background, 34–5
    and father's lunacy, 34–5, 98–100, 130
    financial difficulties, 137–41, 157,
        181–3, 209, 214
    financial maintenance, 147, 153–5,
        157, 159–62, 209–10, 213–17, 220,
        229, 233
    identification of ministers, 6, 40–1,
        121
    imprisonment, 21–4
    letter to landlady, 31–2
    letter to Parton, 179, 200–2
    letter to wife, 181–2, 221–3
    lodgings searched, 19–20

marriage, 107
mental state, 29–34, 42, 47–50, 54,
    56–7, 97, 99–100, 111–12, 116–19,
    124–7, 130–1, 133, 136, 144–5, 149,
    153, 195
and murder weapon, 48–9, 122–3,
    154, 212, 216–17
promissory note, 20, 155, 159, 215, 217
Russian venture, 2, 17–18, 32, 34–6,
    47, 50–6, 101–2, 107–14, 119, 123,
    127–9, 132, 137, 140, 158, 182,
    201–2, 222, 228
speech at trial, 126–30, 145–6
trial, 115–34, 145–6
visitors in jail, 148–53
Bellingham, Mary (née Nevill)
    and Bellingham's trial, 130, 135–6,
        147, 178
    financial problems, 137–41, 155, 215,
        233
    financial support, 181, 199–200, 231–2
    marital tensions, 113–14, 139–43, 182
    marriage, 107
    and millinery business, 136–42, 232–3
    and Russian venture, 2, 52, 55, 110–14,
        182
Berlin decree, 173, 214
Bibby, James, 175
Biblical prophecies, 94–5
Billett, Ann (née Scarbrow), 47, 137–8,
    147, 156, 182
    and Bellingham's mental state, 97–9,
        110–13, 116, 118, 124, 130–1
Billett, Edward, 110
Birch, Samuel, 225–6
Birmingham, 38, 43, 61, 156, 184, 186,
    196, 203, 240
Blackstone, William, 145
Blizzard, Sir William, 229
bludgeon men, 23, 225
Book of Daniel, 94–5, 150
Book of Revelation, 94, 240
Boston, 193, 199
Bourne, John, 47
Bourne, Peter, 231–2
Bow Street magistrates, 18–19, 129, 146,
    158, 211
Bow Street Runners, 19, 156
Brazil, 77, 105, 169, 176–7, 190, 221
Breed, Richard F., 185, 191, 193

Brighton, 29, 69
Brislington lunatic asylum, 240
Bristol, 89, 105
*British Press*, 9, 16
Brougham, Henry, 62, 172, 187, 189, 218
    and repeal of Orders in Council, 4–5,
        197, 210, 213, 216
Brown, William, 185
Brunskill, William, 227–9
Bullion Committee, 91–2
Burdett, Sir Francis, 31, 115
Burgess, Henry, 6, 14–16
Burke, Edmund, 93, 98–9
Burrell, Charles, 16
Butler, George, 68, 73
Butterworth, Joseph, 152–3
Byron, Lord, 225

Cabot, George, 204
Cabot, Henry, 199, 214
Calhoun, James, 188
Calvert, Frances, 29
Campbell, Isabella and Mary, 239
Campbell, John MacLeod, 239
Canada, 230
Canning, George, 42, 82, 84–6, 164
Carlton House, 39, 69
Caroline of Brunswick, Princess, 59,
    80–1, 161
Carr, Lieutenant Colonel Sir Henry,
    237
Case, George, 175
Castlereagh, Lord (Lord Liverpool), 24,
    42, 44, 58, 82, 85–7, 162, 213
    succession to Perceval, 177–8, 197, 230
Catholic Apostolic Church, 238–9
censorship, 65
Challenier, Thomas, 217
charismatic movement, 238–9
Charlton, 60, 235
Chatham, Lord, 87
Chester fair, 138, 192
China, 90
Church of England, 73–4, 238
Churchill, Winston, 87
City of London, 221
City of London militia, 23
Clapham Sect (the Saints), 77–8, 83,
    165, 167–8
Clarence, Duke of, 116

Saints, the, *see* Clapham Sect
Saxony, 88
Scarbrow, Ann, *see* Billett, Ann
Scarbrow, Elizabeth, *see* Bellingham, Elizabeth
Schindler, Oskar, 171
Scotland, 43, 156, 162, 239
Shairpe, Sir Stephen, 54, 128, 132, 232
Shaw, Gabriel, 204
ships
    *Amelia*, 177
    *Blanchard*, 177
    *Chesapeake*, 188
    *Hannah*, 205
    *Hartwell*, 101
    *Hornet*, 213
    HMS *Leopard*, 188
    *Nile*, 176–7
    *Soyuz*, 53, 109
Shoreditch Refuge for the Destitute, 69
shorthand writers, 126, 128, 150
Sicily, 87
Sidmouth, Lord, *see* Addington, Henry
Sierra Leone, 168, 171, 178, 190
Simmons, Dr Samuel, 48, 117
Skagerrak strait, 51
slave trade, 76–82
    illegal, 169–72, 174–8, 180, 187, 189–90, 192, 221, 230
    Liverpool and, 17, 77, 105–6, 108, 137, 169, 175–7
    Perceval and abolition, 7, 9, 78–82, 164, 167–72, 174–8, 180, 241
    Stephen and abolition, 5, 151, 165–70, 172–5, 178, 180, 189–90
    *see also* Abolition Act
slaves, punishment of, 166–7
Sloane, Sir Hans, 166
smallpox, 169
Smith, Adam, 185
Smith, Sydney, 70, 234
Smith, William, 6, 12–13, 164
Smith, Mr, 112, 131
Society of Artists of Great Britain, 98
Southampton, 47, 97, 110
Spain, 173
    and slave trade, 169, 172, 178, 190
    *see also* Peninsular War
speaking in tongues, 238–40

Statham, Richard, 134, 136, 178, 199–200, 231
steam power, 64
Stephen, Anna (née Stent), 165–7
Stephen, James, 150–3, 164–70, 172–5, 181, 189–92
    and Orders in Council, 79, 164, 192, 197, 210, 213, 217, 221
    and slave trade abolition, 5, 151, 165–70, 172–5, 178, 180, 189–90
    *The War in Disguise*, 172–3, 183
Stephen, Sarah (née Wilberforce), 151, 167
Stevens, Eliza, 141
Stevens, Mary, 112–13, 135–45, 147, 154, 178–9, 182, 203, 212–15, 218, 220–3
    and millinery business, 112, 136–42, 159, 214–15, 232–3
    and Parton letter, 179, 200–1
Stoddard, John, 28
Strong, Caleb, 214
sublime, the, 98–9, 211, 218, 220
Sweden, 87, 92

Tarleton, Banastre, 103
Taylor, Michael Angelo, 33
Taylor, William, 49, 121–3
Taylor, William and James, 176
Thames, River, 86, 169, 235
Thistlewood, Thomas, 166
Thornton, Henry, 168
Thorpe, Judge Robert, 171–2, 178, 190, 230
Ticehurst lunatic asylum, 240
Tierney, George, 66, 70, 86
*Times, The*, 27–9, 220
Torres Vedras line, 92, 95
Tower of London, 26
Trafalgar, Battle of, 173
Treaty of Tilsit, 56
Trinidad, 169, 171
Trinity College, Cambridge, 62

United States of America
    and approach to war, 189–93, 208–9, 211, 213–14, 221, 230
    fundamentalism, 64
    Louisiana Purchase, 203
    and slave trade, 77, 105–6, 190–1
    and trade restrictions, 4, 173–4, 179–80, 183–6, 188–93, 198–9, 206–7

van Brienen, Solomon, 52–4
Van Diemen's Land, 177
Venn, Henry and John, 73–4, 77
Vickery, John, 19–20, 22, 34, 38, 48–9,
    114, 123, 131, 138, 154–6, 159–61,
    163–4, 197–8, 200, 202, 215
Vienna, 87

Wagram, Battle of, 87
Walcheren expedition, 87–8
Wales, 36
Walpole, Spencer, 238
Walpole, Thomas, 94
Ward, Robert Plumer, 59, 73, 83, 235–6
Wardle, Gwilym, 66–7
Watkins, Robert, 160
weapons, 36–8
    Bellingham's, 48–9, 122–3, 154, 212,
    216–17
Wellesley, Lord, 69–70, 90, 161–2
Wellington, Duke of, 7, 67, 69, 87–8,
    90–3, 95–6, 170, 237
Wesley, John and Charles, 73–4, 77
West Africa squadron, 171, 190

West Indies, 50, 77–8, 102, 105, 166,
    170, 176–8, 230
Westminster Abbey, 235
Whitbread, Samuel, 42
Whitefoord, Caleb, 98
Wigan, 112, 233
Wilberforce, Sarah, see Stephen, Sarah
Wilberforce, William, 8–9, 74, 76,
    78–82, 151, 167–8, 174, 197
William IV, King, 238
Williams, John, 236
Wilson, Rev. Daniel, 98, 100, 150, 152–3,
    181
Wilson, Fletcher and Melvin, 231
Wilson, John, 204–5
Wilson, Sir Thomas, 60–1
Wilson, Thomas, & Co., 20, 155, 159,
    161, 204–6, 210, 215, 217, 221, 231
Wiltshire, 156, 160
Winchester College, 165
Wordsworth, William and Dorothy, 44

York, Duke of, 66–7, 88
Yorkshire, 36–7, 43, 156